WITHDRAWN

THREE AGES OF MUSICAL THOUGHT

Essays on Ethics and Aesthetics

Da Capo Press Music Reprint Series

MUSIC EDITOR
BEA FRIEDLAND
Ph.D., City University of New York

THREE AGES OF MUSICAL THOUGHT

Essays on Ethics and Aesthetics

by

ERIC WERNER

DA CAPO PRESS • NEW YORK • 1981

Library of Congress Cataloging in Publication Data

Werner, Eric.
  Three ages of musical thought.

  (Da Capo Press music reprint series)
  Reprints of "articles published in various journals
and books between 1941 and 1965."
  CONTENTS: Judaica.—Renaissance.—Mendelssohn.
  1. Music—Philosophy and aesthetics—Addresses,
essays, lectures. I. Title.
ML3845.W47   780'.1   80-28330
ISBN 0-306-76032-0

This Da Capo Press edition of *Three Ages of Musical Thought* assembles
for the first time articles published in various journals and books between
1941 and 1965, reprinted with permission. It includes a preface by the author.

Published by Da Capo Press, Inc.
A Subsidiary of Plenum Publishing Corporation
233 Spring Street, New York, N.Y. 10013

ALTIS MANIBUS PATRIS
IULI WERNER
VINDOBONENSIS,
PROFESSORIS NECNON PHILOSOPHIAE DOCTORIS
NECATI A NOSTRI POPULI INIMICIS
HIC LIBER REVERENTER DEVOTUS EST.

Table of Contents

MENDELSSOHN

Preface

T HE TOPICS OF this volume encompass ancient conceptions of music and their modern interpretation. The subtitle alludes to S. Kierkegaard's thesis *(Either/Or)* of the categorical incompatibility between the ethically and the aesthetically perfect. This thesis was to a certain extent preconceived in biblical Judaism and early Christianity: both judged music according to ethical rather than aesthetic criteria. The individual articles consider questions of music theory, ethics, and cosmology; those studies concerning the relationship between Synagogue and Church may be considered bypaths of my *Sacred Bridge*.

A few comments will not be amiss. The essays selected from previous publications are not simply the *disjecta membra* of a motley conglomerate of writings: the interdependence of Hellenism, Judaism, and Christianity—this writer's lifelong concern—supply the unifying element. Even the three articles on Felix Mendelssohn are apposite; one may see this composer as a latter-day exponent of Judaeo-Christianity, the ancient rivalry between Judaism and Hellenism now replaced by the conflicting demands of German and Jewish allegiances. Not without profound urge did Mendelssohn write his oratorio *Paulus:* he, as well as his father, viewed it as an *apologia pro vita sua.* Judaeo-Christian interdependence, presented as a history of culture *sui generis* rather than a purely musical morphology, constitutes my theme. Jewish "priority" is neither claimed nor implied in these essays; I would hope, rather, that the enormous impact of Christian, Hellenistic, and Moslem thought emerges with clarity.

Let me bring up to date some details in the older articles.

...In "The Conflict between Hellenism and Judaism," the comparison of an Ambrosian with a Nestorian hymn is hardly tenable and not appropriate.

..."The Music of the Dead Sea Scrolls": My hope that the enigmatic signs (or accents?) would soon be unriddled has remained unfulfilled. On the other hand, my assumption of the calendaric basis of the Octoechos has been confirmed by the so-called "Temple Scroll" (not fully published as yet).

..."The Philosophy and Theory of Judaeo-Arabic Literature" (written with I. Sonne) has been excerpted and described in RISM *(Répertoire International des Sources Musicales,)* vol. B IX, 2, Munich 1975, ed. by Prof. Israel Adler. As the full text of the study does not appear in RISM, I welcome its republication here.

...In "Two obscure sources in Reuchlin's 'De accentibus...linguae Hebraicae,'"
I was unable to identify Flavius Mithridates with scholarly precision. This now
becomes possible, thanks to the genealogy given in *Monumenta Judaica*
(Cologne, 1963/4, I, p. 164). This shady personality was the son of the learned
Rabbi Nissim abu al-Fraadj; he subsequently converted to Christianity, taught
Hebrew at Cologne University, and moved to Rome, where in 1517 he was
elevated to the rank of Cardinal by Pope Leo X.

...As the literature on the Dead Scrolls has proliferated in the last decades, I will
cite here only one classic study, *The Scroll of the War of the Sons of Light
Against the Sons of Darkness* by Prof. Yigael Yadin, Jerusalem, London, 1962.

In a wider view, all the essays assembled in this volume deal with essential
parts of Western music's lineage, i.e., with the mainsprings of its tradition. Tradition, as understood here, is heritage, custom, law, living form. If it is dead, it
becomes a museum piece—or it is buried, as a venerable relic is buried, re-
verently, but removed from life. Ever since Arnold Schoenberg laid claim to the
word "traditional" in describing his and his disciples' music, the meaning of tradition has become controversial. Thus we are challenged to examine the tradition or the "main stream" of music *de novo.* And that is as it should be: what
we accept and cherish as enduring values warrants examination, testing, and
reassessment by every generation. Notwithstanding earlier belief, music is not
bound by dogma to fixed rules or principles.

The interaction of Hellenism, Judaism, and Christianity has nourished the
deepest and most powerful roots of our musical tradition. The threefold root
corresponds to the three main concerns of the sponsors in thought and gift: to
the Greeks belongs the glorious feat of having created, out of the ocean of innumerable sounds and noises that surrounded them, a clearly defined island of
individual tones, to be grouped in various scales and modes. The Greeks also
realized the mathematical-acoustical properties of tone, thus inaugurating the
oldest theory of music; they even paved the way towards a musical notation. To
the Jewish-Semitic culture belongs the profound concern with language, the
chanted word, and its intense association with the Holy. To Christianity belongs
the systematization of the—once far more spontaneous—cultic implementation
of music, its synthesis with Greek theory, Hebrew psalmody, and the rise and
growth of Western art music. The respective propensities of these endeavors
suggest the designations arithmogenic (Greek), logogenic (Jewish), and patho-
genic (Christian); art music may be seen as a perfect synthesis of the three,
greater than the sum of its components.

The musical tradition is fundamentally *oral,* notwithstanding the development of notation and the emergence of highly stylized structures in Judaism and
Christianity. As a consequence, many variations of basic tunes coexist, and the
music examples of this volume must be considered approximations of the norm
rather than fixed records of orally transmitted melodies.

Lévi-Strauss and other social scientists observe that the Western world has greatly misunderstood or misinterpreted the Orient—in fact, every non-Western civilization. In respect to music, such Western ethnocentrism distorts the history of the art and obscures the essential continuity of its evolution. The essays in this volume aim to demonstrate the humanistic ideal of spiritual continuity and the synthesis of East and West, thus affirming the sage's insight:

"Wer sich selbst und andre kennt,
Wird auch hier erkennen,
Orient und Okzident
Sind nicht mehr zu trennen."

"Who knows himself and others well
To him it will be plain
Orient and Occident
Are but one domain."

—(Goethe).

Author's Acknowledgments

Grateful acknowledgment for permission to publish the articles contained in this volume is made hereby to the editors and publishers of: *The Hebrew Union College Annual*, Cincinnati; *Acta Musicologica*, Copenhagen; *Atti del Congresso*, Rome; *Journal of the American Musicological Society*, Boston; *The Musical Quarterly*, New York; *The Free Press*, New York; *W.W. Norton & Co.*, New York; Prof. G. Kisch, former editor of *Historia Judaica*, New York; *The Bulletin of the New York Public Library*, New York; *Judaism*, New York; and Dr. I. Eisenstein, editor of *The Reconstructionist*, New York-Philadelphia. To Dr. Bea Friedland, executive editor of Da Capo Press, I feel deep gratitude for her readiness—indeed her suggestion—to republish these essays.

—E.W.

JUDAICA

The Common Ground in the Chant of Church and Synagogue

Reprinted with permission of *Congresso internazionale di musica sacra*, Roma, 1952, pp. 134-148.

While the Occident has always been receptive and susceptible to the great religious teachings of the Orient, none of them originated in the West. It paraphrased and transformed what the Orient offered, it assimilated the ideas to its own forms of thinking and feeling, and sometimes the Occident has succeeded in expanding and deepening originally Oriental conceptions. Yet never was the Occident able to match any of the gigantic symbols of Asia's religions with a creation of its own. Europe did deepen τὴν ὁδὸν τοῦ θεοῦ, it did create, on its own part, ideologies of wonderful purity, logic, beauty, and consequence, but none of them owns the elemental force of the great doctrines of the East. Music is no exception from that rule.

And yet, up to 1920 or so, the question as to the roots of Christian music has been somewhat controversial. Athens or Jerusalem? were the Tenores of the various battlehymns among the scholars. It is not necessary here to elaborate upon the purely Hellenistic theories of Gevaert, Fétis, or Emmanuel — they are today superseded by newer findings. So are the rather naive speculations of Dechevrens or Riemann, who attempted to prove the more or less direct Judeo-Byzantian origin of the venerable chants. Only when scholars, fully familiar with the liturgical as well as musical sources began to re-examine the evidence, the immense complexity of the problem became evident.

We owe this new comprehension of the problem chiefly to three eminent scholars of the first twenty years of the century — all of them dead by now : Peter Wagner and Amédée Gastoué on the Catholic, Abraham Z. Idelsohn, on the Jewish side.

Peter Wagner, in his monumental " Gregorianische Melodien " approached the question of the interdependence of Gregorian and Jewish chants first from the historical angle. While he could not give positive proof of his hypothesis, he at least formulated it clearly in these words :

" Some cantors of the Synagogue probably devoted their art to the service of the Christian Church ". We shall see later on that we know today even some names of Jewish converts, who, being cantors, transmitted Jewish tradition to the Church. In much more convincing manner Wagner demonstrated the influence of synagogal elements and techniques in his third volume, especially with reference to the forms of the Gradual, the Tractus, and the Allelujatic chant. We shall see that many of his theories have been substantiated by recent findings.

Amédée Gastoué devoted a special chapter to Jewish elements in his " L'origine du Chant Romain ", in which he directed attention to the masoretic accents of Scripture and their cantillation in the Synagogue. He concluded that Christian Psalmody was based upon Jewish patterns and gave a most interesting example in his analysis of Psalm 118, its accents and punctuating melisms in Church

3

and Synagogue. Later on, he wrote a series of articles "Chant Grégorien et chant juif" for the "Revue du Chant Grégorien", in which he unfolded the matter in a more extensive way.

Abraham Idelsohn's great contribution to the solution of the problem lies chiefly in the first two volumes of his Thesaurus of Hebrew Oriental Melodies, in which he personally collected and recorded the chants of the Yemenite and Babylonian Jews. To his surprise he discovered close resemblances with Gregorian tunes among these chants, although neither the Yemenite nor the Babylonian Jews had ever been in touch with Christianity ; actually, they were living in strict seclusion, separated even from the rest of world-Jewry. Since the Yemenites had emigrated from Palestine before the destruction of the Second Temple, the idea suggested itself that the identical melodies of Gregorian and Yemenite chant have a common root, namely the practice and tradition of pre- or early Christian Palestine. In twelve learned publications Idelsohn juxtaposed Jewish and Gregorian individual tunes; yet he never realized that such similarities of individual tunes offer little more but ground for conjecture and speculation without giving conclusive evidence. In another essay of his "Die Maqamen der Arabischen Musik" in S. I. M. he was the first one to distinguish between a mode and a scale, and he insisted that a mode be defined as a crystallized — and fictitious — melodic pattern, upon which many various individual tunes are based. P. Wagner himself wrote some reviews of Idelsohn's work and incorporated some of his findings in the last volume of his "Gregorianische Melodien".

Meanwhile the problem has been re-examined as a whole by numerous scholars, mainly by Wachsmann, Besseler, Curt Sachs, E. Wellesz, C. Hoeg, and me.

Klaus Wachsmann gave in his "Untersuchungen zum Vorgregorianischen Gesang" a critical summary of previous studies. He dwells especially on the gnostic notation, connected with Zosimos of Panopolis, also with the origin of the eight modes; he also offers convincing refutation of Gevaert's and Emmanuel's Pan-Hellenic theories. He does occasionally speculate on the interrelation between Hebrew, Byzantine, and Roman chant, without reaching definite conclusions. The work is a fine reference-book and critique of the contemporary theories on pre-Gregorian chant.

Heinrich Besseler made some valuable suggestions concerning the new spirit that arose with Christianity, that influenced all creative work of the first five or six centuries. Some of his formulations are ingenious, e. g., "According to our present knowledge, Psalmody whose dominating significance... is affirmed everywhere, invaded the practice of ancient music as a revolutionizing phenomenon". Or "Most amazing are the newly discovered relations between the chants of isolated Jewish communities in the Orient and Liturgical melodies of the Catholic Church..." I cannot, however, subscribe to Besseler's theory of the Iranian origin of the Antiphon. He makes Mani and Ephraem "honorary Aryans", on most questionable grounds, since both originated in Aramaic countries, and Ephraem was probably a converted Jew. Besides, the Manichaen hymns show exactly the same parallelismus membrorum as the classic Semitic poetry of the Old Testament and of the early Syriac poets.

In his ingenious book "The Rise of Music in the Ancient World", Curt Sachs proposes a number of new theories, perspectives, and vistas. Its greatest value lies in the author's familiarity with the music of the Orient as well as of the Occident. Thus, he was able to demonstrate hidden relations between the Far East, the Near East, between the Islamic and the Hellenistic theories of music. While he only occasionally touches on the interdependence of Gregorian and Hebrew chant, he demonstrates convincingly the interrelation of Egyptian, Assyrian, Hebrew, Syrian, Coptic, and Abyssinian chant. To him the history of the world's music is one indivisible, complex continuum.

Egon Wellesz has devoted his efforts during the last thirty years to incisive studies of the Byzantine chant, besides publishing a goodly number of papers on the chant of Oriental Christianity in general. In his latest large publications "Eastern Elements in Western Chant" and "A History of Byzantine Music and Hymnography" he refers frequently to Jewish elements in Byzantine chant and dedicates an entire chapter to the "Legacy of the Synagogue". Being a pioneer in the study of Byzantine chant, his is the outstanding merit to have recognized early the composite character of Byzantine music, and even more, to have insisted that the study of liturgical music be conducted in close connection with the study of the concomitant liturgy itself. Among his important ideas and theories I mention two, to which I shall return later : he suggests that Hebrew influence came to Byzantine music via the Syrian liturgies and poems; moreover he is convinced, and presents his theory plausibly that certain melismatic chants are remnants of the liturgy of the Temple or the Early Synagogue.

A specialist in early notation is Carsten Hoeg, whose "La notation ecphonétique" has remained the standard-work up to the present day. His discussion of the Hebrew accents is good and up to date, but the Judeo-Arabic sources of early grammarians such as Ibn Balaam, that shed entirely new light on the problem, were unaccessible to him. Together with Wellesz he follows a suggestion of Professor Paul Kahle and Dr. Baumstark, based upon two remarks of Cassiodore, namely that the rabbinic academy in Nisibis and the Nestorian school of biblical exegesis there in the late Fourth century in mutual collaboration evolved the primeval systems of Syrian and Hebrew accents. Moreover, Hoeg traces the lectio solemnis of the Orthodox Church back to the Scriptural cantillation of Oriental Jewry; he feels that the Hellenistic world, while using the *Koine* as its vernacular, imitated in the rendition of the pericopes the Hebrew manner of cantillation and applied it not only to texts of the Old Testament, but also to the new texts of the Christian Church. We shall see later on that this theory has been strongly substantiated on the Jewish side.

Quantum mutati ab illis! is our exclamation, when we consider the abundance of new ideas and theories. And yet, with all these new approaches, we have heard relatively few facts. I except here Drs. Wellesz and Hoeg, since the interrelation of Jewish and Byzantine music is a rather recent aspect of the general problem and they have paid much attention to this matter.

But since these gentlemen are with us and present their own papers, I take now the liberty of speaking of my own endeavors and studies in this field. I shall be brief, but I apologize if I succumb to the danger : Brevis esse laboro obscurus fio.

I. — NEW FINDINGS.

A) For many years I have tried to find conclusive evidence of persons, who transmitted the synagogal tradition to the Church. It was only four years ago, when I eventually discovered some pertinent facts. These facts consist of two epitaphs here in Rome that are by no means unknown, upon the tombstone of early Christian singers. I quote from Rossi's "Roma Sotteranea" (III, p. 239, 242)

> "Hic levitarum primus in ordine vivens
> Davitici cantor carminis iste fuit."

The inscription is found on the tombstone of the archidiaconus Deusdedit, which is the typical convert's Latinization of the Hebrew name Jonathan. The other inscription reads :

> "Prophetam celebrans placido modulamine senem
> Haec fuit insontis vitæ laudata juventus".

The name of the inscription is Redemptus, also a convert's by-name. Both epitaphs originated in the time of Pope Damasus, who, according to Gregory the Great, introduced traditions from Jerusalem. The term "levita" in the first inscription does not stand for Diaconus, as Battifol assumes, since the title is here specified "primus in ordine", which refers to the 24 ranks of Levites of the Temple. The "senex propheta" is obviously David, whose Psalms were considered "prophetia". The "placido modulamine" would justify St. Athanasius' characterization of scriptural recitation as "melodious", which must have been more like the Hebrew-Syrian cantillation than the "severe" style of the Roman Tonus lectionis.

B) An earlier source, Clemens Alexandrinus, contains a passage in his *Pedagogue* in which the author presents contemporary Jewish Psalmody as an exemplar for Christians to follow. He refers to that particular Psalmody as similar to the *Tropos Spondeiacos* of which fortunately Plutarch and Aristides Quintilianus gave us a technical analysis. Based upon this analysis, I was able to trace the *Tropos Spondiacus* in the oldest strata of Gregorian, Byzantine, and Hebrew chant. Among other items, you will find the Gloria of the 14th mass as well as other archaic pieces belonging to that mode. (See exhibit A)

C) The origin of the Octoechos has been a subject of speculation during the last 150 years. Wachsmann, Wellesz, and Baumstark came close to solving the problem of its origin, but the last link always escaped them. Only since we know that the ancient calendar-system of Mesopotamia, Syria, and Palestine was the Pentacontade, it was possible to collect the disiecta membra. A Pentacontade system is 7 weeks plus one day, such as the period between Easter and Pentecost. The calendars of Eastern Christianity have preserved a number of such units, especially the Armenian calendar with three, and the Nestorian with four complete Pentacontades. Inserted in the Pentacontade are seven plus one Sundays. This system dates back to ancient Babylonia and has left its traces in all cultures of the Near East. I was able to demonstrate that the Syrian Octoechos by Severus of Antioch presupposes a complete Pentacontade, namely that *after* Pentecost. The system of eight numerical modes is thus a symbolic reflection of an ancient calendaric institution. The Gnostics, especially the Valentinians, stressed the idea of the Ogdoas, being the Spirit of Sabbatum which represents the Holy Seven, plus One, resulting in the Supreme Deity. Already the apocryphal acts of St. John depict the scene, where Christ, standing in the circle of his twelve disciples, admonishes them to sing and dance around him. I quote the crucial passage :

> " I would be thought, being wholly thought. Amen.
>
> I would be washed, and I would wash,   Amen.
>
> Grace danceth ; I shall pipe; dance ye all.   Amen.
>
> I would mourn, lament ye all.   Amen.
>
> The Ogdoas singeth praise with us.   Amen ".

It can be demonstrated that the idea of the eight "musical days" of the Pentacontade is older than the Psalter, since it contains indications of it, especially in Psalms 6, Psalm 12, and Psalm 29. In my study on the "Origin of the eight modes" I dealt extensively with all these facts and evidences. Thus, we know today that the principle of the Octoechos originated probably in the second millennium before Christ in Asia Minor as a symbolic-calendaric conception.

II. — NEW APPROACHES.

The facts that I shall present to you in the following, are not so much the results of new or hitherto unknown sources, but of a new approach. Convinced as I am of the deep and inherent connection between ancient Christian and ancient Jewish chant, I tried first to establish the time when the respective TEXTS first were introduced into the various liturgies. This led me into a comparative historico-philological study of liturgy, which I hope to present next year as my Book "The Sacred Bridge". Now, as you know, it is sometimes very difficult to establish a terminus a quo for individual liturgical texts. On the other hand, liturgy and music are so inseparable in Church and Synagogue, that they can never be studied separately in a systematical and fruitful way. Thus, I began to concentrate my attention not on individual tunes or texts, but on those entire groups that constitute the framework of the liturgical music of the Church. Since I have little time left, I shall discuss here only my results concerning Plain Psalmody, the Tractus, the Te Deum and similar forms of the Ordinarium and some hymn-types.

It is virtually impossible to touch within these limits upon any of the numerous problems of Psalmody extensively; therefore I must confine myself to *listing* some of the main results of my studies :

a) Roman Catholic tradition distinguishes well between various levels of Psalmody according to the degree of their liturgical occasions : thus, there is a Psalmus in directum at the Weekday Office, but responsorial or antiphonal performance on the Sunday Mass; such criteria are missing in synagogal tradition, where distinction is made only between Weekday and Sabbath or Feast, but none such as that between an office and a Mass. P. Wagner derives many elements of plain Psalmody from the lectionary practice; this is only a *theory* in Gregorian Chant, but an obvious fact in the music of the Synagogue. The scriptural accents were slightly modified and finally resulted in the punctuating melisms such as Mediant, Flexa, and Punctum. In many cases the basic identity is still apparent. (See Exhibit B) where I give a comparative tabulation of the antiphonal psalmtones according to the Commemoratio Brevis and the Oriental Jewish Psalmody. Roman and Jewish Psalmody becomes practically identical in the Lamentations; here all Roman versions have Jewish counterparts, all Jewish versions Roman counterparts. Even the cadences of some of the Psalms on Holy Saturday (e. g., Psalms 14 or 75) that are not in line with the ordinary Psalm-tones, are identical with the congregational " Amen " formula on the Day of Atonement. It can be demonstrated that the entire structure of the liturgy of Holy Saturday was constituted of elements of the Day of Atonement and the Feast of Passover combined. The lessons shall show that most clearly. On the Byzantine and Armenian Psalmodies and their relation to Judaism I shall speak later on, also about the *Tonus Peregrinus.*

b) Already Wagner wrote : " The punctuating melisms, typical of the Tractus, are not of Latin origin... The preservation of numerous archaic elements causes us to say : the real source of the Tractus can be nothing else but the Jewish-synagogal Solo-Psalmody ". Thus far Wagner. Let us for a moment assemble the known *musical* facts of the Tractus. It uses only the II and VIII mode, it consists of recurrent phrases and melisms, that can be reduced to relatively few formulas as Gevaert and Riemann demonstrated, and finally, it displays clearly punctuating melisms. What are these typical melisms? Usually a succession of Climacus, Podatus, Clivis, or of Pressus, Clivis, or of Clivis, Quilisma, Torculus, Clivis. Now, I have demonstrated elsewhere that all tractus without exception have two cadencing melisms in common. These melisms are identical with the Hebrew half-stop and full-stop accents of the prophetic lesson in all Jewish centers. These two melisms run in a sharply contoured line, which I give as my third example. (Exhibit C) They also occur in the oldest responsoria of the Church as well as in the distinctive tune of the Eulogy that precedes and follows the prophetic lesson of the Synagogue. Moreover, the Hebrew passage that carries these recurrent melisms, is " Zion, the house of life ", or " Adonai ", or " forever and ever ". The same or similar words are connected with the melisms of the

7

Latin text, such as, Sion, Israel, Domino, aeternum, Dilecto, etc. Can this astounding identity be a mere coincidence? If we bear in mind that originally the Tractus was considered a second psalm (after the Gradual) and that the solistic Psalmody preceded the antiphonal one, and finally, that the Tractus is an important element of the oldest stratum of the liturgy — the services of Good Friday and Holy saturday — our conclusions are obvious : The Tractus are, next to some psalm-tones and lection-tones, the oldest and best preserved strata of Gregorian chant. They go back to the eulogies connected with the prophetic lesson of the Synagogue. When Jesus recited the *Haftara* from the book of Isaiah, as described in Luke 4, 16-18, he performed it probably like a Tractus, only in a simpler manner. It is interesting to note that the combination of neumes mentioned before, occurs practically without change in all manuscripts down to the Tenth Century.

c) The chants of the Ordinarium originated, as you know, in the centuries between 300 and 1600, and are thus by no means homogeneous in structure, melos, or modal attitude. Yet there are two items that show both in music and in their verbiage distinctly archaic features. While the Te Deum does today not belong to the Ordinarium, I included it since it and the Gloria display many similarities. The text of Te Deum is arranged according to the old Semitic principle of homotony : that means : every line contains the same number of accentuated syllables, not according to quantity, but according to the natural oratorical accent. In the Te Deum we read :

> Té Déum laudámus — Té Dóminum confitémur
>
> Té ætérnum Pátrem — Ómnis Térra venerátur
>
> Tíbi ómnes Ángeli — Tíbi Cǽli et univérsæ Potestátes
>
> Tíbi Chérubim et Séraphim — incessábili vóce proclámant
>
> Sánctus, Sánctus, Sánctus — Dóminus Déus Sabáoth.

Ancient Hebrew and Syriac prayers of the Third or Fourth century show exactly this kind of homotony.

Musically speaking, the Te Deum and the Gloria of the 14th and 15th Mass belong to the same melodic pattern : both represent an archaic type of syllabic, hymnic Psalmody. And in my next example I juxtapose the tone of the Te Deum, that of the 15th Gloria, and that of the Yemenite *Sh'ma*, the oldest core of Hebrew liturgy, and a sample of Yemenite scriptural, cantillation. (Exhibit D). Now I do not claim that a direct process of transfusion took place in these cases, but I am convinced that two of the oldest hymns of the Church and two ancient tones of the Oriental Synagogue all exhibiting a particular type of homotony and the same melodic patterns go back to the same source : namely to that type to which we already directed your attention, the *Tropos Spondeiakos*, which, according to Clemens Alexandrinus, was so reminiscent of Jewish Psalmody.

Another similarity in the Ordinarium presents the famous Sanctus of the 9th Mass. The Jewish liturgy for the High Holy Days has exactly this melody. We hear in a source, called "The Vale of Tears" of the 12th century, that the Jews of Blois, while burned on the stake by the mob that followed the crusaders, intoned that melody, and that the Christians, awed and inspired, bared their heads, and took over this sainted tune. While there are parallel motifs in other Jewish liturgies, this case will bear further study and research, before it is possible to reach definite conclusions — for the case might be just the reverse : the Jews borrowed this chant from the Church, and this would be by no means a singular case! For after the 10th century, Jewry — nilly-willy — began to assimilate to itself Christian texts, poems as well as melodies.

8

d) This is especially discernible in hymn-tunes. When the Jews admitted metrical poems in their liturgy, they had to abandon, at least in these pieces, the free recitative or psalmodic style on which the entire music of the Near East had thrived for so many centuries. Especially the European Jews did a good deal of paraphrasing hymn-tunes of the Church, against all rabbinical injunctions. Hence we must not be surprised to encounter at least the Incipits of such hymns as " Alma redemptoris mater " or " Te lucis ante terminum " in the chants of Spanish, Italian, or even German Jews. Somewhat different is the case of the " Iste confessor " whose almost complete tune can be found in the musical liturgy of all Jewish centers, except the Yemenite ones. Since the Incipit of that hymn also occurs in Byzantine chant, and some of its motifs pervade all of the chants of the High Holy days, we might look for a common source, possibly in old Syrian or Hebrew chant.

The literary antecedents of the text of the Sequence " Dies iræ, dies illa " present a similar but vastly more important case of " wandering ideas and motifs ". My attention was directed to this problem when I examined the late T. Wehofer's study on Romanos' hymn on the Parousia of Christ. I detected in that hymn most of the literary motifs of the " Dies iræ ", but also all of the motifs of a famous Hebrew prayer for New Year. I sought to establish Romanos' extraction, and through Dr. Wellesz' kind assistance I eventually found two Byzantine sources, published by Dr. Maas, which testify to the fact that Romanos was of Jewish parentage and came from Beyrut. My esteemed colleague Dr. Zulay of the Hebrew University in Jerusalem made accessible to me a manuscript of the British Museum, of the early 8th century, which constitutes the first *Hebrew* manuscript of the prayer. The motifs can be traced to various rabbinical sources, especially to the *Tosefta Rosh ha-shana*, which originated in the late Second century. In (Exhibit E) you will find a comparative table of the literary motifs. In Romanos' hymn they follow each other in the same order as in the Hebrew prayer; in the " Dies iræ " we find several deviations from the ancient pattern. In spite of Mone's, Blume's and other hymnologists' efforts to trace the origin of the " Dies iræ " beyond the 13th century, we still do not know, how this significant accumulation of eschatological conceptions came to Italy from Byzantium; for it would be hardly justifiable to consider the Latin composition entirely original, in view of the much older Byzantine and Hebrew poems.

III. — PROBLEMS NEW AND OLD.

In this last section of my paper permit me, Gentlemen, to discuss briefly a few problems that are certainly familiar to you. The reason, why I would like to talk about them is the simple fact that some of these problems assume an entirely different aspect when they are considered from an angle that is not too familiar to you, namely from the view-point of the Science of Judaism. I single out three outstanding questions, on which an entire literature has been written; and I do not pretend that I can at present contribute essentially new facts to their solution. I merely want to draw your attention to certain sources that hitherto have been neglected by many musicologists.

A) The origin of neumatic notation is a classic illustration of my point. Carsten Hoeg has discussed the possible influence of Massoretic scriptural accents upon the development of ecphonetic neumes. I attempted to compare the Protopalestinian accents — known only for about fifty years — to his examples of neumation, based upon the manuscript Sinaiticus 8 and Leimon-Monastery and have had the satisfaction to realize that the basic accents, namely Oxeia, Apostrophoi, Kremaste ap' ezo, and Teleia, correspond well, both in function and in their application, to their Hebrew counterparts.

These Protopalestinian accents, however, show little external similarity to the ecphonetic signs. On the other hand, the Tiberian accents, that were developed after the 8th century, are surprisingly akin, at least *externally*, to the ecphonetic accents. They originated, however, two to three centuries after the first Byzantine sources, and it seeme to me very probable that the Tiberian system is but an elaborated imitation of the older Byzantine pattern. Different is the case of the Proto-palestinian accents; their punctuation of the Text of the Old Testament is based upon very old traditions, and their signs are similar to the old Syriac accents. Hence I have the strong impression that the Syrian and Protopalestinian systems originated simultaneously in an area that became shortly thereafter a battleground between the forces of Nestorianism and those of the Orthodox Church. This would yield the time after 440 and the region between Edessa, Nisibis, Melitene, and the Armenian Ashtishat. The writings of Armenian and Syrian Fathers, such as Sahak, Mesrop, Rabbula, Acacius, and Etznik of Kolb allude to the dogmatic struggle between Byzantium and Syro-Armenian groups. In addition Professor Kahle's interpretation of a passage in Cassiodorus was already mentioned, wherein the Saint refers to a Nestorian and rabbinic school of exegesis in Nisibis, which seem to have collaborated. From there the old Syriac system might have been taken to Byzantium and developed upon more Greek ideas and methods.

B) Indirectly connected with this question is the problem of the Tonus Peregrinus. It seems to me that one should consider this Psalm-tone merely as a special case where the Oriental practice of Double Tenores was permitted to make serious inroads in the logically and theoretically flawless system of the Roman Church. For the principle of two Tenores is nothing extraordinary in Oriental chant. As a matter of fact, we encounter in rabbinical literature at least two allusions to this practice, in particular, when the performance of the *Hallel* is discussed. It so happens, that the model psalm of the Tonus Peregrinus is the first psalm of the Hallel : " In exitu Israel ex Egypto domus Jacob de populo barbaro ". It might interest you to learn that among the Oriental, but also among the Lithuanian Jews this psalm is sung at Passover-time in a tune very much akin to the Tonus Peregrinus. This might be nothing more than a coincidence, but it cannot be a coincidence that the version of the Tonus Peregrinus of the *Antiphonale Sarisburiense* is identical, tone for tone and note for note, with the *Hallel*-tone of the Yemenite Jews — the same text with the same melody! Father Vivell once claimed synagogal origin of the Peregrinus, and Idelsohn's and my findings support perfectly his theory.

C) Turning finally to a problem of general nature, I would like to say a few words concerning the liturgical and musical interdependence of Latin, Armenian, Byzantine, and Jewish rituals.

Musically speaking, there can be no doubt that closest to the Jewish tradition are the archaic strata of Gregorian and Ambrosian chant. Yet, in comparison with the more general structures and archetypes, the identity of *individual* chants in Synagogue and Church, while frequently evident, is not of paramount relevance. In most cases, it was the wonderfully ordering and systematizing genius of the Occidental Church that has preserved the precious and ancient legacy; while the chant of eastern churches was frequently contaminated by Arabic and Turkish influences, and has never been able to bring order into that almost chaotic garden of tunes, modes, and musical symbols. It was the merit of the Latin Church to shape organically the flourishing tunes, even if in many cases its method of systematization had to sacrifice individual details of great beauty. Only in this way was it possible at all to save so much.

There is one exception to this rule : the Byzantine Alleluja. While it is true that the Jubilus is a " mos ecclesiæ orientalis ", and a " canticum

Hebræorum " as St. Ambrosius and St. Isidorus emphasize, I was unable to find Jewish elements in the Jubili of the *Latin Church*. Hence I am convinced that Gennrich and Blume are right, who trace the origin of the Latin Jubili to France and Germany before the 10th century. There is, however, a direct relationship between Byzantine and Jewish Alleluias. What the root of this kinship is, I am unable to say. Possibly the Byzantines received their Alleluias from Syria, where Jewish converts served te Church most faithfully. This matter should be investigated further.

Liturgically, the Armenian tire is most closely related to Judaism; and there are weighty historical reasons fo that strange fact. Yet, I am still unable to account for the many post-biblical Hebraisms that permeate the old Armenian liturgy.

Musically, the Armenian technique of modal variation upon an archaic cantus is also reminiscent of the Synagogue; but this kinship indicates only that the Armenians no less than the Oriental Jews were exposed to the same — basically Arabic — techniques of elaboration upon a given mode. Moreover, this technique is, at least in the Synagogue, not older than the 12th or 13th century and has no significance for the archaic strata of its chant.

Confluence and transformation! These two words spell, what we generally call the history of culture and idea. Spontaneity and order, while fundamentally antagonistic, are the mutually indispensable forces that have imprinted their seal upon the relationship of Orient and Occident. Nowhere are these dynamics of antithetical and synthesizing impulses of greater moment than in the realm of religious art. Its spectrum has more than the customary seven colors. Its rainbow engulfs the whole earth. Its historical symbol throughout the Millennia is the Sacred Bridge.

EXHIBIT A

TROPOS SPONDEIAKOS.

ABBREVIATIONS : HUCA = Hebrew Union College Aunnal.
LU   = Liber usualis.

HUCA 1947, *p.* 427-428

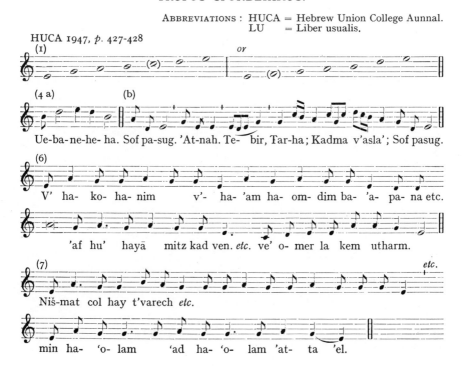

Ue-ba-ne-he- ha. Sof pa-sug. 'At-nah. Te- bir, Tar-ha; Kadma v'asla'; Sof pasug.

V' ha- ko- ha- nim   v'- ha- 'am ha- om- dim ba- 'a- pa- na etc.

'af hu' hayā   mitz kad ven. *etc.* ve' o- mer la kem utharm.

Niš-mat col hay t'varech *etc.*

min ha- 'o- lam   'ad ha- 'o- lam 'at- ta 'el.

(11) Cp. with ♯ 1, 2 a, 6, 4 6, 7, 8, 10. HUCA 1947 *p.* 428

Καὶ ὢν ἐν κόλ- ποις τοῦ Πα - τρός....

ἰ- λάσ- 3η- τι ταῖς ἀ- μαρ- τίαις ἡ- μῶν.

D

Te Deum (first verses)

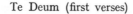

Te De- um lau-da- mus, Te Do- mi- num con-fi- te- mur,

(later verses)

Ve-ne- randum tu- um ve- rum Tu Patris sempi-ternus es Fi- li- us.

Gloria (LU p. 55)

Glo- ri- a in excel- sis De- o... Qui tol- lis pec-ca- ta mundi, *etc.*

su-sci- pe de-pre- ca- ti- o- nem nostram.

Yemenite Sh'ma (IT vol. I p. 71)

(a) *etc.*

Yemenite Thora-cantillation (IT vol. II)

(b)

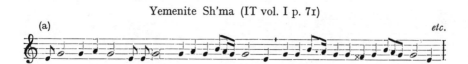

12

C

Responses and Tractus :

Enlogy of the *Haftara*. Friedmann Chasonus, *p.* 82

(1) Tractus « Qui confidunt » LU 500.   (2) Tr. « Saepe expugnaverunt » LU 507.

(3) Resp. «Confitemini Domini LU 674.   (4) Tr. « Cantemus Domini » LU 660.

(5) Tr. « Benedicite » LU 1105.

TABLE I.

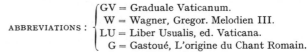

ABBREVIATIONS :
- GV = Graduale Vaticanum.
- W = Wagner, Gregor. Melodien III.
- LU = Liber Usualis, ed. Vaticana.
- G = Gastoué, L'origine du Chant Romain.

Tonus in directum. LU 1178.   Tonus peregrinus. LU 120.

or W 109.

Ist Tone. (a) Office.

(b) Mass. W.

(c) Differentia for VIIIth Tone.

(d) Differentia for II.   Differentia for Antiphone.

Second Tone. (a) Office.

(b) Mass.

Third Tone. (a) Office. LU 111.

Differentiæ. Older form : W 109.

(B) Mass. W

Characteristic Differentia of (b).

Fourth Tone. (a) Office. C 59/60.

(b) or

Other cadence of (a). Other position of IVth Tone. LU 113.

Fifth Tone. (a) Office. Old form. W. Later form. LU 115.

(b) Mass.

or (c) Invitat. of the Easter Vigil. LU 630.

Sixth Tone. (a) Office. Old version. W. (b) Mass. GV.

Seventh Tone. (a) Office. LU 117. or

14

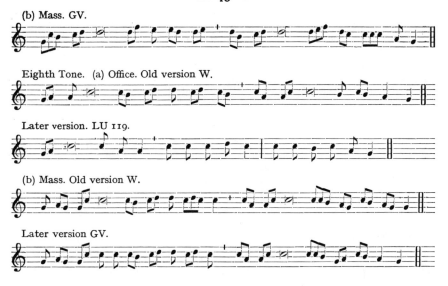

(b) Mass. GV.

Eighth Tone. (a) Office. Old version W.

Later version. LU 119.

(b) Mass. Old version W.

Later version GV.

TABLE 2.

JEWISH PARALLELS.

ABBREVIATIONS :
- IT = a. 3. Idelsohn, Thesaurus of Hebrew, Oriental Melodies, 10 vols.
- EW¹ = E. Werner. Preliminary notes etc. (HUCA 1940).
- — ² Doxology in synagogue o Church (HUCA).
- JM = a. 3. Idelsohn Jewish Music in its historical Development 1946.

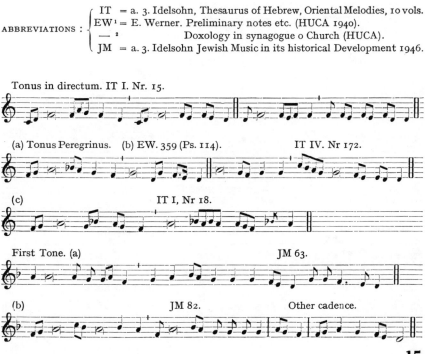

Tonus in directum. IT I. Nr. 15.

(a) Tonus Peregrinus.   (b) EW. 359 (Ps. 114).   IT IV. Nr 172.

(c)   IT I, Nr 18.

First Tone. (a)   JM 63.

(b)   JM 82.   Other cadence.

(c) (d) (e) Accents Merkha-Tebir.

Second Tone. (a) IT II. Nr 41. (b) IT I. Nr 27, 10, etc.

Third Tone. (a) IT IV. Nr 144.

(b) IT I. Nr 14.

Fourth Tone. (a) IT II. Nr 127.

(b) (Transposed) IT II. Nr 58.

Fifth Tone. (a) JM p. 76. (b) IT II p. 75.

Sixth Tone. (a) JM p. 63, Nr 10 (cf. G p. 131) (b) IT II Nr 103.

Seventh Tone. (a) IT I. Nr 49.

(b)

Eighth Tone. (a) IT I. Nr 10.

(b) Transposed! IT IV. Nr 184.

(c) IT IV. Nr 260. (d) Akdamuth.

EXHIBIT A

Hebrew	*Romanos Hymn*	*Dies irae*
The angels shudder, fear and trembling seize them.	ἔλαθε τὰς ἄνω ἐξουσίας δυνάμεις τε καὶ ἀγγέλων τάγματα	Quantus tremor est futurus
Thou dostopen the book of record; Thou dost recall all things long forgotten	Καὶ βίβλοι διανοίγονται καὶ τὰ κρυπτὰ δημοσιεύονται	Liber scriptus proferetur, in quo totum continetur. Quidquid latet, adparebit
The angels shudder; they say : " this is the day of judgment ", for in jutice, not even they are found faultless before Thee.	Καὶ τρέμουσι σύμπαντα οὐδεὶς οὐκ ἐξισχύσει ἀληθείας ἐλεγχούσης Ὅλα τὰ μνήματα σείονται.	
The great Trumpet is sounded	ἐνηχούσης τῆς σάλπιγγος	Tuba mirum spargens sonum
They are not pure before Thee, not even the righteous ones		Quid sum miser tunc diturus... cum vix justus sit securus ?
As the shepherd mustereth his flock, so dost Thou cause to pass, number... every living soul...	Πάντες δὲ οἱ ζῶντες ἁρπαγήσονται ἄθροον συντελεῖται δὲ ἄπαντα	Inter oves locum praesta, et ab hoedis me sequestra
My petitions are not worthy, but penitence, prayer, and charity may avert the evil decree.	ἐν τῷ κόσμῳ τὸν τῆς μετατοίας Καρπὸν ἐπεδειξάμεθα Κἂν εὕρομεν ἔλεος Καὶ χάριν καὶ ἄφεσιν	Preces meae non sunt dignae... Supplicanti parce, Deus.

The Origin of Psalmody

Reprinted with permission of *Hebrew Union College Annual*, 25, 1954, pp. 327-345.

I

PROFESSOR HUIZINGA of Leyden has, with no little ingenuity, shown the close kinship between ritual and play.[1] From Professor Huizinga's work we quote the following significant lines:

> Ritual is seriousness at its highest and holiest. Can it nevertheless be play? We began by saying that all play, both of children and of grown-ups, can be performed in the most perfect seriousness. Does this go so far as to imply that play is still bound up with the sacred emotion of the sacramental act? . . . The play character, therefore, may attach to the sublimest forms of action. Can we now extend the line to ritual and say that the priest performing the rites of sacrifice is only playing? At first sight it seems preposterous, for if you grant it for one religion you must grant it for all. Hence our ideas of ritual, magic, liturgy, sacrament and mystery would all fall into the play-concept.

In the sacred recreation called ritual, psalmody plays a vital part.

What are the musical elements that constitute the chant of psalmody? The systematization offered by the Gregorian scholars will, notwithstanding its rigidity, render us appreciable assistance. In *La Paléographie Musicale*, near the beginning of the third volume, the editors express themselves as follows:

> La structure psalmodique se compose de trois parties: une intonation (initium); une récitation, (tenor), et des cadences; (clausulae, mediantes ou finales), ponctuant, d'après des types mélodiques fixes, les membres de phrase et les phrases.
>
> L'accent est l'expression de ce qu'il y a de plus musical dans language, considéré à ce point de vue, il est une mélodie. Voilà un prémier charactère que nous devons retrouver dans les cantilènes liturgiques.[2]

---

[1] J. Huizinga, *Homo Ludens*, New York, 1950, pp 158 ff.
[2] *La Paléographie Musicale*, III, p. 9 ll.

These sentences set forth explicitly the nature of psalmody. At
the same time they imply something not expressly stated,
namely, the *paralellismus membrorum*, inseparable from all
psalmodic structure.[3] This characteristic has to be grasped before
we can understand the other characteristics, especially that of
musical punctuation.

Occidental psalmody exhibits a close interplay of those
constituent factors. Does the same apply to other psalmodies?
It does, although in other cultures, as well as in certain strata
of the Gregorian chant itself, the separate elements and the
interaction of those elements show not so much fixety. Parallelism, with the major and minor caesuras, remains prerequisite;
similarly the melodic line with a discernible tendency towards
an identifiable tenor; also the syllabic quality uneffaced by any
excess of melismatic phrases. Thus modified, the psalmodic
structure is common to all three monotheistic religions.[4] Yet
modality, stressed though it is in the psalmody of the Jews and
of the Latin Christians, is not always perceptible, particularly
in the oriental Church where the traditions of psalmody were not
so firmly grounded. Likewise in Arabic, Syrian, and oriental
Jewish psalmody, it is sometimes not possible to make out a
particular mode. This is due to the frequent mixture of the
various modal patterns. Moreover, ending as a matter of course
with the same finales — in Gregorian Psalm tones, the general
rule — also does not feature those other psalmodic types.

In all Catholic churches, in Judaism, and in Islam, an
essential ingredient of the ritual is cantillation. The Latin *lectio
solemnis* and the Hebrew chanting of the Pentateuch have
prominent features in common.[5] Both the *lectio solemnis* and
Hebrew cantillation exhibit, besides punctuating melisms, a

---

[3] *Ibid.*, discusses at length the parallelistic nature of psalmody later on.

[4] It is no accident that the monotheistic religions are the main vehicles
of genuine psalmody. Later we shall see that psalmody is rooted in the genius
of the Semitic languages. Since all three monotheistic religions originated in
Semitic countries, this was bound to be the case, no matter how psalmody
was afterward modified by Occidental languages and cultures.

[5] My book, *The Sacred Bridge*, now in press, will discuss this badly
neglected topic.

discernible inclination toward an identifiable tenor and, in most cases, parallelisms. In fact, Hebrew cantillation has developed punctuating melisms further than it has developed plain psalmody. But it is doubtful whether this applied to all times and places. When Judah Halevi stated that "A hundred persons cantillate the Torah as one person, stopping in one moment and continuing simultaneously," he said something that boldly conflicts with the practice of today whether Yemenite or Sephardic or Ashkenazic.[6] The Latin *lectio solemnis*, by contrast, heeds only punctuations of the major kinds. In the Byzantine ecphonetic cantillation, signs of punctuation do occur, but there is no musically identifiable tenor; the ecphonesis being only a *Sprechgesang*, something intermediate between speech and musical tone.[7]

According to historical records, the entrance of psalmody into the ancient Greek and Roman world came as something revolutionary. Persons unfamiliar with it found it astonishing. No uncertainty is left on that score by the Ecclesiastical History of Socrates or by the writings of Diodorus of Tarsus, Clement of Alexandria, Pliny the Younger, even Jerome — those writers who were either pagans or Christians of gentile extraction. No such amazement marks the writings of the Apostles or of others familiar with Jewish or with Syrian ways. Paul treats psalmody as nothing out of the ordinary.

Those to whom psalmody was a wonder contrast it with the music of the theater and of the circus. John Chrysostom pronounced the function of psalmody to be that of producing *compunctio cordis*, contriteness of heart.[8] And: "It is the power as well as the mystery of the Davidic Psalms that they are capable of keeping our mind free from all happenings of daily life."[9] Eusebius speaks of psalmody as a harmony of the soul which generates goodness of conduct even if the singing is unattended by con-

---

[6] Jehuda Halevi, *Kusari*, II, 76, ed. Cassel.
[7] For musical examples, cf. C. Hoeg, *La Notation Ecphonetique*, Copenhagen, 1935.
[8] John Chrysostom, *De Compunctione Cordis*, II, 1.
[9] Andreas of Caesarea in P. G. 106, 1072.

templation.[10] Augustine held psalmody to be a new kind of music which David invented as a mystic device for serving God.[11] Jerome testifies repeatedly to the exquisiteness of hearing vast congregations sing Psalms in such unison that "it all but lifted the roof." The responsorial rendering of Psalms at the church service — men, women, and children participating — is likened by Ambrose to the power of the ocean.[12] The same church father eulogizes psalmody as "the blessing of the people, the praise of God, the exultation of the community, the voice of the Church, the applause of everybody, the enjoyment of freedom."[13] Chrysostom declared that the purpose of psalmody is not art but instruction — such instruction as advances and tranquilizes the soul.[14] Also the Rabbis extol the psalter, but without any amazement at its potencies, except in cabalistic literature where it is considered a powerful mystic tool.

II

Bearing in mind the antiquity of Psalm singing and the paucity of reliable sources, we would do best to trace the development of each of the three constituents separately. While psalmody represents a synthesis of all three, each ingredient is older than the compound. Despite its simple appearance, psalmody is not something elemental. Psalmody is a product of reflection and organization.

A *sine qua non* of psalmody is parallelism. Parallelism, though familiar to us from the Bible and its imitations, began long before the Bible. It shows itself in the ancient literatures of Egypt, Akkad, Babylonia, and Ugarit. It is common to all Semitic and Hamitic languages. The differences among them are differences of degree and quantity, not any differences as regards the presence or the absence of parallelism. Degrees of parallelism

---

[10] Eusebius, Comment. in *Psalmos*, beginning.
[11] Augustine, *De Civitate Dei*, VII, 14.
[12] Ambrose, in P. L. 14, 178.
[13] *Ibid.*, P. L. 14, 924.
[14] Chrystomus, in *Psalm.* 100.

can be illustrated by comparing some pre-biblical samples of
parallelism with the biblical. An Egyptian example is:

> The Lord of truth and father of all gods
> Who made all mankind and created the beasts,
> Lord of what is, who created the fruit tree
> Made herbage and gave life to cattle.[15]

A Sumero-Akkadian example is:

> Who — to her greatness, who can be equal?
> Strong, exalted, splendid are her decrees.
> Istar — to her greatness who can be equal?[16]

A Sumerian example is:

> Let the weapons of battle return to your side,
> Let them produce fear and terror.
> As for him, when he come, verily my great fear
>   will fall upon him,
> Verily his judgment will be confounded, his
>   counsel will be dissipated.[17]

An Akkadian example is:

> I will show Gilgamesh, the joyful man!
> Look thou at him, regard his face.
> He is radiant with manhood, vigor he has.
> With ripeness gorgeous is the whole of his body
> Mightier strength has he than thou,
> Never resting by day or by night.[18]

A Ugaritic example is:

> Thy decree, El, is wise: Wisdom with ever-life
>   thy portion
> Thy decree is: our King's Puissant Baal, Our
>   sovereign second to none;
> All of us must bear this gift, all of us must
>   bear this purse.[19]

---

[15] J. B. Pritchard, *Ancient Near Eastern Texts*, p. 305.
[16] *Ibid.*, p. 383.
[17] *Ibid.*, p. 46.   [18] *Ibid.*, p. 75.   [19] *Ibid.*, p. 133.

Scholars have not always appreciated the full import of parallelism for musical forms. Investigators may have recognized the responsorial or antiphonal refrain as well as other features of psalmody, but they have neglected to trace these back to the parallelistic hemistiches which constitute fully two-thirds of the Bible. Throughout the centuries, the Bible translators have jealously preserved this trait; most of all, Jerome with his three attempts to produce an adequate translation of the Psalms. A glimpse into the learned prefaces with which Jerome introduces these several ventures will demonstrate how earnestly Jerome grappled with the problem of retaining the Hebrew idiomatic structure in a fundamentally different language, and of doing so without introducing into that language too much that was alien. Jerome fully grasped the significance of parallelism.

Parallelism can be traced to primitive beginnings. Professor Lach has endeavored to connect it with repetitions such as those in the speech of small children — da-da, be-be, ma-ma, and the like. Lach's ideas seem to rest on certain hypotheses of the Semitic scholar, the late D. H. Mueller, though Lach does not mention Mueller.[20] Lach's excellent study indicates the lines to follow. There is no denying that every parallelism is a repetition. Yet, between a child's babble and such verses as:

> The sea saw it and fled;
> The Jordan turned backward,
> > or
> I will lift up mine eyes unto the mountains;
> From whence shall my help come?[21]

there stretch what thousands of years!

It is in Hamitic and in Semitic literatures that the earliest recorded instances of parallelism appear. Not a trace of parallelism can be found in Sanskrit or in Old Persian. We might even

---

[20] R. Lach, "Das Wiederholungsprinzip," in *Oester. Akademie der Wissenschaften*, Phil.-Hist. Klasse, 1923–24, also in the same author's *Melöpoïe*, pp. 391, 593, 613 ff.

[21] Psalms 114.3; 121.1 For an exceedingly useful discussion of biblical parallelism, see Theodore H. Robinson, *Poetry and Poets of the Old Testament*, London, 1947, pp. 21–46.

question whether parallelism was the origin of the dichotomic form characterizing so many kinds of metrical melody. The basic requisite of metrical music would exist where each hemistich contained the same number of words or accents. But such was not originally the case. Hardly a single verse of the biblical Psalms shows, in both halves, the same number of words or beats. Whatever may have been the design of ancient Hebrew prosody, if there was any design, it did not entail an equal number of words, still less of syllables, in the two halves of any verse.

While literary parallelism can be traced back to the third millennium before the Christian era, not a vestige of it appears in the literature of the Indo-European languages. Parallelism may nonetheless have prevailed in languages which have not yet been deciphered. Once adopted in the poetry of the Bible, parallelism, by way of translation, entered practically all of the world's literatures. It continues in the modern Occidental literatures though, from these literatures, other poetic devices such as alliteration and isosyllabism have vanished. In Graeco-Christian and Latin Christian literature, as we perceive from the Oxyrhynchus Hymn,[22] and from the *Te Deum* and other Christian poems of the first five Christian centuries, parallelism was deliberately imitated.

Except for some ancient Persian parallelisms which show distinctly Babylonian traces, parallelism was unknown to the vast Indo-European literature of ancient Asia. W. F. Albright aptly admonishes: "Even today few biblical scholars have an adequate appreciation of the importance of the strictly formal element in ancient literary composition."[23] Even musicologists and philologists, when they do not overlook, fail to understand the importance of parallelism and its ramifications for the musical forms to which these gave birth. Winfred Douglas, in an excellent description of musical forms, pronounces of high significance "the principle of inflected monotone, corresponding accurately to the various rhetorical pauses of prose; such as we have in the ancient

---

[22] Apparently most scholars have failed to notice that the Oxyrhynchus Hymn is actually a paraphrase of Psalm 93.

[23] W. F. Albright on Psalm 68 in *HUCA*, Vol. 23, Part One, p. 2.

tones of Lessons, Epistles, . . ."[24] Yet this author, while he discusses the regular pauses, nowhere treats them as corollaries of the parallelistic structure.

All concomitants of parallelism have been shown to exist in the less ancient Semitic tongues. These concomitants include particularly the punctuating melisms, that basic element of psalmody. They likewise include altered vocalization and accent or inflection at the half-stops and at the full-stops. Since we do not know the precise vocalization of the texts in Akkadian or Ugaritic, it is impossible to determine whether those ancient Semitic languages did or did not provide some grammatical indications of the places at which the hemistiches ended. Professor Albright appears of the opinion that some of the later Babylonian texts shift the accents to indicate the crucial points. Hebrew, Biblical Aramaic, Arabic, and Early Syriac do exhibit those characteristics.

More difficult to trace is rendition of one tone per syllable. Such is the case in psalmody whether we do or do not take into account the inclination toward an identifiable tenor. No exact description of ancient psalmody has come down to us except the famous passage in Augustine's *Confessions* where he glories in the music of "una voce dicentes," the ideal of *Koinonia*, the community worship of the early Church.[25] The truth is that an ideal of that kind can be achieved only at the sacrifice of music; plain recitation would inevitably be syllabic. Similar reports in tannaitic sources, dating from a period two hundred years earlier, apprise us how certain Psalms and certain parts of the liturgy were rendered:

> When an adult leads the reciting of the Hallel, the others present respond to each verse: "Hallelujah." When a minor leads, the others repeat after him word for word.[26]

Aside from these passages and a few others like them, we possess no information except such as pertains to singing among

---

[24] Winfred Douglas, *Church Music in History and Practice*, pp. 18 ff. The book is of great value in many respects.

[25] Augustine, *Confessions*, 9.4. Much more insistent in this regard is Athanasius in his Apology to Emperor Constantine, P. G. 25, 616.

[26] Sotah 30b.

the Greeks. Extant notations of Greek melodies indicate that song among the Greeks demanded an all but rigidly syllabic performance. Of melismatic passages with more than two tones per syllable, there is not an intimation. For one thing, Greek singing shows nowhere any bent toward an identifiable tenor. It is entirely unacquainted with parallelism and with that concomitant of parallelism, the punctuating melism. Still, syllabizing psalmody, in some form, must have existed in the Semitic pre-Christian world.

In default of any evidence from history, some non-historical inquiries may prove helpful. In Israel, Dr. Johanna Spector has made more than two thousand tape recordings of Yemenites, Arabs, Iraquis, Copts, Syrians, Kurds, Samaritans, and even Hindus, representing at least five different religions. Among such of those records as I heard, what most impressed me was a choral cantillation of the Yemenites as well as the Kurdish and the Samaritan psalmody. Without anticipating Dr. Spector's conclusions, soon to be published, I noted the following:

1. Cantillation, while commonly performed by a soloist, is for certain poetic portions rendered, in accordance with tradition, choraliter. Where this custom has existed for centuries, as for instance among the Jews of Yemen, the range narrows down to a third or a fourth. The pronunciation is entirely syllabic; melisms occur only at the close or *punctus* of the entire paragraph. In contrast with this, the solo cantillation of those same groups resorts to punctuating melisms in abundance, using them in every verse. The ambitus of the solo goes to a fifth or even a sixth. Group cantillation appears to have been well acclimated to Jewish tradition. Judah Halevi, in the twelfth century, recalls the strong impression created when hundreds, in unison, would cantillate the Pentateuch in a strictly syllabic, even metrical manner.[27]

2. The psalmody of the Kurdish Jews is largely archaic; it employs a hexachord with two conjoint tetrachords. It is not strictly syllabic. Moderately ornate, it rests upon a tenor usually

---

[27] Judah Halevi, *Kusari*, II, 76, ed. Cassel. See also Aloni, תורת המשכילים p. 40. It is highly interesting to note that this mass cantillation often assumes the character of a primitive organum.

in the upper third of the finalis, though occasionally the entire Psalm ends on the confinalis.

What now are the inferences to be drawn with regard to syllabic rendition and its origin? It goes without saying that solo psalmody is older than choral psalmody. We must allow that centuries had to elapse before solo performance could become regulated. After the inception of choral psalmody and of its teaching, other centuries had to elapse before a method of group singing could attain fixety. Group singing would naturally tend toward syllabic rendition or toward an identifiable tenor; in solo performance, a type of psalmody more melodious than that of dry recitation is suggested. Confirmation of this can be found among the fathers of the Church who either exalt in the "melodious tunes" of early psalmody or brusquely oppose all musical appreciation.[28] Basilius writes: "Only for this one reason have the sweet melodies of the Psalms been fashioned: that they who are young and immature, either in years or in spirit, may build and educate their souls while engaged in making music."[29] Methodius observes: "I have no desire to listen to sirens who sing one's epitaph . . . but I do wish to enjoy heavenly voices . . . not as one addicted to licentious songs but as one steeped in the mysteries divine."[30] Augustine reports that Athanasius had instructed his psalmodist to chant with such simplicity "ut pronuntianti vicinior esset quam canenti" (PL 32;800). A similar antipathy, according to the Talmud, prevailed among the Jewish contemporaries. After the destruction of the Temple, the Rabbis showed scant love for musical performance. Their animosity bursts out in such phrases as: "Song in the house, ruin at the threshold," "The ear that listens to music should be torn off."[31]

---

[28] Socrates, Hist. Eccles. II, 8. Augustine, *Sermon Supposit.* Also Jerome, Comment. in *Ep. ad Ephesos*, 284.2.

[29] Basilius, Homilia I in *Psalmos.*

[30] Methodius, *De Libero Arbitrio*, in P. G. 18, 240 ff.

[31] Sotah 48a. See also my study, "The Conflict between Hellenism and Judaism" in *HUCA* 1947, 415–417. Rashi interprets a passage in Sabbath 106b to the effect that a certain remark in the Talmud was superfluous. It was idle and unnecessary *as a song.*

If we examine liturgies such as the Syrian, the Nestorian, or the Jewish, in which choral psalmody has been accorded a minor role, we find that psalmody has remained more melismatic and more flexible and not, like the Latin and Byzantine, rigidly insistent upon one invariable tenor, in the Byzantine theory recognizable as the neume *Ison*. Soloistic traditions abound in psalmodies with two tenors. Even the Gregorian chant incorporated two tenors in its *Tonus Peregrinus*. The plain psalmody of the Gregorian chant and the Byzantine chant must be considered the result of a regressive anti-melismatic movement which itself originated with the advent of choral intonation. Since an entire group cannot, in exact unison, chant melismatic tunes every day in the week, the more florid texture of psalmody that once existed became gradually polished down to a bare framework of *initium, tenor, flexa*, and *punctus*.

Ornate psalmody, at least in some of its samples, appears to date back to an earlier age and to more spontaneous modes of expression. It is necessary to distinguish between such types as are reducible to clausulae of plain psalmody and a more recent type which is predominantly as well as originally, a melismatic chant for festivals. To the first category belong the graduals of ordinary Sundays; to the second, the brilliantly arranged responsoria of masses for the holidays. To trace each category back to its beginnings would be extremely difficult and would demand years of study.[32]

We are confronted here by an important problem. All Christian sources agree that the graduals — that is the Psalm verses sung between the lessons — are a direct heritage from the synagogue.[33] Yet the texts and tunes of the graduals change each Sunday in accordance with the lesson and with the season of the ecclesiastical year. The earliest Jewish source to mention the practice of Psalm singing, before and after the lection from the Torah, is the tractate Soferim,[34] a source far too late for

[32] P. Wagner, *Gregorianische Melodien*, I, 33.

[33] *Ibid.*, I, 81. Also Constitu. Apost. II, 57. See also L. Venetianer in *ZDMG*, Vol. 63, pp. 103 ff.

[34] Soferim, ed. Mueller. Chap. XIV, p. XXIV and pp. 191–194, where all the sources are given together with some suggestions.

our present inquiry. Even if we grant that Soferim describes a practice which was two centuries old when Soferim was composed, the reference would still apply to a period not earlier than the fifth or the beginning of the sixth century C. E. Moreover, if we accept the account in Soferim, the verses recited from the Book of Psalms before and after the Scroll was read, did not change in the course of the year; while, in the Catholic Church, the texts and tunes for the graduals do change. Only one Christian scholar has taken cognizance of the dilemma. Dr. Baumstark suggests that originally, in the synagogal singing of verses from the Psalms, the verses varied from Sabbath to Sabbath as the reading from the Torah varied, but that later the practice was abandoned.[35] Baumstark gives no evidence or source for this conjecture. This being all we know, the origin of the gradual remains an unsolved problem.

All proof is lacking that there was a *public* and *cyclical* reading of sacred scriptures among the Babylonians and the Egyptians or any of the neighboring peoples. Herodotus seems to intimate that there may have been such a practice among the Zoroastrians of ancient Persia. In the old civilization of Mesopotamia, the reading of holy writ belonged to the closely guarded arcanum of the priesthood. As one peruses the collection of ancient texts such as appears, for instance, in Pritchard's *Ancient Near Eastern Texts* and similar works, one cannot fail to recognize the esoteric character of nearly all ancient rites.[36] In the Akkadian and the Egyptian, as well as other cults of the ancient Near East, such as the Ugaritic and Mandaeic, the hymns and psalms were hidden from all except the officiating priests. In this, as in various other respects, it is different with the Psalms of the Bible. These figured in the ritual of the Temple. There was about them nothing cryptic. There were no mysteries to hide, except perhaps the musical intricacies of the Levites who, like any closed guild, were reluctant to part with their professional secrets.[37]

---

[35] A. Baumstark, *Liturgie Comparée*, 3d. edit., p. 51.

[36] T. H. Gaster, *Thespis*, p. 52, n. 30.

[37] C. G. Cumming, *The Assyrian and Hebrew Hymns of Praise*, p. 58.

Where, in ancient literature, can there be found the pattern of parallelism combined with a rendition that is public, regular, cyclical? This is for us an important question. We have seen how parallelism is peculiar to the Hamitic and the Semitic languages, but without a trace in the Hittite. Punctuation does occur in the pericopal reading of the Sanskrit Avesta, but it belonged apparently to the *Yasna*, the Old Persian ritual. Its age is a matter of dispute.[38] By elimination, we thus identify, as the prototype of psalmody, a Canaanite ritual preserved in the Ugaritic poem which goes by the name of "Dawn and Sunset." This ritual has been linked with that for the Feast of the First Fruits.[39] Here, so far as I know, there appears, for the first time, the combination of parallelism, public performance, and recurrence. It stands to reason, of course, that there may have been texts which were considerably older but which have not come down to us. In all events those texts were, without exception, Semitic or Semito-Hamitic.

Already in the ancient Semitic rituals of Babylon and Ugarit, as well as of Israel, responsorial and antiphonal rendition are matter of course The parallelism, with its dichotomic structure and its middle caesura, engenders or at least strongly favors such performance. In the light of what is now known of ancient Semitic rituals, Christian surmises about the monastic origin of antiphony have to be revised.

It is not impossible that Ezra, who introduced the *cyclical public* reading of the Pentateuch, was familiar with the Persian custom, particularly since he lived in Babylonia after the conquest by the Persian king, Cyrus. Ezra may have set a standard for all subsequent millennia, even running counter to the secretiveness of the priesthood in the Second Temple at Jerusalem.[40] Less than four centuries elapsed between Ezra and the rise of Christianity. During that period, the chanted cyclical public reading of the Pentateuch became established and perfected. The cantillation of the Torah was a familiar practice as early

---

[38] *Grundriss der Iranischen Philologie*, II, 3. Personal discussion with Prof. Geiger confirmed these impressions.

[39] T. Gaster. *Thespis*, pp. 231–251.

[40] T. H. Gaster, *op. cit.*, pp. 74 ff.

as the first century before the Christian era. By the third Christian century, the Jewish sages both of Palestine and of Babylonia were stressing the proper divisions and punctuation of biblical verses for purposes of exegesis.[41]

Returning now to psalmody, if we assume the original practice in Judaism to have been a flexible rendering more or less melodious, a change seems to have occurred during the period of the Second Temple. From various sources we learn that the musical rendering of the Psalm had become well regulated. The requirement that every singer undergo five years of training would support this conclusion.[42] That the chant was minutely organized seems indicated by the adage: "If it be a tradition, learn it by heart, word for word, as a song."[43] Still, we do not know whether anything other than oral instruction was invoked for preserving the tradition with such exactness.

III

The third and perhaps the most distinctive element of psalmody resides in the punctuating melisms. What do we mean by punctuating melisms? And what can we say about their origin and their history? There is ample reason for surmising that the melismatic type originated in the Near East, but the first attempts at ecphonetic notation stem from the circles of the Hellenistic grammarians in Alexandria. Though there were earlier efforts at punctuation in Sanskrit, it was the Greek system that got to prevail both in the East and in the West.[44] The musical synthesis of punctuation and melism became the outstanding characteristic of psalmody. But it were erroneous to assume that what occurred was only a simple grafting of the Greek system upon Semitic practice. Forms and ideas do not

[41] *E. g.* in Ned. 37a and b. For a discussion of these passages, Winter und Wuensche, *Jüd. Literatur*, III, p. 491.

[42] Hullin 24a, Arakin II, 6.

[43] Sabbath 106b. Rashi, however, gives a different interpretation. See note 33.

[44] For this and similar information regarding Iranian and Sanskrit, I am indebted to Prof. Bernard Geiger of Columbia University.

follow such mechanical ways. In pre-Christian Judaism, as we have seen, the proper reading of scriptural texts, with the correct separation of words and phrases, was well established. Whether there existed any theory of punctuating melisms we are uninformed. In our survey of ancient psalmody, the visible punctuation will therefore serve as our *terminus a quo.*

We can readily perceive the importance of punctuation for the parallelism favored by the old Semitic tongues. The free distich falls into stichoi by means of the middle caesura (*mediato*, *flexa*, Atnah). All of this has been frequently observed. What has not been observed is that Semitic languages alone employ the elongated, the so-called pausal forms at the caesura and at the full stop. Elongations frequently appear also at the emphasized beginnings of verses in poems. They are called, in Hebrew, Pe'ur (פיאור); in Arabic, *Tafchim.*[45] Falling, as they do, at the major breaks in the sentences, these embellished or lengthened forms may have furnished the linguistic origin of psalmodic melism. Some scholars, such as Bauer-Leander, Robinson, and others, believe that the elongations were specially created for the solemn recital of sacred texts.[46] It is of interest to note that the ancient Indo-European languages, such as Sanskrit and Iranian, do not possess anything comparable to pausal forms or their equivalents, though Sanskrit does possess a kind of ecphonetic punctuation which certainly antedates that of the Masorites, of the Christians, and even of the Alexandrian Greeks.[47]

The lengthened forms were of far-reaching significance for the musical rendering of the text. The full stop and the half close now demand cadences less abrupt and a more gradual falling of the voice. This is the precise function served by the punctuating melisms. As long as strict parallelism is maintained,

---

[45] W. Bacher, *Die Anfaenge der Hebraeischen Grammatik*, pp. 57, 101; also Kusari, II, 80.

[46] Bauer-Leander, *Historische Grammatik der Hebr. Sprache*, p. 186 and note on the subject.

[47] I am indebted for this piece of information to Prof. Bernard Geiger. Cf. also O. Fleischer, *Neumenstudien*, I, Chapters 1 and 2 where, however, no chronological synopsis of the accentual systems is provided.

even a translation can, with the music of psalmody, present a fair simulation of the Semitic style.

All translations of the Bible, from the Septuagint down, take pains to preserve the parallelism even though it could not be done literally or grammatically. It was a contrivance out of accord with the spirit of the new language even when syntactically correct. From the inherently differing principles of the respective languages, discrepancies were bound to arise.[48] The Hebrew verse, whatever its length, rarely falls into more than two parts. Such is by no means true of the Latin or the Greek or, for that matter, the English. Those other languages often require two or three verses where, for the Hebrew, one verse suffices. To illustrate, Ps. 68.5 divides as follows according to the oldest Latin and Hebrew punctuation:

Latin	*English*	*Hebrew*
Cantate Deo	Sing unto God,	שירו לאלהים
Canite nomen ejus:|	Sing praises to His name;	זמרו שמו
preparate viam	Make plain . . . a highway	סלו
ascendenti per deserta;|	that rideth in the desert;	לרכב בערבות
In Domino nomen ejus	Whose name is the Lord,	ביה שמו
et exsultate coram eo. ||	and exult ye before Him.	ועלזו לפניו:

The Latin comes from Jerome's *Psalterium Juxta Hebraeos.* J. M. Harden, who edited a recent edition of this work, points out that the subdivisions in the Codex Hubertinus "agree, on the whole, with the Massoretic divisions of the verses."[49] In the translations, however, melisms are attached to each pausa. Thus we find, for purposes of punctuation, three and even more embellishments in one verse, especially in the psalmody of the Office; while each verse in the Hebrew has not more than one *Atnah* and one *Sof Pasuk* (*punctus*). This could account for the many flourishes which seem to represent the abundant punctua-

---

[48] It is of interest to note that Jerome was well aware of these difficulties as his three or four separate attempts at translating the psalter indicate. Cf. J. M. Harden, *Psalterium Juxta Hebraeos Hieronymi*, London, 1922, especially pp. XXV ff.

[49] *Ibid.*, p. XXVI.

tion in the ancient solo psalmody of the *Tractus*. It was Peter Wagner's contention that, in these melisms, there are vestiges of psalmodic ornamentation going back to ancient Hebrew lore.[50]

IV

Looking at these conclusions from the viewpoint of the musicologist, we may picture psalmodic development as a broad chronological panorama. With allowance for the overlapping inseparable from all organic evolution, the following would approximate the order of its phases:

1. Worship may have originated in the sacred cries which primitive cults emitted for the purpose of inviting friendly forces and of warding off demonic forces. Traces of such invocatory and apotropaic functions seem noticeable in the ancient Shofar.[51]

2. After the creation of a sedentary and, as a rule, hereditary priesthood, there occurred some regulation of these cries and of their transmission.

3. In Sumir, Babylon, and Ancient Egypt, there arose the sacred dialogue and the ritual pantomime and — possibly sequel to these — antiphonal rendition.

4. Originally manifesting, in the Semito-Hamitic languages, the principle of repetition, parallelism became inseparable from poetic diction. Once recognized as such by the singing poets, parallelism got to be musically implemented. This was achieved by means of dichotomic structures and punctuating melisms. It is doubtful whether, in times that ancient, any aesthetic need was felt for a tenor or for two tenors. Considering that all kinds of *flosculi* were indigenous to the music of the Near East, such a sense of need was all the more unlikely..

5. A dual trend, simplification for daily use and elaboration for special occasions, becomes discernible in the ritual of Babylon

[50] P. Wagner, *op. cit.*, p. 368. See also E. Werner, "The Common Ground of the Chant of Church and Synagogue" in *Atti del Congresso Internazionale della Musica Ecclesiastica*, Rome, 1951.

[51] Rosh Hashanah 16b, also Rashi to Rosh Hashanah 37b.

and in that of the Jewish Temple. This continues recognizable in the liturgical music of Jews,' Christians, and Moslems of Europe, America, and Asia. A chant repeated daily would lead to the fixation of a tenor and of a finalis.

6. During an earlier period, that is, during the second millennium before the Christian era, there emerges the system of eight modes or rather of eight preferred modes. Here music exhibits traces of its ancient function as magic. The eight modes bore an ethical symbolism and pointed the way to an outlook in which doctrines regarding music carry an ethical import.[52]

7. The phases thus far enumerated embody the pre-logical forerunners of psalmody. Thenceforth appear the forms and the types which are organized. The oldest of these are such standard practices as refrains and responsoria engendered by the parallelisms embodied in the sacred literature of the Near East.

8. The next two developments must have coincided with the fixation of the biblical canon and with the new procedures of worship in the Temple. Instrumental accompaniments by professional musicians, necessitating a fixed pitch, had momentous results. It was probably during the Maccabean period, in all events not later than the second century before the Christian era, that this took place. The establishment of the canon generated the precise division of verses that provided the stability on which punctuating melisms could rest.

9. The final link in this long chain was ecphonetic notation, indicating either the parallelisms of the original Hebrew with its punctuation or the semi-parallelisms of the translations. This occurred during the fifth and the early sixth of the Christian centuries and simultaneously in the Hebrew, Byzantine, Armenian, Syrian, and Latin orbits.

It is obvious that this development required thousands of years. The earliest sources present the sacred and frequently antiphonal dialogues of the ritual which antedate the second pre-Christian millennium. Prior to that millennium, other millennia were needed to develop the primitive and the part prim-

---

[52] E. Werner, "The Origin of the Eight Modes of Music," in *HUCA*, Vol. 21 (1948).

itive conditions for those dialogues; presupposing, as these do, a fixed calendar, an established ritual, and a professional caste of priests. But, while the magic that preceded psalmody thrived in the occult rites of the initiate, psalmody could attain its full stature only when secrecy was discarded and the indispensable community participation facilitated. It was the democratic spirit of prophetic Judaism — as distinguished from legalistic Judaism — that caused the esoteric to be abandoned. During the fifth and the sixth Christian centuries, the musical psalmody, which had begun in the Second Temple, underwent systematization both among Christians and among Jews.

As we have seen, the tradition of psalmody, while an old one, did not constantly proceed along unvarying ways. Deviations were frequent. This makes it all the more astonishing that so much of the archaic patterns has survived. This persistence seems to indicate that, implemented and strengthened by musical archetypes, the principle of emphasis through repetition, which underlies both psalmody and parallelism, holds a potency assuring its survival for centuries yet to come.

The Oldest Sources of Octave and Octoechos.

Reprinted with permission of *Acta Musicologica,* 20, 1948, pp. 1-9.

1.

Before starting on the subject of this paper, I would like to explain, why I deem this theme of special importance. After all, profound studies about the octave and the Octoechos have been undertaken by greater scholars, and to add one or two more details to our knowledge would in no way warrant a full paper. The main reason, why this matter seems to me to merit most serious examination, is that it demonstrates clearly the intimate relation between music, religion, astronomy, and especially the calendar. This interdependence appears to me a symbol of the truly universal function of music in the life of antiquity, an universalism, which, unfortunately, wast lost early in the Middle Ages.

II.

The term *octave* designates today two entirely different things: (a) the acoustic relation between a fundament tone and its first overtone, the mathematical ratio being 1 : 2. (b) the second meaning of the word octave applies to its being the eighth, or more correctly expressed, the 7 plus 1 tone of the diatonic scale. Today both functions are perfectly identical, and it would be unreasonable to distinguish between them. Yet this identity was, and even is, not always or everywhere valid. The two functions have a different history and a different origin. The theoretical conception of the octave 1:2 is generally ascribed by Pythagoras by Nicomachus, (1) Gaudentius, (2) Jamblichus, (3)

---

(1) Nicomachus, ch. 6, in v. Jan, Musici Scriptores Graeci, Leipzig 1895, p. 249. Also Heraclides Ponticus, ibid. p. 53/.

(2) Gaudentius, in v. Jan, op. cit., p. 340.

(3) Jamblichus, in Vita Pythagorae, ed. Kuester, 18, 81.

Philolaos, (4) and all of their commentators. According to the legend, Pythagoras discovered the relation between music and number in a blacksmith's shop, where he noticed that a heavy hammer produced a lower tone than a lighter one. This led him to invent the monochord, by which device he established the ratio of the octave and that of most of the other intervals. This intuition was glorified by most of the chroniclers of ancient music.

Yet there exists another, much older version of that famous discovery, which reaches deep into the realm of mythology. Ancient Phrygian chroniclers tell us that the great Asian Goddess Rhea Cybele, the Magna Mater or Bona Dea of the Romans, employed in her service dwarfs, (daktyloi), skilled masters of all crafts. (5). These gnomes discovered in the rhythm of their hammers and in the different tone of their anvils the essence of all music, namely the mathematical basis of rhythm and tone. For about twenty years we have had positive knowledge that Cybele, called Kumbaba, belonged to the ancient Hittite Pantheon. That goddess of fertility was adored long before the time of king Hattushilish, the contemporary of King Rammses II. of Egypt. Before that time, the 13th century B. C., the Hittites had build a mighty empire, which reached from North-East Mesopotamia down to Egypt. They were a Non-Semitic, probably an Indo-European people, but used the Akkadian cuneiform script of their neigbors. (6).

The obvious resemblance of the two legends proves that the Pythagorean conception of the relation between music and number is of ancient Asiatic origin. Heretofore it was considered to be a Mediterranean rather than an Asiatic legacy, although at least Porphyry must have known the ancient tradition; for he states that Pythagoras learned the secret of music from the dactyloi. (7). In passing it may be noted that the legend of the musical gnomes might enable us to understand better certain rather strange pictures of Sumerian musicians, who look very much like dwarfs.

The Hittites are memorable in musical history for another, even more important reason: to my knowledge they were the first ones who, admittedly in obscure language, alluded to the existence of eight musical modes. My colleague Prof. Julius Lewy, a renowned Assyriologist, gave me his kind assistance in deciphering certain cuneiform Hittite texts, in one of which we read:

»Know that if thou offerest hymns to the Gods with the help of little Istar, (a musical instrument), it is best to do this eightfold« (or in eight ways or hymns). (KBo IV — KUB XI).

(4) Philolaos, in A. Boeckh's Philolaos des Pythagoreers Lehre etc., Berlin 1819, Fragm. 5.
(5) In Gressmann, Die orientalischen Religionen im hellenistisch-roemischen Zeitalter, p. 59; cf. also Stith Thompson, Motif Index of Folk Literature III., p. 100, »Dwarfs have Music«; also Grimm, Deutsche Mythologie, v. *Daeumlinge — Daktyloi;* also Strabo, lib. X »Studium musicum inde coeptum cum Idaei dactyli modulos crepitus et tinnitu aeris...... in versisicuum ordinem transtulissent«.
(6) Cf. E. Benveniste in Mélanges Syriens I, (Dussaud volume), p. 250 ff.
(7) Porphyrius, Vita Pythagorae, ch. 17, (English in B. S. Guthrie, Pytagoras — source book, 1919, not fully reliable!)

What does this enigmatic precept indicate? Either to chant one hymn eight times, or to offer eight hymns to please the Gods. For the present we shall leave the question unanswered; but we shall later return to it.

III.

What do we know about the octave being the eight tone of the diatonic scale? The oldest literary source which clearly divides the octave into eight tones, seems to be Euclid. (8). But it can be safely assumed that long before him the division of the octave interval into eight tones was familiar to Greek musicians. It is characteristic that again Pythagoras is accredited with the addition of the eighth tone to the former heptachord. This statement comes from so many sources that it merits brief consideration. Nicomachus tells us that Pythagoras added the eighth string to the lyre, which heretofore had had only seven. (9). Philolaos also refers to that great invention of the eighth tone (10) and Gaudentius does what he usually does: he confirms the prior observations. (11). With the exception of Euclid, all these remarks are couched in intentionally obscure, almost mystical language.

Let us remember here again that the acoustic octave was long in existence, before it was identified with the eighth tone of the scale. This fact emerges from the frequent references to older scales, such as Terpander's heptachord. (12). While praising the simplicity and economy of Terpander, Plutarch attempts to explain that Terpander by the omission of one or two tones of the diatonic scale obtained especially fine results. (13). That sounds very much as if somebody would say: »I do not want to spend so much money; it is not that I don't have it, but by saving it I'll be able to buy even better things«. Nor can we really believe Plutarch's argumentation, since Nicomachus, quoting Philolaos, a much older witness than Plutarch, terms the old seven-tone scale as Terpandrian and pre-Pythagorean. (14). There is no doubt that the old heptachord scale has left traces in the music of Asia and Europe; it occurs, in a form practically identical with Plutarch's so-called »Tropos spondeiakos«, a heptatonic scale, in Hebrew, Byzantine, and Gregorian chant. (15). In passing it

---

(8) Cf. Euclid, Sectio Canonis, in v. Jan, op. cit., p. 165 ff. Also I. Duering, Ptolemaios und Porphyrios ueber die Musik, Goeteborg, 1934, p. 64.

(9) Nicomachus, ch. 5 and 7, in v. Jan, op. cit., p. 244, 249.

(10) Philolaos-quotation, in Hagiopolites MS, ed. A. J. Vincent, (Notices et extraits), 1847, p. 270.

(11) Gaudentius, Harmonike Eisagoge, ed. Meibom, p. 14.

(12) Ps. Euclid, Introd. Harm. (Cleonides), ed. Meibom, p. 19; also Ps. Aristotle Problemata XIX, in v. Jan, op. cit., p. 94, probl. 32.

(13) Plutarch, De Musica, ch. XIed. Reinach-Weil, p. 74 ff.

(14) Nicomachus. ch. XII, in v. Jan, op. cit., p. 263/4.

(15) Cf. my study »The Attitude of the Early Church-fathers to Hebrew Psalmody, in Review of Religion, May 1943, p. 349 ff.

should be noted that the Greek term for octave, dia pason, does not say any-thing about the number of tones which the *interval* comprises; and it is only so recent a source as Pseudo-Aristotle, which elucidates the question, whereby again reference is made to the old 7-tone scale. (16). Our first conclusion, then, must be that the mathematical ratio of the octave interval 1:2 is an ancient Asia-tic invention, at least 900 years prior to Pythagoras. The identification of the octave interval 1:2 with the eighth tone of the diatonic scale seems to have taken place at the time of Pythagoras or not long before. Now the question arises: Why had it to be the number eight, which designated the octave? In other words: why was the interval 1:2 divided into *eight* unequal steps? The historic importance of this problem is obvious; for out of this eight-fold di-vision our present diatonic scale was brought into being.

IV.

It has already been acknowledged by some scholars that purely acoustic reasons cannot have caused this particular division; pentatonic, hexatonic, heptatonic divisions are also in evidence, not to mention the divisions into smaller frac-tions, as the chromatic scale, the Hindu, Chinese, and other Eastern systems. We must search for other than acoustic reasons.

To begin with, the number 8 was considered by the Pythagoreans the perfect number for music; (17) but this bare fact does not explain anything. For it might be argued that since the acoustic octave was made by Pythagoras the eighth tone of the scale, it was but natural that his followers should have re-garded the number 8 as the ideal number in music. Hence, we must look for essential corroboration in older sources.

Throughout the ancient Near East the 8 holds the significance of the musical number par excellence. We remember now the enigmatic Hittite injunction, demanding hymns in the eightfold; moreover, in the three of the four recently discovered Babylonian tablets with a cuneiform kind of notation — the latest one I have not seen as yet — the columns are all arranged in 7 plus 1 lines. For our admired Prof. Sachs this constitutes a special triumph, since today it is generally accepted by Assyriologists that these tablets represent some kind of notation, if not exactly that tone-by tone system which Prof. Sachs originally proposed, later withdrew.

From here on we turn to the Hebrews: one of their psalms bears the super-scription: *ban'ginot 'al hashminit.* (18) which is being translated »on Neginot upon Sheminit«, contributing nothing to our understanding of the text. The usual interpretation, sheminit meaning »the eigth« tends to to produce titles like »tunes in the octave«, or »upon an instrument with eight strings«, like the

---

(16) Ps. Aristotle, Probl., in v. Jan, op. cit., p. 94, probl. 32.
(17) Theologoumena Arithmetica, ed. Ast, p. 62, 17—22.
(18) Ps. 6:1.

kithara or lyre; this sounds more acceptable since in another passage mention is made of »kitharas upon the eighth« (19), whatever that means. Neither interpretation is very satisfactory to musicians. But there is an old rabbinic explanation of the passage in question, probably of the 6th cent. C. E., which we must not disregard. R. Saadya Gaon, the great philosopher of the 9th and 10th centuries, quoting an older, rabbinic authority in Arabic, writes:

»This is a hymn of David, in which the regular singers of the Temple were ordered to praise God in the eighth lahan«, (the arabic term for mode). He continues: »the expression *'al hashminit* demonstrates that the Levites used eight modes, so that each time one of their regular groups executed one mode«. (20).

A similar remark comes from R. Petachya, (12th cent.) who reports that the Jews of Baghdad in accordance with the term *'al hashminit* used eight modes for the chanting of the psalms. (21).

That in these cases the number 8 had nothing to do with the octave or the diatonic scale, is evident from the fact that Arabs and Jews employed a system of eight *rhytmic* modes besides the melodic ones; obviously the number eight was artificially imposed upon the system, since there is no equivalent to the octave in rhytm. (22). But this is by far not the only occasion, where the psalms stress the number eight in connection with music.

Ps. 119, an alphabetic acrostich, provides 8 verses for every letter, some of these eight-line stanzas were sung at the Second Temple. If this fact already induces us to think of musical modes, the principle of modality is — in a religious manner — much stronger evident in the ancient commentaries to Ps. 29. The text of that psalm contains the expression »The Voice of God« seven times. Very early was this understood an allusion to the modes of spheric harmony. Ibn Latif, a mystically inclined philosopher, writes thus:

»The science of music envisages 8 melodic modes which differ from each other because of their expansion and contraction...... The eighth mode functions as a genus which comprehends the other seven modes...... The Psalmist has alluded to this cryptically by means of the number 7 in the repetition of the term »God's Voice«...... while the phrase »All say Glory« (Ps. 29, 9) refers to the eighth mode which comprises all of the others. I cannot explain any further«...... (23). See also *Midras' chillim* to Ps. 81.

This kind of mystic-musical emphasis upon the number 8 reached its peak in the first two centuries of the Christian era, under the aegis of a powerful gnostic movement, which tried to combine all of the prevailing ideas of Greek

---

(19) I. Chron. 15, 20.
(20) Saadya's arab. Psalm-commentary, ed. Haneberg, Munich, 1841; also E. Galliner, Saadias Psalmuebersetzung, p. 22; comprehensively treated in Werner-Sonne, Philosophy and Theory of Music in Judaeo-Arabic Literature, in Hebrew Union College Annual, vol. XVI, 1941, p. 295 ff; similar statements by Ibn Latif.
(21) Translation and Text in Literaturblatt des Orients, IV, col. 541, n. 44.
(22) Werner-Sonne, op. cit., Hebrew Union College Annual, vol. XVI, 1941, p. 297 ff.
(23) Ibid., vol. XVII, 1943, p. 552.

as well as of Oriental philosophy in one great synthesis. Indeed, the entire concept of Christian religion may be viewed under this aspect. Of the many relevant passages only two will be quoted:
1. From the apocryphal acts of St. John's, Christ's hymn to his disciples.

> ...I would be thought, being wholly thought. Amen.
> I would be washed, and I would wash. Amen.
> Grace (charis) danceth. I shall pipe; dance ye all. Amen.
> I would mourn; lament ye all. Amen.
> The number Eight (Ogdoas) singeth praise with us. Amen. (24).

This piece originated in the end of the second century. In it, the Ogdoas has attained divine significance; but what is its place in the gnostic system? This is explained about two centuries later in one of the Magic papyri, the so-called eighth (8) Book of Moses. I quote from it:

> »... Stored up in it is the Omnipotent Name, which is the Ogdoas, God, who creates and anministrates everything...... Only by oracle may the great Name be invoked, the Ogdoas...... For without Him nothing can be accomplished; keep secret, o disciple, the 8 symbolic vowels of that Great Name«. (25).

To our surprise we encounter here the famous gnostic vowels as invocation of the Ogdoas; these vowels have already provided some interesting clues to early Christian music, as interpreted by Ruelle, Poirée, and Gastoué. They are 7 or 8 vowels representing either tones or modes. But even this unexpected supplement does not fully clarify the significance of the Ogdoas for music. The first definite clue comes from a strictly theologic source: Tertullian, the West-Roman Church-father writes in his polemics against certain gnostic sects:

> »According to them, the Demiurg, (creator) completes the seven heavens, with his own throne above all. Hence he had the name of *Sabbatum* from the hebdomadal nature of his abode; his mother *Achamoth* had the title Ogdoada, after the precedent of the primeval Ogdoas«. (26).

At first this sounds like a wildly synchretistic fantasy; yet it contains two very ancient conceptions: the seven heavens, above which the Allmighty has His throne, and the calendaric term *Sabbatum*.

V.

The dependence of this passage on Pythagorean musical-cosmological ideas and the Semite Kalendar is obvious; indeed, the Syrian Pythagorean Nicomachus writes in similar terms substituting »star« or »planet« for »heaven«.

---

(24) The Apocryphal New Testament, ed. Montague Rh. James, Oxford 1924, p. 253.
(25) Papyrus mag. Leyden W; quoted from A. Dieterich, Abraxas, p. 194.
(26) Tertullian, Contra Valentinianos, in Ante-Nicean Fathers, vol. III, p. 514.

(27). Similar statements are common to most of the Pythagoreans. We are, however, confronted again with the most important question, why it was the number 8 which assumed so predominant a place in the musical, theological, and cosmological ideas of Near Eastern Hellenism. The Arabs were the first ones to raise this question in blunt terms; but their answer is not fully satisfactory. It says:

»Eight is the perfect number for Music and Astronomy; their are eight stations of the moon; five planets, plus sun and moon, and earth; eight modes of music corresponding to the eight qualities of nature: hot-wet, cold-dry, cold-wet, and hot-dry«. (28).

Since this source originated in the 9th century, it is burdened with the full load of Neo-Pythagoreanism, which found many adepts in Arabic literature. We must go back many centuries if we hope to find pre-Pythagorean explanations. It is precisely here, where the ancient calendar of the Near East provides the decisive clues; I must beg you to permit me a short excursion in which to explain its system. As Prof. and Mrs. Lewy have demonstrated in a learned study, the Assyrians and other ancient nations of Western Asia used originally that so-called pentekontad Calendar. Its unit is not the month, but a period of 7 weeks plus one day, that is, 50 days. Their year consisted of 7 pentekontads (350 days) plus 14 intercalated days. (29). The origin of the pentekontad calendar rests with the conception of seven seasons and seven winds. Each wind corresponded to a God, and above them all throned a supreme deity, later called by the gnostics the Ogdoas. Again we remember the Hittite passage referring to eight hymns. As you probably know, remnants of this calendaric system have survived in both the Jewish and Christian tradition. The period between Easter and Pentecost is such a pentekontad; and originally the Lent-period likewise covered 50 days. Of all Christian churches, The East-Syrian Nestorians have retained most of it: up to the present day they use 4 pentekontades, one for Lent, one after Easter, one after Pentecost, and one from the first sunday in November until Christmas.

The liturgical Octoechos, composed or redacted by Severus of Antioch at the end of the 5th century, was nothing but a hymn-book for the eight sundays of the seven weeks after Pentecost. (30). Baumstark and other prominent Syrian scholars have proved beyond any peradventure of a doubt that the *musical* Octoechos was only an adjustment of eight modes to the eight sundays of the pentekontade. This happened at the end of the 7th century. To the eight sundays of a pentekontad eight modes naturally corresponded, the modes of the musical Octoechos, of the Eastern and Western Churches, of the Armenians no less than of the Ethiopians and Hebrews. It is not necessary to repeat here the

---

(27) Nicomachus, in v. Jan, op. cit., p. 241.
(28) Ikhvan es-Safa, ed. Dieterici, pp. 128—131.
(29) Hildegard and Julius Lewy, The Origin of the Week, in Hebrew Union College Annual, vol. XVII, 1943, p. 41 f., also p. 46, 47, 99—101.
(30) A. Baumstark, Festbrevier und Kirchenjahr der syrischen Jacobiten, p. 44 f, and p. 26.

history of the Octoechos; Baumstark and Jeannin have explored the matter from the philological as well as from the musical point of view. (31). From all sources the fact emerges that the Octoechos is but another of the numerous manifestations, where Liturgy, Calendar, and Music form an inseparable and millenia-old complex entity. While the old rule prescribes that the eight sundays should run the gamut of all the eight modes, no provision was made for a clear identification of the finales of the musical Octoechos with the eight tones of the diatonic scale. This development seems to have taken place in the 10th century, probably under Byzantian influence, since the famous Hagiopolites Ms. of the 13th cent. shows already the consequences of that identification with the eight species of octaves. At any rate, the pontekontad calendar solves the riddle of the origin of the eight modes.

VI.

It remains for us only to sketch the development, during which the »disjecta membra«, viz. the acoustic octave, the eighth tone of the scale, and the eight modes were interlaced in the theory of the Middle Ages. Most of the accomplishments of ancient culture were lost during the storms and migrations, which accompanied the collaps of the Roman Empire. What has survived, was either misunderstood or distorted, and was in most cases falsely provided with the halo of classic Greek scholarship. Thus we are not surprised to find that the conception of the octave as the eighth tone was half-forgotten: in the early West-European theory the hexachord at least for the purposes of Solmization takes the place of the diatonic eight-tone scale.

Gombosi, in his »Studies of early scale-theory« has correctly pointed out that »until the 10th century the species of octaves were in no way connected with the modes of the Church«. And he continues: »Not the range of the octave constitutes the Church-mode, but its finalis and its relation to the area of psalmody«. (32). It is only with Guido, that the octave is again and without ambiguity thought of as the eighth tone of the scale. In his Micrologues he terms that eighth tone the octave, (33) and goes on to say: »For there are seven different tones in music, just as there are seven days in the week«. (34). This calendaric comparison is not astounding, since the term *octava* as eighth day of the week was perfectly familiar to every member of the Roman clergy since Augustine. (35). Even before Guido, the cosmological derivation of the

---

(31) J. C. Jeannin, Melodies Liturgies Syriennes, I. p. 85—94; also Baumstark, op. cit. p. 26, et passim; idem, Geschichte der syrischen Literatur, p. 190, (Paul of Edessa); also Patrologia Orientalis, vol. VI and VII, ed. Brooks.

(32) O. Gombosi, in Acta Musicologica, X, 1938, p. 155.

(33) Guido Ar., Micrologus, ch. V.

(34) Ibid., ch. VII. »Nam sicut septem dies sunt in hebdomada, ita septem voces sunt in musica«.

(35) Augustine, Sermo de Tempore CXI, 1. »Hodie octavae dicuntur infantium......«

number 8 in music was not entirely forgotten: Aurelianus Reomensis links the number of the modes with astronomical and kalendaric observations. (36). From Guido on the identity of the acoustic with the eighth tone of the scale is firmly reestablished; likewise the modes of the Octoechos were arranged in a diatonic octave. In this scheme the eighth mode always presented the greatest difficulties. (37).

VII.

Let us now summarize the results of our investigation:

(1) The discovery of the acoustic octave, that is, the ratio 1:2, took place many centuries before the division of the octave interval into 8 unequal steps. The relation between tone and number was found probably before the second millenium B. C. in the Near East.

(2) To the historic or legendary Pythagoras the elements of musico-mathematic science were handed down in Asia Minor or through documents originating there. Probably before, or at his time, the diatonic octave, the eighth tone of the scale was superimposed upon the octave-*interval*, dividing it into 8 tones.

(3) The reasons for this superposition of the number 8 upon the interval 1:2 and the number of modes in antiquity were of kalendaric and liturgic, but not of musical nature.

(4) These conceptions, which were of decisive influence for the constitution of the Octoechos and its historic antecedents, originated in the Pentekontad kalendar of 7 weeks with eight holy days, to which the 8 modes were applied.

(5) At the peak of the hellenistic-Asiatic gnosis the musical 8 attained the rank of divinity, called Ogdoas. Chants in its honor were to be sung in the order of the 7 or 8 gnostic vowels.

(6) The application of the 8 to the diatonic scale and the Octoechos were entirely unrelated to one another. From Euclid's time until the 10th cent. C. E. the originally identical conception had lost its meaning; it was only by a series of misunderstandings of the medieval theorists that the diatonic octave-scale and the 8 Church-modes were linked together again. The identity of the octave-*interval* with the eighth tone of the scale, however, has, with century-long interruptions remained intact, and proved to be the backbone of European as well as of Near Eastern music.

(7) A last question ought to be anticipated: Is it not astounding that a kalendaric system should have influenced a musical system so decisively? That answer is simple: the influence of the calendar did not reach music directly. It was the liturgy which had to follow the kalendar, as it still does in the Christian and Jewish ecclesiastical year. Music, being the liturgical art par excellence, could not escape the constant pattern of the liturgy.

---

(36) Aurel, Reomensis, in Gerbert, Scriptores I., p. 40.
(37) O. Gombosi, op. cit., p. 168 ff.

The Conflict Between Hellenism and Judaism in the Music of the Early Christian Church

Reprinted with permission of *Hebrew Union College Annual,* 20, 1947, pp. 407-470.

CONTENTS:

Introduction.

THE problem with which we shall deal in the following pages, is an old one. Since musical history was first written, it has been a subject of inquiry. In the Middle Ages that history was narrowly regarded as an ecclesiastical matter and was viewed from a theological basis. Only in the Renaissance, when Ornitoparch, Glarean, and Tinctoris ventured a more secular treatment of musical history, do we encounter the beginnings of a systematic search for the primary sources of ancient music. During the nineteenth century the historic-philological method was applied to these sources, combined with profound musicological analysis by scholars such as Bellermann, von Jan, Gevaert, and others. Their efforts led to concrete and significant results, although they overemphazised the Greek-Hellenistic stratum in the music of the early Church. The theological writers of the early Middle Ages were all but neglected, however, and many valuable clues in their writings were therefore overlooked. The new trend of cultural and religious history has rectified that onesidedness and a more balanced portrait of the problem can now be drawn.

The "territorialistic" approach of scholars like Rostovzteff, Strzygowski, and Herzfeld has produced many fine results and has taught us a series of lessons which are now in some respects in direct opposition to the concepts and methods of former schools. Their main principles are:

(1) Hellenism cannot be separated from the culture of the Near East;

(2) But the historic development of Asia Minor during the seven or eight centuries of Hellenism must be understood as a continuation of previous millenia, not as an entirely new era.[1]

(3) The ancient traditions of the Near East have often been transformed into, and disguised as, Hellenistic "Pseudomorphoses" (Spengler).

---

[1] Cf. Strzygowski, *Asiens Bildende Kunst*, p. 596.

(4) The all-important religious tendencies of the time should not be evaluated in ecclesiastical or systematic terms exclusively, as was done by Schuerer; for the ancient, indigenous traditions were stubborn and capable of deceptive adjustments to new ideas and forms.

A complete musicological study ought, then, to investigate our problem on the basis of the three different levels on which the musical contest between Hellenism and Judaism took place, namely: the practice of rendition; melodic tradition and structure; philosophical and theological attitudes. The key to the solution of the entire question would be a comprehensive analysis of the ethnic and local musical traditions of the peoples in the Hellenistic sphere and epoch. Unfortunately our knowledge of their music is quite insufficient, since almost all of our sources spring from the philosophic-theologic realm, whose authors showed little interest in an unbiased representation of the lore of the *dii minorum gentium*.

In spite of this handicap I shall endeavour to utilize Syrian-Aramaean sources, insofar as they are accessible to me; musicologists have heretofore examined them too little. This writer is firmly convinced that the Syrian and Northwest Mesopotamian countries played a far greater role in the development of Church music than is generally recognized.

It is true that the Syrians were not a very creative people, and that their function was mainly that of translator and go-between. Just because of this we must carefully trace that function, for it is our only opportunity to appraise the relative shares of Judaism and Hellenism in the music of the Syrian Church.

In general it seems amiss to search for every detailed indication of some single "influence" or other. Asiatic culture grew not in years or decades, but in centuries and millennia. We cannot and should not evaluate the whole fabric from individual wefts or threads. Consequently, this study does not pretend to be more than an introduction to the far greater complex of liturgico-musical interrelations between Church and Synagogue.

The Sources.

Hellenistic

What we know about the Hellenistic music of the Near East comes to us through three channels of information, viz. Greek, Jewish, and Christian, none of which even pretended to be objective. The authors of our historic sources were:[2]

a. The Greek intellectuals who spoke with condescension and occasionally with contempt of all music which did not strictly follow the "pure and straight" ($\sigma\epsilon\mu\nu\acute{o}\tau\eta\varsigma$) path of classic Greek music.[3] It was their ever-repeated lament that the standard of Hellenistic music had fallen far below the level of a serious art. This indictment is even today echoed by modern scholars such as Riemann and Reinach, although our conceptions of the "purity" of classic Greek music have undergone considerable modification.[4] For the mixture of Hellenic and Near East lore, the ancient authors show little regard, and we have to interpret their remarks with a good deal of caution.

b. The Jewish intellectuals, our second category of sources, viewed with enmity and with great fear, the ever-broadening inroads of Hellenism in Jewish life. If the bias of the Greek authors rested upon esthetic-philosophic reasons, the sharp prejudice of the rabbis, on the other hand, was caused by a burning desire to erect a protective "fence around the Law," which prevented them from attaining any objective attitude. Considering the vast number of Greek terms even in the talmudic language, it must be admitted that their fears were not altogether groundless.

[2] Dealing with a symbiosis of several nations during a period of seven or eight centuries, it was necessary to simplify the manifold sources into a few main categories. Since most of the really relevant sources will be discussed in detail later on, the danger of over-simplification is not too imminent.

[3] Cf. Plutarch, *De Musica*, ch. 17, quoting Plato.

[4] Cf. H. Riemann, *Handbuch der Musikgeschichte*, I. 1, p. 163 ff., also Th. Reinach, article "Musica" in Daremberg-Saglio, *Dictionnaire des antiquités grecques et romaines*, vol. 3, 2, p. 2074–2088. A far more positive attitude toward the music of Hellenism in W. Vetter's article on "Music" in Pauly-Wissowa, *Realenzyklopaedie des klassischen Altertums*.

c. The authors of the Christian Church during the four centuries of unfolding Christianity displayed a slowly changing attitude. At the outset their conception of the spiritual value of Hellenistic culture was all but identical with the orthodox Jewish, but gradually they came to terms with it, and finally — just before the final collapse of the Roman Empire — they began to appreciate its nobler implications. This generalization reckons with many exceptions, but the victory of the Gentile-Hellenistic Church over the Judaeo-Christian sects in Nicea 325 clearly demonstrates the spiritual trend of the times. We shall see, later on, that the Church even absorbed some Hellenistic tunes and musical ideas, incorporating them in its older Judaeo-Syrian stratum.

In general our sources pay more attention to instrumental music than to songs. We must not assume, however, that this instrumental music was independent of vocal rendition. Quite to the contrary, vocal music is taken as a matter of course, since the ancient nations could hardly conceive of any music whose chief element was not song. The instrument is merely the variable element. It is in this sense that we hear of the various types of music which accompanied the religious ceremonies. The chanted words formed the liturgy, the instruments added the specific color.

Music in the Hellenistic cults — of secular music we know next to nothing — had manifold functions. The most characteristic were: accompaniment of sacrificial worship; apotropaic protection from evil gods; epiclese; katharsis before and initiation into the mysteries; funeral; magic and sorcery.

The most frequent sacrifices were solemn libations. Plutarch relates that these libations were accompanied and dignified by a sacred paean.[5] On another occasion he offers a rationalistic explanation when he assumes that music was played during the sacrifices to cover up the groaning of the beasts or, in the Cartha-

---

[5] Plutarch, *Quaest. conviv.* 7, 7, 4, #712: τὸν δὲ αὐλὸν οὐδὲ βουλομένοις ἀπώσασθαι τῆς τραπέζης ἔστιν· αἱ γὰρ σπονδαὶ ποθοῦσιν, αὐτὸν ἄμα τῷ στεφάνῳ καὶ συνεπιφθέγγεται τῷ παιᾶνι τὸ θεῖον. About origin and conception of the paean, see F. Schwenn, "Gebet und Opfer" in *Religionswissenschaftliche Bibliothek*, ed. W. Streitberg, Heidelberg 1927, p. 18 f.

ginian sacrifices to Saturn, the crying of the children.[6] Actually, the function of music in all these cases was apotropaic — a principle which holds true even of some of the Temple music of Jerusalem. The *sistra* of the Egyptians to drive away the evil Typhon, the bells of the Phrygians to chase away hostile shadows and Demons, even the *paamonim* on the garment of the High Priest, when he entered the Holy of Holies[7] and hundreds of other illustrations demonstrate, beyond any doubt, the basically magic and apotropaic power of music.[8] The efficacy of music for the purpose of epiclese was a strongly implemented belief of all polytheistic religions. Music invokes the Gods to render help and assistance to the praying person. In the cult of Rhea Cybele, one of the most popular religions of Asia Minor, cymbals and bells played a significant, clearly epiclectic part.[9] The theory has been proposed that the Shofar and the trumpets in the older strata of the Bible had exactly the same purpose.[10] The Christian Arnobius ridicules this type of music, asking the pagans whether they want to awaken their sleeping Gods.[11] The analogy of this polemic with the famous passage in I Ki. 18.28, where Elijah mocks the priests of Baal and asks whether their God is travelling or asleep, is obvious.

The kathartic power of music was one of the chief tenets of Pythagoreanism; and this idea is one of the few conceptions of

---

[6] Plutarch, *De superstitione* 13, #171. The question is fully discussed in J. Quasten, *Musik und Gesang in den Kulten der heidnischen Antike und der christlichen Fruehzeit*, p. 36 ff.

[7] Ex. 28.35. The best interpretations of that mysterious passage in H. Gressmann, *Musik und Musikinstrumente im Alten Testament*, p. 6 ff., where also the older literature is given. Of recent scholars Curt Sachs "History of Music Instruments" and Solomon Finesinger "The Musical Instruments of the Bible" in *HUCA* 1926, follow in principle Gressmann's explanation.

[8] See also Blas. Ugolinus, *Thesaurus Antiquitatum Sacrarum*, vol. 32, p. 1057. f.

[9] *Ibid.* Nonnus Dionysius:

Πρώτῳ μὲν θέτο δῶρα κυβηλίδος ὄργανα 'Ρείης
Κύμβαλα χαλκεόνωντα, καὶ αἴολα δέρματα νεβρῶν.

[10] Cf. Gressmann, *op. cit.*, p. 9.

[11] Cf. Arnobius, *Adversus nationes* in Corpus scriptorum ecclesiasticorum latinorum 4, 265 ff.

musical ethos, which has survived up to the present day, (e. g. in the fire and water ordeal in "The Magic Flute" by Mozart.) The martyrium of St. Theodotus relates that at the holy baths and baptisms, which formed an important part of the cult of Artemis and the *Magna Mater* (Kybele) in Asia Minor, flutes and tympana, or hand-drums were played.[12] So worldly an author as Ovid tells us that, on such occasions, the Phrygians "howl and the flute is played furiously, while soft hands (of the priestesses) beat the bull's hide" (drums).[13]

Flutes and Cymbals were also in evidence at funerals in all of the cults of Asia Minor and even in Palestine. In general, there is an abundance of documents testifying to the use of these instruments in all the mysteries and synchretistic religions of the Near East.[14]

Only in the last 60–70 years have documents of musical sorcery been uncovered; most of them stem from Egypt and Hellenistic Babylonia.[15] As we know through Blau's penetrating studies, Jewry did not keep itself free from these superstitious practices.[16] Most probably the recitation of these texts was

---

[12] Martyrium Theodoti in *Studi e Testi* 6, 70. (de Cavalieri): . . . αὐλῶν γὰρ καὶ κυμβάλων ἦχος ἐθεωρεῖτο καὶ γυναικῶν ὀρχισμοὶ λελυμένους ἐχουσῶν τοὺς πλοκάμους ὥ σ π ε ρ μ α ι ν ά δ ε s.

[13] *Fasti* 4: "Exululant comites, furiosaque tibia flatur
Et feriunt molles taurea terga manus."

[14] By far the best accumulation of ancient sources about the use of percussion instruments in antiquity is still the extensive treatise of Friedrich Adolph Laempe in Ugolini *Thes. Antiqu. Sacr.* vol. 32, col. 867–1092, where hundreds of quotations are given.

[15] The original Greek text in M. Berthelot and Ch. Ruelle, *Collection des anciens alchimistes grecs*, II 219, 434. Also Ch. Wessely, *Neue Zauberpapyri*, Kais. Akademie der Wissenschaften, Vienna, 1893; C. Hoeg, *La theorie de la musique byzantine*, in Revue des études grecques, 1922, p. 321–334), and, most extensively, Klaus Wachsmann, *Untersuchungen zum Vorgregorianischen Gesang*, Regensburg, 1935, p. 50–77. It cannot be said that our present knowledge permits an exact evaluation of these magic manuscripts in terms of music. Not even knowing whether or not Zosimos of Panopolis, our main source, was a Christian, we should be most cautious in our hypothesis, especially since patristic literature shows not the slightest trace of any influence of such alchimistic-magic sects.

[16] Cf. L. Blau. *Alt-Juedisches Zauberwesen*, Strasbourg 1898.

accompanied by music, since most of them are found around the gnostic alphabet and differently arranged vowels, and are often concluded by Hallelujahs. We know today that these arrangements had a musical connotation which the Jews had learned from the Babylonian gnostics and Manichaeaens of the third to seventh centuries.[17]

We have, in the previous pages, attempted to give a brief synopsis of the descriptive sources of Hellenistic music, written in Greek and Latin. Unfortunately, nothing of Aramean literature has come down to us which might shed some light upon our problem. Hence, we can match the gentile sources only with the reports given by Jewish and Christian authors. They are, however, hardly ever descriptive in the true sense of the word, inasmuch as both pursue decidedly theological ends and are strongly biased against anything that does not conform to their ceremonial and theological concepts.

JEWISH SOURCES

Instrumental music in general, and Greek music in particular is described as euphonious (קלפונון = καλλίφωνον) in contemporary rabbinic writings.[18] The rabbis even considered the Greek language the one most fitted for song.[19] Numerous musical terms, borrowed from the Greek language demonstrate clearly how deeply the culture of Hellenism had penetrated the daily life of Palestine. Only a few illustrations need be quoted:

קתרות = κιϑαρα	(lyre)	
נימין = νημα	(strings)[20]	
פסנתרין = ψαλτήριον	(string-instrument)	
פנדורא = παδοῦρα	(instrument with 3 strings?)	

---

[17] This is the contention of P. A. Gastoué which today cannot seriously be disputed. Cf. P. Gastoué, *Les Origines du Chant Romain*, p. 27–33; also Dom Leclercq, article "Alphabeth vocalique" in *Dictionnaire d'archeologie chretienne*.

[18] Cf. S. Krauss, *Talmudische Archaeologie* III, p. 276, n. 43.

[19] Cf. j *Sota* 7, 2, 21.

[20] Cf. Krauss, *op. cit.* III, p. 85.

סומפוניא = συμφωνία   (consonance, ensemble, perhaps
                                                   bagpipe?)[21]
הדראולים = ὕδραυλις   (water-organ)
כרבלין = χοραῦλαι   (a choir of flute-players; perhaps
                                                   organ)[22]
אירוס = αἰρός   (aes-ris) (ball made of ore)[23]

It is characteristic that Greek musical terms are used almost exclusively for instruments, their parts, their tuning, etc. The Hebrew vocabulary was perfectly sufficient to express all of the nuances of *vocal* music. Indeed, the Hebrew language has an abundance of terms for describing vocal forms, melodies, range, volume, etc.

Surrounded by so many Greek elements, it is understandable that the spiritual leaders of Judaism considered Hellenic music a medium of temptation to abandon Israel's faith. Most significant in this respect is the Talmudic statement: The apostasy of R. Elisha ben Abuyah was due to the Greek melodies (or to the Greek instruments which were always in his house).[24] The prohibition against attending, on the eve of Passover, an *epikomon*, a festal procession with flutes and cymbals and probably Greek songs, may also stem from the fear of the assimilation of Hellenistic customs. In the Talmudic treatise *Sukkah* 50b, we read occasionally about the musical instruments significant of the cults of Asia Minor.

After the destruction of the Temple, instrumental music was banished in Judaism.* The rabbis usually based this injunction upon Is. 24.9 and Hos. 9.1; yet it is clear that the two reasons for the rabbinic opposition to instrumental music were of a quite different nature. Philo, as well as the Sibyllines, both representative of Hellenistic Judaism, display contempt for any musical instrument. In both cases spiritual worship is regarded as more exalted than any sensuous ceremo-

[21] *Ibid.* p. 86–88.
[22] *Ibid.* p. 91.
[23] *Ibid.* p. 93.
[24] b *Chagiga* 15 b.
* As a demonstration of mourning over that disaster.

nial.²⁵ Philo, in particular, emphasized the value of spiritual hymns and praises (ὑμνοὶ καὶ εὐδαιμονισμοί)²⁶ even when they are not actually pronounced by "tongue or mouth," prayers which only the deity can hear (τῇ δε ἄνεν γλώσσης καὶ στόματος μόνη ψυχῇ . . . ὧν ἓν μόνον οὗς ἀντιλαμβάνεται τὸ Θεῖον).²⁷ In much stronger terms the Sibyl turns against the pagan type of music: "They (the faithful) do not pour blood of sacrifices upon the altar; no tympanon is sounded, nor cymbals, nor the aulos with its many holes, instruments full of frenzied tones, not the whistling of a pan's pipe is heard, imitating the serpent, nor the trumpet calling to war in wild tones."²⁸ This passage reveals much better than all the rabbinic explanations the actual situation. It is a remarkable fact that the three instruments mentioned were considered unsuitable for the Temple service: the *aulos* (חליל), the *tympanon* (תף), and the cymbals (צלצלים). These played a considerable part in the Psalter; yet the rabbis had a low estimate of them. Hugo Gressmann was the first to realize this strange fact, without offering any concrete explanation.²⁹ The later antagonism toward these instruments probably had the following reason: all three instruments were sacred attributes of Kybele, as is shown in our pictures. Illustration I displays a priest of Kybele; in the left upper corner we see the

²⁵ Cf. Philo, *De spec. leg.* II#193 (V 114 Cohn-Wendland).
   Idem., De spec. leg. I #28.
   Idem., De plantatione #148.
²⁶ *Idem., De vita Moysis* II #239.
²⁷ *Idem., De spec. leg.* I, #271. Against this conception turns Paul in I Cor., 14, 14–19; Rom. 10, 9–11. Without mentioning Philo's name, it is obvious that Paul considers Philo's ideal of silent prayer insufficient.
²⁸ Oracula Sibyllina 8, 113, (147 ed. Geffken) . . . τύμπανον οὐκ ἠχεῖ, οὐ κύμβαλον . . . . οὐκ αὐλὸς πολύτρητος, ἔχοντα φρενοβλάβον αὐδην, οὐ σκολιοῦ σύριγμα φέρον μίμημα δράκοντος, οὐ σαλπίγξ πολέμων αγγέλτρια βαρβαρόφωνος.
²⁹ Cf. Gressmann, *op. cit.*, p. 29. He writes: "Die Floete, die in aelterer Zeit auch bei religioesen Gelegenheiten wie Wallfahrten und Festreigen Verwendung fand, wurde spaeter infolge religioeser Scheu aus dem Kultus entfernt. In der Chronik fehlt sie ganz, nach dem Talmud spielt sie beim Gottesdienst nur eine beschraenkte Rolle . . . . Das spaeter fixierte Gesetz hat die Floeten ebenso wie den Reigen um den Altar . . . mit Stillschweigen uebergangen."

I. PRIEST OF KYBELE

cymbals; in the right upper corner the *tympanon*; beneath it is a phrygian flute. Illustration 2 depicts the holy tree of Attis, the lover of Kybele. All kinds of sacred emblems are hanging from the tree: on its left branch we see two cymbals, from its right branch hangs a flute, and in the crown a *tympanon* is hidden. The Greek and Latin sources are full of allusions to these instruments as the originally Asiatic accessories of the orgiastic cults of the *Magna Mater*. If this application made the instruments suspicious to the Jewish authorites, it must have been their use in the Jewish synchretistic ceremonies of Zeus

2. THE HOLY TREE OF ATTIS

Sabazios. There the serpent, together with the flute and the
cymbals, held central significance. Our illustration 3, a repro-
duction of a so-called Sabazios hand, shows the serpent beneath
the thumb; on the left side of the hand we see a *kymbalon* and
the back of the hand rests upon a *tympanon*. This explains the
allusions of the Sibyl who, like the rabbis, felt horror and contempt for these renegade Jews and their customs.[30]

Gradually other instruments — originally very popular and

[30] About this sect see Gressmann, *Die orientalischen Religionen im Hellenistisch-roemischen Zeitalter*, p. 110–124; also P. Reitzensten, *Die hellenisti-
schen Mysterienreligionen*, p. 105–108; and F. Cumont, *Acad. des Inscript.
Comptes rendus* 1906, p. 63. The best epigraphic sources in Ramsay's comprehensive work: *The Cities and Bishoprics of Phrygia*, I, p. 639–653. Two of
the arch-priestesses of Zeus Sabazios were the Jewesses Julia Severa and
Servenia Cornuta.

3. SABAZIOS HAND

used frequently in the Temple — were considered suspicious and unclean through their use in synchretistic religions; hence the rabbis frowned upon most of them, even upon their noblest representative, the *kinnor*.[31]

---

[31] כנור שמנגנין בו לצים in b. Sanhedrin 101a.

Vocal music, however, if of a sacred nature, was exempt from these inhibitions. Since its texts were exclusively in the Hebrew or Aramean idiom, derived from Scripture, the songs were not likely to become a medium of synchretism.

CHRISTIAN SOURCES

Up to the third century, the Christian sources reflect almost the same attitude toward Hellenistic music as contemporary Judaism. The very same distrust of instrumental accompaniment in religious ceremonies, the same horror of flute, tympanon, and cymbal, the accessories of the orgiastic mysteries, are here in evidence. Clement of Alexandria may be quoted first, since he was in many respects a Hellenist, and certainly not a Judeo-Christian. He wrote: "One makes noise with cymbals and tympana, one rages ($\pi\epsilon\rho\iota\psi o\varphi o\upsilon\mu\acute{\epsilon}\nu o\iota$) and rants with instruments of frenzy; .... The flute belongs to those superstitious men who run to idolatry. But we will banish these instruments even from our sober decent meals."[32] Arnobius, likewise a Gentile Christian, follows the same trend, as does Gregory of Nazianz, always referring to the "sounding ore" (*aeris tinitibus* — cymbals) and the "tones of the flute" (*tibiarum sonis*).[33]

Some of the Church Fathers, especially Clement of Alexandria, and occasionally Chrysostom, used Philo's allegory where he likens the human tongue to the God-praising lyre.[34]

That vocal music is more pleasing to God and more suitable for Christians, was assumed by all the Church Fathers without exception. In one instance, however, they had to be even more circumspect than the rabbis. Their vernacular consisted of the ancient languages, and the danger of the infiltration of Greek or Latin pagan influences was much more imminent to them than to the rabbis. Wherefore, they tried to restrict the texts of their

[32] Cf. Clement of Alex., *Paedagogus* II, 4.

[33] Arnobius, *Adversus Nationes, in Corpus script. eccl. lat.* 4, 270; also Gregory of Nazianz, *Oratio* 5, 25, in PG 35, col. 708/9.

[34] Clement of Alex., *Paedag.* 2, 4; Eusebius *in Ps.* 91, (PG 23, 1172); Chrysostom *in Ps.* 149, (PG 55, 494).

songs to Biblical passages, chiefly from the Psalter, as did the contemporary rabbis.

In the course of time, Hellenistic and Aramaic-Asiatic forces made gradual but significant inroads into the liturgy of the Church and wrought a profound change upon its attitude toward syncretism. We know that the *"Kyrie Eleison"* of the Mass is a transformation of an original Helios-Mithra hymn.[35] As we shall see later on, a piece of Hellenistic composition, the Nemesis hymn of Mesomedes, was later incorporated in a *Kyrie*.[36] Recognizing the pagan origin of both text and melody (sun hymn; Nemesis hymn) we may readily conclude that the Church gave up its once intransigent puritanism. Another indication of this strategic retreat are the numerous paintings, mosaics, etc., in which Christ is identified with Orpheus or sometimes with Orpheus and David.[37]

On the other hand, the musical terminology and structure of the Armenian and Nestorian songs show a considerable amount of Semitic and Hellenistic traits superimposed upon the native lore. Here we need only refer to the studies of the late Komitas Kevorkian in which this gifted scholar offered the first scientific accounts of Armenian Church music.[38] It appears that the Armenian Church, in particular, has preserved an astonishing amount of ancient tradition, both in its liturgy and music. We intend to deal extensively with this highly intriguing problem elsewhere.

Another example may illustrate how complicated the interrelation between Hellenism and Asia proper actually was. One of the most famous legends told by Greek authors about Pythagoras relates the following: When listening to a group of black-

[35] Cf. F. J. Doelger, *Sol Salutis*, Muenster 1930, p. 5, 78/9, *et passim*. The Catholic scholar treats the delicate subject with a frankness which is as admirable as his profundity.

[36] Cf. *Kyriale Vaticanum*, Nr. VI, "Kyrie rex genitor."

[37] Cf. R. Eisler, *Orphisch-Dionysische Mysteriengedanken*, pp. 15, 46, 353, 395, *et passim*; also O. Ursprung, *Katholische Kirchenmusik*, p. 9.

[38] In *Sammelbaende der Internationalen Musikgesellschaft*, I, 1899–1900, p. 54 ff.; also the same author's *Musique populaire armenienne*, Paris 1925; see also E. Wellesz, *Die armenische Messe und ihre Musik*, in Jahrbuch Peters, Leipzig 1920.

smiths, who were beating the iron upon anvils of different sizes, Pythagoras discovered the correlation between number and tone, cosmos and music.[39] Actually this legend reaches back to a far earlier era. It is told that the Idaian Mother ($\mu\acute{\eta}\tau\eta\rho$ 'Ιδαΐα = Cybele) had as servants dwarfs ($\delta\acute{\alpha}\kappa\tau\upsilon\lambda\upsilon\iota = —$ "Daeumlinge"), skilled masters of all crafts. These gnomes discovered in the rhythm of their hammers, in the different tones of their anvils, the essence of music, rhythm, and melody.[40] The recent discovery that Kybele belonged to the ancient Hittite Pantheon[41] gives a new significance to the obvious similitude of the two legends. It proves that the Pythagorean conception of the invention of music and its mathematical ramifications are of ancient Oriental origin. Heretofore this was considered to be a Mediterranean rather than an Asiatic legacy. We can now discern three phases: 1. The development of the conception of music in Asia; 2. Its migration via the Mediterranean to Greece, and 3. The return of Pythagoreanism to Asia Minor under the aegis of Hellenism. How dominant this philosophy became in Asia Minor is demonstrated by the fact that the three greatest theorists of that period, namely Aristides Quintilianus (second century A. D.), Philodemus of Gadara (first century), and Nikomachus of Geraza (second century A. D.) were all hellenized Syrians or Palestinians.

Christianity, after some hesitation, accepted their theories and digested them in a great synthesis of Orient and Occident, of which the erudite Boethius and the saintly Cassiodorus, in their books on music, were the first and most influential champions. Only after this synthesis was it possible that this ancient Oriental heritage of both the liturgy and the music of the Church

---

[39] Cf. Gaudentios, 'Αρμονικὴ 'Εισαγωγή, ch. 11, in v. Jan's *Scriptores Graeci de Musica*, p. 340, often repeated by ancient and medieval authors.

[40] Cf. H. Gressmann, *op. cit.*[30] p. 59; also Stith Thompson, *Motif-Index of Folk Literature* vol. III, p. 100: "Dwarfs have music;" and Grimm, *Deutsche Mythologie*, v. "Daeumlinge-Daktyloi." The last reference was kindly given to me by Dr. Theodore Gaster.

[41] Cf. H. Gressmann, *op. cit.*[30], p. 58; also E. Benveniste in *Mélanges syriens* I., (Dussaud-Festschrift) p. 250 ff., where a Ras Shamra inscription is quoted.

could be forgotten, until modern science rediscovered the deepest and most genuine strata of early Christianity.

Since Hellenistic ideas reached deep into East Syria and Persia, it would be a mistake to leave these regions outside the scope of our investigation. Indeed, there is increasing evidence that the early hymns of the Syrian Church reflect to a considerable degree the musico-literary technique and structure of Hellenistic patterns. Thanks to Parisot's and Jeannin's works on the hymns of the Syrian Churches, we possess a better understanding of the actual precepts which effectuated the synthesis of the Aramean and the Greek spirit in the Christian sphere.[42]

MUSICAL SOURCES

Among the few authentic documents at our disposal, we must distinguish between primary sources, such as have been transmitted to us in musical notation, and secondary ones, which are either insecurely established or based on modern reconstruction. We shall give only the musical text; analysis and comparative treatment will be given in the following chapter. This musical source material has been selected as representative of the different melodic styles and of the various types of performance.

1a. *Skolion* of Seikilos, of Tralles in Asia Minor. (1st-2nd cent. A. D.) (Notated.)

[42] Dom J. Parisot, *Rapport sur une mission scientifique* etc., Paris 1899; Dom J. C. Jeannin, *Melodies syriennes et chaldéennes*, 1924–28; also *Oriens Christianus*, N. S. 3, 1913, #3. In broad historical aspects the problem is treated by E. Wellesz, *Aufgaben und Probleme auf dem Gebiete der byzantinischen und orientalischen Kirchenmusik*, 1923, p. 95 ff., and A. Baumstark, *Die christlichen Literaturen des Orients*, p. 119. The ancient ethnic traditions of East Syria and Iran underwent a decisive transformation under the hands of Graeco-Syrian monks. It is with this thought in mind that we shall later on attempt to analyse the structure of some of the Aramaean hymns. While no ancient or even medieval documents of these melodies are extant, it may be assumed that they belong essentially to a fairly old stratum. Their occasional resemblances to Gregorian formulas seem to confirm such an assumption. See our illustrations 9a, b, 10a, b; *infra* p. 429.

65

1b. Antiphon *hosanna filio David*, of the Roman Church.
(Notated.)[43]

2a. Helios hymn of Mesomedes. (Greek-Syrian composer,
ca. 130 A. D.) (Notated.)[44]

2b. Responsorium *Accipiens Simeon* of the Roman Church.
(Notated.)[45]

---

[43] Quoted after A. Gastoué, *Les Origines du Chant Romaine*, p. 40/1,
who gives the best transcription.

[44] Quoted by C. Sachs, *Musik der Antike*, in Buecken's *Handbuch der
Musikwissenschaft*, p. 16.

[45] *Liber usualis*, Paris and Tournai, p. 1253.

gra - ti - as   a - gnus be - ne - dix - it Do - mi - num.

Si - me - on   pu - e - rum in ma - ni - bus

3a. Nemesis hymn of Mesomedes. (Notated.)[46]
3b. Kyrie VI ti tone (Notated.)[47]

4. Christian hymn from Oxyrynchos in Egypt. (3rd century.)
    (Notated.)[48]

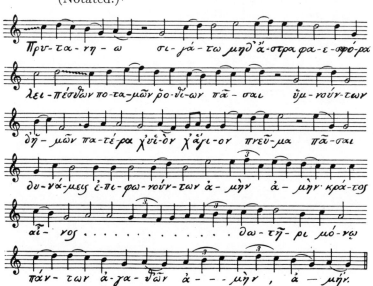

---

[46] Cf. C. Sachs, *op. cit*, p. 13.   [47] *Liber usualis*, p. 29; cf. *supra* note 36.
[48] Quoted by H. Besseler, Musik des Mittelalters, in Buecken's *Handbuch der Musikwissenschaft*, p. 45 ff.

5. Toni Psalmorum of the Roman Church, compared with
   Hebrew Psalmódies.[49]

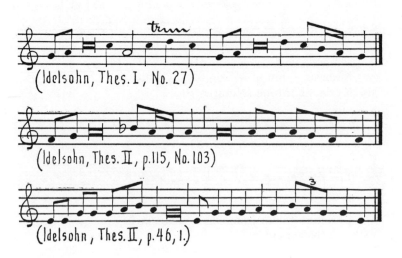

(Idelsohn, Thes. I , No. 27)

(Idelsohn, Thes. II , p.115, No. 103)

(Idelsohn , Thes. II , p. 46, 1.)

---

[49] Quoted by *Graduale Romanum* and E. Werner, *Preliminary Notes for a Comparative Study of Catholic and Jewish Musical Punctuation*, in HUCA, XV, 1940.

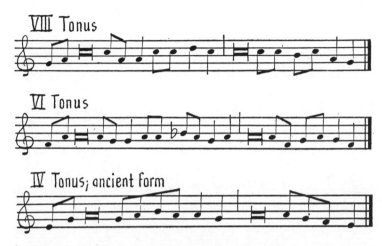

VIII Tonus

VI Tonus

IV Tonus; ancient form

6. Ancient version of the '*Abodah* of *Yom Kippur*. (Oral Tradition.)[50]

Vehakohanim tune.

'Ve - ha - ko - ha - nim   ve - ho - om   ho - ôm - dim

bo - a - zo - ro,   ke - she - ho - yu sho - me - im es. ha - shêm

7. The *Tropos Spondeiakos* after Clement of Alexandria and Plutarch, compared with Jewish and Christian chants. (Reconstruction by E. W.)[51]

(1)

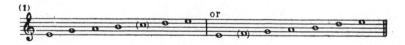

or

[50] Quoted by Idelsohn, *Manual of Musical Illustrations*, (from Ms 4 E #81 in the Library of the Hebrew Union College.)
[51] Tabulation of the *Tropos Spondiacos*, quoted in excerpt from E. Werner,

69

(2)

Cum sanc-to spi-ri-tu, in glo-ri-a Dei Pa-tris. A - - men.

(3)

V'-ha-ko-ha-nim v'-ha-'am ha-'om-dim ba-'a-za-ra *etc.*

'af hu 'ha-ya mitz-kad ven ve' o-mer la - - hem.__

(6)

Καὶ ὢν ἐν κόλ-ποις τοῦ Πα - - - τρὸς - - - -

ἱ-λάσ-θη - - - τι ταῖς ἁ-μαρ-τί-αις ἡ-μῶν.

8a. *Te Deum*, after the Ambrosian version. (Notated.)[52]
8b. *Shema'* of the Yemenite Jews. (Oral Tradition.)[53]

(3)

(a) Antiphonale Ambros.

Te De-um lau-da-mus, te Do-mi-num con - fi-

te - mur, tu rex glo-ri-ae Chris-te.

"The Doxology in Synagogue and Church," 333 ff., where all sources are given. (In *HUCA* vol. XIX., 1946.) See also my article "The Attitude of the Church-Fathers Towards Hebrew Psalmody" in *Review of Religion*, May 1943.

[52] Antiphonale Ambrosianum, or Liber Usualis, p. 1471, *in slightly-different version.*

[53] Cf. Idelsohn, *Thesaurus*, I, (Yemenites), p. 71.

9a. Nestorian Psalmody (Oral.)[54]
9b. Psalmody of Yemenite Jews. (Oral.)[55]
9c. Mode of lamentations of the Roman Church.[56]

10a. Nestorian Hymn. (Oral.)
10b. Gregorian Hymn. (Notated.)
10c. Maronite Kedushah. (Oral.)
10d. East Syrian psalmody. (Oral.)[57]
10e. Song of Songs; cantillation of the Persian Jews. (Oral.)[58]

[54] Cf. Dom Parisot, *op. cit.*, #321.
[55] Cf. Idelsohn, *Jewish Music in its Historic Development*, p. 63, #9.
[56] Cf. Oscar Fleischer, *Neumenstudien*, II.. p. 22/3.
[57] Cf. Parisot, *op. cit.* Nrs. 350; 62; 316; *Lib. usualis* p. 261.
[58] Cf. Idelsohn, *Jewish Music*, p. 52, #2.

THE LEVELS

The practice of musical performance

Before we examine these musical sources in detail, we should acquaint ourselves with the manner in which music was actually performed in the era of the disintegrating culture of antiquity. In the synopsis of Hellenistic music given above, its role in the mystery cults has been emphazised but these were by no means the only occasions when music played a significant part. At the symposia, in the theatron, at secular processions and parades, and in real concerts and recitals, vocal and instrumental music was very much in evidence. Ascetic tendencies independent of Christianity, on the other hand, repudiated music completely. It is an historic irony that the Neo-Pythagoreans, the followers of the idolized inventor of music, led the battle for a "spiritualized" music (the harmony of the spheres), such as could not be heard by human senses at all.

Between these extremes the young Church had to find its way. The third century marked the turning point in the Church's attitude toward instrumental music; it was being tolerated, if not welcomed. Even a canonical book, Revelations, visualized the host of elders ($\pi\rho\epsilon\sigma\beta\acute{\upsilon}\tau\epsilon\rho o\iota$) prostrate before the Lamb and playing, with harps, the "new song."[59] Clement of Alexandria defended the playing of the lyre by quoting the great example of King David.[60] As in most cases, he patterned his ideas on Philo, who excepted the lyre from the accusation of sensuality.[61] The first authoritative injunction against instrumental music appeared in the Canones of St. Basil, which were written towards the end of the fourth century.[62]

Two questions with regard to musical performance arise: Who sang the prayers and hymns in Church and how were they rendered? As to the first question, the ideal of the early Church was, according to the Apostolic literature, the $\kappa o\iota\nu\omega\nu\acute{\iota}a$ i. e. the congregation singing in unison with one or more men functioning as precentors. This community singing was led by psalmists, anagnostes, lectors, deacons, and other clergymen. Our most reliable testimonies come from the Apostolic Constitution,[63] Cyril of Jerusalem,[64] and the pilgriming woman, Aetheria Sylvia.[65] Judging from this evidence, the lectors' and psalmists' function was well-nigh identical with that of the שליח צבור in rabbinic literature. In fact, it has long been surmised that the

---

[59] Revel 5.8. Cf. also the famous passage of the Thomas Acts where the female Hebrew flute-player enchants the apostle into prophetic ecstasy. See H. Gressmann, *Die Musikinstrumente des AT*, p. 16.

[60] Clement of Al., *Paedagog.* 2, 4.

[61] Philo, Leg. Alleg. I, 5, #14; (I., 64 ed. Cohn). Later on, he likens the lyre to the Universe and the microcosm of the human soul.

[62] Cf. F. Leitner, *Der Volksgesang im juedischen und christlichen Altertum*, p. 261, who quotes W. Riedel, *Die Kirchenrechtsquellen des Patriarchats Alexandrien*, 1900.

[63] Const. Apost. ed. Funk, III, 11, 1; VIII., 10, 10; II., 28, 5; VI., 17, 2; VII., 45, 2, *et passim.*

[64] PG 33, 804.

[65] *Peregrinatio Silviae*, ed. Heraeus, cap. 34, 73.

early Church recruited its cantors from among Jewish prose-
lytes.[66]

There are two documents which demonstrate the truth of
this assumption beyond any doubt and shed new light upon the
matter:

A. The Roman epitaph of a Christian singer of the fifth
century:

Hic levitarum primus in ordine vivens
Davitici cantor carminis iste fuit.

This inscription is found on the tombstone of an archdeacon
named *Deusdedit* (= Jonathan). Here is surely one Christian
cantor who had been a Jew.[67]

B. The epitaph of the lector *Redemptus* (another typical
proselyte name):

Prophetam celebrans placido modulamine senem.

He was obviously a fifth century Judaeo-Christian reader, or
cantor of Scripture, who sang the "Prophet" in pleasing cantillation. E. M. Kaufmann suggests that the "Prophet" is David,
whose Psalms qualified him to be considered a prophet by the
Church.[68]

The "pleasing cantillation" would justify Athanasius' characterization of recitation of Scripture as "melodious";[69] today's
tonus lectionis is, on the other hand, no more than an emphatic
speaking with semi-musical cadences. Leitner is evidently right
when he links the Athanasius passage to the Hebrew-Syrian
type of melodic cantillation.[70]

Two other types of musical rendition in the Church, the
responsorium and the antiphony, were likewise of Jewish origin.
There is no need to cite the numerous ecclesiastical authors who
claim the invention of both forms for Christianity: The passages
I Chr. 30.20, Neh. 12.27, and Ps. 136 make it perfectly clear

---

[66] Cf. P. Wagner, *Gregorianische Melodien*, I., p. 17 ff.

[67] Cf. De Rossi, *Roma Sotteranea* III., p 239, 242.

[68] Cf. E. M. Kaufmann, *Handbuch der altchristlichen Epigraphik*,
p. 272.

[69] Cf. Athanasius, *Ep. ad Marcellum* 12, in PG 27, 24.

[70] Cf. E. F. Leitner, *op. cit.* p. 196.

that both the response and the antiphony were details of a well established Jewish heritage which the Church adopted.[71]

The participation of women in the congregational singing of Synagogue and Church warrants special consideration. Marcion had formed a female choir, and Paulus of Samosata, also a gnostic, composed psalms for women singers.[72] Significantly, the antagonism toward the female voice became violent only in the gnostic crisis of the Church. P. Quasten's hypothesis, that the practice of the gnostics was the decisive reason for the complete prohibition of female activity in the common liturgy, is quite unconvincing.[73] After all, the Paulinian rule αἱ γυναῖκες ἐν ταῖς ἐκκλησίαις σιγάτωσαν (let the women be silent in the holy assembly) in I Cor. 14.34 was written long before gnosticism came on the Christian scene. When finally the Didascalia of the 318 Fathers gave the Apostolic rule a legal formulation, there were still voices raised in defence of female choirs.[74]

The underlying reason was of a different nature. It becomes obvious when we compare the background of the defenders of women singers with that of their oppenents in the fourth and fifth centuries. In the opposition were: Tertullian (North Africa), Jerome (Rome, Palestine), Cyril of Jerusalem (Greece, Jerusalem), and Isidor of Pelusium (Greece).[75] The defenders were: Marcion (Black Sea), Ephrem Syrus (Nisibis), Bardesanes and his son Harmonius (Edessa). This tabulation seems to indicate that the Western regions were more puritanic than the Syrians. To be sure, gnostics had no monopoly on female singing as is shown by the example of Ephraem, who instituted women's choirs. This practice spread all over Asia Minor. The Arabic "canones of the Apostle" even admits female lectors and dea-

---

[71] We refer here to the basic forms, not to their later elaborations in the occident. About European transformations see *infra* p. 447 ff.

[72] Leitner, *op. cit.* p. 263.

[73] Cf. P. Quasten, *op. cit.*, p. 123 ff.

[74] *Ibid.* p. 124.

[75] Isidor's reasons against female singing are almost literally identical with the talmudic formulation. (קול באשה ערוה, b. *Ber. 24a*): Τῇ δὲ τοῦ μέλους ἡδύτητι εἰς ἐρεθισμὸν παθημάτων χρώμενοι...; quoted by P. Quasten, *op. cit.* p. 121.

cons.[76] A kind of compromise attitude is found in the Syrian "Testament of the Lord," (fifth century) which permits a female response to the psalm intoned by a male precentor.[77] This is quite analogous to the statement of a Babylonian Amora, R. Joseph who accepted responses by women but not their leading the songs.[78] The very same practice is described by Aetherea Sylvia as a usage of the Church at Jerusalem in the fourth century.[79] All in all, those countries, where orgiastic ceremonies had not been too popular took a stronger stand against female singers than did those provinces where women had always participated actively in licentious folk ceremonies.

What were the texts of the hymns, psalms and songs, which were written about in such exalted language in the many reports and epistles of the first six centuries?

The question can be answered only by referring to the spirit of early Christian liturgy. Paul's categories of prayer (I Tim. 2.1) δέησις — בקשה; προσευχή — תפלה, שבח; ἐντεύξις — תחנון; εὐχαριστία — הודאה do not quite coincide with his categories of liturgical songs, ψαλμοὶ, ὑμνοὶ, ὠδαὶ πνευματικαί (Eph. 5.19; Col. 3.16). Many scholars have attempted to interpret the last three terms from a liturgical, others from a literary or poetic point of view. The difficulty lies chiefly in the ambiguous term *hymnos*, since Biblical pieces like the canticles, as well as post-Biblical spontaneous utterances and Apocryphal compositions were all termed hymns.[80] According to Origen who based a whole theory of oration upon Paul's categories, προσευχή stands always for praise and is usually couched in hymnic form.[81] All of these distinctions are, of course, familiar terms of

[76] *Ibid.* p. 120.　　　[77] *Ibid.* p. 119.　　　[78] b *Sota* 48 a.

[79] Cf. *Peregrinatio Silviae*, 24, 1:... "descendent omnes monazontes et parthenae, et non solum hii, sed et laici praeter viri et mulieres ... dicuntur hymni et psalmi responduntur ..."

[80] The literature on the question see in Leitner, *op. cit.* p. 78; also P. Wagner, *op. cit.* I, p. 6, and E. Werner, "The Attitude of the Church Fathers towards Hebrew Psalmody," in *Review of Religion*, May 1943.

[81] Cf. Origen, *De Oratione*, cap. 4, 9, 13, 14, 33; (PG 11); *Contra Celsum* I, 8, cap. 37, (PG 11, 1574). This is borne out by Chrysostom, *Ep. ad Col.* III, 9,2: Αἱ γὰρ ἄνω δυνάμεις ὑμνοῦσιν οὐ ψάλλουσιν. (The higher powers [angels] sing hymns, not psalms.)

rabbinic literature. If it were possible to identify them with the musical categories, then *hymnos* would correspond to the poetic laudation of the congregation (שיר); *psalmos*, to the psalm (of the Psalter or a recent composition of the same kind); and ᾠδὴ πνευματική to the spontaneous song, born of the religious impulse of the moment. This ecstatic type of musical prayer was frequently juxtaposed with the equally enthusiastic *glossolalia* (talking in tongues).[82]

Both the scriptural and post-Biblical hymns became very popular.[83] In the third century, they were already so well established that the gnostics used the hymnic form for propagandizing their doctrines. The Syrian and Asiatic Greek heretics expecially were masters of the hymn. Ephrem, as a result, decided to fight beauty with beauty and his hymns served as most effective counter propaganda for the orthodox Church.[84] In addition, to thwart this kind of heresy and its artistic lure, the Council of Laodicea (360–381) strictly prohibited the singing of any non-scriptural text in the Christian liturgy.[85] Most of the older hymns were therefore lost during the subsequent centuries and the majority of present day hymns stem from a more recent time. Later on the Churches modified their policy and admitted non-scriptural hymns to a limited degree. The real homestead of the hymn remained the Syrian and Byzantine Churches which also have the largest hymnals.

The two outstanding attributes of these Aramean compositions were: (1) almost excessive use of the contrafact practice — singing an old melody to new verses or *vice versa*; and (2) the introduction of isosyllabic meters, in which the syllables, not the accents of each line, are counted. This new poetic scheme was

[82] Cf. E. Werner, *op. cit.*, p. 341.

[83] CF. Leitner, *op. cit.* p. 125–28.

[84] According to Sozomenus, *hist. eccl.* 3, 16, Ephraem imitated the Gnostic Harmonius. Cf, also Dom Jeannin, *Melodies liturgiques syriennes et chaldéennes*, I. p. 144. The original text is first given in Assemani, *Bibliotheca Orient.*, I. 47 ff., where also the Syriac musical terminology is discussed.

[85] Cf. P. Wagner, *op. cit.*, I. p. 43 f. Jewish history knows of an identical prohibition of non-scriptural texts in the liturgy of the Karaitic sect.

of far reaching consequence in the literature of the Western Church.[86]

The former was an old practice of Semitic music. Many of the enigmatic superscriptions of Psalms (22; 56; 57; 58; 60; etc.) refer to the tunes or initial lines of then popular songs. In post-biblical literature, the Judeo-Arabic term *lahan* designated this contrafact practice. [87] The Byzantine Church also made use of the device, which was called εἰρμός; most probably this form stems from the Syrians. For we read in Ephrem's ,hymns that some of them were to be sung according to tunes of his antagonist Bardesanes.[88] Whether or not it was the prior form, the Syrian *riš-qolo* is fully identical with the Byzantine εἰρμός.

The invention of a new metrical system by the Syrian poets is of great consequence for our study. It is inseparably linked with the development of Church music and, as it seems to this writer, also with that of the Synagogue. For it was due to the new metrical scheme of the Syrians that the corresponding music also was forced into metric structure. This conception of music is much closer akin to Hellenistic than to original Jewish theory and practice. The superabundance of metrical hymns in the Aramean Churches demanded strongly rhythmic tunes which had been known to the Greeks for centuries but entered synagogal music only in the ninth century when the *piyyut* conquered the liturgy. The question remains, however, whether the Syrians were really the inventors of the new poetic style. Since W. Meyer has demonstrated their priority, we must at least assume it. We shall discuss this matter later from a broader viewpoint.

---

[86] Cf. W. Meyer, "Anfang und Ursprung der lateinischen und griechischen rhythmischen Dichtung" in *Abhandlungen der k. Bayerischen Akademie der Wissenschaften*, I. Kl. XVII 1885, p. 108 ff. "Von den semitischen Christen ist mit dem Christentum die rhythmische Dichtungsform zu den lateinischen und griechischen Christen gewandert." See also H. Grimme, *Der Strophenbau in den Gedichten Ephraems (Anhang)*, Freiburg, (Switzerland) 1893.

[87] Cf. Werner-Sonne; The Philosophy and Theory of Music in Judaeo-Arabic Literature" I, in HUCA 1941, p. 296 ff. Also K. Wachsmann, *op. cit.* p. 51 ff.

[88] Ephraem Syrus, *opera*, ed. Benedict, vol. VI, p. 128, end of the 65th homily, (*adversus scrutatores*); where he adds ܟܕܒܕܒ ܟܐܘܣܐ. ܠܠ ܡܕ. Also Assemani, *Bibl. Or.* I, p. 47/8.

Another peculiarity of the Aramean pieces deserves a brief description: their preference for half-choirs, when responses or antiphones were sung. We have already mentioned the Biblical origin of these forms, but it seems that they were organized and cultivated in Syria before they became wholly integrated in the Roman or Byzantine plainsong. This conclusion is not only based upon the ever repeated Patristic statements that the Greco-Syrian monks Flavian and Diodorus (of Antioch and Tarsus) invented and fostered the antiphonic practice[89] but also upon new and fully convincing evidence which has been produced by P. Odilo Heiming. This scholar has demonstrated that many of the Syriac hymn manuscripts were actually arranged for half-choruses. Beyond this fact, Heiming investigated the leading stanzas and compared them with Byzantine patterns. The result displays an intricate interrelation between Syria and Byzantium, where the Eastern wave met the Western wave.[90]

Melos and Rhythm.

(I) The three archetypes of early Church music can be defined according to one single criterion: the relation between tone and word. Considering psalmody but an elaborate form of cantillation or *ekphonesis*, that old and venerable category is characterized by the organic links which bind the syntactic structure of the scriptural text to its musical formulation. The individual word is of no relevance; only the whole sentence with its caesura and cadence makes a musical unit. The parallellism of Scripture which has carefully been preserved in all translations created the dichotomic structure of musical psalmody.

If we compare No. 5 (p. 426) with either 2b or 3b (p. 425)

---

[89] Cf. Sozomenus, *Hist. eccl.* 3, 20, (PG 76, 1100); also Theodore of Mopsuestia, PG 139, 1390. The first Christian author to claim the Syrian origin of the antiphon is Socrates, *Hist. Eccl.* VI., ch. 8, (PG 67, 889). It should not be forgotten that, at the time referred to (ca. 270), Jewry was predominant in Antioch and probably had introduced there the old familiar antiphonal practice.

[90] Cf. P. Odilo Heiming, *Syrische Enjane und Griechische Kanones*, Muenster 1932, p. 40 ff.

the difference is plain and fundamental. In psalmody we find melodic movement only on special significant places of the sentence: in the beginning, at the pause (*'Atnah*), and in the final cadence. The rest of the sentence is recited upon the *ténor* without any melos. There is no discernible *ténor* in the other two examples, however, nor any clear dichotomy, nor its charac-teristic attributes, the punctuating or final melisms. The melody, while closely bound to the words, if not to single syllables, flows more freely and is more autonomous. Now psalmody is a direct Jewish heritage of the Church. This is also true of the *lectio solemnis*, the cantillation of Scripture. Not only are these two elements, the core of the ancient musical liturgy, common to both Synagogue and Church, they also are by far the best preserved and most authentic features. For the first attempts at musical notation in Judaism and Christianity concerned them-selves with the fixation of these two forms. The musical organi-zation of the Jewish raw material, however, remained the task of the different Churches and varied considerably with the individual ethnic traditions. Even here we find occasionally Hel-lenistically inspired fragments; our Ex. 2a and b give such an instance. Parts of the Helios-hymn of Mesomedes were inte-grated in the response "Accipiens Simeon" for the feast of purification. Note the parallelisms in ex. 5a, b (p. 426/27).

(II) Much more complex is the genesis of the second arche-type, the hymnic syllabic composition. This form is linked to the syllable or the word rather than to the sentence. No *ténor* of recitation, hardly a *pausa*, and seldom a final melism in the cadence, occur in hymnic forms. But its music is a faithful expression of the metrical poem, since it obeys in all details the accents of the text. If we desire to understand its history, our first task must be the study of the hymn meters. But we meet with serious difficulties. Hellenistic poetry was based upon the system of quantity, but the earliest Aramean and Greek-Chris-tian hymns do not observe this scheme. Let us compare Ex. 4, the earliest musical document of Christianity, the Oxyrynchos-hymn, with Ex. 10 c, a, and b [a Syrian Qedusha, a Nestorian and Gregorian hymn,] with regard to their texts: (Cf. *supra* p. 425, 429.)

4. (Oxyrynchos hymn)[91]

Πρυτανήω σιγάτω μηδ' ἄστρα φαέσφορα λειπέσθων
ποταμῶν ῥοθίων πᾶσαι ὑμνούντων δ' ἡμῶν
πατέρα χ' υἱόν χ' ἅγιον πνεῦμα πᾶσαι δυνάμεις
ἐπιφωνούντων, ἀμὴν ἀμὴν; κράτος αἶνος . . .
σωτῆρι μόνῳ πάντων ἀγαθῶν ἀμὴν . . . ἀμήν.

Ex. 10 c. (pentasyllabic meter) perhaps $\smile - \smile \smile -$

> qadiš qadišat
> qadiš b'kul 'edon
> aloho m'šabho
> m'qadaš l'qadiše
>
> d'men srofe d'nuro
> bravmo metqadaš
> v'men krubē d'ḥilē
> b'hedro metbaraḥ

Ex. 10 a. (octosyllabic meter) probably $\smile - \smile - \smile - \smile -$[92]

> šagdinan mar l'allahuṭāḥ
> valnāšutāḥ dla pulāgā.

Ex. 10 b. (Octosyllabic meter) scheme $\smile - \smile - \smile - \smile \smile$[93]

> Lucis creator optime
> Lucem dierum proferens
> Primordinis lucis novae
> Mundi parans originem
>
> Qui mane junctum vesperi
> Diem vocari praecipis
> Illabitur tetrum chaos
> Audi preces cum fletibus
> etc.

---

[91] Cf. H. Abert, "Ein neuentdeckter fruehchristlicher Hymnus," in *Zeitschrift fuer Musikwissenschaft* IV, 1922; p. 524 ff. Also O. Ursprung, Der Hymnus aus Oxyrynchus, in *Theologie und Glaube*, XVIII, 1926, p. 387 ff. The original text in facsimile in *The Oxyrynchos Papyri* XV, ed. B. Greenfell and A. S. Hunt, London 1922, #1786, p. 21 ff.

[92] Cf. Dom Parisot, *op. cit.* #62, p. 67; #350, p. 240.

[93] *Liber usualis*, p. 261.

81

The first text is at least partially based upon the old principle of quantity, while the following three hymns show no trace of quantity. There might be some doubt concerning the Syrian text, since we do not know its original correct accentuation, but in the Latin hymn, the accentuation is evident. The Syrian and Latin texts have, however, one principle in common: their verses always contain the same number of syllables. This scheme finally replaced the classic conception of meter both in the Roman and in the Greek Churches.

It is generally assumed that the Syrian practice of numbering syllables was of no influence upon Hebrew poetry, which counted accents rather than syllables. This writer has found, however, that some of the oldest *piyyutim* followed the Syrian scheme. Here are two examples;[94]

(Decasyllabus)

(a)

במידה תיכנת לו מים גם דם

חיות חציו מים וגם חציו דם

דולף הוא צונים אם כיזבו מימיו

ולוקה בזיבה אם יזובו דמיו

etc.

(b) Strict heptasyllabus. ("Ephraem's meter") $\simeq \acute{-} \,\_\, \cup \,\acute{-}\, \_\, \_\, \cup \,\acute{-}$[95]

מטל מלכים בהזילו

ימטוב חלב בהיגדלו

יעקב ירש בחבלו

מתן אדם ירחיב לו

etc.

There probably existed older sources of the same literary type before the era of the *piyyutim* quoted above (seventh century). It is only through the findings in the Geniza that we know the *Maḥzor Yannai* at all. Nonetheless, the priority of the Syrians in using the syllabic type can hardly be doubted.[96]

---

[94] Cf. Maḥzor Yannai, ed. Davidson and L. Ginzberg, p. 15, line 29 etc.

[95] Cf. *Studies of the Research Institute for Hebrew Poetry*, vol. II. p. 227, Jerusalem 1936.

[96] G. Reese, in his splendid work, "*Music in the Middle Ages*," p. 68, gives a definition of Syriac meters which can easily lead to misunderstandings. He

Again, there are indications which point to Hellenism as the agent under whose aegis the Syrians evolved their system. The historian, Sozomen, in his biography of Ephrem Syrus writes: "Harmonius, the son of Bardesanes, having been well instructed in Grecian literature, was the first who subjected his native language to meters and musical laws, (πρῶτον μέτροις καὶ νόμοις μουσικοῖς τὴν πάτριον φωνὴν ὑπαγαγεῖν) and adapted it to choirs of singers, as the Syrians now commonly chant; not indeed using the writings of Harmonius, but his tunes."[97] This passage would suggest the Syrian hymnodists as heirs of the Greek tradition. Indeed, when we consider that Judaism kept itself free from such metric conceptions until the sixth or even the seventh century, while living all of the time in close contact with Aramean Christianity, there is perhaps some reason to doubt the genuineness of Syrian hymnody. This suspicion becomes even stronger when we contemplate the rapidity with which the Syrian type swept all over the Western and Eastern Church. To be sure, the contemporaries of Ephrem and the champions of the new form in the Roman orbit, such as Ambrose, did not immediately abandon the traditional quantity system, but neither Augustin nor Gregory I heeded quantity any longer.[98] Had the new system been entirely alien to Romans and Greeks it would have encountered much more opposition than it actually did.

writes: "Correspondence between lines being obtained through equality not in the total number of syllables in each but in the number of tonic accents." This point is not at all certain. W. Meyer, *op. cit.*, p. 115, writes: "Durch jenes semitische Vorbild wurden diese Voelker angeregt, die Quantitaet der Silben nicht mehr zu beachten, ... dagegen auf die Silbenzahl zu achten ..." and p. 108: "Dennoch ist nicht der Wortakzent an die Stelle der Versakzente getreten; .... dagegen wird die Silbenzahl der Zeilen berechnet und mit einigen Schwankungen eine bestimmte Zahl festgehalten." The whole theory needs still further elucidation; it is based upon Pitra's erroneous conjecture that the Syriac and Byzantine hymns with acrostics and isosyllabic verses are a legacy of the Synagogue. The more recent literature on the problem, e. g. Hoelscher's *Syrische Verskunst* was not accessible to me. See also E. Wellesz, *op. cit.* [42] p. 48-60.

[97] Cf. Sozomen, *Life of Ephraem*, III., ch. 16.

[98] Cf. W. Meyer, *op. cit.* p. 119. Note the psalmodic type of the *"Te Deum,"* ex. 8a! (*supra* p. 428.)

Another factor must be considered: the type of melody. When we compare the oldest Latin hymn melodies with those of the Syrians, we find some surprising analogies in their flow and structure.

Cf. No. 10a and 10b; (p. 430) they follow the same pattern.

Their rhythmic identity, dependent upon the octosyllabic scheme of the Syriac and of the Roman hymn, needs no further elaboration. If we search for the Greek models of the Syriac meters, the closest likeness presents the anacreontic pattern with Ephrem's heptasyllabic meter. The following example is taken from August Hahn's work, who first ventured the conjecture that Harmonius borrowed this meter from Anacreon:[99]

'Η γῆ μέλαινα πίνει
Πίνει δὲ δένδρε' αὐτην, etc.

or:

Μυθῖναι δ'ἐνὶ νήσῳ
Μεγίστῃ διέπουσιν

(*Rossbach-Westphal,*
Griechische Metrik III., p. 493)

These Greek rhythms (*Acatalectic Pherecrateus; logaoedic Tripody*) were used for popular processions. It seems that the women sang them at the mystery cults, often in strophic responses.[100] Let us, in this connection, remember that Ephrem, after whom that very meter is named in Syria, taught it to women in responsorial style.[101]

---

[99] Cf. Augustus Hahn, *Chrestomathia Syriaca*, sive S. Ephraemi carmina selecta, Leipzig 1825; see also H. Burgess, *Select hymns and homilies by Ephraem Syrus*, London 1853, p. XLVII.

[100] A. Rossbach and R. Westphal, *Griechische Metrik*, III, p. 494-96. The poem, by Yannai, quoted supra p. 440 is likewise a heptasyllabus, and its meter a logaoedic tripody.

[101] Yet Asseman already doubts the originality of Ephraem's heptasyllabus; he writes: "Errant quoque, qui unum dumtaxat carminum genus, videlicet septem syllabarum, Ephraemo tribuunt . . ." (I. p. 61) And: "Hallucinantur enim, qui Ephraemum asserunt excogitasse versus heptasyllabos,

Contemporary Jewish literature offers neither isosyllabic poems nor strophes nor even descriptions of such types of hymns before the sixth or seventh century. This fact admits of one conclusion only: The hymn form is originally alien to Judaism and is a Greco-Syrian element in the music of the Church.

(III) In the third archetype, the melismatic style, the melos has no immediate relation to the word. This is the oldest form of "absolute" music, entirely emancipated from meter, syllable, word, or sentence. What is its origin? After all, singing without words was not such a common practice in antiquity; even today, coloratura-singing is a rather extraordinary thing. In the Church it is invariably connected with the jubilant rendition of the Alleluja; which fact alone suggests Jewish origin. The acclamation *Hallelujah* may have had, as I have suggested elsewhere, a definite liturgical function, to give the uninitiated, primitive listeners the opportunity of joining the proclamation of God's praise.[102] Gradually it loosened itself from its original context and, used as spontaneous acclamation, together with its pneumatic color, led to a certain disembodiment, to a spiritualization of the Hallelujah. The last step was the omission of the word *Hallelujah* itself, in whose place only its vowels were sung — AEOUIA, to be changed later to EUOUAE.

In Judeo-Christian circles the acclamation was very popular, as the "Odes of Solomon" show, of which each ends with an independent Hallelujah. In the same way it was sung in the gentile Church, as the following passage illustrates:

> "A Hebrew word they (the Christians of Antioch) added to every verse as from one mouth, so that one could believe they were not a multitude of men, but one reasonable, united being, uttering a wonderful sound . . . . . ."[103]

Narsetem hexasyllabos, Balaeum pentasyllabos . . . , nam longe ante hos auctores iam Syri carminibus huiusmodi utebantur ut Bardesanes et Harmonius." (*Ibid.*)

[102] For a full discussion of the Hallelujah see my study "The Doxology in Church and Synagogue" in HUCA 1946, p. 323 ff.

[103] Cyprian Antiochenus, ed. Maurinorum, Venice 1728, CCCX; quoted after J. Doelger, *Sol Salutis*, p. 132. Compare with these passages the conception of *Numbers Rabba* ch. 2, 24.

These facts and testimonies indicate the "additional" character of the Hallelujah; it grew as an expansion of a verse or of an entire psalmody. Cassian's statement confirms this conception: "Some of them (monks) felt that they ought to prolong the . . . psalms themselves by melodies of antiphones and by *adding certain melisms.*"[104] In other words: *the melismatic, wordless Jubili are mere expansions of final melisms in the psalmody.* This theory can be further confirmed by comparing certain final melisms of the oldest Jewish strata with similar, extended Allelujas of the Church.

In these four illustrations the history of the Jubilus is clearly reflected: a) is a very common Jewish psalmody formula, familiar in the Occidental as well as in the Oriental Synagogue; b) and c) are two final melisms of the Gregorian Chant, miniature expansions of the original mode; d) gives a splendidly extended version of a *versus allelujaticus.*

The technique of the melismatic ecstatic singing was imitated in synchretistic circles where it was used for magical purposes. The imitation, however, poor and inorganic, presents a bizarre

---

[104] Cf. Cassian in PL 59, 77: "Quidam enim vicenos seu tricenos psalmos, et hos ipsos antiphonarum protelatos melodiis et adjunctione quarundam modulationun debere singulis noctibus censuerunt."

picture. Compare the fragment of a gnostic-magic incantation
with a Gregorian passage:

After P. Gastoné, *op.cit.*, p. 29.

a)   Gnostic-magic papyons Berlin I.

b)   After P. Wagner, III, p. 387.

The almost howling monotony of both examples is obvious.
It might be due to the idea that certain intervals or tonal figures,
if repeated over and over again, can exert a strong magic appeal,
even more than stubbornly reiterated words or vowels, which
were also the common stock in trade of magic papyri. The
Gregorian example is perhaps a lost wave of that synchretistic
practice which somehow crept into the authentic songs of the
Church. Dom Leclercq describes the curious passages of the
incantations as "remnants of hymns, in which one can recognize a mixture of elements Jewish, pagan, and Christian." But,
he goes on to declare, "we will not be too bold if we imagine in
them (pressentir) translations or pasticchios of Bardesanes
Syriac hymns".[105] This conjecture seems hardly convincing
since the analysis of Syrian hymns indicates their strongly
metrical character. The magic pieces show no discernible rhythm
nor meter and convey, in general, a rather amorphous, not to
say chaotic impression.

From the very outset the *melismatic* type was identified
with religious ecstasy. Created by spontaneous emotion, it was
frequently rendered as improvisation, both in Synagogue and
Church. When the Western Church attempted to systematize
its songs according to the misunderstood teachings of Greek

---

[105] Dom Leclercq, in *Dictionnaire d'archeologie chretienne*, art. "Alphabeth
vocalique des Gnostiques."

theorists, it was the melismatic type which suffered most.[106] Forced into the Procrustean bed of the eight Church tones, it was modified and mutilated. Still, we must consider this a cheap price for its essential preservation: without the occidental arrangement it would have disappeared altogether.

Thus we realize, as in the case of psalmody, a Jewish heritage preserved in the Church by means of Greek theories and systems.

(IV) We have sketched in the previous pages the origin and the structure of the three *urformen* which constituted the backbone of the Church's musical liturgy: psalmody, hymn, and melismatic song. In addition to these types we encounter, at a fairly early stage, certain mixed forms which blended psalmodic elements with melismatic or syllabic hymnic features. They are common to the oldest strata of the Roman, Greek, Syrian, Nestorian, and Armenian chant, but developed independently according to the customs and requirements of their specific liturgies. An ancient Jewish instance is ex. 6 (p. 427).

In the Roman plainsong we find many of these hybrid structures, the most interesting of which are the tunes of the *Ordinarium Missae*, the *Tractus*, the Gradual-Response, the later Antiphones, and the Lamentations, a special version of the *Lectio Solemnis*. In most of these compositions, Jewish and Hellenistic elements were merged in various degrees, generally blended to a perfect unity. In contradistinction to the Eastern Churches, Rome was quite conservative, when it came to changes in, or modifications of, its liturgical traditions. As far as we can see today, there were few, if any, other formative forces besides the Hebrew and the Greek which constitute the nucleus of the Roman chant. Only in the eight and ninth century did West European notions (Gallic, Germanic, Irish) begin to make inroads into the rigid body of Roman tradition.

---

[106] Cf. P. Wagner, *op. cit.*, I., p. 57. "The highly developed type of musical punctuation may very well have its origin in the practice of Jewish precentors;" also G. Reese, *op. cit.*, p. 63. "The singing of the Alleluia was doubtless taken over from the Synagogue;" also K. Wachsmann, *op. cit.*, p. 118: "Ihre Bedeutung (of the ancient Jewish chants) hat nunmehr den Weg in die Literatur gefunden, die die belegte Gemeinsamkeit juedischer und gregorianischer Weisen allenthalben anerkennt und ihrem Bestande einverleibt hat."

a. The tunes of the *Ordinarium Missae* (the nuclear prayers of the Mass). Here a rare opportunity of comparing Hellenistic with Jewish impulses presents itself; No. 3a and 3b juxtaposed the Nemesis hymn of Mesomedes, a Hellenistic piece of the second Christian century, with the *Kyrie* VI of the Gregorian tradition. In the Greek composition the relation between tone and word is strictly syllabic — one tone to each syllable; but the Christian version of the same melody uses punctuating and final melisms. In short, it adjusts the Hellenistic passage to the more Hebraic melismatic character of the *Kyrie*. Quite the reverse development is discernible in the assimilation of an original Hebrew motif to another *Kyrie* piece. Idelsohn was the first to compare the two compositions but without much elaboration.[107]

The Jewish cantillation contains certain initial and final melisms. While its melody has been essentially left untouched by the Church, it has been well-nigh divested of its flourishes by the syllabic distribution of the new Latin words to the ancient Hebrew tune.

In both cases the Church has balanced Hellenistic against Jewish elements by adding or effacing the typically Oriental melisms.

b. Not always was the process as smooth as here, nor the result as well composed. This is especially obvious in some of the antiphones, where the rigidly parallellistic structure of the

---

[107] Idelsohn, *Jewish Music in its Historical Development,* p. 40, 47

Scriptural verses often disturbed the flow of Hellenistic melody. Classic examples of this forced adaptation are Ex. 1a and 1b.

The easy going drinking song of Seikilos was pressed into the distich:

> Hosanna filio David; benedictus qui venit in nomine
>   Domini.
> Rex Israel: Hosanna in excelis.

Here, a good deal of the Hellenistic melody has been absorbed, but the Christian arrangers, as was their custom, insisted upon emphasizing the *pausa* in each verse. Thus they had to add a pausal melism for the words *David* and *Israel*.[108] The adaptation tried, moreover, to stress the twofold *Hosanna* of the first and second verse by the identical musical phrase, thereby cramping the flow of the Greek cadence.

c. Another archaic form of the plainsong, the *Tractus*, reveals prevailing Hebrew elements. Its style is very florid, like that of *Ḥazanut* and it is indeed performed by a soloist during the Mass. It probably antedates all other music of the Mass, except the Hallelujah.[109] P. Wagner has pointed out that the roots of the *Tractus* lie deeply in the solo psalmody of the Synagogue, especially in the punctuating melisms of cantillation. Two arguments put forth by this illustrious scholar make his thesis most plausible: The fact that the *Tractus* texts (with few late exceptions) are exclusively Biblical, and the identity of some of their melodies with chants of the Yemenite Jews. Here we add one more sign of their Jewish origin: the use of certain recurrent melodic patterns which are not at all based upon the systematic scales as the Greeks knew them. These melodic clauses are a most characteristic element of ancient Jewish modality.[110] As all students of the plainsong knew, the melodies of the *Tractus* belong only to two modes, the II and VIII. They do not organically fit into the two modes, but were

---

[108] This becomes even more obvious through the neume *tristropha* upon *Israel*, which always indicates a simplification of an originally melismatic texture to a more syllabic phrasing. Cf. P. Wagner, *op. cit.*, II, p. 123 ff.

[109] Cf. P. Wagner, *op. cit.*, III., p. 366 ff.

[110] Cf. E. Werner, "Leading Motifs in Synagogue and Plain Song," in *Papers of the American Musicological Society*, vol. 1946, Detroit Congress.

forced into that system, alien to Hebrew music, by the Medieval theorists of the Church.

d. The punctuating melisms which play so great a part in cantillation and psalmody were a driving force of agressive power. The old singers of the Church were so accustomed to them that these little flourishes were dragged by them into originally Hellenistic melodies of clearly syllabic character. The famous hymn of Oxyrynchos, the oldest musical document of Christianity, is a case in point. A comparison of No. 4 with a classical Greek composition like Ex. 2a evidences certain fundamental divergencies. The text of the hymn proper ends with "Amen, Amen" followed by a small doxology beginning with κράτος αἶνος and ending with πάντων ἀγαθῶν ἀμήν, ἀμήν. In all these endings, we encounter the typical final melisms of Jewish psalmody although, in melody and structure, the piece is distinctly Hellenistic, even written in the Greek letter notation. We quote here the charactistic passages (p. 425).

The question then arises: How did the Egyptian Christians come to be acquainted with Jewish psalmody and its practice? Fortunately, this question can now be answered satisfactorily. Clement of Alexandria, an older contemporary of the Oxyrynchos hymn wrote:

> "Further, among the ancient Greeks, in their banquets over the brimming cups, a song was sung called a *skolion* after the manner of the Hebrew Psalms, altogether raising the paean with the voice."[111] — indicating his knowledge of Hebrew Psalmody.

Later on, Clement gives some hints about that mode of psalmody, and this writer essayed, by comparing Clement's statements

[111] Clement of Alex., *Paedagogue*, II, ch. 4. For a full discussion of that significant passage, see E. Werner, "Notes on the Attitude of the Early Church Fathers towards Hebrew Psalmody" in *Review of Religion*, May 1943, p. 349, where also numerous musical illustrations are quoted.

with those of Plutarch, Aristides Quintilianus, and others, to reconstruct the *Tropos Spondeiakos*, the mode alluded to. No. 7 shows the occurrence of that melodic type in Hebrew as well as in Roman and Syrian psalmody. In most of the corresponding examples (see n. 111), the final melisms are outstanding and color the cadence much in the same way as in the Hymn of Oxyrynchos. (Cf. *supra* p. 427, 428.)

e. Perhaps the most interesting instance of the Roman policy of balancing Hellenistic and Jewish features against each other is the case of the Lamentations. Liturgically, they belong to one of the oldest strata of Christian worship. Musically, the tradition is variegated, heterogeneous, and not always authentic. Of the numerous versions we select two, both of which occur also in Jewish cantillation:

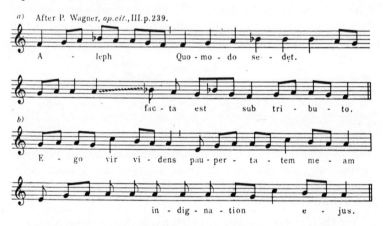

a) After P. Wagner, *op.cit.*, III. p. 239.

A - leph   Quo - mo - do   se - det.

fac - ta   est   sub   tri - bu - to.

b)

E - go   vir   vi - dens   pau - per - ta - tem   me - am

in - dig - na - tion   e - jus.

Originally, the cantillation of the Yemenite Jews (ex. 9b) was full of the little melisms demanded by the disjunctive accents of Scripture and has been preserved in that form. While the Church has adopted the characteristic mode, it rigidly simplified it and retained only the punctuating melisms of *pausa* and *punctus* (*'Atnah — Sof Pasuk*). (Cf. *supra* p. 429.)

Again we behold the Jewish gem in Greek setting, as often before. Notwithstanding the obvious melodic identities, the deeper reasons for the Christian modifications must not be overlooked. But it is not possible within the scope of this study to examine the manifold causes which, in the course of centuries, engendered a kind of stylistic unity within the traditional music of the Churches as well as that of the Synagogue. Here only a theory can be offered without full implementation. That organic unity was forged on the two levels of practical music and theological speculation.

In the realm of practical music (*musica humana*), the two main causes which made for homogeneity of style were (a) the associative power of certain melodic types and (b) the organization of musical notation. In the oldest layers of Church music, we encounter sorts of primitive leading motifs which set the pattern for later compositions. While this development is especially visible in the Gradual-Responses of the Gregorian Chant, an analogous principle prevails also in the music of the Synagogue. The origin of this technique is probably purely musical; it is but natural to imitate older tunes, particularly when they are surrounded by an aura of holiness. Once this practice was established, a further element was added, which lent a new significance to the leading-motifs: they were used to serve as *hermeneutic expressions* of the various texts to which they were applied.[112] Venturing a drastic anachronism, one might say: the leading-motifs functioned as "cross references" in the extended liturgies of the Churches and the Synagogue.

In Judaism, the leading-motifs have become so familiar to every worshipper that he automatically associates certain tunes with entire holydays whose liturgy they permeate. The *Missinai* tunes were among the factors which helped to create the unique atmosphere of the Jewish holyday service. While the plainsong never reached this unity of style, there is evidence enough that it was aspired to and in certain forms also achieved, notably in the Roman Gradual-Responses, the Greek εἱρμοί, and the Syrian *enyane* and *riš-qole*.[113] The influx of the various ethnic groups and of their tunes prevented the Gregorian Chant from

[112] Cf. my article on "Leading Motifs in Synagogue and Plain Song," *supra* n. 110.

[113] Cf. P. Wagner, *op. cit.*, III., p. 376 ff.: "The technique of wandering melisms is an ancient heritage of Synagogue psalmody"; *ibid.* p. 396. On the *hirmoi* and the related Syrian forms, see G. Reese, *op. cit.*, pp. 66, 78 ff.

becoming completely homogeneous; but it obviated also a potential monotony. The more nationalistically-minded Byzantine and Syrian Churches did not fully escape that monotony. Judaism, on the other hand, avoided such sameness of style due to its migrations and its various regional *minhagim.*

The other factor contributive to the unification of musical style was undoubtedly the notation. We meet here with a situation not at all unique in the centuries of slowly disintegrating antiquity. While the Greeks had developed an exact system of musical notation, it had been so completely forgotten, that in the seventh century Isidorus Hispalensis could write: "Unless tunes are preserved by memory, they perish, since they cannot be written."[114] Yet the Oxyrynchos hymn was written in the Greek notation as late as the third century. As in other fields of culture, most of the accomplishments of Greek music were thrown overboard by zealous religious, and perhaps ethnic fanatics who had arisen in and with Christianity. To be sure, a new notation had to be organized; but it did not begin where the Greeks had left off. Its oldest documents can be traced to the seventh century, and there were probably earlier attempts.[115] Still, there remains a lacuna of almost three centuries, which we are unable to bridge.

It is not surprising that the new system was vastly different from the Greek conception, for it had to serve another purpose. The Greek notation had to define each tone, since its music was syllabic-rhythmic, and its phrases not melismatic. The Church required a method by which the most venerable element of liturgical music could be fixed, namely the cantillation of the scriptural lesson and psalmody. The Greek system, with its minute description of every tone, would have proved very cumbersome, had it been applied to the new task. *Phrases* or *syntactic units* had to be provided with notation, not individual

[114] In Gerbert, *Scriptores de musica sacra* I, 20 a: "Nisi enim ab homine memoria teneantur, soni pereunt, quia scribi non possunt."

[115] The notation of the Cod. Ephraemi Syri, (Nat. Libr., Paris, Greek div. Cod. resc. 9) is, according to recent examinations, considerably younger than the text of the palimpsest, which originated in the 5th century. Cf. C. Hoeg, *La Notation ekphonétique*, Copenhagen, p. 107/8/

syllables. Hence the ecphonetic origin of the Greek and Roman neumes. Indeed, the primitive neumes, which stood for entire phrases of both text and music, were much more practical for their purpose than any other system.

It was O. Fleischer who in his *Neumenstudien* proved indisputably the common origin of the Hebrew, Armenian, Hindu, Greek, and Roman systems of accentuation. F. Praetorius investigated the origin of the Hebrew *Te'amim*, claiming that the Massorites borrowed the ecphonetic system from Greek evangeliars. He offered no real proof for this contention.[116] Since Kahle's penetrating studies (*Masoreten des Ostens* and *Masoreten des Westens*) we know that the relations were by no means that simple and onesided. According to his theory, a Nestorian school of scribes and exegetes was the first to set up a system of ecphonetic signs applied to Scriptural texts. He also suggests an interrelation between the Nestorians and the Rabbinic academy at Nisibis.[117] That there existed an intimate connection between the Syrian and the earliest Hebrew accents cannot be doubted, since their similarity is evident. Unfortunately the musical tradition of the Syriac accents had been lost for many centuries, as we learn from Bar Hebraeus.[118]

In my study on "Musical Punctuation," the theory was presented that the earliest Masoretic accents were a combination of signs borrowed from the contemporaneous Syriac system and the older Hebrew cheironomic tradition. Be that as it may, Syriac and Hebrew elements must have played a decisive role

---

[116] Cf. F. Praetorius, *Ueber die Herkunft der hebraeischen Akzente*, and Reply to Renee Gregory, Berlin 1901/2. See also E. Werner "Preliminary notes . . . on Catholic and Jewish Musical Punctuation" in HUCA 1940, p. 338 ff.

[117] Cf. Cassiodor, De inst. divin. litterarum in PL 70, 1105: . . . "sicut apud Alexandriam multo tempore fuisse traditur institutum, nunc etiam in Nisibi civitate Syrorum ab Hebraeis sedulo fertur exponi, collatis expensis in urbe Romana professos doctores scholae potius acciperent Christianae . . " See also P. Kahle, *Masoreten des Westens*, p. 52.

[118] Cf. Moberg, *Bar Hebraeus' Buch der Strahlen*, II p. 108; also Th. Weiss, *Zur ostsyrischen Laut-und Akzentlehre*, 1935, p. 29 ff. Also E. Wellesz, "Die byzantinischen Lektionszeichen" in *Zeitschrift fuer Musikwissenschaft* 11, 1929, p. 527; and E. Werner, *op. cit.*,[116] p. 339.

in the genesis of the new ecphonetic system which became the starting point of our modern musical notåtion.

Once again, the course of events followed the general pattern: pure Greek culture was abolished, and the new conceptions, on which the entire development of Church music depended, came from Aramaic-Hebrew sources. And again we realize how the Asiatic raw material was polished and rearranged by the application of Greek methods. They systematized but also mutilated the originally syntactic function of the Semitic notation, yielding to the ever increasing demands for exactitude and precision. The decisive break with the principle of ecphonetic notation occurred with the introduction of the first horizontal staff in order to define an exact musical pitch, a *note fixée* for the early neumes. This happened in Western Europe some time in the ninth century.[119] Neither the Byzantine nor the Syriac nor the Hebrew systems followed Rome in this ingenious adventure: their neumes retained their primitive phrasing character almost to this day. Had it not been for the didactic manuals for the choristers (*Papadikai*), the Byzantian neumes would today be as undecipherable as the Syriac system whose signs lost all meaning once the oral tradition had disappeared. A somewhat better knowledge is preserved of the old Armenian system which, in numerous points resembles the early Masoretic accents.

The individual systems of notation — Hebrew, Byzantine, Syriac, Roman, etc. — contributed much, by isolating their music from that of other Churches, to a crystallization of the style, of which they are a part. It is perhaps not an idle speculation to contemplate the course of musical history, if there had not been ten systems but only one system of notation. It is a safe guess that, in such a case, the Oriental forces would be much more in evidence than they are today. For, during the first millenium of Christianity, wave after wave came from Asia throwing men, ideas, and traditions on the shores of Europe. We can appreciate

[119] The Latin neumes borrowed a good deal from the primitive grammatical accents (which served as models for some of them) and the Byzantine and Hebrew accents. But the relationship is rather complex. While, e. g., the Latin *quilisma* equals the Byzantine κύλισμα which in turn is identical with the Hebrew šalšelet, their functions are clearly different.

such a hypothetical case in the history of art where no barrier of language or notation isolated the East from the West. The Basilika, the Romanesque style, the Mosaics of Ravenna, the Christian manuscript illustrations of the first seven centuries — all these came from Asia and were transformed in the Mediterranean orbit, not always to their advantage.[120] The policy which governed these transformations and pseudomorphoses, however, was determined on the highest level, the dogmatic-religious.

The Attitude of the Authorities in Academy, Synagogue, and Church.

In the intellectual world of declining antiquity, there was considerable controversy about the nature and the true purpose of music. These discussions took place in the sphere of a philosophy which considered music in terms of either a science or a moral power. We know of only a few deviations from this general path, and these originated chiefly in Syria and Palestine; Philodem of Gedara and the Syrian Jamblichos do not quite fit into the musical philosophy of the Hellenistic era. To the men of the Academy as well as to the Neo-Pythagoreans and the Neo-Platonists, music was an abstract *episteme* which, if applied wisely and correctly, could lead the adept into the highest spheres of metaphysical knowledge. Hence music was considered by these thinkers a cathartic force.[121] Few of these men knew much about Jewish doctrines and customs; and it is characteristic that even Plutarch likened the God of the Jews to Dionysos, seriously believing that the "feast of drawing water" during Sukkoth was a kind of Bacchanalia.[122] Jewish music, too, seemed to him bacchic and orgiastic, and consequently unacceptable from the philosophical or ethical point of view. Nor

[120] Cf. J. Strzygowski's monumental work *"Asiens Bildende Kunst,"* p. 715 f., also p. 501 ff. See also the same author's "Ravenna als Vorort aramaeischer Kunst" in *Oriens Christianus*, N. F. V. 83 ff.

[121] Cf. Werner-Sonne, *op. cit.*[87], p. 274 ff.

[122] Plutarch, *Quaest. conviv.* IV, 5–6. Also in Reinach, *Texts d'auteurs Grec et Romains relatif au Judaisme*, p. 144: "εἰκὸς δὲ Βακχείαν εἶναι τὰ ποιούμενα."

was he the only writer of the time who felt so; it would be easy to duplicate his remarks by quotations from many lesser authors.

In general, the attitude of the Hellenistic philosophers showed a Janus-Head. One side viewed music as a science, like any other, to be taught by rational methods. It had certain links with the order of the universe and with its microcosmic reflection, the human soul. This is the Pythagorean conception. The other side emphazised the more elemental, emotional forces of music in connection with its supposed magical powers. This is the Orphic-Dionysic ideology. At the very end of the Hellenistic era, a great philosopher attempted a synthesis of both concepts. Plotinus wrote:

> "The tune of an incantation, a significant cry, ... these have . . . . power over the soul drawing it with the force of . . . . . tragic sounds, for it is the reasonless soul, not the will or wisdom, that is beguiled by music, a form of sorcery which raises no question, whose enchantement, indeed, is welcomed . . . . . Similarly with regard to prayers: the powers that answer to incantations do not act by will . . . . . The prayer is answered by the mere fact that part and other part (of the cosmos) are wrought to one tone like a musical string which, plucked at one end, vibrates at the other also."[123]

The entire history of music could be represented as an incessant struggle between these two conceptions, the Orphic-tragic (Romanticism) and the Pythagorean (Medievalism, Classicism). In the music of the Church, these two conceptions are frequently at odds. Still, it is not possible simply to identify the Orphic-Dionysic style with the Orient, the scientific Pythagorean with the West; for both come from Asia and both have been assimilated by the Occident. For example: the inclusion of musical science in the Seven Liberal Arts did not, as generally assumed, originate in the Western orbit, but in Nisibis, as Th. Hermann had demonstrated.[124]

[123] Cf. St. Mackenna, *Plotinus on the Nature of the Soul*, (Fourth Ennead), 1924, p. 96. The metaphor of the string is borrowed from Philo, *De Somn.* III. 212.

[124] Against P. H. Lang, *Music in Western Civilization*, p. 59. The author includes Greece and even the oldest strata of plainsong in Western Civiliza-

The Rabbis were not influenced by these speculations to a very great extent. To them music was either a מלאכה, an occupation, or a חכמה, a science.[125] As an art it had only one legitimate function: to praise God. As a science it was part of the propedeutics, analogous to the Western *quadrivium educationis*, together with mechanics, astronomy, optics, and mathematics.

Concerning the music of Hellenism, the Rabbinic position was unequivocal: they viewed it with the greatest suspicion, rightly connecting it with the orgiastic cults of Asia Minor. The statement that Greek tunes had caused the apostasy of a famous Rabbi, quoted above, speaks for itself.

The early Church held, at least in the first two centuries, exactly the same principles as normative Judaism. But under the impact of Eastern Gnosticism and philosophic Hellenism it had to modify its rigid position. Yet it was a well-planned, strategic retreat, and sight of the ultimate goals was never lost.

The first weakening of these principles concerned instrumental music. In Byzantium, where the Emperor was *de facto* the head of the Church, kitharody survived and later on the organ conquered the court if not the liturgy. In fact, the organ was considered the secular instrument *par excellence*. The clergy, however, opposed its use in church and consequently no documents of instrumental music have survived in Byzantium.

Another instance of the flexible policy of the authorities is the case of non-scriptural hymns. Although the Council of Laodicea had banned them, they had a strong revival and eventually became the greatest contribution of the Eastern churches to Christian liturgy.

A characteristic aspect of that complex evolution is reflected in the varying viewpoints of the ecclesiastic authorities with regard to Jewish forms of prayer and song. In contradistinction to the generally expressed veneration for the Psalter or the canticles of the OT there were warnings not to relapse into

tion but neglects entirely the oriental basis of the whole mediterranean culture. Cf. Th. Hermann, "Die Schule von Nisibis vom 5.–7. Jahrhundert" in *Zeitschrift fuer neutestamentl. Wissenschaft* XXV, 1926, p. 89–126.

[125] See *supra* n. 121, *op. cit.*, p. 272 ff.

modum Judaeorum precandi.[126] Diodorus of Tarsus, a learned monk, complained bitterly that the Church was imitating Jewish songs and asked of what use the many Hebrew words and Psalmodies could be.[127] Chrysostom also assailed the Jews because of their instrumental music in the Temple, which in his opinion was only a divine concession to their weakness and stupidity. He warned Christians against imitating Jewish practices and customs.[128]

Nor is that all. The great Eastern authors all seemed to fear the spell of Judaism. In all of their apologetic writings, warnings against just such temptations were sounded. During the incessant schisms within Eastern Christianity, no terms of abuse were so common as "Judaizer" or simply "Jew."[129]

This apprehension is absent in the leading circles of the Western Church. The Popes, Damasus and Coelestine championed the psalmodic forms, especially the responses and antiphones, borrowed from Jewish tradition.[130] We have already seen that Damasus imported Jewish singers to the Occident;[131] and Jerome encouraged St. Paula to study the Hebrew language. She achieved such a mastery of Hebrew *ita ut psalmos Hebraice caneret.*[132] Apparently the Western authorities did not feel the need of impugning the survival of Jewish traditional forms in the liturgy of the Church. This more tolerant attitude was due to two causes of entirely diverse nature.

In the first place, the Roman Church was much more conservative than the Eastern sects. This fact is reflected in its whole tradition and is well-known to every student of comparative liturgy. Since the oldest forms are all of Jewish origin, they have

---

[126] Cf. Cyrill of Jerusalem, *Catech. Mystag.* V, PG 33, 1118 ff.

[127] Diodor of Tarsus, in Harnack, *Texts und Untersuchungen, Neue Folge,* VI., p. 35.

[128] Cf. Chrysostom, *Homily in Ps.* 150, (PG 55, 497) and In Ps. 149, 2, (PG 55, 494.)

[129] Cf. J. Parkes, *The Conflict of the Church and the Synagogue,* p. 300 ff.

[130] PL 128, 74; 225; also Jerome, *ep. 20 Ad Damasum.*

[131] See *supra* p. 432.

[132] Jerome, *ep. 108, in PL* 22, 902. Even Thomas Aquinas praised the ancient Jewish practice of psalmody although he opposed the use of instruments "lest the Church become judaized." *Summa* 2, 2; quaest. 91, art. 2).

survived in the Latin Church by virtue of its consistent tradition-
alism. The intonations of the Hebrew letters *Aleph*, *Beth*, etc. at
the beginning of the verses of Lamentations, or the correct
(non-Latin) accentuation of Hebrew proper names in the Gregorian chant are proofs of that inheritance. In the second place,
a danger was absent in the Western orbit which beset many of
the Asiatic Churches: The close proximity of great Jewish
centers, whose eruditional and numerical powers were feared as
inducements to Judaizing. Dr. James Parkes sums up this
antagonism in the following words:

> "The only explanation of his (Chrysostome's) bitterness
> . . . . is the too close fellowship between Jews and Christians
> in Antioch . . . . . It must be recognized that the ways of
> thinking of Jew and Christian were very similar . . . . The
> Jews of the East were in a much more powerful position
> than their Western brethren for influencing their neighbors.
> Europe at this period contained no great intellectual Jewish
> center. Jewish scholars were largely concentrated in Pales-
> tine and Babylon."[133]

Certainly the Roman Fathers were in no way more tolerant
than their Eastern colleagues when it came to *actions* against
the Jews. But they were more conservative in matters of liturgical tradition and less perturbed by the threat of Jewish influence. Besides, the Eastern Christian population was more
familiar with, and therefore more positively opposed to, Jewish
customs and institutions.

THE FORCES

A. Static Forces

While this disquisition deals mainly with music of religious
character, it would be a mistake to neglect secular impulses
which have often, in ecclesiastical disguise, determined the style
of whole liturgies. It is, to quote just one instance, quite impossible for a student not to recognize the difference between
Eastern and Western theologians. Although they belonged to
one Church before the schism, their ways of thinking were vastly

---

[133] Cf. J. Parkes, *op. cit.*, p. 164, 274 ff.

disparate. Thus, the dialectics of a Syrian Church Father resemble much more the midrashic or talmudic style of reasoning than the more factual Latin argumentation, notwithstanding his violent contempt for everything Jewish.

We shall now seek to show the static tendencies at work. They were sometimes of ethnic or local character, sometimes reflecting the usual conservatism of religious authorities.

These tendencies were strongest in the Roman and Armenian Churches. This is evident in the preservation of the oldest musical strata side by side with more recent features. In Rome, this conservatism was due to the statesmanlike policy of the Church which held the ethnic forces in balance. Only during a period of transition did regional traditions arise, such as the Gallican, Mozarabic, or German, in the fields of liturgy or musical notation. Finally they all were superseded by the centralizing policy of the Roman Hierarchy.

Here a basic fact should be observed, important for the understanding of musical history: the Roman Church created in its liturgy the monumental framework which subsequent centuries filled with an abundance of artistic forms. As soon as the level of art music was reached, the different styles of it reflected the varying tendencies of the periods. Gothic, Renaissance, Barock, Classicism, and even Romanticism could evolve and express themselves in Church music. Even the secular music of Europe was fed by the Gregorian Chant well into the 17th century. Yet its foundation remained unchanged.

No such development is noticeable in the Eastern Churches. There the level remained more or less static in the folk-song stage, and no art-music enriched the liturgy. Nor is it possible to discern definite stylistic changes or evolutions. This cannot be due to the divergent organization or theology of the Churches, since none of them, not even the Roman enclave in the Near East, has ever created or performed any art-music comparable to the European accomplishments. The conclusion is inevitable that not religious or dogmatic principles but *ethnic* forces determined the stagnation in the East, the evolution in the West.

The very same partition goes through Jewish liturgical music.

102

The musical style of the oriental and Levantine Jews remained stationary and only in exceptional cases rose above the level of folklore. European and especially Ashkenazic Jewry accomplished its first artistic creations in the *Missinai-tunes* of the late Middle Ages.[134] Subsequently, the liturgical music of European Jewry reflected in its course most of the tendencies and stylistic changes of the Christian Church music.

Returning to the Eastern Churches, we find in the music of the Armenian Church a decidedly folkloristic character, quite unlike the Gregorian Chant, where every folk song was subjected to consistent stylization. The terminology, notation, and rendition of Armenian psalmody are akin to Hebrew cantillation in its earliest stages. Other phases of Armenian sacred music reflect the manifold features of its turbulent national history. Byzantine, Syrian, Turkish, and Russian elements were molded into a not too homogeneous popular style.

The West Syrian Churches successfully resisted the sway of their Arab environment, at least in their musical traditions. Their chants represent a decidedly older and differently organized style than those of their Arab neighbors. Again the Church was the preserving power, in this case supported by the ancient cultural bonds with Byzantium and Palestine.

Quite different is the nature and history of the Nestorian liturgy and its music. Its oldest sources, foremost its calendar and its lectionary, show traces of very ancient and authentic tradition.[135] The musical influences, as far as they can be determined, seem to be more secular than ecclesiastic in origin. It is

---

[134] These, in turn, betray certain traces of Burgundian composers of the 13th–14th centuries. On the other hand, the liturgy of the Church absorbed Jewish ideas well up to the 12th century. This can be seen in the sequence "Dies irae," whose substance is all but identical with the *piyyut* ונתנה תקף. Both have a common root, probably an Aramaic *Seliḥah*, which entered the Byzantine liturgy on the Christian side, and the Ashkenazic liturgy on the Jewish side. Cf. A. Kaminka, "Der Kirchenhymnus *Dies irae* und seine Beziehungen zu hebraeischen Bussgebeten" in *Freie Jued. Lehrerstimme*, IV., p. 67.

[135] Cf. A. Baumstark, *Nichtevangelische Syrische Perikopenordnungen des ersten Jahrtausends*, in Liturgiegeschichtliche Forschungen III, Muenster 1921, ch. III. See also the identities 9a, c, and 10a, b, *supra* p. 429!

Iranian culture, whose superior creative power slowly squeezed out of East Syrian Christianity the more systematic but weaker Byzantian forces, and this in spite of the great tradition of the Nisibis Academy. Here local perseverence prevailed over the infiltration from the West. True, Nestorian doctrine and liturgical forms are Christian; but, under the surface, old Iranian ideas were at work for many centuries.

While the Persians had a musical culture of their own, it was neither highly developed before the Arabian epoch nor was it supported by the Iranian Mazda religion. The Persian kings had to import music and musicians; even the crown-prince Bahrām Ghūr (ca. 430) was sent by Yezdegerd I to the Arabian Lakmid court, in Al-Ḥī ra, to be educated in music.[136] Later on the young prince colonized ten thousand singers and dancers "from Hindustan all over the country."[137] Thus Persian civilization does not seem to have created as much music as sculpture or architecture. This lack becomes conspicuous in Christian worship where the Syrian liturgy is celebrated by and for a semi-Persian population. We have already mentioned the great academy at Nisibis where Scripture and its interpretation were scientifically studied.[138] Its founders were Bar Saoumâ and Narsai, both Syrians.[139] Narsai's liturgy and homilies lack almost all references to singing, excepting the cantillation of Scripture. Even the *Sanctus* is, in his

[136] Cf. H. G. Farmer, *Historical Facts for the Arabian Musical Influence*, p. 52. It is here that the recent findings of Iranian art would let us expect parallel discoveries in music. But these expectations have not been fulfilled as yet and are not likely to be realized. The reasons are manifold, and not only lack of musical notation. E. Wellesz, following Strzygowski's ingenious lead, promised decisive musical discoveries through careful study of Manichaean-Soghdic manuscripts. Yet these manuscripts originated in a time, when Byzantians, Armenians, Romans, and Jews had already well developed their respective ecphonetic notations. Beyond this nothing has been established to vindicate the great hopes which were set upon Iranian music.

[137] Cf. H. G. Farmer, *op. cit.*, p. 271, quoting Mirkhwand *"Raudat al-Safa"* I. II. 357. The Persian text in *Histoire des Sassanides*, Paris, 1843, p. 217.

[138] E. Sachau, Die Chronik von Arbela, p. 91 ff., in *Sitzungsberichte der Preussischen Akademie der Wissenschaften, Hist. Phil. Klasse,* 1915.

[139] *Ibid.* p. 86. Cf. also Chabot, (Schola Nisibena) in *Journal Asiatique* 1896, vol. 8, p. 43 ff.

liturgy, a curt answer of the people. Edmund Bishop makes this pertinent observation:

"It is only necessary to read the early chapters of the first formal Western treatise on liturgy, the *De officiis ecclesiasticis* of St. Isidor of Seville, to see how great is the contrast. The note of Church song is continually struck, and singing in one form or another is dwelt on by him again and again. It is hard to believe that, if singing had been any prominent feature in the celebration of the East Syrian Mass of Narsai's day, that rhetorical writer would have passed it over in silence. It seems much more probable that both he and Isidor spoke naturally and that each renders, the one by his reticence, the other by his abundance, the actual state of things around him."[140]

The cause for that silent type of worship, in which the κοινωνία apparently did not play a great part, is probably Mazdaism and its individualistic-esoteric liturgy. All this was anti-Hellenic and anti-Jewish propagated by the Sassanides.[141]

The Nestorian Church was surrounded by adversaries. Considered heretic by the Syrian and Byzantine Church, it felt the hard rule of the Sassanide dynasty which attempted to impose Mazdaism upon it, and in its turn, it looked upon the Jews of Mesopotamia as its enemies, theologically and nationally. Cantillation of Scripture, the oldest musical tradition, was preserved while new elements, due to constant internal and external pressure, could not survive.* The theology was under the spell of the West, its liturgical forms under the influence of the East, chiefly Iran. This antinomy of forces, theological doctrine vs. folk custom, resulted in a stalemate and ultimately in the century long stagnation of Nestorianism.

[140] Cf. Dom R. H. Connolly and E. Bishop, The Liturgical Homilies of Narsai, in *Texts and Studies*, vol. VIII., p. 117, Cambridge 1916.

[141] C. Sachs' statement "The Persians had been under strong Hellenistic influence until the dynasty of the Seleucides (226–641) brought a nationalist Anti-Greek reaction." (*Rise of Music in the Ancient World*, p. 278) is wholly ununderstandable to me. I suppose the author had the Sassanides in mind, when he wrote "Seleucides." I suspect that the Iranian cult of the *chtonic* deities, which must be adored in silence, was the reason for the lack of music. Cf. F. Cumont, *Oriental religions*, p. 151 ff.

* Note the resemblance of ex. 10 d and 10 e (p. 430) (instances of cantillation).

B. Dynamic Forces

After the collapse of the West Roman *imperium*, only one great
state was capable of carrying the banner of Christianity through
the ruins of the old Commonwealth, namely, Byzantium. The
Roman Church limited its activities in Europe to missionary
tasks until the tenth century, while Byzantium expanded north-
ward and its Church conquered Russia. Byzantine liturgy and
music became the pattern of the Russian Orthodox Church.

Its music displays, besides old slavonic features, both Hellenistic and Jewish traits. The bulk of the *Známmeny Rospéw*
(orthodox song) is syllabic, like Hellenistic and early Byzantine
music, but final melisms, borrowed from psalmody, occur regularly. The modality corresponds to Byzantine and to Western
Oriental systems.[142] This also holds true for other slavonic
Church music, in particular for Macedonian and Bulgarian
Chant. There we encounter even the Hellenic-Jewish *Tropos
Spondeiacos* alluded to by Clement of Alexandria.[143]

There is still another element common to the music of
Byzantium, of the Arabs, Turks, South East Russians, and of
the Eastern Jews: the Phrygian Mode with augmented second.
The Arabic *maqamat Hijāz* and *Husseini* contain this characteristic interval, and it is equally familar in Turkish folk songs,
Byzantine, and Russian chants. The Eastern Jews believe —
erroneously — that this mode, called *Ahava Rabba*, originated
in Palestine in pre-Christian times. We do not know the actual
source of that expressive mode, but there are many indications
that it is not very old, possibly not older than the invasion of
the Turks in the twelfth century.

Under the cloak of Hellenistic scholarship, Byzantium succeeded in transmitting a good deal of its musical practice to the
Western Church. Today some scholars are convinced that also
the western system of the eight Church tones evolved in Byzantium, before it was transmitted to, and transformed in, Italy
and France. If the western structure of Church tones came via

[142] Cf. P. Panoff, *Die altslavische Volks- und Kirchenmusik*, in Buecken,
Handbuch der Musikwissenschaft, p. 14.
[143] See *supra* p. 422, also the examples 16, 17, 18, 22 in Panoff's work.

Byzantium, it certainly did not originate there; no Middle-Greek treatises on music prior to the eleventh century are extant. The little we do know of their musical theories has reached us through Syriac, occasionally through Arabic sources. The main feature of that system, the eight Church tones, occurs first in 'Syriac sources where it had an originally liturgical connotation.[144] Farmer has investigated some of these sources and has reached the conclusion that Syrians, Jews, and pre-Islamic Arabs shared the theory of modality and stimulated its systematization.[145]

This writer came to the same conclusion when he found that some of the most important terms of Byzantine musical theory, the *enechemata*, were borrowed from the Hebrew. They were paradigms, used for the different modes of final or punctuating melisms, mostly words derived from the Hebrew *Nin'ua'*. Also in Hebrew, the word has a musical significance.[146]

Here we are confronted with one of the thorniest problems of musicology: namely the genesis of the *Octoechos*, or the principle of the eight modes of the Church. An extensive research of this question would warrant a voluminous study and reach far beyond the scope of this article. Nonetheless, the problem is of such great consequence, that a brief excursus is mandatory.

In modern musicology, there are three principle trends of thinking with regard to this subject: (1) The older view, as represented by Gevaert, Reinach, Jeannin, and most of the French scholars. These consider the Syro-Byzantine conception of the eight modes a natural derivation from the classic Greek system of the *harmoniai*. (2) In sharp contradistinction thereto, R. Lachmann, A. Baumstark, K. Wachsmann, and H. G. Farmer emphasize the liturgic-cultic origin of the Syrian *Octoechos* and doubt, at least as regards the first five centuries, a decisive Greek influence upon the modality of pre-Gregorian chant which, in their opinion, was almost wholly Oriental in form and substance.

---

[144] Cf. E. W. Brooks, *James of Edessa*, p. 6; the Hymns of Severus of Antioch, in *Patrologia Orientalis*, VI, 1911, and VII, 1911, p. 759–802.

[145] Cf. H. G. Farmer, *op. cit.*, pp. 55, 60, 163/4, 307.

[146] Cf. E. Werner, "The Psalmodic Formula Neannoe and its Origin," in *Musical Quarterly*, Jan. 1942, p. 93 ff.

(3) A mediating position is held by scholars like Curt Sachs, Peter Wagner, E. Wellesz, G. Reese, U. Bomm and others, who assume that the systems of all modes were the results of constant repetition of certain melodic formulae. These passages of sacred folk-lore crystallized in the course of centuries to fixed phrases, the nuclear cells of the modes. These were then superimposed upon recurrent liturgical rubrics and connected (erroneously!) with the Greek *harmoniai*.[147]

With due deference to the fine work of these scholars, I venture to say that an important aspect of the problem has been neglected altogether, namely, the link which connected music with popular superstition and magic. It was certainly not the Neo-pythagorean speculations about corresponding proportions between the Universe, music, and soul that created the eightfold modality of the Church tones. Their ideas, subtle and even sublime as they were, lacked popular appeal and, foremost of all, practical applicability. Simple popular belief and superstition, on the other hand, displayed much greater vigor and has, at all times, been a fertile soil of popular art.

In ancient and in medieval times, the number eight held great musical significance throughout the Orient, *quite aside from the conception of the octave*.[148] The Psalter knows the term *Sheminith*. Was it an instrument with eight strings? We do not know. It might have been a mode or a system of modes, as rabbinic literature seems to indicate. These early medieval authors derived the eight (or seven) modes from the eight (or seven) "voices" of God mentioned in Ps. 29. The eightfold alphabetic acrostic of Ps. 119 was rendered in responsorial fashion. Cantor and congregation alternated seven times, but each eighth verse was finished in melismatic cadence. Saadya Gaon, in his commentary upon the Psalms (in Arabic) states, while discussing Ps. 6.1, that there had been eight modes of psalmody. Some more instances are cited in Steinschneider, *Hebrew Liter-*

[147] A good bibliography on the question in G. Reese, *op. cit.*, p. 422–3; also K. Wachsmann, *op. cit.*, p. 78–100.

[148] Even in classic Greek terminology the term διὰ πασῶν shows no reference to the number 8. The same holds true of the Arabic term *bill-kull* which is a literal translation of the Greek διὰ πασῶν.

ture, p. 536 f.[149] Jews and Arabs knew even of eight *rhythmic* modes. There it is quite obvious that the number eight was artificially imposed upon the rhythmic modes since, for rhythm, an equivalent to the octave does not exist. In the *Ikhvan es-Safa*, (ninth century), we probably have the clue to the prevalence of the number eight. According to the *Ikhvan*, eight is the perfect number for music and astronomy.[150] Among the Syrians, the term *Octoechos* occurs first as a liturgical designation for eight successive Sundays after Pentecost; only later on it assumed a musical connotation. Was the liturgical *Octoechos* a remnant of an older extended *Pentacontad*, such as the East-Syrian Nestorians and the Armenians have preserved in their calendars?

It is generally known that the number four, too, is of outstanding musical value. The Greek *tetrachordon* is just one aspect of many, when we consider the manifold folkloristic relations between the four humors, seasons, temperaments, colours, elements, animal tendencies, etc., to music, which were fully familiar to the peoples of the Near East.[151]

In view of these facts, I am convinced that the numbers four and eight were understood as musical *a priori* by everybody, not only by intellectuals. Perhaps the division of the octave into eight tones and two tetrachords was already *a consequence* of that primitive belief in the numbers four and eight. Actually, numerous other divisions of the octave are known to comparative musicology. Once the modes were systematized, the numbers four and eight dominated the entire system. Thus, we may yet find a common popular root for the two tetrachords, the eight *harmoniai*, and the *Octoechos*.[152]

[149] Cf. Werner-Sonne, *op. cit.*, I, p. 297 ff. and II. 552.

[150] *Ibid*. I. p. 298, n. 155.

[151] *Ibid*. I. p. 276 ff.; also H. G. Farmer *Sa'adyah Gaon on the Influence of Music*, p. 9, tabulation "The Fourfold Things." This conception was already familiar to Ambrose, for we read in *De XLII Mansionibus Filiorum Israel*: "Quaternioni enim sunt omnia, punctum, linea, superficies, et soliditas, mensurae universorum. Insunt etiam potissimae symphoniae musicae." (PL 17, 12.) Whether he refers here to the first four overtones, or to the *tetrachordon*, or to the four *harmoniai*, is not quite clear.

[152] The significance of the numbers 4 and 8 in the musical culture of many lands cannot be based upon mathematical divisions of strings or other in-

The theory of modality proved to be one of the strongest progressive forces in the development of European music up to the time of the Renaissance. Without it, no harmony or polyphony would have come into being. And again we observe Jewish and Syrian ideas receiving the final formulation via Byzantium, through the remainders of Hellenistic scholarship, and through Roman systematization.

C. Results and Prospects

Concluding our investigation, it will not be amiss to cull the chief fruits.

1. The post-Biblical hostility of Rabbinic Judaism toward all instrumental music was not so much an expression of grief over the loss of the Temple and land as a policy of defense for Judaism against pagan cults, particularly against the orgiastic mysteries of Asia Minor, wherein certain musical instruments were recognized attributes of the deities.

2. The very same reasons caused the early Church to view every kind of instrumental music with suspicion, the more so, if that music was of Hellenistic origin.

3. The musical raw material of the Churches was of Hebrew and Syrian origin, except the hymnic forms, a new type created by an intricate interrelation and interreaction between the Syrian and the Hellenistic spirit.

4. The systematization of all of these forms was the result of century-long work done by European theorists, yet the principles of the various systems again originated in Palestine, Syria, and Mesopotamia. The modal conceptions of the Near East were confused with the Greek *harmoniai*, resulting in a highly artificial structure of Church tones into which the old tunes frequently do not fit.

struments, since we find this conception likewise in rather primitive vocal tradition. The inference is that these numbers represented the elements of music based upon popular (superstitious) belief. Later on the musicians used these numbers for the most natural division of their tonal system, and the philosophers rationalized and systematized the popular conception in their cosmic-mathematical speculations.

5. The same development is discernible in the history of musical notation. The earliest systems came from East-Syria, Jewish-Babylonia and Palestine, and were transformed by the Byzantine and Latin Churches in accordance with the various languages and practical needs. The Eastern Churches preserved a few traces of their notation only through an oral tradition or lost that knowledge entirely. Rudiments of the primitive systems are still recognizable in Roman and Greek plainsong.

6. The Western Church was conservative and rigid in its liturgy, while the Eastern Churches were more flexible, except the Armenian and Nestorian. Hence the Roman Church has preserved more Jewish elements, since these belong to the oldest strata. In the Syrian and Byzantine liturgies the chief forms are syllabic hymns; in the Roman realm, psalmodies, responses, and melismatic songs. The Eastern churches reflect more of the influence of Hellenism than the Roman Church does.

7. The liturgy of Judaism developed migrating melisms which, in both Synagogue and Gregorian Chant, occasionally assumed the function of leading motifs with hermeneutic purpose.

8. In the East Syrian Churches, Iranian influence is discernible. Due to Persian indifference towards music, it did not essentially change the Syrian chant, except perhaps for some traits of Nestorian liturgical music.

9. The basic philosophy and esthetics of music originated in Asia Minor and Mesopotamia, certainly before 1500 B. C. These ideas were brought to Greece, there transformed and systematized, and carried back to Asia Minor where they were absorbed by early Christianity and Hellenistic Judaism. Syrians and Jews transmitted these ideas to the Arabs who in turn built upon them their philosophy of music.

10. Under the aegis of the Byzantine Church, the Hellenistic syllabic hymns invaded the Russian liturgy while the old Jewish forms of cantillation, psalmody and melismatic songs were neglected in it.

All that remains is for us to outline a sketch of some of the tasks still to be performed. We shall not really understand the tremendous waves of incipient and decaying cultures at the break-

111

down of antiquity, unless we know more of their creations. *Saxa loquuntur*: but that language is not always unequivocal! Only if we possess historical, literary, artistic, and musical documents of these great civilizations, shall we be prepared to evaluate their heritage and what was worthy of becoming a heritage.

In our field three unsolved, interrelated problems loom in the background of all investigations: the musical sources of ancient Iran, the music-theoretical documents of the pre-Islamic, non-Christian Near and Middle East, and a comparative study of the Armenian Church music, wherein the historical and liturgical aspects are not to be neglected. Important spadework has been done in all three fields and we may look forward to significant discoveries in the near future which are bound to shed much new light upon a hitherto obscure subject, the interrelation between Judaism and the churches of the East.

"If I Speak in the Tongues of Men..."
St. Paul's Attitude to Music

Reprinted with permission of *Journal of the American Musicological Society,* 13, 1960, pp. 18-23.

THIS CELEBRATED PASSAGE (I Cor. 13:1) has often been quoted, many tracts have been written about it, and more sermons preached. Yet I have been unable to find in all the commentaries, ancient, mediaeval, or modern, an explanation of this musical metaphor, which so contemptuously speaks of instrumental music. Even vocal sounds uttered "without love" (ἀγάπην δὲ μὴ ἔχω) are decried. At first blush our passage reads quite easily, almost like a commonplace. For the postulate of love was nothing extraordinary or novel at a time when many a rabbinical treatise culminated in this demand for transcendent love.[1] But the descending gradation

> tongues of men
> tongues of angels
> sounding brass
> tinkling cymbal

was, when it was pronounced, a revolutionary conception. For the metaphor was couched when the Temple in Jerusalem still stood with all its ceremonial music, instrumental and vocal. Did Paul not set aside with one stroke the age-old and venerated glory of the Temple, exactly as he had set aside the Law? Voices of men, even angelic choirs seemed worthless to him when bereft of

[1] For examples of such statements, *cf.* G. F. Moore, *Judaism,* Vol. II, pp. 85ff; also Hillel's dictum: "Be of the disciples of Aaron, loving and pursuing peace, loving all creatures and drawing them near to the Law" (*Abot* I: 12)

love—not to speak of instrumental strains! In the above gradation, Paul cites what seemed to him the lowest instruments of the Jewish or pagan orchestra, viz. "the tinkling cymbal." Yet the cymbal was in the Temple of his time a highly respected instrument, for it served almost as a kind of conductor's baton. According to the Mishna (*Tamid* VII: 3) the signals of the cymbal served as cues for the vocal and instrumental performance of the Levites. The Mishna mentions even one of the cymbal-players of the Second Temple, Ben Arsa, by name. What, then, were Paul's reasons for so drastic an *Umwertung aller Werte?*

In order fully to understand any one passage, we must read it in its full context. The Corinthians, whom Paul addressed, were somewhat one-sided, not to say biased, in their scale of "spiritual gifts." In ch. 12, Paul lists these gifts, (verses 4-11), and it seems to this writer that the apostle's gradation is again a descending one: from "the utterance of wisdom" (λόγος σοφίας) down to the "interpretation of tongues" (ἑρμηνεία γλωσσῶν). Then, as often today, ecstatic utterances such as *glossolaly* (speaking in tongues), or miracle-working stood in higher esteem with the gentile Christians of Corinth, than sober instruction and teaching of ethics. Hence, the apostle had to deal most cautiously with a group of neophytes, filled with eager expectations. (I Cor. 14:1-23). These early Christians believed that with good will everybody could become his own prophet, healer, or miracle-worker. Paul recognized the danger and faced it squarely. He taught the Corinthians that their scale of spiritual gifts was much too narrow (ch. 12:14-26). Thereafter he challenged them:

"Are all apostles? Are all prophets? Are all teachers? Do all work miracles? Do all possess gifts of healing? Do all speak in tongues? Do all interpret? But they all earnestly desire the higher gifts."

The apostle has not yet climaxed his harangue; but instead of a prophetic or doctrinal message he shows to the Corinthians, who were losing their sense of measure, "a more excellent way"—and he commences his sublime hymn on the power of love (I Cor. 13:1-13). The special significance of Paul's term for love (ἀγάπη), is still being debated by theologians, but as this is no theological paper, we shall (with Lietzmann, Bultmann, Klausner and others) understand it as love in the widest sense of the word.

The love which Paul glorifies, should not only bind man to God, but also man to fellow-man, and even to fellow-creature. This was, of course, nothing new, either in thought or in formulation. For Jesus had stressed these "laws of love" most emphatically. (Cf. Matt. 22:37-40.) Yet even then, the two commandments mentioned by Christ were nothing but literal quotations from the Old Testament, and among the most celebrated ones. (Deut. 6:5; and Lev. 19:18.)

The apostle goes further; he exalts love as the most timeless spiritual gift. The gifts of tongues, of prophecy, and of knowledge will pass away, but love never ends. Paul, however, makes it plain that he neither will nor can grant to the good Corinthians those spiritual gifts, which they crave, be they miracle-working or healing or prophecying. Love is higher than any of these gifts and of timeless value. The preamble to this hymnic manifesto is our musical metaphor. What makes it so bold is the transition from the spiritual gifts to "the tongues of men and angels"; it strikes us as unexpected and almost incoherent.

The transition is, as it were, subterranean. In order to appreciate it, we must take into consideration the attitude of the Jewish and Greek groups of Paul's time towards music in general, and to its different types in particular.

Paul was brought up as a Pharisee. He says of himself: "I am a Pharisee, a son of Pharisees." (Acts 23:6).[2] This statement implies that he and his ancestors were adherents of the Pharisaic sect. Indeed, he prides himself of having been a disciple of the great Rabban Gamaliel. (Acts 22:3). How did the Pharisees regard music? A few references will answer this question. (a) The apostasy of E. Elisha ben Abuya was attributed (by his colleagues) to the Greek instruments which were always in his home, and to Greek tunes always in his mouth. (b) The rabbis held a particularly low opinion of certain instruments: the *halil* (a primitive clarinet, or a kind of αὐλός) the *toph*, a tamburine or hand-drum, usually played by women, and the *tziltzelim* (cymbals). A bronze gong, called *ayrus* (Roman *aes*, Aramaic *ris*, hellenist *aes-ris*) was used in the

[2] The term "Pharisee" is used here in the sense in which Paul and modern comparative history of religion have understood it, not in the derogatory meaning frequently found in the Gospels.

Temple on festive occasions and at solemn weddings. It was probably the instrument most contemptible to the rabbis. (c) Philo and the Sibyls expressed strong antagonism to all cymbals and similar noise-making instruments. (*De vita Moysis* II, #239; *Oracula Sibyllina*, ed. Geffcken, 8, #113.)

Many reasons for the Pharisee's anti-musical attitude may be presented: their inclination to puritanism, their original opposition to the Sadducean hierarchy in the Temple, and others. I am inclined to believe, however, that the real cause of this antagonism is to be found in the Pharisaic abhorrence of each and every kind of syncretism. Just these three instruments (clarinet, cymbal, gong, or drum) were inseparably bound to the mystery cults of Asia Minor. Whether the divinity worshipped in these cults was the ancient Kybele, the Syrian-Babylonian Ishtar, or the Roman Magna Mater, did not interest the rabbis: they knew that all these female deities protected as well as symbolized the principle of fertility; also, that their cults were by nature orgiastic. That was enough for them.

The Corinthian group, which the apostle addressed, was composed of adherents of these fertility-cults; indeed, we find strong allusions to their licentiousness in Paul's epistle. (ch. 5; 6:9-11: 7:1-6; 10:7-9.) In the last-mentioned passage idolatry is coupled with whoredom!

The apostle, however, is not content with disparaging solely the instruments used for the mystery-cults; he adds another musical metaphor which indiscriminately attacks all instruments (I Cor. 14:6-9).

Now, brethren, if I come to you speaking in tongues, how shall I benefit you unless I bring you some revelation or knowledge or prophecy or teaching? If even lifeless (ἄψυχα, properly "soulless") instruments, such as the flute or the harp, do not give distinct notes, how will anyone know what is played?

Again spoken like a true Pharisee! For this sect was actually opposed to all and every instrumental music well before the Temple's destruction. They had no power to abolish it, for the jurisdiction of the Temple rested safely in the hands of the Sadducees, a hereditary hierarchy. Pharisaic dicta such as "Music in the house, ruin at the threshold," or "the ear that listens to (instrumental) music should be torn out," are significant in themselves. More important are the reasons—both the real reasons and the given ones—of this hostility.

Contemporary with Paul's activities were the syncretistic Jewish sects in Asia Minor, especially in Phrygia. There the worship of Zeus Sabazios was ministered by Jewish priestesses. Even some of their Roman names have come down to us—Julia Severa or Servenia Cornuta. Indispensable to this heretic ritual was the use of musical instruments, especially of κύμβαλον, τύμπανον and gong. Yet, the priestly authorities in Jerusalem could not excommunicate those sectarians: they identified themselves as Jews and paid the Temple-Tax faithfully. In contrast to the authorities of the Temple (the Sadduceans), the Pharisees turned away from these perversions of Jewish monotheism with horror and contempt. Such abusive practices made all instrumental music suspect, even that of the Temple. As soon as the Temple fell under the incendiary missiles of Roman catapults, and all sacrificial ritual had to be abolished, the Phari-

115

sees came to power. They did not hesitate to prohibit all instrumental music, liturgical or secular. The way by which they could legally justify this negation of a millenary tradition is interesting enough, but does not concern us here.

How differently had a poet of the aristocracy felt about this very issue 200 years before!

The Siracide (Jesus ben ben Sirach Simon ben Eleazar) advises young men of his time in the niceties of urbane behavior:

Do not disturb the musicians!
Where there is music,
Do not pour out speech,
And be not importunate in showing thy wisdom;
As a ruby shines in its golden setting,
So is the musician's ensemble at a banquet of wine
As the splendour of the precious emerald in a frame of gold,
So are melodies of musicians in a feast of wine.
Listen in silence,
And they, modest, will be rewarded by good will.

(Ecclesiasticus, 32:3-8)

Can we wonder at the austere Pharisee's banishment of this charming book from the Canon of the Bible? And yet, the views of the early Christian leaders, certainly those of Paul and his disciples, ran parallel with those of the puritans. A surprising confirmation of this thesis (which the author has first expressed in 1943) has come from the Dead Sea Scrolls, which were written during the period of flourishing Hellenism (180 B.C.—A.D. 200).

The Dead Sea Scrolls, however, are anything but Hellenistic in spirit. They represent the thinking of neither Pharisees nor Sadducees, but are closest to the sentiments of the dissident sect of Essenism, a move-

ment of ascetic character. The Essenes and their many splinter-groups were certainly puritans as well in their morality, which viewed the life of normal man as "wicked," as in their emphasis upon strict discipline among themselves. Indeed, we must consider Essenism in general, and the sect of Khirbet Qumran (where the Dead Sea Scrolls and the cloister of the group were discovered) in particular, as the prototype of organized monasticism.

It is curious and noteworthy that in the Dead Sea Scrolls passages occur which we can find in Paul's writings. Some of them deal with music. Exactly as the apostle uses names of instruments for metaphors and similes, so do the Dead Sea Scrolls.

I will sing with understanding
And all my music shall be for the glory of God.
My lyre and harp shall be
For this holy fixed Order,
And the flute of my lips
I will raise in His just circle.

(Manual of Discipline, ch.x)

The incipit of this passage is identical with I Cor. 14:15; the Hebrew term "understanding" encompasses both the "spirit" (πνεῦμα) and "mind" (νοῦς), the word chosen by Paul. If this verse does not yet prove the purely rhetorical usage of musical terms, then the following will convince the most literal-minded reader:

But suddenly I saw
That there was no distress
To tear me with pain.
I played then my harp
With sounds of redemption,
My lyre to joyful strains,
Yea, I blew the pipe and the flute
In ceaseless praise.

(Hymns of Thanksgiving, ch. XI)

116

Whether or not the writer of these verses could have played all four instruments, it is obvious that this ensemble of praise is nothing but poetic license. Really meant here is the chanted prayer, the "hymns, psalms and spiritual songs" of which Paul speaks (Eph. 5:19; Col. 3:16). The Essenes, however, could dispense with spoken or chanted worship. As we know from Philo, they practiced also silent prayer—prayer in thought—a custom unacceptable to the missionary Paul. Not only are instruments "soundless" and "indistinct" to him, but also silent prayer. He recognizes only prayer through words as, in I Cor. 14:9, "If you utter speech in a tongue that is not intelligible, how will anyone know what is said?" And again:

I will pray with the spirit and I will pray with the mind also; I will sing with the spirit and I will sing with the mind also; Otherwise, if you give thanks with the spirit alone, how can anyone in the position of an outsider [i.e., pagan or unlearned] say the Amen to your thanksgiving, when he does not know what you are saying? [A veiled attack upon the Philonic concept of silent prayer.]
(I Cor. 14:15-16)

It is clear that wordless prayer and, so, all "soulless" sounds, including instrumental music, are meaningless to him—even prayer "in tongues" does not fulfill its proper purpose. There remains only the chanted prayer; inseparably linked to scriptural "psalms, hymns, and spiritual songs." It is possible to infer from this attitude that even the wordless Jubili or ecstatic songs without words did not meet with his approval. All this reflects again the rabbinic doctrine of prayer.

Viewed from the more detached angle of history of religion, Paul's hostility towards each and every kind of instrumental music appears as a paradox. Unfolded on that higher level, it deserves a further explanation and solution.

Paul, a Jew of the Diaspora, was linked to the world of Hellenism by Greek customs, ideas, even by language: it was his natural and congenital home. The then dominant Hellenistic philosophy was the school of stoicism, and it attracted Paul by many of its conceptions. Yet both Pharisaic Judaism and incipient Christianity opposed this philosophy. During his formative years, especially during his years of study under Rabban Gamaliel, Paul seems to have forgotten his leanings toward the Stoa. Then, on the road to Damascus, there befell the dramatic conversion, that transformed his further life. As apostle to the Gentiles Paul sought—and recovered—his erstwhile rapport with Hellenistic thought. With one exception however: in the eternal conflict of values, between the Greek admiration of beauty, perfection, of elegant moderation in life and art, and the Pharisaic transcendent awe of the ethical postulate, he chose the latter. He disparaged the Jewish Law, mainstay of the Pharisees, and replaced it with his own doctrine of sin and redemption. But still, he insisted upon a number of Jewish *conventions*, retaining, so to speak, the empty shell of rabbinic Judaism: women shall not speak or sing in the churches; they shall cover their heads, lest they exhibit their hair and attract the lust of men; after the thanksgiving prayer even the uninitiated must add their Amen; psalmody and prophecy remain for him important constituents of Christian life and worship; and finally, instrumental music, soulless, and even unclean through syncretistic misuse, must not be heard in the service. The

117

Law has lost its validity for him and his adherents; Love and Grace supersede it. Yet many of the old mores remain intact. They are the mores of the Pharisees. Hellenistic thought is blended with Jewish practices. However, the guiding idea of this seemingly contradictory system emerges pure: no mystery-cults, but the one mysterium of Jesus.

Jewish Institute of Religion

Musical Aspects of the
Dead Sea Scrolls

Reprinted with permission of *Musical Quarterly,* 43, 1957, pp. 21-37.

WHATEVER the final verdict on the now controversial Dead Sea
Scrolls will be, it is sure to clarify many a point in the interplay of
Judaism and Hellenism that is now obscure. The actual discoveries in the
fields of theology, archaeology, and history have yielded a large crop of
hypotheses. A number of important facts, however, stand out by now.
Far from troubled Jerusalem and its cauldron of power politics there
lived in a remote part of the Holy Land, sometime between 150 B.C. and
150 A.D. — the actual dates are heatedly debated — a group of pious
collectivists, the Essenes. They produced a most interesting sort of literature. By thought and word they opposed the synthesizing and fermenting
spirit of Hellenism. In their discipline they anticipated Christian monasticism: in accordance with an established rule they lived in freely
chosen poverty and obedience to their superior brethren, the majority in
self-imposed chastity. Before entering the order definitely their novices
had to bind themselves with a tentative vow, a sort of *votum mobile*. The
scrolls of this mysterious order, discovered in Khirbet Qumran near the
Dead Sea, reveal a school of thought of which hitherto very little was
known.

It is not even certain whether the group's recently excavated "mother-
house" belonged to the "classic" Essene sect or to one of its many off-
shoots; but its inhabitants must have been closely akin to that ascetic-
collectivist fraternity, of which Philo, Josephus, and the Gospels speak so
sympathetically.

The scrolls themselves are of unalloyed Hebrew nature and show few,
if any, traces of Hellenistic infiltration. The same isolationist trend appears later in the early Judaeo-Christian Church. Both groups, the

21

Essenes and the Judaeo-Christians, were eventually crushed between the major forces of rabbinic Judaism and Gentile Christianity.

Of the published scrolls at least four contain musical references. They bear on the history of musical notation, the use of instruments, and the evolution of the antiphon.

I

The so-called St. Mark's Scroll of the book of Isaiah contains a number of marginal signs, five of which occur repeatedly. They seem to have no direct reference to the text, but perhaps to its rendition. That the signs had an ecphonetic-punctuating function might have occurred to some scholars. Yet owing to the lack of any internal (or external) evidence the hypothesis was never clearly expressed. Characteristic of the caution and restraint of the scholars is such a passage as: "Scattered through the Isaiah scroll are interesting marginal markings, probably inserted at a later time, perhaps to mark off sections used for reading by the sect which owned the manuscripts."[1] Five years later the same author permits himself a more extensive description:

> Most striking, however, are several very elaborate and mysterious signs in the margins of these two manuscripts [Isaiah and Habakkuk Commentary]. The meaning of all these signs has not yet been satisfactorily explained. Some of them may mark passages selected for public reading or regarded as especially significant for doctrine. Some may possibly call attention to errors in copying that require correction. Some are so elaborate as to tempt one to regard them as mere idle "doodling" by an absent-minded scribe or student, but of course such an explanation can be entertained only as a last resort. For a convincing solution of the problem we may have to wait until comparable examples of the same kind of marking have been found in other manuscripts.[2]

It is true that there has been some speculation about whether these markings were not the primitive forerunners of the later Masoretic accentuation, the ecphonetic notation of Hebrew Scripture. Such a hypothesis would attribute to these signs a punctuating and possibly a musical function. In the absence of any similar or at least comparable signs in other manuscripts this conjecture could not be upheld.

The ten marginal signs are given here:[3]

[1] Cf. *The Dead Sea Scrolls, Vol. I. The Isaiah Manuscript and the Habakkuk Commentary,* ed. M. Burrows, New Haven, 1950, p. xvi.

[2] Millar Burrows, *The Dead Sea Scrolls,* New York, 1955, p. 99.

[3] Quoted after the source mentioned in note 1.

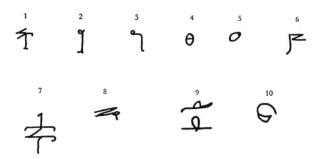

At first blush the idea of comparing these marks with Masoretic accents looks promising. Yet the signs themselves are different from Masoretic accents contained in the plethora of manuscripts examined, just as Burrows indicated. The present writer has searched for similar signs among Roman, Syrian, and Armenian neumes, but with negative result.

Then I came across a relatively recent book on the neumes of the Old Slavonic and Bulgarian Church; it revealed some astonishing parallels. I refer to Mme. R. Paralikova Verdeil's fine study, *La musique Byzantine chez les Bulgares et les Russes*.[4] The following comparisons are based upon her book.

Of the many Slavonic neumes, five are either identical in shape with, or very similar to, signs found in the Dead Sea Scrolls. The Byzantine-Slavonic neumes are:

These paleo-Byzantine neumes are found in Cod. Laura 67, Cod. 1753/4 of Chartres,[5] in an anonymous manuscript of the Mt. Athos monastery, and in ancient Slavonic codices. The system to which these signs belong is the so-called *notation Kontakarienne*, which bears that name because of its application to Byzantine *Kontakia*, a hymn type of the 5th-7th centuries. This writer has elsewhere drawn attention to the

[4] Published as *Monumenta Musicae Byzantinae Subsidia, Vol. III*, Copenhagen and Boston, 1953.

[5] Destroyed in 1944 during the bombardment of Chartres.

strong influence of Syriac and Hebrew poetry upon the Byzantine *Kontakion*.[6] The most famous poet-composer of *Kontakia* was the great Romanos, a converted Syrian Jew. This type of *Kontakia* notation was used, according to Mme. Verdeil, during the 9th and 10th centuries in Byzantium. It has, at least in the oldest Slavonic manuscripts, preserved its original forms.[7] A comparison of some of these neumes with signs from the Dead Sea Scrolls yields the following tabulation:

If we dare at all to proceed beyond this bare statement of paleographic evidence, we must constantly be mindful of the two possible alternatives, which exclude each other mutually: 1) the similarity is the result of sheer coincidence; or 2) the similarity has a historical foundation. The latter assumption would imply a direct or indirect relationship between the Dead Sea Scrolls and Byzantine or paleo-Slavonic manuscripts. *Tertium non datur!*

However, at the present stage of scrutiny, with just a part of the manuscripts published, it is futile to pursue our investigation further. At least two more hurdles must be cleared before we can reach even tentative conclusions. Paleographic evidence will have to ascertain whether the marginal signs were written by a later hand than the text itself; and the scholars will have to search for similar markings in all the scrolls and

[6] Cf. E. Werner, *Hebrew and Oriental Christian Metrical Hymns*, in *Hebrew Union College Annual*, Vol. XXIII, Pt. II, pp. 415-25.

[7] Cf. P. Verdeil, *op. cit.*, p. 113.

fragments, which seem, after all, to display a common authority and doctrine.

If we could assume, with Drs. Zeitlin and Kahle, that the medieval Jewish sect of the Karaites had, at one time or another, known and even handled some of the scrolls, our path would be easier.[8] The problem of a common historical origin of paleo-Byzantine neumes and Dead Sea Scrolls signs would not seem insurmountable, for the Karaites settled in Byzantium, later in the Crimea and Southeast Russia. One of their authorities in the 10th century, Al Qirqisani, knew of Hebrew scrolls in Southeast Palestine; moreover, they were already then traced back to the "cave-dwellers" *(Al Maghariyah)*, the Arabic sobriquet for the Essenes.[9] There seems to be little doubt that some enigmatic connection existed between the Qumran sect and the Karaites; but what the Karaites had to do with the manuscripts, if they really had access to them, is still problematical.[10]

For the moment there remains only the question whether the signs in the scrolls *could* have had any notational or, to be specific, ecphonetic function. While there is nothing to contradict such an assumption *a priori,* our answer must necessarily depend upon our stand towards the two principal alternatives stated above. Although five of the signs are repetitive, it would be rash to assume any ecphonetic significance on that evidence alone. Should newer discoveries from Khirbet Qumran or its environment contain identical or even similar signs, then we might have to weigh the hypothesis that all such markings constitute primitive attempts at lectionary notation. Such a conjecture would indeed revolutionize our views on the origin of neumes.

II

Musical instruments and their use are mentioned repeatedly in the scrolls called *The War of the Children of Light against the Children of Darkness* and the *Manual of Discipline.* The names of the instruments are the same as those that so often appear in the Psalter. Even their usage appears, at first blush, to be patterned according to the standard phrases, familiar to every student of the Old Testament. But this similarity is only

[8] Cf. M. Burrows, *The Dead Sea Scrolls,* p. 298.

[9] Cf. A. Dupont-Sommer, *The Jewish Sect of Qumran and the Essenes,* London, 1954, p. 74ff.

[10] P. Kahle, *The Karaites and the manuscripts from the Cave,* in *Vetus Testamentum,* Leyden, 1953, pp. 82-84.

superficial. For among these backward-harking phrases there sounds an unexpected new note, a type of thought and speech that is known to us from New Testament literature.

One of the characteristic passages of the hymn that concludes the *Manual of Discipline* reads:

Dupont-Sommer's translation	Burrows's translation
I will sing with knowledge	I will sing with knowledge
And all my lyre will vibrate	And all my music shall be for the
of the Glory of God	Glory of God
And my lute and my harp	My lyre and harp shall be
for the holy Order of which	for this holy fixed Order
He is the author	And the flute of my lips
And I will raise the flute	I will raise
of my lips on account	In His just circle.[12]
Of his righteous cord.[11]	

The "lute" of Dupont-Sommer's translation and also his "vibrating lyre" are perhaps a little periphrastic. The "holy fixed Order" refers to the succession of weeks, months, and holy days, indeed to the Essene luni-solar calendar, in which they took great pride.[13] Of greater interest than these terminological differences are expressions like "I will sing with knowledge"; for the very same phrase occurs in Paul's First Epistle to the Corinthians,[14] while it is absent in the Old Testament. And Clement of Rome, the third Bishop, stressed, like the sect of the scrolls, the holy fixed Order, according to which all worship should be regulated.[15]

It is at this point that the question arises: does the hymnodist refer to real instruments or are they imaginary ornaments of his poetry? Did he refer to a veritable *symphonia sacra?* For his outburst has a certain flavor which reminds us of similar allegorical passages in Paul, Philo, and the post-apostolic literature.

The trouble with all these references to musical instruments is that they usually were meant as well as understood *metaphorically.* A few examples will illustrate this point:

[11] Dupont-Sommer, *op. cit.*, p. 139.

[12] M. Burrows, *ibid.*, p. 385.

[13] Philo reports the very same fact about the Therapeutes in Egypt, who celebrated the Pannychis (the Pentecontad), of which the system of Octoechos is the lasting musical symbol. Cf. E. Werner, *The Origin of the Eight Modes of Music*, in *Hebrew Union College Annual*, 1948.

[14] I. Cor. 14:15.

[15] Clement of Rome, I. Ep. to the Corinthians, ch. 40.

Philo of Alexandria was an older contemporary of Jesus and a sympathizer with the Therapeutes, the Egyptian branch of the Essenes. He likens the soul to a well attuned lyre,[16] and even speaks of "the lyre of the soul."[17] In general he thinks that no instrument can attain the expressive dignity of the human voice.[18] And St. Paul, in a famous diatribe, while not directly speaking against instruments, compares them unfavorably with song, song of the spirit and of understanding:

> Though I speak with the tongues of men and of angels, and have not charity, I am becoming as sounding brass, or a tinkling cymbal.[19]
>
> And even things without life giving sound, whether pipe or harp . . . how shall it be known what is piped or harped?[20]
>
> What is it then? I will pray with the spirit, and I will pray with the understanding also: I will sing with the spirit, and I will sing with the understanding also.[21]

In the same way the idea of "singing with understanding" or "knowledge" is stressed in the *Manual of Discipline*.

More radically it is expressed in the *Hymns of Thanksgiving*, the breviary of the unknown sect of Qumran.

> Thou has put praises in my mouth
> and on my tongue rejoicing,
> and the circumcising of my lips in place of loud praise,
> that I may sing of thy steadfast love . . .[22]

This seems to allude to silent worship as implied in the expression *Hash-shaim* (silent or secret ones), an epithet of the Essenes.[23] And again, we remember Paul's refutation of this type of prayer in I. Cor. 14:16-18. It is not unlikely that he had the Essenes in mind.

St. Paul's indifference to, and Philo's lukewarm allegorization of, musical instruments speak the same language as the passages from the Dead Sea Scrolls. Indeed, how is it possible to interpret the following verse in any but an allegorical way?

[16] Philo, ed. Cohn-Wendland (*Quod Deus sit,* II, 61).
[17] Philo, *ibid.* (*De Fuga et Inventione,* III, 115).
[18] Philo (*De Posteritate Caini,* XXXI, 104 f.).
[19] I. Cor. 13:1.
[20] I. Cor. 14:7.
[21] I. Cor. 14:15.
[22] Cf. M. Burrows, *ibid.,* p. 413.
[23] Cf. F. Coneybeare, *Philo about the Contemplative Life,* Oxford, 1895, p. 247.

> My adversaries roared forth their complaint [against me]
> With a lyre, accompanied by mocking songs.[24]

It seems that the poet is alluding to a verse of Lamentations (3:14): "I was a derision to all my people; and their mocking song all the day."

Such expressions would lead us to understand the passages dealing with musical instruments in a purely allegorical way. This interpretation would certainly suit the puritanic-ascetic type of worship described in most of the scrolls. For the sect of Qumran strongly opposed every kind of sacrifice; instrumental music, on the other hand, as practiced by the Temple's orchestra, was invariably understood as an organic accessory of the sacrificial cult. Without sacrifice the instruments had no cultic value. Hence we might dismiss the passages with reference to instruments as mere allegories.

This rule has, however, an important exception: the scroll of the *War of the Children of Light against the Children of Darkness*. This strange document purports to set down the battle order in the apocalyptic war between the forces of Good and Evil. Tactical positions, banners, lines of attack and defense, even the trumpets and signal-horns are described in minute detail. Various types of metal trumpets are referred to, all named according to their military functions, whereas the ram's horns (*shofars*) are less diversified.

The translation of the musical or semi-musical terms is by no means definite and no more than an approximation, for many Hebrew terms are unfamiliar to scholars. The words themselves are known, of course, but their technical significance is still a matter of conjecture.

Equally controversial is the question whether the entire scroll was more than an eschatological fantasy; but, fantasy or war-ritual, the group that is glorified therein — or that glorified itself — seems to have been active in matters musical. A passage such as this:

> . . . the name of the commander of the fifty and names of the commanders of its tens; on the standard of the ten they shall write "Songs of God with a Harp of Ten strings" and the name of the commander of the ten . . .

demonstrates the deep reverence in which the musical terms of Scripture

[24] Quoted from M. Wallenstein's excellent translation, in *Bulletin of the John Ryland Library*, Manchester, Vol. 38, No. 1, p. 254.

were held. For when this was written, the "harp of ten strings," the biblical *asor,* was most probably obsolete.[25]

In this case, however, the *asor* was mentioned as a symbol of the squad of ten, not as a real musical instrument. This writer is convinced that the old number symbolism, whereby each musical instrument had its numerical and cosmological significance, was revived in Jewish sects under neo-Pythagorean influence. Such an assumption appears the more plausible in that the *Manual of Discipline,* too, stresses calendaric-cosmological ideas and principles. The Essenes leaned strongly to such speculations. Later, we encounter those speculations again in the gnosticism of the first three Christian centuries.[26]

The trumpets, on the other hand, are viewed and treated as real instruments. The signals and the manner of their performance are described in detail. At the moment we can only speculate on the full significance of those apocalyptic trumpet-blasts, in which the War-Scroll abounds. Certainly, they cannot be simply dismissed as allegorical or symbolical, since technical terms were employed that have direct application to real instruments. We quote one of many such passages:

> Then the priests shall sound on the trumpets a *prolonged* note, the signal for putting the battle in array . . . When they are standing in three lines, the priests shall sound for them a second call, a *quiet and sustained* note, the signal for advancing . . . Then they shall take hold of their weapons, and the priests shall sound on the six trumpets of the slain [?] a *sharp and agitated* [broken] note to direct the battle . . . and the Levites and all those who have the ram's horns shall sound in unison a great war blast . . . the priests shall sound for them on the trumpets of return [?] a *quiet, prolonged, and sustained* note . . .[27]

The War-Scroll contains many such passages and is full of interesting details. Each trumpet (or set of trumpets) has a function of its own, such as "trumpets of ambush," "trumpets of the slain," (?) "trumpets of return," etc., which may be understood with reference to their signals at the varying phases of the actual battle. All these tactical regulations are couched in a strangely archaic language. They remind the reader — no doubt intentionally so — of certain military accounts as they occur in the historical books of the Old Testament.[28] Yet these books were at least

[25] The instrument, a cittern with 10 strings, a close relative of the psalterium, is referred to in Ps. 92:4; 33:2; 144:9.

[26] Cf. E. Werner, *The Origin of the Eight Modes of Music.*

[27] Cf. M. Burrows, *ibid.,* p. 398 (Mr. Burrows's translation).

[28] The War-Scroll actually quotes the passages Num. 10:9.

three or four centuries old when the War-Scroll was being composed. The functions of these war-trumpets correspond roughly with the ordinances as set down in Lev. 23:24; Lev. 25:9; Num. 10:2-10; and especially Jos. 6:4-6, 8-9, 13, 16, 20. The *loci classici* are:

Num. 10:8	And the sons of Aaron, the priests, shall blow with the trumpets; and they shall be to you for an ordinance for ever throughout your generations.
II. Chron. 5:12	Also the Levites which were the singers . . . having cymbals and psalteries and harps, stood at the east end of the altar, and with them a hundred and twenty priests sounding with trumpets.
II. Chron. 7:6	And the priests waited on their offices: the Levites also with instruments of music of the Lord . . .; and the priests sounded trumpets before them . . .
II. Chron. 13:12	And, behold, God Himself is with us for our captain, and His priests with sounding trumpets to cry alarm against you.
II. Chron. 13:14	And when Judah looked back, behold, the battle was before and behind: and they cried unto the Lord, and the priests sounded with the trumpets.

The biblical rule ascribes the singing and "musick-making" to the Levites, the blowing of trumpets to the priests (Aaronides). In fact the trumpet *(hasosra)* was *the* priestly instrument. The *shofar* was usually blown by the Levites and only occasionally also by priests.

The War-Scroll distinguishes equally sharply between priests and Levites:

> One priest shall go before the men of the rank to strengthen their hands in the battle; and in the hands of the other six shall be the trumpets of assembly, the memorial trumpets, the trumpets of the war-blast, the trumpets of pursuit, and the trumpets of re-assembly. And when the priests go forth to the space between the ranks there shall go with them seven Levites holding in their hands the seven ram's horns of jubilee, and three officers of the Levites before the priests and the Levites. Then the priests shall sound the two trumpets of assembly.[29]

The various numbers, six, seven, three, two, appear to have a theo-cratic-cosmological significance. But exactly what this significance was, we do not know. The book of Revelation, which offers many points for

[29] Burrows, *ibid.*, p. 397.

comparison, also contains a vision of seven trumpets, yet here they are sounded by angels in the eschatological war between Christ and Antichrist.

Within a brief essay it is not possible to enter into a prolonged discussion of the various technical terms. Most recently Yigal Yadin, a high officer in the Israeli army as well as an outstanding archaeologist, has published an extensive monograph on the War-Scroll. He offers in three chapters dedicated to the trumpets and their signals a profound analysis of the various problems raised by the terminology of the manuscript.[30] Many of his explanations are cogent and conclusive, others no more than hypothetical. In some cases he seems to have passed by important clues.

What are these clues? In our opinion, they are all concerned with the technique of trumpet-blowing as presumed by the author of the scroll. A few quotations in my own translation and with my interpretation of musical terms (printed in italics) may indicate the problems of the manner of performance alluded to in the manuscript.

> 1) "And they [the priests] shall sound a steady *sostenuto legato* signal"
>
> 2) ". . . they shall sound a sharp *staccato* repeated signal" (the Hebrew term suggests here a constant breaking or interrupting of tone, which might be understood as double or triple tonguing)
>
> 3) ". . . they [the priests] shall blow [on six trumpets], *as if with one voice, a great war-blast . . .*"

These battle regulations all reckon with unison blowing of the trumpets. This is even emphasized:

> "Then the priests shall sound a long-held tone . . ."
> "And the priests shall sound a second blast, a tone *sostenuto legato* . . ."
> "And the Levites and the whole people . . . shall sound *in unison* a great war-blast . . ."[31]

Some of these descriptions read like paraphrases of biblical verses, such as:

> "And it came even to pass, as the trumpeters and singers
> were as one, to make *one sound* [as in unison]
> to be heard in praising and thanking the Lord . . ."[32]

---

[30] Yigal Yadin, *Megillat Milehemet*, Jerusalem, 1955 (in Hebrew).

[31] All these passages occur in the War-Scroll VIII, 3-10; in attempting to give a translation of my own, I was most ably assisted by Dr. A. Giat, to whom I am indebted.

[32] II. Chron. 5:13.

The term unison *(qol ehad)* is used both in this Old Testament passage and the War-Scroll.

What do such specifications teach us? When technical terms convey ideas such as legato, staccato, sostenuto, tonguing, etc., we must assume a considerable skill in blowing. But even more important is the evidence of definable notes and pitches. For it is not possible for two or more trumpets to produce a unison sound "as with one voice" unless the trumpeters were able to regulate the pitch with considerable accuracy. This, at least, proves decisively that the Temple trumpets had a number of definable notes and phrases. The sound of the signals themselves must have been rather shrill, since the Temple trumpets belonged to the family of the short, two-foot instruments.[33]

Another angle of the problem with which these priestly war-trumpets confront us concerns their names: they are called trumpets of assembly, of the war-blast over the slain, of ambush, of pursuit, and of re-assembly. Are we to understand that different kinds of trumpets were envisaged for these respective functions? This seems a rather fantastic assumption. And yet, the alternative interpretation that each of these designations stands for one kind of signal or another is contradicted by passages like these: "After that, the priests shall sound for them on the trumpets of return a steady sostenuto legato tone." "The priests shall sound on the six trumpets of the slain a sharp staccato signal."

If the designation "trumpets of return" or "trumpets of the slain" refers to fixed sets of signals, why was it necessary to describe the call as a "steady sostenuto legato" or "sharp staccato"? The answer to this question seems to lie in the position in space of the various sets of trumpets. Perhaps each set was envisaged at a different place as well as a different phase of the battle, and it would be irrelevant whether the battle actually took place or was just a fantasy of the author of the scroll. To him a corps of skilled trumpeters was simply a requirement of the battle.

III

Philo of Alexandria has left us in his famous *De vita contemplativa* a detailed description of the life and mores of the Therapeutes. It is generally known that the sect of Qumran was closely akin to that Egyptian branch of the Essenes which was called Therapeutes. Philo's account, partly quoted by Eusebius three centuries later, mentions in a

[33] Cf. Curt Sachs, *Geist und Werden der Musikinstrumente,* Berlin, 1929, p. 152.

famous passage the practice of antiphony of men and women. Unfortunately, he does not quote any of their prayers or hymns, although he stresses that they "were of many meters and tunes." The song of the Red Sea, Exodus 15, is the only biblical canticle mentioned in Philo's description; it was not only chanted, but it was danced in a sacred pantomime.

Actually, this often quoted passage constitutes but a part of the general report concerning the Therapeutes' musical liturgy. The antecedent part of the description, much less known, goes into details of the hymns sung at the sect's worship.

This portion reads as follows:

> . . . the President [of the sacred banquet] rises and sings a hymn composed as an address to God, either a new one of his composition or an old one by poets of the past, who have left behind them hymns in many meters and melodies, hexameters and iambics, lyrics suitable for processions [*prosodion*] or libations [*paraspondeion*] and before the altars or for the chorus whilst standing [*stasimon*] or dancing, set in most flexible stanzas well proportioned [*strophais polystrophois eu diamemetremenon*] for the various turns. After him all the others follow in turn as they are arranged in proper order, while the rest listen silently except when they are obliged to sing the refrains and closing verses [*akroteleutia kai ephymnia*]: then they sound forth, all men and women together. [34]

This description would indicate an intonation of a (new or old) canticle by the senior, in metrical style or otherwise, while various groups follow in turn until the entire congregation joins them in the refrain or the closing line.

The sacred banquet celebrated every seven weeks (in intervals of a pentecontad) was concluded by a vigil-nocturn *(pannychis)*.[35]

If we now compare with the ritual of the Therapeutes the rules, statutes, and poems pertaining to the sect of the Dead Sea Scrolls, certain conspicuous resemblances strike the reader. Among the regulations, identical in both sources, which concern the sacred banquet, we find such items as: "The presiding priest shall stretch out his hand first of

[34] Cf. Philo, *De vita contemplativa*, M. 484 (Loeb Class. Library, Philo, Vol. X, p. 162-3). Some of the terms are somewhat ambiguous. (My translation. E. W.) A very similar description is offered in Clement of Alexandria, *Pedagogue*, II, §4.

[35] Coneybeare, *Philo about the Contemplative Life*, p. 101 ff, seems to understand this as a reference to Pentecost; actually, however, there is no valid reason for this assumption, since the ancient pentecontad-calendar appears to have been used by the Therapeutes. Cf. Eric Werner, *The Origin of the Eight Modes of Music*, where all sources are given.

all to bless [or to thank] God with the first fruits of bread or of wine . . ." "The novice shall not come into touch with the banquet of the Many before he has completed his second year in the midst of the members of the Community . . ."[36] It is superfluous to point out the similarity with the Mass, divided into the *missa fidelium* and *missa catechumenorum;* the latter part corresponds here to the role of the novices in the service.

The *Manual of Discipline* states the rules of the nightly study of the Law and the habitual prayers. Dupont-Sommer comments on these rules: "In these sacred vigils they read the Law, commented on it, and praised God. This was no doubt a heavy obligation for men who passed their whole days in manual toil; for, as we know, they labored from morning to evening . . . One can easily understand why from time to time one of them would be tempted to stretch out and go to sleep. But woe betide him!"[37]

For the rule prescribed thirty days' punishment for such an offense. Here we are reminded of an early monastic controversy dealing with the admissibility of *troparia* and *octoechos.* The monk of this 5th-century anecdote was severely reprimanded by his abbot for always drowsing during the vigils.[38] This no doubt typical case happened in an Egyptian monastery; the sleepy but musical monk could keep awake only by frequent singing during the night's service.

There has been occasion to mention the collection of poems, called *Hymns of Thanksgiving* after their incipit (and presumable refrain): "I thank thee, O Lord" or "I bless thee, O Lord." In addition, some poetic sections are contained in other scrolls, as in the *Manual of Discipline,* the *War of the Sons of Light,* and others. It will be interesting and instructive to examine these poems against those mentioned in Philo's accounts. It might be well to point out that the poems do not constitute hymns in the accepted sense but are free compositions, like the biblical canticles.

None of these poems shows — as of now — any evidence of metrical composition. Unless the meters were exceedingly complex, which is unlikely, we must assume that no metrical style was used. Refrains and

[36] Cf. Dupont-Sommer, *op. cit.,* pp. 99-100.

[37] *Ibid.,* p. 103.

[38] Cf. Yochanan Rufos de Mayuma in *Patrologia Orientalis,* VII, 180 ff. Also E. Werner, *The Origin of the Eight Modes,* pp. 232-3.

occasional strophic structure, however, are noticeable and not uncommon. If Philo's terminology is applied, *akroteleutia* and *ephymnia* (refrains and emphatic closing verses) seem to play a part in the structure of these pieces. Since we do not know anything about the way in which these texts were chanted, we cannot, of course, determine whether they were of stationary *(stasima)* or processional *(prosodia)* character. We do know, however, that these hymns were regularly chanted and that they constituted a kind of breviary. Says the poet in the *Manual of Discipline:*

> When I begin to put forth my hands and my feet
> I will bless His name;
> When I begin to go out or come in
> When I sit down or stand up
> And as I lie on my couch, I will sing aloud to Him.
> I will bless Him with an offering of the utterance of my lips
> More than the oblation spread out by men
> Before I raise my hand to satisfy myself
> With the delights of what the world produces,
> In domination of fear and terror
> The place of distress with desolation,
> I will bless Him, giving special thanks . . .
> When distress is let loose I will praise Him
> And when I am delivered I will sing praise also . . .
> With thanksgiving I will open my mouth . . .
> Blessed art thou, O my God
> Who opened to knowledge the heart of thy servant . . .[39]

The last line is an almost literal quotation from an ancient prayer. Furthermore, the often repeated "I will bless him" is to be understood as a kind of refrain, which opens every new stanza.

To the musicologist, the *Hymns of Thanksgiving* are even more interesting. For he should regard them as the missing links in the gradual evolution from plain psalmodic-responsorial style to the full rounded form of the antiphon.

The formal structure of the classic antiphon can be described as roughly a ternary form ABA, in which A is a prefatory verse of Scripture and B is usually an inserted verse from the Psalter or the canticles. Often the last A is replaced by the Lesser Doxology *(Gloria Patri)* or

<hr>

[39] Cf. M. Burrows, *ibid.,* pp. 385-87. Dr. Sukkenig's hypothesis that the "Teacher of Righteousness," the central figure of the scrolls, was the author of these hymns, is very plausible.

an Alleluia. The most characteristic feature is the combination of scriptural quotation with choral refrain.[40]

A number of the *Hymns of Thanksgiving* represent an intermediate stage in the evolution towards the antiphon form. One cannot yet discern a clear structure, nor are the "hymns" conceived in ternary form. Yet the elements of refrain and quotation are already combined in these poems. For example:

> I thank thee, O Lord
> For thou holdest my soul in the hurdles of life [I. Sam. 25:29]
> and thou shelterest me from all the snares of the pit . . .
> And from the wreckers who seek my life, because
> I adhere to thy covenant.
> And they are but a vain brood and a tribe of Belial . . .
> Thou wilt ensnare the feet of those who spread a net against me [Ps. 9:16]
> They will fall into the entanglements they have
> hidden for my soul, but my foot standeth in an even place [Ps. 7:16]
> In the congregations will I bless thy name . . . [Ps. 26:12][41]

I have omitted some of the free poetic outbursts of the hymnodist between these quotations. Almost every one of these *Hymns of Thanksgiving* is couched in this mixture of refrains, free poetry, and scriptural quotation. This juxtaposition of quotation and original poetry presages the split in early Christian hymnody: the conservative policy of the Roman Church, which for the first five or six centuries championed a strict biblicistic chant and form against the free, didactic-homiletic hymns of the Eastern Churches, culminated in the edicts of the Council of Laodicea.[42]

We may well imagine the performance of such a hymn. The presiding senior of the sacred banquet intoned the hymn, and, whenever a familiar quotation occurred, the congregation joined him in traditional chant; eventually they all sang the refrain or closing verse. Philo-Eusebius speak even of antiphonal chant between men and women but in the Dead Sea Scroll there is no evidence of such a practice. Such hymns and psalms were the patterns upon which the monastic offices of later centuries elaborated in their extensive services.

---

[40] This rough simplification will do justice only to the antiphons of the First Millennium and their usual method of performance.

[41] Translation and annotation after M. Wallenstein, *Hymns from the Judean Scrolls*, Manchester, 1950, pp. 9-13.

[42] Cf. Lou H. Silberman, *Language and Structure in the Hodayot*, in *Journal of Biblical Literature*, Vol. 75, June, 1956.

The foregoing remarks should be viewed only as a first report on a search for musical references in the scrolls. A number of scrolls or fragments of scrolls have not been opened or not been published as yet; and it is quite possible that the unpublished manuscripts will enrich our knowledge with new findings. The new facts cited and interpreted here seem to add unexpected data to our meager corpus of information about music in the Hellenistic era. Yet it is only fair to admit that every new discovery raises more questions than it answers.

The Philosophy and Theory of Music in Judaeo-Arabic Literature

Reprinted with permission of *Hebrew Union College Annual*, 16, 1941, pp. 251-319.

I

THE POSITION OF MUSIC IN THE JEWISH CULTURE OF THE MIDDLE AGES.

REGRETTABLE as it may be, we know very little about the musical theory and philosophy of the medieval Jewish authors. Nonetheless, it would be a gross exaggeration were we to assert a total lack of musical literature in medieval Judaism. Statements have frequently been made to this effect, although a few glimpses into Steinschneider's bibliographies could teach us better.[1] We cannot deny, however, that by comparison with

*For technical reasons, it was impossible to publish, in this issue of the *HUCA*, the Hebrew texts, their translations, and the critical apparatus prepared by Dr. Sonne. These will be used later, in the continuation of this article. Sections I to V of the present instalment are the work of Werner; the appendix was prepared by Sonne: while section VI was written by both authors in close collaboration. Dr. Werner is greatly indebted to Dr. Sonne for his numerous suggestions, his helpful counsel, and his unflagging interest in this onerous task.

The Texts to which we refer are the following:
  Honein-Alharizi, *The Maxims of the Philosophers* (מוסרי הפילוסופים),
    Text A.
  Saadya Gaon, *Emunot Vede'ot* (Ibn Tibbon's and anonymous translations),
    Text B 1, 2.
  Moses Maimonides, *Responsum concerning Music*; the *Eight Chapters*,
    Text C 1, 2.
  Shemtob Falaquera, *Rešit Hokma*; *Hamebakkesh*, Text D 1, 2.
  Isaac Ibn Latif, *Ginze Hammelek*, Text E.
  Moses Abulafia, (quoted by Shemtob ben Isaac, cf. Steinschneider, *Hebr. Bibliographie* XIX, 43. Also Steinschneider's *Hebr. Uebers.*, 410, 689), Text F.
  Isaiah ben Isaac, *Commentary on Avicenna's Al-kanun*, Text G.

[1] I refer here to such erroneous statements as that made by Miss Lentschner, in the *Reconstructionist*, Nov. 10, 1939.

the great and comprehensive literature on music among the Arabs, and with the efforts of the Western theorists of the 10th to the 14th century, the Jews have shown but a scant interest in this subject.

What are the reasons for this neglect? Many answers have been offered, but none can satisfy us completely. Let us examine them one by one. This apparent indifference cannot be due to a dearth of musical accomplishment; for we know that the Jews created and developed the best part of their traditional liturgical music in those very centuries.[2] Nor can the chief reason be the absence of an established musical notation. For neither the Arabs nor the European theorists possessed a fully developed system of notation until the twelfth century, and even then the Arabic system was no more than a primitive tablature based on their favorite instrument, the 'ud.[3] For all that, the theoretical achievements of the Arabs are both remarkable and extensive.

Adequately to explain the paradox we must briefly notice the general attitude of scholars, Jewish as well as non-Jewish, toward the music of their times and their environment. For it was these scholars whose views on music either fostered or impeded the growth of musical disquisition.

In the Middle Ages, music was supposed to be not so much a practical art as a *"scientia"* well embedded in the *quadrivium educationis*[4] which contained the four mathematical sciences,

---

[2] Of the literature on the development of traditional chant, we note only the following: Idelsohn, *Thesaurus*, vols. 2, 4, 5, 7, 9, 10, and *Jewish Music in Its Historical development* pp. 132–200. Birnbaum, *Liturgische Studien* II. Nettl, *Alte juedische Spielleute und Musiker*. Vogelstein-Rieger, *Geschichte der Juden in Rom* II, 120 ff. Steinschneider, *Hebr. Uebersetzungen*, p. 698 ff. Werner, *Die hebr. Intonationen des B. Marcello*, in *MGWJ* 1937. Idem, *Notes on Jewish and Catholic Musical Punctuation*, in *HUCA* 1940.

[3] Cf. H. G. Farmer, *History of Arabian Music*, p. 95, and *Facts for the Arabian Musical Influence*, pp. 305–16.

[4] About the number of the sciences in the Jewish world cf. Guedemann, *Das Juedische Erziehungswesen waehrend der Spanisch-Arabischen Epoche*, p. 38 n. 1. The inclusion of music in the *quadrivium* dates back to M. Varro. Augustine opposes the general practice of the science of music, when saying: "Aliud igitur putas esse artem, aliud scientiam. Siquidem et in sola ratione

viz. Arithmetic, Geometry, Astronomy, and Music. Boethius
made this classification fairly common. His works *De Institutione
Musica* and *De Institutione Arithmetica* belonged to the standard
books of the Middle Ages. He gave the classic definition of Music
from which eight hundred years of musical theory drew.[5] According to Boethius, Music has the following genera: (1) *Musica
mundana* representing the movements of the heavenly spheres
and the order of the elements and seasons. This Music is inseparably connected with the mathematical order of the universe.
(2) *Musica humana* is the power which links body and soul in a
kind of mathematical harmony, mirroring the macrocosmic
Musica mundana in the microcosm of human existence.[6] (3) *Musica instrumentalis* is music in our own sense of the term, namely,
the art of musical composition yielding music which can be
heard and felt. Such music is not "real" in the Platonic sense
but only an *imitatio Musicae mundanae*. Its task is to unify the
movements of the soul and to attune them into a perfect harmony. It is the lowest form of Music.[7] Quite different is Cassiodorus' division into *scientia harmonica, rhythmica et metrica*. Here
we find no reference to melody or to musical forms; everything
is dealt with *"more arithmetico."* This purely abstract method
did not, however, deter the monk, Cassiodorus, from a strictly
theological interpretation of the effect which music has upon the
human soul.[8]

Regino of Pruem formulated the classification *musica arti-
ficialis et naturalis*, also resorting to ecclesiastical speculation.
Here natural Music is that which emanates from God's creatures,

esse potest, ars autem rationi jungit imitationem." Cf. *Patr. Lat.* (*Migne*)
XXXII, 1086.

⁵ Cf. G. Pietzsch, *Die Klassifikation der Musik von Boethius bis Ugolino
von Orvieto*, p. 40.

⁶ *Ibid.*, p. 42.

⁷ Boethius' formula "quibusdam instrumentis ut in citharis vel tibiis"
is perhaps an allusion to 1 Sam. 10.5.

⁸ Cassiodorus closely follows the allegorical representations of the late
Alexandrian school, which claimed a personal affinity, almost identity between Orpheus, David, and Jesus, although Cassiodorus himself did not go
quite so far. Cf. Pietzsch, *op. cit.*, 14.

while artificial Music is performed upon instruments devised
by man.[9]

The influence of the Arabic theorists, especially of Alfarabi,
is recognizable in Gundissalinus' (ca. 1150) classification into
musica speculativa et activa whereby a rigid distinction is drawn
between the meditative (philosophy) and the active (singing,
playing) capacity of the musician.[10]

In all of these definitions, the theoretical viewpoint greatly
prevails over practical musical performance. Considering the
enormous part which authority played in mediaeval thinking,
we need not to be surprised that the definitions mentioned were
quoted recurrently.[11] This is equally true of the world of the Near
East; and Spengler is certainly right in calling Plato, Aristotle,
and Pythagoras the prophets of the Western orbit, including
Syria and Arabia. "Whatever could be traced back to them was
inevitably thought to be the truth."[12]

Judaism also, to a certain degree, accepted those Greek sages
as authorities, but set high above them the Bible and the talmudic Rabbis.[13] Still, in the attitude toward music, we may
find a considerable difference between the Jewish scholars of
Central and Eastern Europe on the one hand, and the Hebrew
sources of the Arabic sphere on the other. While Jewish scholars
within the domains of Arabic culture participated in all phases
of that culture, even in the secular and the artistic, the rest of
European Jewry had to limit itself to theological and exegetic
studies based exclusively on rabbinic doctrines. Those Rabbis
knew of musical art only the traditional elements of the synagogal
chant and were interested in the proper rendition of music purely

[9] *Ibid.*, 64.

[10] Cf. L. Baur, *D. Gundissalinus' De Divisione Philosophiae* in *Beitraegen
zur Philosophie des Mittelalters* IV, pp. 96–102. *See also* Pietzsch, *op. cit.*, p. 79.

[11] Cf. Clemens Baeumker, *Geist und Form in der Mittelalterlichen Philosophie*, p. 60.

[12] Spengler, *Der Untergang des Abendlandes* II, 303. However, Spengler is
quite mistaken in some of his conclusions concerning the invention of "working hypothesies."

[13] "The understanding of Aristotle is the highest a man can ever achieve,
excepting the wisdom of the prophets." (Maimonides to Samuel ibn Tibbon,
cf. Steinschneider, Hebr. Uebers. 40/41.)

from the rabbinic point of view.[14] It even seems that the boundary
line between the two different attitudes corresponds to the geo-
graphic frontier between the Spanish and the Parisian areas.
R. Joseph ibn Caspi, a learned writer of Provence which was then
the exact line of demarcation between Spain and France, says:
למנצח בנגינותי אשר אלו המות ר"ל שניונות. ולמנצח הם מלות שיריות ר"ל
ממלאכת השיר הנהוגית בכלי הניגון העשוים להעיר הנפש המשכלת המכונה
בימי קדם מוסיקא אבל נאבדה החכמה הזה.[15]

Accordingly, we limit this study to the Jewish sources within
the Arabic sphere among whose intellectuals the scholastic works
on musical theory were almost common property. Judaeo-Arabic
literature placed music among the sciences at a fairly early time.
Already the Karaite Nissim ben Noah in the ninth, David
Almokammez in the tenth, and Bachya ibn Pakuda during the
eleventh century mention music as a part of scientific study.[16]
Much more is to be said about Joseph ibn 'Aknin, the disciple
of Maimonides who, differing appreciably from his almost anti-
musical master, gave in his *"Tabb-ul-nufus"* (Recreation of Souls)
a precise description of the curriculum of musical studies prevalent in his day. We shall later deal with this work in detail.
Suffice it for the present to cite a remark interesting for its inde-
pendence of judgement. In Ibn 'Aknin, Music finds a place after
the study of Writing, Torah, Mishna, Grammar, Poetry, Talmud,
Philosophy of Religion, Logic, Mathematics, Optics, and Astronomy.[17] And he continues: "The practice of this science (Music)
precedes the theory. The former must come chronologically first,
because its healing power cannot show itself except by its actual
performance. Thus theoretical speculation is in place only after
practical accomplishment. The priority of practice is imposed by

[14] Cf. Epstein, *Die Wormser Minhagbuecher*, p. xxii, *Sefer Hasidim*, #302,
also Idelsohn, *Jewish Music* chap. viii.

[15] Cf. Joseph ibn Caspi, אדני כסף, ed. Last, p. 120. Note that the author
does not refer to the traditional cantillation of the Psalms, but to the חכמה
(science) of Music.

[16] Cf. Guedemann, *op. cit.*, (note 4), p. 158.

[17] Cf. David Kaufmann, *Gesammelte Schriften* III., p. 343. *See also* שפתי
ישנים, p. 7. Cf. also Steinschneider's words about Ibn Aknin in *Hebr. Uebers.*,
p. 33, and *HB* XIV, 10, 38.

law and nature."[18] To give precedence, even chronological precedence, to *ars*, perhaps even to *usus* before *scientia*, was by no means a common view. The great Roger Bacon was of quite a different opinion: "In the same manner as children can understand the mathematical method of figuring or counting, it will be easier and even necessary for them to understand numbers before singing, because in the relationship of numbers to each other, all the ideas of musical numbers serve as explanatory examples."[19]

A singular position concerning the place of music is taken by Yehuda Halevy. In his *Cusari* he deals with music as part of astronomy and the calendar (II #64–65). But he also links it with metrics and with poetry (II #70–73), later with natural science (IV #24–25), and finally with the speculative disciplines (V #12).[20] Apparently his ideas about musical science are based on Alfarabi and Ibn Sina with whom music similarly occupies a double position, subsumed partly under grammar and partly under the speculative and natural sciences. Hence, we need not wonder that this ideology appears in remote occidental scholars like Vincent of St. Beauvais or Roger Bacon, both of whom are well conversant with Alfarabi and Avicenna.[21]

Yehuda Alharizi, an older contemporary of Ibn 'Aknin, proposed, in a translation from Arabic sources, a concise curriculum

[18] Like his Arabian and Latin fellow-theorists, Ibn 'Aknin identifies the science of Music with musical theory, the art of music with musical practice. Cf. H. Edelstein, *Die Musikanschauung des Augustinus nach seiner Schrift De Musica*, pp. 75–81.

[19] Cf. Roger Bacon, *Opus Maius*, N. E. by J. H. Bridges, Oxford 1897, pp. 100, 178/79, 237/8.

[20] Cassel (*Cusari*) p. 393, claims that Yehuda Halevy while enumerating several disciplines, makes veiled allusions to some works of Aristotle. I cannot agree with him; for Aristotle did not write about Music in his *quaestiones mechanicae* (genuine?) nor in his *De Coloribus*. About the influence of the Pseudo-Aristotelian *Problems, see infra*, chap. III.

[21] At least one of Vincent's works was available to the Jews; cf. Steinschneider, *Hebr. Uebers.* #299. About Alfarabi-quotations in Vincent's work *see* Pietzsch, *op. cit.*, p. 30. Roger Bacon, too, quotes Alfarabi's writings on Music: Cf. his *Opus maius*, transl. by R. B. Burke, I, 259/60.

of learning. In his מוסרי הפילוסופים § 11 he states: "Aristotle says concerning education: The first matter in which a teacher should instruct his disciple is Greek script. In the second year he may teach Grammar and Metrics; in the third year Law and Religion; in the fourth year, Reckoning; in the fifth year, Mathematics; in the sixth, Astronomy; in the seventh, Pharmacology (Medicine); in the eighth, Music; in the ninth Logic. In the tenth year, he may proceed to Philosophy. The disciple shall learn these ten sciences in ten years, each in one year."[22] We see with amazement that secular science occupies a larger part than religion in this educational program. Yet soon thereafter the reaction toward a more religious attitude followed which finally culminated in a limited ban, pronounced by R. Solomon ben Aderet (1305), upon all secular studies.

An inkling of this more orthodox feeling is to be found in the curriculum, suggested by Yehuda b. Samuel b. Abbas in his book "Yair Natib" (Illumination of the Path).[23] According to this author, the student ought first to become familiar with the Bible, the Talmud, and the writings of the best rabbinical authorities." Then may follow the study of Geometry, of Optics, and of Music. Of the latter science, some parts ought to be studied in conjunction with Medicine, because of pulsation and its rhythm."

Three decades later, Shem-Tob Falaquera could still, in the face of orthodox reaction, emphasize in his Reshit Ḥokma the pursuit of the secular sciences, including music. But in his later book, the didactic novel Mebakkesh, he had to qualify his program with the cautious admonition: "Take care and beware lest thou forget the words of Scripture. Believe nothing of the statements based only on the conclusions of reason which might contradict Scripture. For the faithful, belief in Scripture is paramount, since Scripture comes from God and is above the syllogisms of mere reason." Then he proceeds: "The student may study Bible, Mishna, and Talmud for five years . . . Afterwards the diligent disciple leaves his master in order to study, with

---

[22] Guedemann, op. cit., (note 4), p. 37/8.
[23] Ibid., p. 146. The work is still in MS, available in the Bodleiana.

another teacher, the science of Mathematics, which he will pursue in this order: Arithmetic, Geometry, Optics, Astronomy,
and Music."[24] We may recognze here the growing prevalence of
orthodoxy which placed the study of Bible and Talmud above
everything else. This swing to the dominance of the Bible was
accompanied by the decline of Arabic scholarship. Thus the
Cabalist, Abraham b. Isaac of Granada (ca. 1400), could discern
reference to the secular sciences in the same scriptural verse,[25]
in which talmudic interpretation saw an allusion to the six
sedarim of the *Mishna*.[26]

וְהָיָה אֱמוּנַת עִתֶּיךָ חֹסֶן יְשׁוּעֹת חָכְמַת
וְדַעַת יִרְאַת ה' הִיא אוֹצָרוֹ:

Abraham ben Isaac interprets the verse as follows: "Certainty
(אמונת) means Arithmetic, Fate (עתיך) means Astronomy, Strength
(חוסן) means Geometry, Salvation (ישועת) means Music, as it is
written: (II Ki. 3.15) 'But now bring me a minstrel. And it came
to pass, when the musician played, that the hand of the Lord
came upon him.' Wisdom (חכמת) means Ethics" *etc.*[27]

The upshot of this antisecular dogmatism was the practice
of referring interminably to the music of the Temple, which
served as a keyhole through which the Jews peeped into the outer
musical world. But since these passages are not of much consequence for our subject, we cite here only a few, hoping that these
will shed light on the opinions of the medieval Jewish scholars.

[24] *Ibid.*, p. 156/7.
[25] *Ibid.*, p. 41, quoted from Abraham b. Isaac's work ברית מנוחה cited by
Shabbetai Bass, שפתי ישנים introduction, p. 7b.
[26] The talmudic passage is from Šab. 31b. The allusion is to Isa. 33.6.

[27] שפתי ישנים, ז' ובספר ברית מנוחה פרק י' א' על פסוק והיה אמונת עתך וגו' אמונ'ת
רמז למספר. עת'ך רמז לתכונה. חוס'ן רמז לתשבורת. ישועו'ת רמז לניגון כמ'ש: ועתה קחו לי
מנגן וגו' והיי עילו רוח ה'. חכמ'ת רמז למדות. ודע'ת רמז לטבע. יראת ה' היא אוצרו רמז
להחכמת האלהים. כאמרם אין סוסרין ראשי פרקים אלא לאב'ר וכו': I was, however, unable to locate the original passage in the ברית מנוחה (Ed. Amsterdam 1648,
Ed. Warsaw 1883). Yet Azulay states that he once saw a copy of the MS
of this work which contained twice the material of the printed book. The
first printed source of our passage is undoubtedly Moses Bottarel, introduction to his commentary on the ספר יצירה (Ed. Warsaw, p. 24). About the
prophetic virtue of music see *Infra*, ch. III.

Of the older exegetes, it is Saadya who, commenting on the Psalms, deals frequently with musical terms and expressions.[28] Yet, with all of his output, he does not enlighten us much about contemporary musical theory. In his chief work, *Emunoth Wede'ot*, he gives a terse, but interesting description of the musical modes of his milieu.[29]

In Italy, Serahya b. Isaac, a contemporary of Manuello of Rome interprets Prov. 9:1 as follows: "The seven sciences are the four mathematical ones, viz. Arithmetics, Geometry, Music, and Astronomy, and the three philosophical ones, viz. Physics, Metaphysics, and Politics."[30] Manuello himself in his exegesis of Proverbs seizes the opportunity for bitter complaint about the decay of musical art and science. His words (to Prov. 26.16) are: "Truly a miracle that we still possess the twenty-four books of Scripture! It is very probable that Physics, Metaphysics, and the other sciences, of which Plato and Aristotle are today said to be the masters belonged originally to Solomon. Indeed, we see that Music, an excellent science and art, was at home originally in our religion, performed by men like Asaph, David, and Samuel. But today nobody among us knows anything about it. It has been left to the exclusive possession of the Christians."[31]

We have cursorily sketched the place of musical science in the Jewish system of education during the Middle Ages.[32] In so doing, we have encountered two questions of major importance.

A. Did Hebrew theory, like Western Civilisation between the 8th and the 12th century develop a system of musical notation? The answer is — unfortunately — "No." Hebrew theory

---

[28] Abraham Ibn Ezra curtly recognizes Saadya's musical Knowledge in the words: במנים אומר הגאון כמו מינים ויאמר ר' אדונים שהוא אחד והטעם כלי נינון אחד, ודברי הגאון אמת ...(שפת יתר), Ed. Pressburg, p. 32).

[29] Cf. our Texts B, 1, 2.

[30] Guedemann, *Geschichte des Erziehungswesens und der Cultur der Juden in Italien*, p. 160.

[31] *Ibid.*, p. 120. Cf. also Manuello's caustic verse: (Div. VI, 49) מה אומרת חכמת הניגון אל הנוצרים. :גנוב גונבתי מארץ העברים: (Gen. 40.15).

[32] Salomon Almoli, already under the spell of the Renaissance, does not quite belong to the Middle Ages proper. In his מאסף לכל המחנות he compromises between religious and secular sciences, suggesting a very elaborated and ambitious educational program. Cf. Steinschneider, *Hebr. Uebers.* #9.

closely followed the Arabic lead which never created a truly
popular or practical notation, limiting itself to some inconse-
quential sporadic attempts.[33] The Arabs likewise failed to use
full harmonies — at least full harmonies in the European sense.
Although they knew of chords, they seldom went beyond a complex heterophony.[34] Thus, the Jewish and Arabic theory of
consonances was little more than a matter of mathematical
speculation.[35]

B. Did Hebrew theory contribute in any way to the advance-
ment of medieval musical science? Here the answer is: Directly,
No; indirectly, Yes. And it was a Jewish figure of significance
who furthered the theory of music by devious ways. Gersonides
(= Ralbag = Leo Hebraeus) wrote a Latin treatise *De Numeris
Harmonicis* the title of which is somewhat misleading, inasmuch
as it does not deal with the numbers of the overtones. Actually,
it lays the foundation for the new rhythmic theory of Monsignore
Philipp de Vitry, the outstanding personality of the *"Ars nova"*—
a much misunderstood work with which we shall elsewhere deal
extensively.[36]

[33] The discussion about the clarity and the value of the Arabic notation
is still going on. Kiesewetter, a hundred years ago, condemned it sharply.
(*Musik der Araber*, p. 66–68) He wrote:
 *"Allein, es scheint den Orientalen zu allen Zeiten die Eitelkeit eigen gewesen
 zu sein, das sich ihnen darbietende Einfachere und Leichtere von der Hand zu
 weisen, um kuenstlichere, . . . auf die Bewunderung der Laien berechnete
 Erklaerungen und Methoden aufzusuchen.*
H. G. Farmer, in our day defends the Arabic system of notation and calls it
a letter-notation, not a tablature. He furthermore attempts to prove that this
complex and awkward system influenced the European notation of Hucbald
and his followers. Cf. *History of Arabian Music*, p. 95, also *An Old Moorish
Lute-Tutor*, p. 27.
 [34] *Infra*, chap. v on Harmony!
 [35] Cf. G. Reese's excellent work on the *Music of the Middle Ages*, p. 118,
where he states: "In the Middle Ages, Music was looked upon as a branch of
Mathematics, — a view that never has been and probably never will be altogether discarded, since there is much truth in it."
 [36] The term *numerus harmonicus* has already been used as ארך הנגינות by
Abraham Ibn Ezra, as we see in his ספר המספר ed. Silberberg, p. 47 ff. The
editor of Gersonides' work, Joseph Carlebach, admits freely, (p. 142, note 3).
that he was unable to detect the musical implications of Gersonides' book,
This was due to the misleading title which is a musical as well as a mathe-

After this digression, we resume our discussion of the Hebrew conception of music, as expressed by the few medieval sources which are immediately available.[37]

> *Musica est exercitium arithmeticum occultum nescientis se numerare animi. Errant enim qui nihil in anima fieri putant, cuius ipsa non sit conscia.* — LEIBNITZ.[38]

II

DEFINITION AND CLASSIFICATION OF MUSIC

In general, medieval Jewish literature knows of two more or less opposing conceptions of music, between which a third, an eclectic conception attempts to mediate. Since the Jews were largely under the spell of Arabic writers in all secular issues, we need not marvel that views of music which appear in Arabic theory should be identical with Jewish views. Ancient Greek ideas, in turn, dominated the Arabs. As a result, those Greek principles are to be encountered again and again in Hebrew literature. The

---

matical term. The solution of this problem, i. e., the relation of the book to musical theory lies, we believe, in the system of rhythmic division and notation, as created by Philipp de Vitry. I cannot fully explain here the importance of Gersonides' thesis for Vitry's sytem, but in my opinion there is no doubt that it conceded the strictly mathematical foundation of Vitry's *quatre prolations*. I shall explain the real meaning of Ralbag's great contribution to the new system of the *ars nova* in a special study.

[37] Of the MSS which were not available to us we mention the following:
Abu'l Salt's treatise on Music, MS P 1037, cf. Steinschneider, *Hebr. Uebers.* p. 855.

Yehuda b. Isaac, cf. Steinschn. *Hebr. Uebers.* p. 970, and notes 158,159.

Anonymous treatise כללים ממושיקא MS Halberstam 49 f. 388, cf. Steinschn. *ibid.* note 58.

I am convinced, however, basing my belief on Aubry's *Iter Hispanicum*, (*Sammelbde. d. Internat. Musik-Gesellschaft* 1906/7) and the latest discoveries of Higini Angles, (Cf. *Mus. Quarterly* 1940 p. 524) that some Judaeo-Arabic MSS on Music still repose undiscovered in the libraries of Spain, probably in Toledo, in Cordova, or in the Escurial.

[38] *Epistolae ad div.*, ed. Korthold, p. 239.

representatives of the three ancient attitudes were: (1) The Neo-
Platonists and the Pythagoreans, (2) the Aristoxenians, and
(3) mediating between the two, the followers of the Peripatetic
school of Aristotle. Since the last, employing in his ideas on
music elements of both the Pythagoreans and Aristoxenians,[39]
was considered by the Arabs one of the highest authorities on
everything but matters religious, we find his ideas, sometimes
modified, sometimes amplified, in both the Arabic and the Jewish
treatises on musical theory. For all that, the old dispute between
the Neoplatonists and Pythagoreans on the one hand, and the
Aristoxenians on the other, outlasted all attempts at mediation.
And that perennial controversy — even if in an indirect way —
determined not a few of the Arabic and the Jewish notions. Since
we shall frequently refer to those antithetical conceptions, we
think it suitable to explain briefly the chief differences between
them.

According to the Pythagoreans, the human soul is in constant
motion. This motion is defined by certain numerical proportions
which attend the harmonic relations of the tones.[40] Therefore,
certain tunes evoke corresponding motions of the listener's soul.
The mathematical analogy between the ratios of the soul's motion, the vibration of strings, and finally the movements of the
heavenly bodies, constitutes the basis upon which rests the
principle of ethical power — ἐπανόρθωσις τῶν ἠθῶν. The idea of
the moral *katharsis* of the emotions,[41] as proclaimed by Aristotle
and his followers, is closely related to the older Pythagorean
ideology. The connection between body and soul is improved
and "harmonized" by properly selected tunes, and this involves
also the idea of music as effective medical treatment. The motions
of the celestial bodies, of the *Macrocosmos*, are supposed to be

[39] On Aristotle and Music cf. A Kahl, *Die Philosophie d. Musik nach
Arist.* H. Abert, *Die Lehre vom Ethos in d. Griech. Musik* §§4 and 5; Th. Reinach, *La Musique Greque*; W. Vetter, *Die antike Musik in d. Beleuchtung
durch Arist.* (in *Archiv fuer Musikwissenschaft* 1936, 2) — to quote only the
best and most recent studies.
[40] Cl. Ptolemaeus, *Harmonica*, III, chap. iv.
[41] We are using in this study the term *emotion* in place of the more correct,
but unusual *affectus*. The terms are not quite identical, however, and we apologize for this lack of correctness.

paralleled by those of the soul.[42] Thus a complicated numerical calculation in musical astrology begins to take shape.[43]

Much more practical was the ideology of the Aristoxenians. The Aristoxenians approached music entirely from the acoustic point of view, relying upon the ear rather than upon mathematics. The conception of a human microcosm, brought into harmony with the universal macrocosm by means of music, was not among the teachings which the Aristoxenians stressed.[44] The Platonic, and still more, the Aristotelian theories attempt to reconcile the aforementioned philosophies by conceding the effect of music upon the human soul, but cautiously avoiding definite commitments concerning mathematical and astronomical concepts.

Many of these speculations entered into Hebrew literature. Even in the realm of definitions and classifications of music we shall encounter some of them and shall compare them with Jewish and Arabic statements.

However, a word of caution may be in place. The ideas with which this study is concerned refer to the somewhat *artificial* music of the Arabs and the Jews and do not necessarily apply to their genuine folk-music. We have every reason to assume that the folksong of the Near East, as we know it today, with all of its tendencies toward the ecstatic and the wild, (in short, toward the Dionysic) is not much different from that which prevailed in the Middle Ages. The artistic music with which we are dealing, was originally under suspicion by the vast majority of the orthodox, chiefly on account of its secular attitude and its patronage

---

[42] Cf. Plato, *Timaeus*, 34 B.

[43] If H. Abert in his *Lehre vom Ethos in d. griech. Musik* disposes of this entire system with the words "gelehrte Tifteleien" (learned hairsplitting), then let us remember the enormous influence of this great conception upon philosophy, aesthetics, music, and astronomy until Newton. Even in such sober books as those of the modern astronomer Eddington we may find speculations, which are closely related to Pythagorean ideas. At any rate, Abert's rash statement could hardly be sustained in our times.

[44] Cf. Westphal-Rossbach, *Die musischen Kuenste der Hellenen*; (still the best paraphrased edition of Aristoxenos). Also Winnington-Ingram, *Aristoxenos and the Intervals*, (in *Classical Quarterly* 1932, p. 195). H. Abert, *op. cit.*, and Laloy, *Aristoxène de Tarent*.

by the courts of the Caliphs.[45] Nonetheless, in the course of centuries, it gained popularity and strongly influenced the music of the people. Perhaps there occurred a certain assimilation to popular taste. Still, the simple Arab or Jew did not trouble much about musical theories, certainly no more than the average American troubles about musical science today.

In general it is a science (חכמה) of propaedeutics, seeking powers that go far beyond the aims of the other sciences. The other sciences comprise merely knowledge and information.[46]

Following the Platonic principle that knowledge conduces to virtue, we read: "Music leads to spiritual knowledge."[47] It is sometimes called "An occupation" (מלאכה).[48] Above all, it is supposed "to be a mathematical science, involving arithmetical and geometrical proportions."[49]

Much more simply and with deliberate restraint, Bottarel defines it thus: "חכמת השיר והניגון — this is Music; the science of melody, the motion of ascending and descending tones, as well as the study of intervals."[50] Quite in the same vein, which is closely Aristoxenian, Izaiah b. Isaac states in his commentary to Avicenna's *Al-kanun*: "The task of Music is the composition of *laḥanim*.[51] The elements of which the *laḥanim* consist are divisible into two groups: 1. the individual tones (נעימות), and 2. structure or shape (חבור). The first one is the matter (חומר) and the second is the form of completed melodies (לחנים)."[52] Yehuda Halevy

---

[45] Cf. Julian Ribera, *Music in Ancient Arabia and Spain*, chap. iii (end), vi (end), p. 72 *et passim*.

[46] *Infra*, chaps. iii and iv.

[47] Cf. Texts A, XIX, 13. Beethoven's proud words: "*Musik ist hoehere Offenbarung als alle Weisheit und Philosophie*" expresses exactly the same idea. *See infra* appendix of translated passages!

[48] Cf. Texts A, XIX, 24. *See infra* appendix of translated passages!

[49] Cf. Abr. Ibn Ezra: "והדרך השלישי ערכי חכמת הנגינות והיא חכמה מפוארת מאד כי ערכיה מורכבים מערכי החשבון וערכי המדות... (cf. Silberberg, ספר המספר des Ibn Ezra, Hebr. part, p. 46.)

[50] Cf. Bottarel, Comment. on the *Sefer Yezirah*. (according to the ברית מנוחה of Abr. of Granada.)

[51] For all following terms cf. *infra* chap. VI., (Terminology).

[52] Cf. Texts G, #2. Compare with it the first definition of Aristides Quintilianus: "Music is the science of the melodies and of their parts and properties." (Arist. Quint. ed. Meibom. p. 6.) *See infra* appendix of translated passages!

recognizes both of the Pythagorean aspects of music, the ethical
as well as the mathematical. "Music was then (in David's time)
a perfect art. It wielded that influence upon the soul which we
attribute to it, namely, that of moving the soul from one mood
to another." Again: "Measures, weights, the proportions of
various movements, the harmony of Music, everything is in
number." (ספר).[53] Likewise following the Greek trend of thought
is the definition to be found in Honein-Alharizi's *"Maxims of
the Philosophers"*: "Music is an art which links every species
with its own . . . it stirs up that which is at rest and brings to
rest that which is in motion."[54] The difference of opinion mentioned in the discussion of the Greek Schools can also be found
in the *classification* of music in which, we believe, the genuine
spirit of the Greek authors still lives, though somewhat faded
and obscured. Jewish literature, as well as Arabic literature,
knows of three ways of classification: 1. by separating theory
and practice, 2. by distinguishing between natural and artificial
music, and 3. by noting the effects upon the listener. Ibn 'Aknin
represents the first category; likewise Falaquera who offers in
his *Rešit Hokma* almost the same text as Ibn 'Aknin. We shall
later refer to that classification as a classic example of the continuity and virtual identity of the Greek-Arabic-Hebrew-Latin
tradition of musical philosophy. The second method is employed
chiefly by Saadya Gaon and his commentators, especially Abraham b. Ḥiyya, the Pseudo-Bereḥya, and the three disciples of
Frat Maimon, viz. Jacob b. Ḥayyim, Salomon b. Yehuda and
Nathanael Caspi.[55] Saadya himself, in the introduction of his
Emunot W'de'ot divides music into natural and artificial types.[56]
The third method, which is somewhat frequent in Arabic literature, is employed by Honein-Alharizi, by the *Ikhvan es-Safa* and

[53] Cf. Yehuda Halevy, *Cusari*, ed. Cassel, II §65 and IV. §25.
[54] Cf. Texts A, XX, 4. It is not by matter of chance Euclid, the Pythagorean,
who is here credited with such a statement. Compare with this maxim Texts
A XVIII 3, and Aristides Quintilian, (ed. Meibom), p. 107, where the same
characteristic is affirmed. *See infra* appendix of translated passages!
[55] Cf. Steinschneider, *HB* XIII, p. 36 ff.
[56] Cf. Texts B 1. See also Jacob Guttmann, *Die Religionsphilosophie des
Saadya Gaon*, p. 286. A very similar classification is given by Cassiodorus,
Patrol. Lat. LXX, 1208 ff.

by Alfarabi.[57] It is, as we shall presently see, the favorite method of the Arabic writers. In Honein-Alharizi's *"Maxims of the Philosophers"* we read: "There are three sorts of arts: 1. those in which speech preponderates over action; 2. those in which there is more action than speech; 3. those again in which speech and action are equipollent. To the first belongs the telling of stories and fables . . . The arts in which there is more action than speech are represented by the physician . . . The art of Music is that in which action is equipollent to speech. Music, therefore, is the best art, provided that its speech comports entirely with its works, as in the case of a lute-player whose melody corresponds with his movements."[58]

This evaluation of music is obviously based on hermeneutic principles. We find similar ideas in Pseudo-Aristotle's *Problems* XIX, 27. And quite unequivocally the authentic Aristotle states: "We approve of the classification of all tunes and melodies . . . into such as possess *ethos* ($\dot{\eta}\vartheta\iota\kappa\alpha\dot{\iota}$), such as express energetic action ($\pi\rho\alpha\kappa\tau\iota\kappa\alpha\dot{\iota}$) and such as evoke enthusiasm ($\dot{\epsilon}\nu\vartheta o\upsilon\sigma\iota\alpha\sigma$-$\tau\iota\kappa\alpha\dot{\iota}$)."[59] Classification on the basis of expression appears also in Alfarabi, in Ghazzali, in the *Ikhvan es-Safa*, and, above all, in the *Kitab al Aghani*, that rich treasury of musical facts and theories extant among the Arabs.[60] To that "expressionistic" classification we shall occasionally revert.

Of those three ways of classifying music, there is no doubt that, down to the seventeenth century, the first method, representing a very old tradition, wielded the strongest influence upon Western civilisation.

In order to exhibit the steady stream of tradition within the science of music, we compare, in the following pages, the classi-

---

[57] Cf. Texts A XIX, 1, 2 *et Passim.* XVIII, *passim. See infra* appendix of translated passages!

[58] Cf. Texts A XIX, 24. *See infra* appendix!

[59] Cf. Aristotle, Politics VIII, 6, 1341 B 32.

[60] Alfarabi, *Kitab al musiqi*, ed. D'Erlanger, I., p. 13.

Al-Gazzali, in Ribera, *op. cit.*, p. 90.

Die Enzyklopaedie der Lauteren Brueder, (*Ikhvan es-Safa* — encycl. of the Brethren of Purity) ed. Dieterici, chap. Music.

Kitab al-Aghani, in Ribera, *op. cit.* p. 89, *et passim.*

fications of music proposed by a Greek (Aristides Quintilianus), an Arab (Alfarabi), a Jew (Falaquera), and a Spanish Christian (Dom. Gundissalinus).[61]

TABLE 1

ARISTIDES QUINTILIANUS (ED. MEIBOM, P. 7 FF.)

Music as a whole admits of subdivision into a theoretical part and a practical part.

The theoretical part is that, in the first place, which comprehends, with precision and exactness, the technical rules. These include the highest postulates as well as the derivatives. This part also undertakes observations relating to the highest, the most general principles; which means the elements and their ultimate source in Nature as well as their consonance with the things of Existence.

The practical part is that which, operating in accordance with the technical rules, pursues the end and aim to which music is dedicated; wherefore this part is characterized as pedagogical.

The theoretical part admits of subdivision into the physical (the natural) and the technical (artificial). One portion of the physical comprises the doctrine of numbers. The other portion

[61] The sources of our tabulation:
1. Aristides Quintilianus *De Musica*, translated by R. Schaefke, p. 167. *Idem*, ed. Meibom, pp. 7/8.
2. Alfarabi, *De Ortu Scientiarum*, ed. Baeumker, in *Beitr. zur Philos. des Mittelalters* XX, pp. 3/ff.
   Alfarabi, *De Scientiis*, in Farmer, *Alfarabi's Arabic-Latin Writings on Music*, pp. 21–31.
3. Falaquera, *Reshit Ḥokma*, cf. Texts E 1.
4. D. Gundissalinus, *De Divisione Philosophiae*, ed. L. Baur (in *Beitr. zur Philos. d. Mittelalters* IV., pp. 96–102). Here Aristides is recognised as source of Alfarabi. Cf. pp. 240–46.
   That Falaquera translated almost literally Alfarabi's *De Scientiis*, (Ihsa' al-'ulum), is well known, cf. Brockelmann, *Geschichte d. arab. Literatur, I. Supplem.*, p. 377; *see also* L. Straus in *MGWJ* 1936.

bears the same terminology as the genus which includes it, namely, "physical." It is this latter portion that undertakes the surmises regarding the things of Existence. The divisions of the technical are Harmony, Rythm, and Meter.

The practical part subdivides into:

1. The application of the aforementioned three technical divisions to the process of musical composition.

2. Directions as to the manner in which these divisions should be presented.

The subdivisions of the first point are: Construction of Melodies, Formation of Rythm, and Poetry. The following is the systematic classification according to Schaefke, *Aristides Quintilianus*, p. 67.

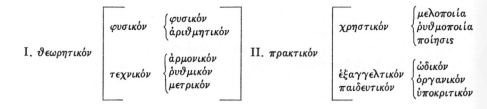

TABLE 2

ALFARABI, IHSA'AL-'ULUM (DE SCIENTIIS), ED. FARMER, GLASGOW 1934

"Scientia vero musice, comprehendit in summa, cognitionem specierum armoniarum; et illud ex quo componuntur, et illud ad quod componuntur, et qualiter componuntur, et quibus modis oportet . . . Et illud quidem quod hoc nomine cognoscitur, est due scientiae. Quam una est scientia musice activa, et secunda scientia musice speculativa. Musica quidem activa, est illa cuius proprietas est ut inveniat species armoniarum sensativarum in instrumentis que preparata sunt eis aut per naturam aut per artem. Instrumenta quidem naturalia, sunt epiglotis, . . . deinde nasus. Et artificialia sunt sicut fistule et cithare, et alia. Et opifex quidem musice active, non format neumas, et armonias, et omnia accidentia eorum, nisi secundum quod sunt in instrumentis quorum acceptio consueta est in eis. Et speculativa quidem dat scientiam eorum, et sunt rationata, et dat causas totius ex quo componuntur armoniae, non secundum quod sunt in materia . . . et secundum quod sunt remota ab omni instrumento et materia . . . Et dividitur scientia musice speculativa, in partes magnas quinque. Prima eorum, est sermo de principiis, et primis quorum proprietas est ut administrentur in inventione eius quod est in hac scientia . . . Et secunda est sermo de dispositionibus huius artis, et est sermo in inveniendo neumas, et cognitione numerum neumatum quot sint, et quot species eorum . . . Et tertia est sermo de convenientia que declaratur in radicibus cum sermonibus et demonstrationibus . . . Et quarta est sermo de speciebus casuum naturalium qui sunt pondera neumatum. Et quinta est de compositione armoniarum in summa, deinde de compositione armoniarum integrarum . . . in sermonibus metricis . . . et qualitate artis eorum secundum unamquamque intentionem armoniarum, et docet dispositiones quibus fiunt penetrabiliores, et magis ultime in ultimitate intentionis ad quam facte sunt.''

TABLE 3

FALAQUERA, RESHIT ḤOKMA (ED. DAVID, P. 46–47)

The science of Music falls into two divisions, that of theory and that of practice.

Musical practice consists in producing audible tones by means of instruments, natural and artificial. A natural instrument is the throat and the organs of the mouth together with the adjacent nasal passages. Artificial instruments are such as harps, psalteries and the like.

The expert at musical practice devises such melodies and harmonies as are customarily extracted from musical instruments because they are latent in those instruments.

Musical theory yields systematic knowledge regarding the causes of melodies and their relationships. It considers melodies not as physically mediated but melodies in general — detached from all instrumentation or material embodiment. It ponders melody in the abstract, as something heard, regardless of the instrument or the organism that may function incidentally.

Musical theory admits, in turn, of five large subdivisions:

1. The first discourses on the principles used by investigators, on the manner in which those principles are employed, on the way in which research is initiated and the steps by which it is brought to completion, and on the proper methods of inquiry.

2. The second discourses on the elements, that is, on the manner in which melodies are produced as well as on the number and the variety of their modes. This division explains the proportions which melodies bear toward one another. It provides the needed demonstrations. It also considers the various dispositions and sequences by means of which melodies are constructed, thus enabling one engaged in musical composition to choose what he desires.

3. The third division deals with the consonance between the aforementioned elements, discourses, and proofs on the one hand. On the other hand, it deals with the instruments devised for this art and with the production of melodies and their instrumental performance according to the proportions and the sequences explained in division two.

4. The fourth division discourses on the various musical patterns in nature by which melodies are measured, i. e. rhythmic qualities.

5. The fifth division discourses upon the construction of music in its completeness, that is, the adaptation of melodies to words composed with meter and rythm. This division also ponders the question of rendition in accordance with musical intent. It considers what melodies are suitable and adapted to the respective purposes for which songs are designed.

Systematic classification (E. W.) gives us the following:

THEORY	PRACTICE
1. Principles	1. Teaching of music, to be played on instruments, either natural or artificial.
2. Arithmetical elements	
3. Rules of instrumental composition	
4. Rhythmic measures and modes	2. Practical composition of tunes.
5. Composition of metrical tunes	

TABLE 4

DOM. GUNDISSALINUS, DE DIVISIONE PHILOSOPHIAE
(ED. L. BAUR, P. 98)

(In this text we have adapted the common Latin orthography for the sake of convenience.)

Partes vero alias habet theorica, alias practica. Partes practicae sunt tres: scientia de acuto sono et scientia de gravi et scientia de medio. De his enim tractat ostendens utilitatem eorum et comparationes inter se, et quomodo ex eis componuntur cantilenae.

Partes vero theoricae sunt quinque, quarum prima est scientia de principiis et primis, quae debent administrari in acceptione eius . . . secunda est doctrina de dispositionibus huius artis, scil. inveniendi neumata et cognoscendi numeros eorum . . ., tertia est doctrina de convenientia principiorum et de sermonibus et demonstrationibus specierum, instrumentorum artificialium . . ., quarta est doctrina de speciebus casum naturalium, quae sunt pondera neumatum. Quinta est doctrina de compositione armoniarum in summa; deinde de compositione armoniarum integrarum, scil. illarum, quae sunt positae in sermonibus metricis compositis secundum ordinem . . . et qualitatem artis eorum secundum unamquamque intentionem armoniarum. Systematic classification. (E. W.)

THEORETICA	PRACTICA
1. Principia	De acuto sono
2. Dispositiones arithmeticae	De gravi sono
3. Convenientia et compositio	De medio sono
musicae instrumentalis	utilitates tonorum ac modorum
4. Elementa rhythmica	Melopoiia practica
5. Compositio cantuum metricorum	

Surveying Gundissalinus' classifications, we realize that he, eclectic as he was, employed all three methods of classification. In the quotation above, he copies Alfarabi's *De Scientiis* almost verbatim. Again, in the paragraphs preceding this quotation, he uses Boethius' famous classification of *musica mundana, humana et instrumentalis*. In the paragraphs following this quotation, he employs the evaluative classification given by Alfarabi in

De Ortu Scientiarum[62] and by earlier sources, e. g. Isidor's Etymology.[63]

It is clear that Alfarabi had already altered the Greek source somewhat and, what is more, that Gundissalinus had apparently gotten matters mixed. Incidentally, we may mention that Gundissalinus collaborated with a Jewish translator, Johannes Hispalensis.[64]

As a whole, however, we recognize the uninterrupted flow of musical philosophy from the Greeks down to such late medieval authors as Johannes de Muris or Ugolino de Orvieto — through Syrian, Arabic, Jewish, and Spanish writers.

III

PHILOSOPHY OF MUSIC

Since music belongs to the propaedeutic sciences, it is frequently associated with physics. In fact, the interest of Arabic and Jewish philosophers in acoustics exerted a fruitful influence upon the development of musical theory and philosophy. Accordingly, before entering upon the discussion of their philosophical ideas, we shall give a short account of acoustic theories as set forth by the medieval philosophers. In general, these rest upon a valid empirical foundation which, without the help of our modern exact sciences, sometimes lead to surprisingly correct conclusions regarding the nature of sound and of tone.

As with the other natural sciences, the ancient Greeks were the recognized teachers in this field. According to Aristotle, his disciples, and commentators, especially Porphyry, sound is a movement of the air, caused by the percussion of objects that are struck. With the diffusion of the vibrating air in three dimensions — according to Priscian — sound, carried by the air, reaches the ear, unless it is dulled by excessive distances or

---

[62] Recently Alfarabi's authorship for *De Ortu Scientiarum* has been disputed, cf. Farmer, "A Further Arab-Latin writer on Music" in *JRAS* 1933.

[63] Cf. L. Baur, *op.cit.*, p. 247.

[64] Cf. Steinschneider, *Hebr. Uebers.*, pp. 261, 282, 292.

obstructed.[65] Sound, in contradistinction to music, is due to an unregulated multiplicity of tones. This comes fairly near to our modern acoustic theories.[66]

Turning from the physical to the physiological, we meet the somewhat strange conception that music affects the "humors" of the human body. Here the Arabs and the Jews went far beyond the original Greek idea. The Greeks, as we have seen, asserted a close relationship between music and medicine, ascribing to music a distinctly therapeutic effect both upon body and upon soul. But, while Plato, Aristotle, and the Neo-Platonists were content to state the fact, explaining it by the cathartic and sedative influence of the musical art, the Arabic and the Jewish philosophers went boldly and almost materialistically into physiological details. They emphasized the effect of music on the humors, blood, phlegm, yellow bile, and black bile. Let us compare some of the most significant statements on these points. Leaving aside the many legends of the Greeks, Arabs, and Jews, telling how music cured some highly phantastic ailments, we turn to the ideas which lie behind these stories.

The Greeks linked medicine and music in two different ways:

1. The Pythagoreans consider number and proportion as instruments of the imitative principle ($\mu\iota\mu\eta\sigma\iota\varsigma$) which prevails in all of the arts. This is somewhat similar to the thought of the Aristotelians.[67] Thus Music, Medicine and Mathematics employ the same fundamentals; Music in rhythms, intervals and proportions, Medicine in the proportion of the humors and medicaments, and, particularly, in the mysterious ratios of human pulsation,[68] while in Mathematics, number and proportion are

[65] On the ancient theory of acoustics see: C. v. Jan, *Musici scriptores Graeci*, 3–35, 50 ff.; E. Hommel, *Untersuchungen zur Hebr. Lautlehre*, p. 35 ff.; Diels, *Ueber d. Physikalische System d. Straton*, p. 144; D. Kaufmann, *Die Sinne*, p. 127 ff.

[66] Cf. Saadya, *Emunot W'De'ot*, ed. Slucki, p. 4. (introduction.) Also Alfarabi, *Kitab al musiqi*, ed. D'Erlanger, I., p. 80. (Henceforth *Kitab*.)

[67] Cf. Aristotle, *Metaphysic* I., 6, 987 b 11., οἱ μὲν γὰρ Πυθαγόρειοι μιμή- σει τὰ ὄντα φασὶν εἶναι τῶν ἀριθμῶν.

[68] Aristides Quint. elaborates upon the theory of pulsation in true Pythagorean spirit: "The pulsation which corresponds to normal circumstances — analogous to the octave 1:2, or to the fifth 2:3, or to the fourth 3:4, — does

the working material itself. Plato expresses similar ideas in his *Timaeus*.

2. The other link between Music and Medicine is more physiological. It is based chiefly on the term *Katharsis* in a medical sense. Aristotle as well as Galen use this word with the connotation of "purgation." Considering how Jacob Bernays has exhibited the predominantly medical background of the entire cathartic idea, we could characterize this principle as that of a treatment basically homoepathic.[69] The Neo-Platonists, Proclos and Jamblichos, accepted Aristotle's explanation. Cure was accomplished, according to the *Aristotelian* prescription, by playing, before the insane corybantes, frantic melodies on the orgiastic instrument, the Phrygian *aulos*. Thus, *Katharsis* was brought about *homoepathically*. The *Pythagoreans*, however, preferred the playing of solemn, soothing melodies for the maniacal listeners in order to impress upon their disorganized souls, the magically numerical and cosmic order, attuning them, as it were, to the proportions of the Universe. This is the type of *Katharsis* that is *allopathic*.[70]

The literature of the Arabs and the Jews discusses only the *allopathic* form of treatment although, in their philosophy, cathartic elements still play a part. But, for therapeutic purposes, Arabs and Jews seem to have relied entirely on Pythagorean principles, which they stressed to the limits of the absurd. Being good physicians, keen observers, and consistent logicians, the Arabs zealously embodied everything in their Pythagorean con-

---

not necessarily endanger life ... Those pulsations, however, which present themselves in an entirely non-consonant ratio ..., are dangerous and may bring death." (ed. Meibom, p. 127.) The entire medieval theory is full of similar statements. Cf. Boethius, *De musica*, (Patr. Lat. LXIII, 1170) who is the chief source for all further speculation.

[69] Aristotle, Pol. VIII, 1341 b 32. We give here part of his report:

"We see that if those insane persons (ἐνϑουσιαστικοί) listen to enthusiastic melodies which intoxicate their souls, they are brought back to themselves again, so that their catharsis takes place exactly like a medical treatment." He relates how corybantes were cured by listening to corybantic tunes. (*Ibid.*, 1340 b 8.)

[70] Aristides *Quint.* ed. Meibom, (henceforth *AQM*), pp. 103–107.

cept. Accordingly, each musical mode, even each string of their chief instrument, the 'ud, had to be seen *sub specie mundi*. The four seasons, the four humors, the four cardinal virtues, and the four elements had to be embodied in their musical theory.[71]

We find in Honein-Alharizi's *Maxims of the Philosophers* a characteristic statement: "The reason for our making four strings is their correspondence to the four temperaments of which man is composed."[72] The author goes on to associate with every string of the 'ud a special effect upon some special humor. No less specific is Falaquera, and also Saadya who, in his *Emunot wede'ot* chapter 10 (end), connects every rhythmical mode (Arab. *naghama*, Hebr. נגינה, נעימה) with one humor and one virtue respectively. Since Saadya explains certain technical points in that passage, we shall deal extensively with his statements later on. A highly important source for our subject is also the *Ikhvan es-Safa* from which Saadya may possibly have borrowed.[73]

We quote now a few sentences from the *Ikhvan es-Safa* by way of illustration:

"The musicians restrict the number of the strings of the lute to four,[74] neither more nor less, in order that their work might

---

[71] Although Greek literature offered the basis for the scheme, it was the more radical Arabs and Jews who tried to link anything and everything to their musical system. Whatever the Christian writers wrote in this fashion was always borrowed from the Arabs, even with the help of Arabic words. Thus, in Odo de Clugny's and in Hucbald's writings occur words like *scembs*, *kaphe*, *neth*, *caemar*, clearly recognisable as Arabic terms. Yet the Christian authors do not know their origin or their meanings. Cf. Gerbert, *Scriptores* I, 249. Even in our day it could happen that a scholar like G. Lange, (on his article on solmization, *SIMG*, I, 539 ff.) did not recognize the Arabic origin of Odo's syllables.

[72] Cf. Texts A XX, 1, and D 2, third question. *See infra* appendix of translated passages!

[73] Cf. Jacob Guttmann, *Die Religionsphilosophie des Saadya Gaon*, p. 287 ff., stresses the almost verbal similarity of the *Ikhvan* with Saadya's text in the musical portion. Since Honein is older than both Saadya and the *Ikhvan*, we have to look for a common (probably Syrian) source, from which all the three authors drew. Cf. Baumstark, *Aristoteles bei den Syrern*, I., pp. x–xii.

[74] Cf. Farmer, *An old Moorish Lute-tutor*, p. 38: "Ziryab claimed to have added a fifth string to the lute . . . Naturally, he had to connect it with the cosmic scheme and hence associated it with a fifth nature — the soul. What

resemble the things of sublunar nature in imitation of God's wisdom.

> "The treble string is like the element of fire, its tone being hot and violent.
> "The second string is like the element of air; its tone corresponds to the humidity of air and to its softness.
> "The third string is like the element of water; its tone suggests water-like moisture and coolness.
> The bass string is like the heaviness and thickness of the element earth."

Subsequently, the treble string corresponds to the yellow bile, the second string to the blood, the third string to the saliva, the bass string to the black bile, as elaborately explained.

Our source continues: "If one employs these tones in appropriate melodies and uses these melodies at those times of the night or day the nature of which is opposed to the nature of a virulent disease . . ., they assuage the sickness, breaking up its force and relieving the sick ones of their pains."[75]

Thus music was generally considered a strictly allopathic, pain-relieving, or invigorating medicine corresponding to the mixtures of the humors and of the elements. Ibn-Sina refers to these matters frequently in his *Alkanun*.[76] Throughout Arabic literature, the Pythagorean relationship between Astronomy, Music, and Medicine is consistently maintained.

Falaquera's *Mebbakkesh* (39b) closely follows these ideas. This work is a poetic revision of his aforementioned earlier work

would have prompted this association? In the Pseudo-Aristotelian *De Mundo* (393a) we find a fifth element,— ether, which occurs in the *De Musica* of Aristides Quintilianus."

[75] *Ikhvan es-Safa*, ed. Dieterici, (henceforth Diet.) Die Propaedeutik der Araber, pp. 126–28. Also *infra*, appendix of translated passages.

[76] The medico-musical system, as accepted by Arabs and Jews, admits of this tabulation.

STRING	ELEMENT	HUMOUR	QUALITY	SEASON
Zīr, (treble)	fire	yellow bile	hot	summer
Mathnā, (2nd)	air	blood	humid	spring
Mathlath, (3rd)	water	phlegm	cold	winter
Bam, (bass)	earth	black bile	dry	autumn

Rešit Ḥokma, with a stronger emphasis on the Pythagorean
point of view.[77]

The Christian theorists of the thirteenth and fourteenth
century, perhaps even earlier, adopted Judaeo-Arabic concepts
to such an extent that a considerable influx of semitic theory
into the medieval world can not be denied. As an important
translator from the Arabic, we have already mentioned Gundissalinus. We give one other example by quoting a passage of
Aegidius Zamorensis, an author of the thirteenth century, who
in his *Ars Musica* says:[78] "The joining of the elements comes to
resemble a harmony such as results from a fitting consonance
of strings and a clear combination of tones. The seasons likewise
correspond to the elements and vice versa. Air corresponds to
Spring, Fire to Summer, Earth to Autumn, Water to Winter.
Thus the eternal God grants us seasons, linked with most fitting
melodies, in order to alleviate man's labors. Air, furthermore
corresponds to Blood, Fire and Summer to Yellow Bile, Earth
and Autumn to Black Bile, Water and Winter to Phlegm . . ."

From here it is only a short step, in fact an imperceptible
gradation to a detailed and elaborate theory of the influence of
music upon the individual emotions. We also find in the Jewish

---

[77] On the relation between Falaquera, Ibn 'Aknin, and Alfarabi, *see*
Farmer, *Alfarabi's Arabic-Latin Writings on Music*, p. 6, 57, where a very
clear picture is given. Also Steinschneider, *Hebr. Uebers.*, §12. Thus, Guedemann's assertion of an allegedly Averroes-influence is no longer tenable.

[78] Cf. Gerbert, *Scriptores* II, 376. Of the many fitting instances we selected
just this one in order to refute Pietzsch' statement "that this treatise, in contradistinction to the others previously mentioned, does not show a recognizable
influence by the Arabian theory" (*op. cit.* p. 95). The connection with the
medico-musical theories of the Arabs is quite unmistakable. However, the
general extent of Arabic influence upon Western theory is still greatly disputed
and some caution in this matter is certainly desirable. Cf. the controversy
between K. Schlesinger and H. G. Farmer in his book, *Historical facts for the
influence of Ar. Music. See also* O. Ursprung, *Um die Frage nach d. arab. Ein-
fluss auf d. abendlaendische Mus. d. Mittelalters,* in *Zeitschrift f. Mus.-Wiss.*
1934, p. 129 ff., with whose conclusions we disagree entirely. Cf. Ribera, *op.
cit.* chaps. vii–xii. A brief and cautious summary of this disputed question in
Reese, *op. cit.*, p. 118 ff., 245 *et passim*. In Ath. Kircher's *Musurgia universalis,*
(17th cent.!) we find all of the Graeco-Arabic ideas taken up and elaborated.
(*Liber diacriticus, Erothema* VI–VIII).

and Arabic authors originally Greek doctrines expanded and augmented. It seems however that, in this field, the oriental nations preferred less of system and more of detail, fewer explanations and more plain statements. There are even more significant differences which we shall consider presently.

We are confronted now with a perennial problem of philosophy and aesthetics, a problem which concerns us today as much as it did three thousand years ago, and a problem which is unlikely ever to be solved objectively. Since it cannot be our task to discuss that problem here, we shall only describe the different attitudes toward the problem found in Greek, Arabic, and Hebrew Literature.

The problem to which we refer poses two chief questions which we shall cite cursorily:

1. Does music express emotions, and if so, how?
2. Does music evoke emotions, and if so, how?

We may, again in a cursory way, name the first question as one relating to the expressive powers of music and the other as relating to the impressive powers. The very approach to these problems differs and shows unique characteristics for Greek, Jewish, and Arabic authors, although the answers frequently sound similar. But these apparently similar answers must not deceive us about the fundamentally different attitudes assumed. The Greeks consider the issue either from the psychological-ethical side exemplified by the Pythagoreans, Platonists, Aristotelians, or from the purely aesthetic-formalistic side as exemplified by the Sceptics and the Sophists. Both questions are answered in the affirmative by the first group, while the Sophists deny at least the first question and restrict their affirmative answer of the second to a few cases. They explain the influence of music upon the emotions by a materialistic theory of the association of words and ideas.[79] Furthermore, the Greeks are

[79] Cf. Abert, *op. cit.*, §4, 5, 9, 11. The problem itself has created an enormous literature, of which we can not here give a comprehensive bibliography. We mention only the works, in which such bibliographies may be found: A. Aber, *Handbuch d. Musikliteratur*, pp. 470–90; E. Kurth, *Musikpsychologie*, (Index). It was this perennial problem, which created the famous struggle for and against Richard Wagner.

far more interested in the second question than in the first. Both questions were answered in the affirmative by Aristotle. To the first he applied the principle of μίμησις, i. e. imitation of the emotions. In dealing with the second, he modifies and even contradicts Plato's explicit evaluation or negation of certain modes and their *ethos*.[80]

Very clear in this respect is the doctrine of Aristoxenos, a disciple of Aristotle, who probably gave the first characterization of the three τρόποι (styles) viz. the *systaltic*, the *diastaltic*, and the *hesychastic*. The first is described as paralysing human energy. It includes love-songs as well as funereal lamentations. The second is strong and virile, spurs to action and thus becomes the heroic style employed in tragedy. The last is in between. It indicates and at the same time stimulates balance of mind and feeling.[81] We notice here, as a decisive criterion, the effect which music has upon human *will-power*. A *priori* Aristoxenos assumes that music *expresses* the same *ethos* which it is to *evoke* in the listener. In all cases, only such music is supposed to be good which arouses ethical powers and eventually dissipates emotions that are harmful or evil.[82] In short, the Greeks aim not to evoke stormy or violent feelings but to banish them, thus creating a happy philosophical balance of the soul.

Quite different is the Arabic approach and different again the Jewish approach. It is here that we find perhaps the only really important departure of the Jewish attitude from Arabic influence in the entire realm of musical problems. The Arabic writers either consider the question in its psycho-physiological, even in its materialistic aspect, or view it from the lofty tower of their metaphysical or mystical speculations.[83] If we ask which attitude

[80] Cf. Plato, Pol. III, 398 C–402. Aristotle, Pol. VIII, 7, 1342 a, b.

[81] Cf. H. Abert, *op. cit.*, pp. 67–69.

[82] Cf. Plutarch, *Quaest. conviv.* III, 8th question., c. 2. "The wailing-song and the funeral-flute excite pain and bring about tears, but afterwards attune the soul to compassion, gradually mitigating and annihilating the painful emotion."

[83] Cf. *Arabian Nights*, ed. Lane, p. 400: "Ibn Sina hath asserted that the lover's remedy consisteth in melodious sounds, And the company of one like his beloved . . ." *Ibid.*, p. 129, 302, *et passim*. Compare with this Shakespeare, *Twelfth Night*, I act, 1st scene: "If Music be the food of love, play on! . . ."

in Arabia was not that of the esoteric scholars but that of the people in general, there can be no doubt that the materialistic concept represented the common outlook.[84] The Arabs in general prefer emotional excitement to eudaemonic pacification. The philosophers discarded the sentiment of the masses and adopted much of the Greek ideology even if with some change of emphasis. However, the question of expression in music is deemed important by Alfarabi, though all but disregarded by the Greeks whose distinction between expressive and impressive Alfarabi had adopted.[85]

Arabic thinkers raised no issue about harmful and unpleasant emotions: "Other good melodies evoke such emotions as satisfaction, ire, clemency, cruelty, fear, sadness, regret, and other passions."[86]

While we find some aesthetic speculations in Arabic theory, Hebrew theory, though differing but slightly, is not concerned with aesthetics at all. This, to be sure, is nothing but an *argumentum e silentio*. Yet, considering the scantiness of Jewish literature in this field, the fact that genuinely aesthetic statements are altogether lacking, might hold some significance. The Jews set another principle as their highest, namely that of the כונה. This applies to medieval scholasticism as well as to the literature of the Cabalists and the Ḥasidim.[87]

[84] Cf. Doughty's statement about the polar nature of Arabic culture which is both rude and refined, containing materialistic and mystic elements at the same time. Also: "Music is in constant connection with everything intoxicating: wine, love, and ecstasy . . ." (Lachmann, *Musik des Orients*, pp. 98–101.)

[85] *Kitab* I, p. 13; also Texts A XX, 3. *See infra* appendix of translated passages.

[86] *Kitab* II., p. 89 ff.

[87] It is with regret that we have to record the lack of serious scholarly efforts in the difficult field of musical elements pervading the literature of the Cabalists and the Ḥasidim. Yet some useful references are given in Idelsohn, *Jewish Music*, pp. 410–434, and *Thesaurus*, vol. X, introduction; A. v. Thimus, *Die harmomikale Symbolik des Altertums*, 2 vols., a very interesting and stimulating, if somewhat confused book, filled with polyhistoric knowledge; A. Farwell, "The Sonata form and the Cabbala," (in *Musical Quarterly* 1941,1); E. Hommel, *op. cit.*, pp. xvi, xxvi, 31, 33, 70, 127, *et passim*.

This antinomy between the Arabic and the Jewish conception of music becomes most perceptible in Maimonides. What we have said about the state of Arabic music in his time sheds a new light on his known *responsum*. It becomes clear that Maimonides had in mind chiefly the exciting and sensual songs of the Arabs and the Arabian Jews.[88]

Maimonides makes three distinctions: 1) He admits that there are some few connoisseurs who study Music as a suitable means of reaching a higher wisdom (the Greek διανóη-σις). But, he continues, one must not base one's conclusions on these individual cases. The laws of the Torah were written not for exceptional people but for the majority. 2) The prohibition of secular music is based on Hos. 9.1; Isa. 5.12; Amos 6.5; and Ber. 24a, emphasizing that, in most instances, music does nothing but excite lust. It makes no difference whether the texts of the songs are in Arabic or in Hebrew; for not the language, but only the content of utterances matters. The Jewish people must become a holy nation, and must avoid everything which does not lead to perfection. 3) The music which is mentioned and even recommended by the Gaonim is of a purely religious character and consists of psalms, hymns, and songs of exultation. Secular music ought not to be tolerated; surely not when it is performed in a tavern and by all means not when performed by a singing female. Elsewhere, however, music as a therapeutic measure[89] recieves Maimonides' commendation.

All that separates the ideology of Jewish philosophers from the Arabic view is clearly recognizable in this *responsum*. Maimonides endorses *religious* music. He wishes to eliminate all secular music regardless of the few individuals who study such music in order to achieve a higher wisdom. He stresses the biblical and talmudic tradition and opposes the fashion of his time. In his preoccupation with the religio-ethical effects, Maimonides completely ignores aesthetic appreciation. (The same is true

[88] *Infra* appendix of translated passages. Goldziher, in *MGWJ* 1873 omits consideration of the tendency of Arabic music at the time of Maimonides.

[89] Here it is the *physician* Maimonides who speaks, the faithful disciple of the great Arabic tradition of medicine. Also *infra* appendix of translated passages. Cf. Maimonides, שמנה פרקים, ed. Gorfinkle, p. 30.

as we know, of his attitude toward poetry.)[90] On the whole,
Maimonides faithfully reflects the *Platonic* and not the *Aristotelian* viewpoint. Like Plato he gives an ethical evaluation rather
than an aesthetic classification.[91] Still there are also some deviations. The highest aim of the Greek philosopher-artist is the
world of Ideas. Music is only an instrument for ethical education,[92] and has all but lost its religious function. The highest
goal of Maimonides, on the other hand, is the intellectual and
ethical perfection which leads to the prophetic perception of
the Divine. Music may, in some cases, conduct one to this goal.
Nonetheless, music has no place in ethical training. Thus there

[90] Many centuries later, a truly Christian philosopher, a stranger to his
own contemporaries, displayed a somewhat similar attitude toward music.
In Kierkegaard's *Entweder Oder* we meet striking resemblances to Maimonides.
But the Danish thinker grants us a choice only between the beautiful and the
good, which becomes not a little difficult, when Kierkegaard makes Mozart
his champion of beauty.

[91] We set the typical statments of both Plato and Maimonides side by
side.

Plato, Legg. II 668 A, Pol. III. 398 C,
Pol. II. 376 E, Legg. II. 669 *etc.*

Maimonides, Responsum on Music

Then, when anyone says that Music
is to be judged by pleasure this cannot be admitted; and if there be any
Music of which pleasure is the criterion, such Music is not to be sought
out or deemed to have any real excellence but only that other kind of
Music, which is an imitation of the
good. The chief place of Music is in
the *paideia*. (Transl. by Jowett, IV,
p. 197.)

Secular Music is to be prohibited, because it arouses lust and wickedness.
Music of a religious character and
Music leading to ethical wisdom is
permitted. The only decisive criterion
of Music's value is its religious-ethical
essence. The chief place of Music is
in the synagogue, and generally, in
worship.

[92]*Au fond* Plato seems to have cherished the same ideas as Maimonides
regarding the religious functions of Music, although he is not quite as outspoken on this issue, and clothes his conception in the form of a historical
report. He says: "Among us and our forefathers ... Music was divided into
various classes and styles; one class of song was that of prayers to the gods,
which bore the name of *hymns*; contrasted with this was another class, best
called *dirges*; *paeans* formed another; and yet another was the *dithyramb*,
named, I fancy, after Dionysos"... (Plato, *Legg.* III, Transl. by Bury, vol. I,
p. 245)

are two different levels on which music appears as a spiritual force. It is hard to avoid associating the position of Maimonides with the function of music in the troops of ancient prophets, where it aroused the נבואה, the prophetic inspiration.[93] Maimonides refers in fact to the story of the prophet Elisha: "But now bring me a minstrel. And it came to pass, when the minstrel played, that the hand of the Lord came upon him."[94] This incident is mentioned in the philosophies of music throughout the ages, together with references to David, Miriam, and Asaph. The Church Fathers took over the practice and passed it on to the philosophers as an irrefutable proof that music has divine potentialities.[95] Jewish literature also refers to this frequently.

We shall limit ourselves to three quotations which elucidate and confirm our interpretation of Maimonides' allusion.

1. Isaac ben Abraham Latif, *Ginze Hamelek*, chap. 15.
"After this science (Geometry) there follows the science of Music which is a propaedeutic one, leading to improvement of the psychological disposition as well as to

[93] Maimonides mentions the story of Elisha while discussing the nature of prophecy. Cf. *More* II, 32. Cf. Plotinus' great conception of the chanted prayer: "The tune of an incantation, a significant cry ... these too have a power over the soul ... similarly with regard to prayers; the prayer is answered by the mere fact that one part and the other part (of the All) are wrought in to one tone like a musical string which, plucked at one end, vibrates at the other also ..." (Mackenna, *Plotinus on the Nature of the Soul*, p. 96.)

[94] Dr. Morgenstern, in his illuminating "Amos-studies III," looks upon the Elisha story from quite a different angle: "And in order to divine for them as requested Elisha proceeded to work himself into a state of ecstasy, in accordance with the customary technique of the professional prophets, by having a musician play in his presence. The significance of this procedure is unmistakable. Within two years after the death of Elijah Elisha had fallen from the high level of prophetic standards and technique of his great master to the much lower level of the professional prophets ..." (*HUCA* XV., p. 228.)

[95] Of the innumerable references to the stories of David or Elisha, we mention here only three of the most characteristic ones from Christian sources.

(1) *Joanni Damasceni vita a Joanne Hierosolymitano conscripta* (*Patr Graeca, vol.* 94, 473.)

(2) Regino Prumiensis, (d. 915) in *Patr. Lat.*, vol. 132, 490.

(3) Roger Bacon, *Opus maius*, (transl. by R. B. Burke, I., 259 ff.). Here the philosopher confounds the name Elisha with Elijah!

understanding of some of the higher intellectual principles, as was manifest in the case of Elisha, when he said:
'But now bring me a minstrel'. . ."[96]
2. With more elaboration, Ibn 'Aḳnin states: "And we
discover that those who desire the spirit of prophecy employ musical instruments, playing them when they desire
the vision. The instruments bring about keenness of mind
and judgement, and invigorate the mental faculties for
the reception of spiritual wisdom. It is said: 'Thou wilt
come to Gibeah'. . ." Here Ibn Aḳnin refers to the story
of Saul and the prophets. (I. Sam. 10.5). Then he continues: "And Elisha, the prophet, could not attain to the
prophetic vision, because he was in a rage against the
king of Israel, and the prophetic vision did not come
because passion had prevailed over spiritual perception.
Therefore he told them: 'Bring me a minstrel'. . . "[97]
3. Then there is Falaquera who, in his *Mebbakesh*, as-
signs a primacy to the religious function of music as he
had not done in his earlier work *Rešit Ḥokma*. Falaquera
stresses this point as follows: "Know, my son, that one
of the reasons why the wise men cultivated the science
of music was their use of it in their temples of worship,
when they brought their offerings. They also employed
melodies for their prayers and for the praise of the Creator. Some of these tunes affected the heart to such an
extent that whoever heard them concentrated his mind,
repented, and turned away from his sins." Later he reports: "They assert also that as soon as the soul hears
music congenial to its own nature . . ., it yearns for its
Creator, longing to reach Him. It subsequently contemns
the miseries . . . of the temporal world . . . and meditates
upon the world supernal."[98]

When it comes to the *doctrine of virtue*, the interrelationship
between philosophy and music becomes even more pronounced.
A realm almost mystical opens up before us when we consider
the Neo-Platonic philosophy of the movements of the soul as
affected by music. Here Greek, Arabic, and Jewish views converge. We confront an eclectic syndrome of ideas from Plato,
Aristotle, Porphyry, and Plotinus. In one and the same work,[98a]

[96] *See* our Texts E.
[97] Cf. Guedemann, *op. cit.* p. 97 /8.
[98] *See* our Texts D 2.
[98a] Honein — Alharizi's *Maxims of the Philosophers.*

we may find the views of all four philosophers resting peacefully side by side. We give but one example: "Living in solitude, the soul sings plaintive melodies (emphasizing the vanity of the world) whereby it reminds itself of its own superior world. As soon as Nature (the physical world) sees this . . . she presents herself in various forms, introduced one by one to the soul, until she finally succeeds in recapturing the soul. The latter, busy with wordly affairs, soon forsakes its own true essence and abandons that which is sublime in composition and in the rhythm of artistic molodies. At last . . ., the soul is entirely submerged in Nature's ocean.[99]

Very similar ideas may be found in Aristides Quintilianus who describes the soul's solitude, the cathartic influence of music upon it, and the temptations, such as those offered by tawdry pleasures,[100] that keep it from perfection.

Alongside of this grand and lofty vision, we find strictly Platonic theories like those in chapter 19:15,[101] and particularly 19:11, which illustrate doctrines stressed in the *Republic*.[102] Aristotelian thoughts are also not missing: "As soon as the melody disappears, the hearers remember it and yearn for it and do not find repose until they have repeated it several times, by which repetition the soul finally obtains rest, pleasure, and relief."[103] Completely Aristotelian also are maxims 19:19, and 18:5, all in the *Maxims of the Philosophers*.

The materialistic views seem to be genuinely Arabic.[104] In the

---

[99] *See* our Texts A XVIII, 8. This thought might in a more general form occur in Schopenhauer's *Welt als Wille und Vorstellung*. Cf. Rosenthal in *HUCA* XV., p. 468. *See infra* appendix of translated passages.

[100] Cf. *AQM*, p. 184.

[101] Cf. Plato, *Timaeus* 67 B; also Gellius, *Noctes Atticae* V., 15.

[102] The famous passages of Plato's *Republic* III 398 C ff. breathes quite the same spirit, also Legg. II. 669 C. It was these intolerant statements that provoked the sharp opposition of Aristotle and Aristoxenos.

[103] Cf. Ps.-Aristotle, *Problems* XIX., 5, 40.

[104] Cf. Lange, *The History of Materialism*, (transl. by Thomas), p. 177. "Mohammedanism is more favorable to materialism than Chrisianity or Judaism." Also p. 181: "They (the Arabs) set to work with a independent feeling for exact observation, and developed especially the doctrine of life, which stands in so close a connection with the problems of materialism."

Hebrew sources, such are almost entirely missing.[105] Details about
the individual virtues, so extensively pondered by the Greeks, are
but rarely found in Jewish literature. On the other hand, the
Arabs, particularly Alfarabi and Ghazzali, reared a considerable
hierarchy of the virtues that music was believed to promote.[106]
Once more, it is Saadya who follows the Arabic way. The virtues,
according to Saadya, are power to reign, fortitude, humility,
joy, and sorrow(!). Saadya closely connects these virtues with
the physiological theory which we have already noticed, the
theory of the effect which music has upon the humors. In general,
Saadya follows the *Maxims of the Philosophers* (20,1) and shows
striking similarities to the *Ikhvan*.[107] However, he does not refer
to those virtues which Plato "standardized:"[108] σοφία, σωφρο-
σύνη, δικαιοσύνη, ἀνδρεία. As for the rest, Hebrew literature
prefers to stress the virtues that are dianoetic or prophetic,
apparently assuming that the practical virtues, the ordinary or
civic ones, were already achieved by the performance of the
מצוות.

If we ask which element of music was supposed to possess
the greater ethical power, melody or rhythm, we must answer
without hesitation: rhythm. On this point, Arabs, Greeks, and
Jews agree completely. That this view has generally been accepted, we can see from all of the later Greek and Arabic writers.[109] Saadya's entire theory is based on the rhythmical constructions common in Arabic theory.[110]

---

[105] The only inklings of materialistic reasoning are such as might be found
in Saadya and Falaquera. Yet, in both instances, the materialistic trend of
thought is more than counterbalanced by a strong emphasis on religious principles.

[106] Cf. Ribera, *op. cit.*, p. 90 ff.

[107] *Supra*, note 73.

[108] Plato, *Res publica*, (Pol.) IV., 441 C. *See also* Texts A XVIII, 6.

[109] Aristotle, *Poetics* chap. i, also *AQM* p. 31 very clearly.

[110] This fact has been overlooked by all writers on Saadya; perhaps because
the passage about Music is a "rather dark one" (Steinschneider), "offers
difficulties" (Guttmann), "has not been properly explained" (Malter.) In
view of Saadya's emphasis upon rhythm, the statement of P. Gradenwitz
(in *MGWJ* 1936, p. 463) that the Rabbis unanimously objected to rhythmical
music, cannot be upheld.

The *Maxims of the Philosophers* recount manifold and varied effects, supposedly produced by music, but not belonging to the category of philosophy or *ethos*. It is not easy to bring these "tall stories" under a common denominator. In most cases we find that these tales are ancient and famous. We cite here a few examples:

The stories of the magic effect of music upon animals are very old and go back to the legends of Orpheus and Arion. They belong to the Pythagorean stock in trade.[111] Rams, dogs, dolphins, swans, and — grasshoppers! — were considered music producing creatures.[112] We find the grasshopper story repeated in Falaquera's *Mebakkesh*; it goes back to Strabo, Diodorus, and Pausanias.[113] Plato and Plutarch, as well as all of the others, mention the correct explanation, namely the sound resulting from the rapid vibration of the wings. That camels are stimulated by music, as told throughout Arabic literature, is probably based upon the fact that camel drivers used specially rhythmical songs to keep their animals going.[114]

Other legends tell of the invigorating effect of music upon entire armies, upon individual warriors, and upon race horses, and the like.[115] In most cases the explanation is simple: the equable rhythm of martial music and the shattering blasts of trumpets operate as directive signals effecting a coordination of movement among the hearers.[116]

---

[111] In all of these legends magical ideas play an obvious part. A good collection of all of the Greek musical myths is to be found in Burney's *General History of Music*, I., p. 150 ff. *See also* Combarieu, *Musique et Magie*.

[112] Tragedy means "song of the goat;" Dolphins are glorified with regard to music by Pliny, IX., cap. 1, Herodotus, and Plutarch. Swans, the prophetic birds, are considered most musical by Plato, (*Phaidon*), Aelian, and many others. Cf. Burney, *loc cit. See also* W. Bacher, *Nizami's Alexanderbuch*, pp. 78–80.

[113] Cf. Burney, *op. cit.*, p. 161.

[114] Cf. Diet., p. 103. Also Texts A XIX, 6; Bacher, *op. cit.*, and Texts D 2. *Infra* appendix of translated passages.

[115] All these stories are probably as old as music itself. We shall consider the sources of some of our anecdotes in chap. VII.

[116] *See* our Texts A XX. 5, 6. *et passim. Infra* appendix of translated passages.

The comparison between the effects of music and of wine appears many times and in many places and is, beyond doubt, very ancient. Our first record seems to come directly from Pseudo-Aristotle (Probl. XIX,43). More outspoken is Plutarch: "We see that wine, like music, having intensified courage and strength, calms and soothes reason, so that when one has overcome drunkenness, one finds one's self at rest."[117] It is an old saying: *Cantores amant humores.*[118]

IV

THE HARMONY OF THE SPHERES

Closely related to the *ethos* doctrine is the venerable principle of the harmony of the spheres.[119] This ancient and beautiful conception was, as we know, one of the key-stones of Pythagorean cosmology. But today it has begun to appear that the idea of sounding spheres originated much earlier, in Egyptian, perhaps also in Babylonian culture. Apparently, it belonged to the *esoteric* doctrines of the priestly classes. Only in Greek philosophy does this conception step out into the light of public discussion. The Greeks incorporated the idea into the general principle of harmony within the universe and within the human soul.

For Plato's cosmogony, harmony in its widest sense is an indispensable element.[120] Plato's allusion to the dance of the stars and to their perfect proportions represents a distinctly Pythagorean trend of thought. Aristotle was the only great philosopher

[117] Plutarch, *Quaest. conviv.* III., qu. 8, c 2.

[118] Cf. Mose ibn Ezra, *Sepher ha-Taršiš*, ed. Ginzburg, Berlin 1886, p. 31: היה מזין לקול ערב בעוגבו ושכרה על דבר נונן וזמר ולחנו נפלו עופות ומאין רשתות נתפשו אקו וזמר ...

[119] How inseparably these two conceptions are connected may be seen. in the following juxtaposition of sentences: "*Coelum ipsum sub harmoniae modulatione revolvitur. Musica movet affectus.*" (Isidorus Hisp. in *Gerbert, Script.* I 20 b.)

[120] Cf. Plato, *Timaeus* 34 B ff. Pol. VII, 530. The word χορεῖον used in *Timaeus* 40 c can be understood only as the rhythmic motion of the heavenly bodies.

of his time who energetically combated the idea, although he did acknowledge its fascinating beauty.[121] Of the later thinkers, the Neo-Platonists and the Pythagoreans again stressed this conception. Thence it found its way into the astronomy and the music of the dying ancient world.[122] Ptolemy and Aristides Quintilianus fashioned very concrete and mathematically elaborate systems, of cosmic harmony, developing some of the ideas of Nicomachus of Gerasa.[123] The last mentioned was one of the many Syrian writers who formed the bridge between Greece and Arabia over which Pythagorean doctrines traveled.[124]

The theory of cosmic harmony was not altogether as popular with the Arabs or with the Jews as it had been with the Greeks. Hence the concept of *spheric* harmony, fitting so beautifully into the general ἁρμονία κόσμου of the Greek philosophers, while accepted and mentioned by the Arabs, was not greeted by them with much enthusiasm.[125] Alfarabi, for one, opposed it. He vents his feelings against this doctrine in the words: "The opinion of the Pythagoreans that the planets and stars produce harmonious sounds in their courses is erroneous."[126] Nevertheless, most of the Arabic authors adhered to the ancient idea, notwithstanding Alfarabi's great prestige. It became a cherished tradition abandoned unwillingly, even when not accorded much weight.

Different from this is the attitude to be found in Hebrew literature. Allusions to the harmony of the spheres appear already in the Bible. The Talmud also accepts the theory, though not

---

[121] Cf. Aristotle, *De caelo*, chap. ix, 290b 12.

[122] Cf. Heath, *Aristarchus*, pp. 105–115.

[123] Cf. Ptolemy, *Harmonics*, ed. Duering, III., chap. xvi–ixx; *AQM* III., pp. 145–155; Nicomachus Gerasenus in v. Jan, *Script.*, pp. 230–43, 272, 276–80, *et passim*. A survey of the entire ideology is given in Piper, *Mythologie und Symbolik der christlichen Kunst*, I., pp. 245–75.

[124] It is significant that three of the most important authors on music in Greek were Syrians, viz. Nicomachus of Gerasa, (ca. 100 A.D.), Porphyrius of Tyrus, (ca. 260 A.D.), and Jamblichus of Coelesyria, (Palestine, ca. 310 A.D.). *Also infra* in Chap. vi.

[125] Except the *Ikhvan* which, being fervently Pythagorean, stresses to the utmost the conception of spheric harmony. Cf. Diet., pp. 162 ff. On Al-Kindi's attitude *see* Steinschneider, *Alfarabi*, p. 80.

[126] Cf. *Kitab*, I., p. 28.

in a straightforward unequivocal way.[127] Jewish literature, accordingly, links the harmony of the spheres to biblical and talmudical authorities rather than to a supposed harmony of the universe. If a Jewish writer was, in addition, inclined toward Pythagorean ideas, he would naturally support those ideas with the available biblical statements. Philo is the most vigorous advocate of the Pythagorean idea among the earlier Jewish philosophers. To him, the heavens are the archetype for all musical instruments. The purpose of the musical structure of the cosmos is to provide the accompaniment for hymns of praise. The seven planets are compared to the seven strings of the lyre.[128]

Among the texts considered in this article, only Falaquera (in his *Mebakkesh*) and Latif affirm the harmony of the spheres, though the latter alone supports the theory by biblical citations.[129] In his earlier work *Rešit Ḥokmah* Falaquera follows Ibn 'Aḳnin almost verbatim or rather Ibn 'Aḳnin's source, Alfarabi's *De Scientiis*, not even mentioning cosmic harmony.[130] It appears that Falaquera later became more friendly to the old Pythagorean theory. As for Latif, it is characteristic that he constantly emphasizes the esoteric nature of his ruminations: "The psalmist has spoken cryptically . . . I can explain no more . . . This speculation can be grasped only by those who are initiated into both sciences."[131] The Neo-Platonists, Moses ibn Ezra and Abraham ibn Ezra, both accepted the doctrine. The first acclaims it in his poems;[132] the latter, less ardent, is content with one or two

---

[127] Ps. 19.1; 93.4, 96.11, 97.6. Job 38.7, 38.37. Ezek. 1.4, 1.22. bJoma 20b, 21a.

[128] Cf. Philo, *De somn.* III., 212/13. Ὁ τοίνυν οὐρανός, τὸ μουσικῆς ἀρχέτυπον ὄργανον, ἄκρως ἡρμόσθαι δοκεῖ δὲ οὐδὲν ἕτερον ἢ ἵνα οἱ ἐπὶ τιμῆι τοῦ τῶν ὅλων πατρὸς αἰδόμενοι ὕμνοι μουσικῶς ἐπιψάλλοντα. Elsewhere he states that the idea of cosmic harmony has been developed by the Chaldeans. *See also* H. Abert, *Die Musikanschauung des Mittelalters*, p. 39 ff. Also I. Heinemann's article Philo in Pauly-Wissowa's *Realencycl. des klassischen Altertums*.

[129] Cf. our Texts D 1.

[130] Cf. Brockelmann, *op. cit.* Supplem. I, p. 377. Also *infra* chap. VII. The decisive word in that matter was spoken by Farmer, *Alfarabi's Arabic-Latin Writings on Music.*

[131] Cf. our Texts E.

[132] Moses ibn Ezra writes in a piyut for (שחרית) . . . קדושה לר' ה' מלאכת צבא שוכני שמים בזמר יענו בקול.

mentions of it. Strangely enough, of all biblical passages alluding
to cosmic harmony, Abraham ibn Ezra chooses Ps. 93.4, while
he misses such inviting opportunities as those offered by Job 38.7
or 38.37.[133] Simon Duran also broaches the ancient idea in the
same connection.[134]

The most consistent and significant opponent of the entire
doctrine is Maimonides; in his *Moreh* he unequivocally expresses
his antagonism.[135] Thus we arrive at the surprising conclusion
that philosophers of the greatest consequence in their respective
lands viz. Aristotle, Alfarabi, and Maimonides were sceptical of
or even inimical to the theory of cosmic harmony. To what extent
the latter two did or did not follow Aristotle in that question, is
a problem with which we shall not deal. Yet the attitude of these
thinkers did not deter later generations from returning to the
old Pythagorean track. In Hebrew literature, however, Maimonides almost set a standard on this issue, so that the principle of

---

[133] Cf. Abr. ibn Ezra to Ps. 93.4. ‏מקולות מים רבים: יותר מקולות מים רבים‎,
‏שהם אדירים שהם משברי ים יותר אדיר השם במרום וזה לאות כי לגלגלים קולות וכן כתוב‎
‏ביחזקאל כקול מים רבים ואלה הקולות לא ישמעו החרשים כאשר לא יביטו העורים מעשה‎
‏השם נוראים‎'. To Job 38.7 he says simply: ‏'ותנועתם היא רנתם ותרועותם‎'. To Job
38.37 ‏'...מי אוטרים‎ ‏מי יספר: פירושו מספיר מי שם אותם כספיר כענין כראי מוצק ויש‎'.
[134] Cf. Simon Duran, *Magen Abot*, 52 ff.
[135] Maimonides, *More* II, #8, (chap. xxxii.) We may realize here to what
an extent the different translations of a single Scriptural verse have influenced
philosophy. The passage, Job 38.37 says: ‏'מי יספר שחקים בחכמה ונבלי שמים מי‎
‏ישכיב‎'. Vulgate: *Quis enarrabit coelorum rationem, et concentum coeli quis
dormire faciat?* Authorized version: Who can number the clouds in wisdom? —
or who can stay the bottles of heaven? The interpretation of the Vulgate may
be found also in Hebrew literature; Cf. Abr. ibn Daud, Commentary on *Sefer
Yezirah*, chap. i, f. 27, col. 3, where ‏נבלי שמים‎ is derived from ‏נבל וכנור‎. *See also*
Steinschneider *HB* XIII, 35. The Christian philosophers refer to the Vulgate
version, which is their chief basis for the doctrine of spheric harmony. Cf.
Boethius, *De Musica, Patr. Lat.* LXIII, 1171. Also Aurel. Reomensis, in
Gerbert, *Scriptores* I., 32, who refers to the passage from *Job* and to the seven
voces of the planets, linking them to the eight musical modes of the Church.
This idea occurs also in cabalistic literature in connection with Ps. 29.2–9,
where the seven voices of God are interpreted in quite the same manner.
Allusions to the astro-musical idea are very frequent. Kepler himself defended
this theory in his *Harmonice mundi*, and Shakespeare refers to it in the beautiful passage, *The Merchant of Venice*, Act V, sc. 1.

spheric harmony was abandoned by most of his followers.[136] It appeared instead in the camp of his antagonists, i. e. in the literature of the Cabalists. There it received the utmost elaboration throughout the following centuries. We cannot discuss these sources here, for the position of music in the esoteric literature of the Jews would take a special study. It may suffice to refer to the many commentaries on the *Sefer Yeẓirah* and on the Zohar, in all of which the principle of spheric harmony plays an important part.[137]

V

MUSICAL THEORY

The struggles over the esthetics of music present a spectacle of fiery dispute. Alongside of the conflict over the respective rankings of secular music and sacred music, the theory of music was itself a field of debate. Theory in the middle ages, though always lagging behind living music, either dominated living music or did not concern itself with the practice of music at all.

Up to this point, we have surveyed not musical theory proper but, so to speak, the theory of theory, i. e. the philosophy of music. We occasionally inserted a word of caution that, so far as we know anything about the subject, it is difficult to harmonize the speculations of the philosophers with actual practice. Instead of receiving the bread of living craftsmanship, we have sometimes been fed with the stones of speculation. But now we have finished our study of mixed ideologies and may proceed to consider musical theory itself. As music formulated its own autonomous laws, many of the ideas which were often the product of mystic speculation yielded to common sense. The full fruits of this painful process did not mature until the seventeenth cen-

---

[136] Cf. Steinschneider, *Alfarabi*, p. 244, (note to p. 80.)

[137] Cf. A. v. Thimus, *Die Harmonikale Symbolik des Altertums*. The entire second volume is devoted to the acoustic and harmonic ideas of cabalistic literature. I have to confess, however, that, in spite of the tremendous amount of material, accumulated by the author, and the many astonishing ideas he presents, the work as a whole did not convince me.

tury. Meanwhile music lost its universal all-embracing import, and that loss was by no means trivial.

Pythagoreanism (which may certainly be called a religion) and likewise Judaism forced all musical thinking into a cast-iron frame of cosmological, ethical, and theological postulates, ignoring the aesthetic entirely. Early Christianity and Islam faithfully imitated this ascetic pattern. Not until the tenth century do we find the inception of independent thinking among the musical theorists of the Christians, Arabs, and Jews. Even these base their ideas, without exception, upon the ancient Greek assumptions.

In concrete musical descriptions, our original sources are poor. Whenever we are in need of additional knowledge we have to turn to Arabic literature for analogies. There is, besides, almost an entire lack of musical notation. Later we shall deal with the very few instances of notation extant.

TONAL SYSTEM, INTERVALS AND THEIR CALCULATION

We must distinguish between the theoretical system of the scale, and that of the usual modes (*Gebrauchstonleiter*). From our Hebrew sources we know only of a diatonic system of eight tones within the octave.[138] Of chromatic systems we have no sign at all, which does not mean of course that such did not exist. The eight tones were naturally connected with numerological speculations in the manner of the Greeks and Arabs. While we are well informed about the computation of the intervals within the theoretical system, we know almost nothing about the structure of the usual modes. That modes existed and were regarded as an important part of music, we shall show later on. But beyond this, everything is obscure.

---

[138] Cf. Latif's (Texts E) Interpretation of Ps. 29.4–9; all of this is paralleled by the Christian interpretation of Vergil's verse: (Aen. VI, 545 f.)

"*Nec non Thraeicius longa cum veste sacerdos*
obloquitur numeris septem discrimina vocum"

This quotation descends through most of the Christian theorists down to the XVth century. *See infra* appendix of translated passages!

Arabic literature on the theory of music is more extensive than Hebrew literature on that topic. Still, it is difficult to acquire from the numerous descriptions of Arabic music by Arabic writers anything like a consistent picture while, owing to the dearth of extant sources, the situation with the Hebrew writers is still worse. Jews as well as Arabs speak clearly and unequivocally only in one regard, namely, in matters involving mathematics — above all, in the computation of intervals; this being a field in which the Arabs, chiefly Alfarabi have pioneered. We regret that we can not credit the Jews with having equalled or excelled them. Quite to the contrary!

Jewish calculation of intervals is as complex as it is poor by comparison with the methods of Euclid or Nicomachus, not to mention a master like Ptolemy. This calculation is based upon the Euclidian division of the fundamental string into overtones (superparticulars) which produces the intervals. With the octave, ($\delta\iota\grave{\alpha}\ \pi\alpha\sigma\tilde{\omega}\nu$ = בכול אשר יחס = bi-l-kull) the fifth and the fourth the chief concern, the imperfect consonances are neglected. The Arabs were in this respect much more thorough, for they employed, besides the division of the octave, also the various divisions of the fourth, from which Alfarabi deduced the three favorite genera of Arabic music based strictly on Greek theory.[139] The Arabs also knew the mathematical proportions of all of the other intervals within the octave itself. The Jews added to this simple division a great deal of somewhat clumsy calculation attempting to formulate the mathematical rule of the progression of overtones, $\frac{n+1}{n}$ (Fifth = $1+1/2 = 3/2$, Fourth = $1+1/3 = 4/3$).[140] One of our sources, Isaiah ben Isaac, could not express himself as technically as he perhaps wished, because his work, a commentary to Ibn Sina's *Alkanun*, was not for musicians or mathematicians but for physicians. An advance beyond Isaiah ben Isaac is achieved by Abulafia who investigates the relations of the two

---

[139] *Kitab*, p. 55.

[140] Cf. Texts G.

Farmer's remark (*Facts on Arabian musical influence*, p. 68.) about the "thoughtful animadversion of Euclid by Isaiah b. Isaac" is well-meant, but gives the Hebrew author undeserved credit. *See infra* appendix of translated passages!

consonances (combined proportions) to each other.[141] He too neglects the intervals of the third and the sixth, probably because these intervals were of no consequence in a music which lacked chords almost entirely.[142]

CONSONANCE AND DISSONANCE

To this subject, our only reference is one passage in Isaiah ben Isaac. The octave, of course, is considered the perfect consonance. Some hidden allusions to the value of the various consonances or dissonances are scattered through cabalistic literature.[143] Already in the manuscripts of the fifteenth century, the entire Western theory of consonances is accepted by the Jews.

MODES, TROPI, STRUCTURAL LAWS OF MELODY

a) *Modes of melody*. We have evidence of the existence of various melodic modes in the theory of the Jews. In fact, it would be almost a miracle if the Jews did not employ modes, for we know today that the principle of modality was prevalent in the entire world of the Near and Middle East, including Greece. Saadya tries hard to prove that already the Levites of the Temple used a system of eight distinct modes for their rendition of the Psalms.[144] Elsewhere Saadya states that certain Psalms had to be sung in specific and unchangeable modes, in accordance with their respective superscriptions.[145] The theory of modality is more

---

[141] Cf. Texts F. *See infra* appendix of translated passages!

[142] *Infra* on Harmonies!

[143] Cf. A. v. Thimus, *op. cit.*, chap. 3 and 4. Kiesewetter's contemptuous remark, (*op. cit.*, p. 25) that the Arabs valued the consonances only according to their arithmetical relationship is unacceptable. For one thing the Arabs employed other criteria as well, such as the psychological effectiveness of intervals and scales. On the other hand, the arithmetical criterion is ample, since the more perfect consonance is always represented by the simpler proportion. *See a'so* R. Lachmann, *op. cit.*, p. 51.

[144] Galliner, *Saadya's Psalmuebersetzung*, p. 22. Also S. H. Margulies, *Saadya's Psalmuebersetzungen*, pp. 13, 22.

[145] E. Cohn in *Magazin fuer die Wissenschaft des Judentums* 1881, p. 65 /66. "Die zweite Anordnung war, dass gewisse Psalmen nach einer bestimmten

clearly announced by Latif who connects the tone of the octave
with the eighth mode and, at the same time, with the super-
scription 'Al Hašminit.[146] Nowhere can we find a definition of the
term "mode" (נגינה, נעימה, קול, מין הניגון, נענוע, Arab. *naghama*,
aṣābi', *maqām*.).[147] Modern musicology identifies "mode" with
the Arabic *Maqam*, or the *Byzantine-Syriac* ἦχος = *ikhadia* of
which Idelsohn gives a highly valuable description.[148] Mode may
be explained, in short, as a fixed pattern of a melody containing
certain motives. These have the respective functions of beginning,
ending, conjunction, and disjunction.[149] The composer's task is
that of arranging the pre-existing motives according to his ideas
and according to the rules of the respective *Maqam*, embellish-
ing them and grouping them. The composer has to adhere, however, to the particular properties of his chosen *Maqam*. Thus,
"*Maqam* exists only in the sense of a Platonic idea" (R. Lachmann).[150] The individual melodies (לחן = Ar. *laḥan*; נגינה = Ar.

Tonari, die nicht veraendert werden durfte, gesungen werden sollten, je nachdem eine solche Melodie in der Ueberschrift angedeutet ist. Der Ausdruck
נגינות bezeugt *eine bestimmte* Sangesweise."

[146] Cf. Texts E. *See infra* appendix of translated passages.

[147] *Infra* on Terminology. Cf. also Idelsohn in *MGWJ* 1913, 314 ff., and
Bacher in *REJ* Vol. 50, viii ff.

[148] Cf. Idelsohn in *SIMG* XV, p. 11 ff. The vast field of modality contains
an equally large literature of which we can cite here only the standard works:

> Syrian modality   : Dom Jeannin, *Les chants liturgiques de Syrie*
> Byzantine modality: Wellesz, *Byzantin. Musik*
> Arabian modality : Idelsohn in *SIMG, loc. cit.*
> v. Hornbostel in *SIMG* VIII, p. 1 ff.
> R. Lachmann, *op. cit.*
> R. Lach, "Die vergleichende Musikwissenschaft," in
> *Sitzungsberichten der Akad. d. Wissensch.*, Wien,
> vol. 200, 1924.
> Gregorian modality: P. Wagner, *Die Greg. Melodien*, III.
> A. Gastoue, *l'origine du Chant Romaine.*
> Jewish modality   : *Thesaurus*, I, IV, V, VII. (Idelsohn)
> Werner, "Preliminary Notes," in *HUCA* 1940.

[149] This system is closely related to the idea of the Bible accents, (נגינות)
which are also divided into conjunctive, disjunctive, and ending signs.

[150] Lachmann, *op. cit.*, p. 59.

ghinā) are but the various images of the Platonic idea.[151] Some
scholars are of the opinion that this principle of strict modality
was not genuinely Arabic, but was imported from Byzantium,
Syria, and Persia. Although this seems improbable, considering
the fact that the entire music of the Near and Middle East is
based upon this principle, we cannot render a final judgement
until the many manuscripts of the early Islamic period which
deal with music, become available for our use.[152]

b) *The Number of the Modes.* In the older literature we hear,
almost invariably, of *eight modes.* We are, of course, inclined,
to associate the number eight with the eight tones of the diatonic
scale, thus ascribing to each tone its own mode. However, we
must consider, first, that the octave can be divided variously,
e. g. into five, twelve, seventeen, or even twenty-four parts. All
of these divisions do indeed occur. Secondly, it is not certain at
all that these modes were connected with the eight tones of the
scale, even of the diatonic scale. Thirdly, as we shall see later
on, there were eight rhythmic modes besides the melodic ones.
Here it is quite obvious that the number eight was artificially
imposed upon the rhythmic modes since, for rhythm, an equivalent to the octave does not exist. Moreover, we have evidence
that originally the Arabs employed ten rhythmic modes[153] (Arab.
iqa'at), but reduced them to eight, to those eight modes (Arab.
naghamat — Hebr. *ne'imah, ninnu'ah*) to which Saadya and the
Ikhvan es-Safa refer so extensively.[154] In the last mentioned

---

[151] *Infra, see* Terminology. The term *lahan* has been adopted by Hebrew
poets to indicate the appropriated melodies of their *piyutim,* quite as the
early Protestant hymn-writers adapted their new texts to already well known
popular songs. ("Contrafacts.") On the term *lahan see also* Dukes in the
Literaturblatt d. Orient IV, 539–542, where he quotes the following interesting
passage of Simon Duran, *Magen Abot* 55b. הטעמים והם מיני הלחנים והנה נשאר לנו
במיני הלחנים ג' והאחד הובדל לקריאת התורה, והב', לקריאת הנביאים וזה יש בו שני מינים
קרובים זה לזה כי קריאת ההפטורה אינה כקריאת שאר הנביאים. והג' קריאת ג' ספרים תהלים,
משלי, איוב. ושאר הלחנים כנון הנוטים לשיר והנוטים לתמרור שהם מיני הפיוטים כלם יש
מהם קדומים כמו שירי ר' עליעזר הקלירי... ויש מהם נתחדשו בארצות ספרד לקחום
המשוררים משירי הישמעאלים הם ערבים הרבה מושכים הלב...
[152] Ribera, *op. cit.,* 77, n. 13. Also Farmer, *Facts* etc., p. 57, and *Encyclo-
paedie des Islam,* article "Musiqi."
[153] Ribera, *ibid.,* 79, also *Kitab,* pp. 150–58.
[154] Cf. Texts B 1, 2; *see also infra* the appendix of translated passages.

work we find the clue for the prevalence of the number eight. According to the *Ikhvan*, eight is the perfect number for Music and Astonomy. Nature herself reveals eight qualities: hot, cold, wet and dry; and, in combination, hot-wet, cold-dry, cold-wet, and hot-dry. There are also eight astronomical stages.[155] Here again we encounter the influence of cosmological views upon musical theory.

c) Details of the Modes, Musical Notation. We know very little about the musical details of these modes. Their classification with regard to their effects upon the emotions are not of much aid. In Hebrew literature we have thus far only two sources which give unmistakable indication as to the notes by which the modes were expressed. Unfortunately both are relatively late. Of the Ms. Jehudah ben Isaac (early 15th century) which contains some concrete remarks,[156] there is, according to Idelsohn, a copy in the Hebrew Union College Library at Cincinnati. But I was not able to locate this rare manuscript.[157] Steinschneider quotes some sentences of the manuscript which include the Latin soffeggio-names of the tones, *Ut, Re, Mi, Fa*, and the like.[158] This would indicate that the diatonic system was the basis at least for musical theory, perhaps also for practice. Such an assumption is supported by the oldest Hebrew musical manuscript, an elegy on the death of Moses containing neumes of the

---

[155] Cf. Dieterici, pp. 128–31. "True, there are many things according to the numbers 2, 3, 5, 6, 7, 8, 9, 10. Yet we intend to awaken the slumbering ones from their carelessness by emphasizing the eight and, at the same time, to explain that those who prefer and represent the seven and its advantages, are right only in part and not in general . . ." We met the same problem in the exegesis of Ps. 29, *supra* note 135 and 138.

[156] Steinschneider, *Hebr. Uebersetzungen*, p. 970, n. 159.

[157] Idelsohn, *Jewish Music*, chap. x, note 21.

[158] The famous polyhistor and friend of Pascal and Descartes, Pere Mersenne, gives an interesting tabulation of the Greek and Latin names of musical tones, comparing them with the ten Cabalistic Sefirot and the ten Divine Names. In his study *De Musica Hebraeorum*, (*Thesaurus Ugolini*, Venice 1767, vol. 32, col. 531-33) Father Mersenne quotes some anonymous cabalistic authors who had apparently a perfect knowledge of the entire of musical theory. But since he fails to mention names or sources, we cannot evaluate his statements.

13th century.[159] The melody here is devoid of all chromatisms,
which in turn well comports with Ribera's conviction that
Arabic (and Jewish) music of the 11th–13th centuries used the
diatonic scale now employed in the occident.[160] Thus *modern*
Arabic music would have to be regarded merely as a corruption
of a classic style.[160a] But we cannot follow Ribera to that extent.
Musical traditions in the Near East have, according to our
knowledge, been jealously guarded and protected.[161] These contradictory views can be reconciled by the fact somewhat overlooked that, when Arabic culture reached its greatest splendor,
theory and artistic music, on the one hand, and popular music
on the other, were not at all identical. It may well be that
"learned" music avoided chromatisms, while the chromatic music
of the common people survived. We have reason to assume that
the popular modes of those times made as extensive a use of
half-tones as they do today. So long as we do not possess more
Hebrew manuscripts containing musical notation, we are free
to suppose that, in practice, music employed both diatonic and
chromatic elements. Theory, however, at least in the Hebrew
sources, seems entirely to have ignored chromatic usage, although
it knew such to be possible.[162] The assumption of this divergence

---

[159] Cf. A. Friedlaender, *Facts and Theories Relating to Hebrew Music*,
pp. 13–16, which includes a photograph of the MS. *See also* the *Elkan Adler
Catalogue MS #4096*, where a more extensive analysis is given. It is regrettable
that we could not secure an exact and enlarged photostat of the MS, inasmuch
as we do not fully agree with Friedlaender's interpretation of the clef. A
thorough investigation of this valuable and unique MS is much to be desired.

[160] Ribera, *op. cit.*, p. 77. We cannot enter here into a discussion, whether
or not the Latin syllables *Ut, Re, Mi, Fa* etc, are of Arabic origin, as Farmer
has it. (*Facts* etc. pp. 72–82.) Also, *An old Moorish lute tutor* 27.

[160a] It makes ample use of half- and even of quarter-tones.

[161] Best proofs for this are the works which show clearly the close connection between Gregorian, Byzantine, Syrian and Oriental Jewish chants.
Supra note 148. A comprehensive work on the music of the entire Near East
(including the Gregorian chant) is a desideratum.

[162] Cf. Texts G. The Arabian attempts at a musical notation from Al-
Kindi up to Safi ad-Din were only complex tablatures based on the *'ud*. Hence,
they can hardly indicate any chromatism at all, even if there were such a
thing in the artistic and "recognized" music of those times. *See also infra*
appendix of translated passages!

between popular and artistic music would also account for the many contradictory statements *a propos* the theory of rhythm.

RHYTHMIC MODES

It is the rhythmic modes which present the greatest diffi-culties to the occidental musician. These rhythmic-metric for-mulae, though alike in principle throughout the entire Near and Middle East, varied considerably at different times and places. Moreover, the Arabic modes frequently kept their names while changing their patterns. That is why remarks of the 12th and 13th centuries contradict descriptions of the 9th century and the 10th century.[163]

Saadya gives in his '*Emunot Wede'ot* (chap. X) an extensive account of the modes as he knew them. In addition to the original Arabic text, we possess two Hebrew translations, one by Ibn Tibbon, and another by Abraham b. Ḥiyyah and, of the chapter dealing with music, an anonymous paraphrase published by Steinschneider.[164] These four versions of Saadya's text give us a clear picture of his theory of rhythm. As J. Guttmann first pointed out, the *Ikhvan es-Safa* contains very similar, almost identical observations.[165] Probably both Saadya and the *Ikhvan*, being contemporaries, drew from an older authority, possibly Al-Kindi.[166] Recent investigations point to Syrian literature as the intermediary between Byzantine and early Arabic sources.[167]

Saadya (and his unknown source) borrowed their modes from the metrical theory of the Arabs.[168] This is not surprising, since

[163] Ribera, *op. cit.*, p. 80 ff. Also Farmer, *History of Arabic Music*, p. 147, who says: "It is clear from the great *Kitab al Aghani* that an alteration took place in the rhythmic modes . . ."

[164] Cf. Texts B 1, 2.

[165] Cf. J. Guttmann, *op. cit.*, pp. 286–88.

[166] Farmer, *History of Arabic Music*, p. 150. *See also* Ahlwardt's *Catalogue of the Berlin MSS*, #5530.

[167] Bar-Hebraeus' description of the modes shows definite resemblances to Al-Kindi's or Saadya's presentations, although he refers to earlier Syrian sources. Cf. Bar Hebraeus, *Ethikon*, (*De la Cause Naturelle des Modes*, ed. Bedjan, pp. 69 ff.). *See also* Dom *Jeannin*, *op. cit.* I., 21.

[168] Saadya emphasizes the *mixture* of several modes as healthful; cf. *AQM*, pp. 30–31: "It is the mixtures of medicaments which bring about complete

the Greeks, notwithstanding their distinctly different prosody, did the very same. We cite here only three instances typical both of the Arabs and of the Greeks. (1) The metrical basis of the theory of musical rhythm; (2) The existence of eight rhythmic modes; (3) The principle of the χρόνος πρῶτος (unit of measure).[169] The single open or closed syllable was such a unit for the Greeks, the Jews, and the Arabs. Later, the original designations of the properties of the syllable had to serve for musical purposes as well. They could indicate rest and motion, heaviness and lightness, depth and height.[170] Subsequently, part of this metrical system, complex as it was, became integrated with Arabic musical theory.[171] Many of its rhythmic patterns, however, are possible only theoretically and were not in practical

remedy. Quite similarly, one single tune can do but little for the uplifting (κατόρθωσις) of the soul. The best influence comes from that Music which is mixed and composed of all the various styles. "*See also* Ps.-Aristotle, *Problems* XIX, 38, 43.

[169] These resemblances ought to be investigated further both by linguists and by musicologists. They have the following foundations:

(1) The single syllable as the metrical and musical unit. Cf. Westphal-Rossbach, *Griechische Rhythmik*, I 69–95.

(2) Aristoxenos' description of eight rhythmic-metrical modes, analogous to the Arabic system. Also the principle of conjunctive, disjunctive and mixed rhythms. Cf. Westphal-Rossbach, *op. cit.*, I 91 ff., and *Kitab*, pp. 152–156.

(3) The principle of *Chronos protos*, the unit of measure, can be found in Aristoxenos as well as in Aristides Quint. It is well known to the Arabic theorists like Alfarabi, the *Kitab al Aghani*, and others. *See also* Martianus Capella in Westphal-Rossbach, *op. cit.*, p. 85 /86. The Arab. passages in Kosegarten, *Ali Ispahanensis liber cantilenarum*, p. 127; and *Kitab* p. 152. Such scholars as Dechevrens, Jeannin, Gastoué have even attempted to introduce the term *Chronos Protos* into their evaluation of the Gregorian chant, and have received widespread approval.

[170] We find the same attitude, regarding music as a mere part of metrical poetry, in St. Augustine's *De Musica* VI. Cf. Edelstein, *Die Musikanschauungen Augustin's*. We must not forget that the great philosopher of the Church was not a "Roman" but a Semitic Carthaginian.

[171] J. Guttmann and even Malter, in their books on Saadya, have entirely misunderstood the rhythmic emphasis of Saadya's musical theory, probably because of the ambiguous terminology, with its many pitfalls.

use.[172] The highly practical rule of the *Chronos protos*, employed already by Saadya, was of course preserved.[173]

For the explanation of Saadya's schemes, we depend to a degree upon the more complete description of the *Ikhvan*. Saadya renders only the first "halves" of the modes. Moreover, the *Ikhvan* is an excellent aid for eliminating the numerous mistranslations in the Hebrew text which obscured the basic ideas. Hence we arrive at the following system:

First mode: ♩ ♩ ♩ | ♩ (♩) ♫ (♩) | ♩ ♩ ♩
Second mode: ♩ ♩ ♩ | ♩ ♩ (♩ ♫) | ♩ ♩ ♩
Third mode: ♫ ♩ | ♫ ♫ | (*Makhuri*)
Fourth mode: ♫♫ (♩) | ♫♫ |
Fifth mode: ♩ ♫ | ♫ ♫ | (*Ramal*)
Sixth mode: ♫♫ ♩ ♩   (*Ramal legère*)
Seventh mode: ♫ ♩ ♫ ♩
Eighth mode: ♩ ♩ ♩. ♪ | ♩ ♩ ♩ ♪ | (*Hedjaz*)

Practically all Arabic authors agree that these eight modes go back to four principal patterns, which appear in two versions, a slow one (*taqil*) and a swift one (*kamil*). We need not discuss here the complex Arabic theory of conjunctive and disjunctive rhythms, since these are not mentioned in Hebrew sources.[174]

On the relation between metrical poetry and music in the actual performance of Psalms, *Piyutim*, and *Pismonim*, we have in medieval Hebrew literature only a few comments. Most of these sources share Yehuda Halevy's view, as expressed in his *Cusari* II §70, where he discusses the subject of metrical melo-

---

[172] Cf. *Kitab*, p. 152–57.

[173] Cf. Texts B 1, 2. "There are two beats between which there is no time for another beat . . ."

[174] Diet., p. 140; also Mas'udi in Ribera, *op. cit.*, p. 79 ff. Ribera's tabulation of the principal modes, however, agrees but partially with the descriptions of both the *Ikhvan* and Saadya. Idelsohn's representation of these modes refers to the modern Arabian terminology and practice. (*Jewish Music in its Historical Development*, pp. 114–117.)

dies.[175] We may conclude that, though it has at times been over-looked, musical and metrical theories in Hebrew literature are closely interwoven and can hardly be separated from each other.

CHORDS AND HARMONY

This much disputed question can be answered briefly. We have indubitable proof of the existence of chords, although these are mentioned in only one Hebrew source. Moses Abulafia distinguishes between two kinds of tonal connections. The first consists of the relation of two successive, discrete tones to each other; the second consists of a simultaneous striking of two different tones, with a chord as the result. (קול מזוג)[176] The inhabitants of the Near East used that species of primitive harmony, obtained primarily by striking the "bordun" strings of their lutes.[177] Going far beyond this, Farmer quotes a passage of Ibn Sina which can hardly be understood as other than a description of the early *organum*.[178] Our passage likewise adds to the evidence, already convincing, that chords were known and utilized in the Near East. But they were rather an exception than a common feature.

VI. TERMINOLOGY

The investigation of Hebrew musical sources involves certain difficulties not the least of which is the terminology. Speaking with but slight exaggeration, our knowledge of musical cultures outside of the European sphere depends to a considerable degree

---

[175] Cf. Samuel ibn Tibbon's introduction to the commentary on *Ḳohelet*. *See also* A. de Rossi, מאור עינים § 60, (end) R. S. Archivolti devotes a part of his ערוגת הבשם to this question. (chap. xxxi) Further references may be found in Cassel's edition of the *Cusari*, p. 170, note 5.

[176] Cf. Texts F. Also *infra* appendix of translated passages.

[177] A short but comprehensive discussion of the question of chords in the music of the Near East may be found in Lachmann, *Musik des Orients*, pp. 85–92. Also Collangette in the *Journal Asiatique* 1904–06. From the standpoint of the various musical instruments C. Sachs discusses the matter in his monumental *History of Musical Instruments*, pp. 248 ff.

[178] Cf. Farmer, *Facts etc.*, pp. 104, 108, 112, where he quotes many corroborative statements by Arabian authors.

upon our understanding of the musical terms used in the various languages. The inconspicuous rank which music occupied in the Jewish scientific world of the Middle Ages is shown by the rudimentary development of musical nomenclature. It is characteristic that a Hebrew dictionary of philosophical and scientific terms, composed at the end of the XIVth century, contains only one musical item, namely נעימה.[179] As a matter of fact, almost all of the other terms in use are of a vague, general character and not scientifically exact. Since music was considered part of mathematics, we have in Hebrew terminology, as in the Greek and Latin, a considerable number of auxiliary expressions, borrowed principally from mathematics. These are usually combined with genuine musical terms, but are sometimes omitted by ellipsis.

Below, we attempt to list the Hebrew terms occuring most frequently in our texts, placing them in a comparative tabulation, together with their Greek, Latin, Arabic, and English equivalents. Naturally, complete identity of these words in five languages with all of their implications can hardly be expected. The Greek expressions are taken from the sources edited by C. v. Jan. (*Musici Scriptores Graeci*). In addition, we included Aristides Quintilianus and Cl. Ptolemaeus. The Latin terms are those which occur regularly in Gerbert *Scriptores*. The Arabic words and their transliteration are taken from the works of Farmer and D'Erlanger.

---

[179] Menahem ben Abraham Bonafos, *Sefer Hagedarim*, (Book of Definitions), Salonica 1567. About the author cf. Gross, *Gallia Judaica*, 467.

A. MUSICAL TERMS

HEBREW	GREEK	LATIN	ARAB	ENGLISH
(E) זמר	μελῳδία	musica, cantus	ghinā'	song, music, musical instrument[180]
(B2) נגינה, נגן,	φθόγγος	sonus, tonus, vox	ṭanīn	trill, tone, musical note[181]
לחן	νόμος, μέλος	modus, tonus,	laḥn,	mode, tune, melody[182]
מוסיקאה	μουσική,	musica	mūsīqī	music
מוסיקאה	μέλος			
נימה	χορδή	chorda, nervus	darb	string
(A. XX.) משקל,	ῥυθμός, ἀγωγή	rhythmus,	īqā', awzān	meter, rhythm, measurement
נ. המשקל נקראת		mensura, ordo		
נגן, לחן,	μέλος	tonus, melodia	laḥn	melody, tune
(D2) מנגן	μουσικός	musicus	mūsīqār	musician
נגמה	μέλος, νόμος, ἁρμονία	modus, vox,	nagham	mode, tune, music

[180] Dunash Ibn Tamim, Commentary on *Sefer Yezirah*, London 1902, 4 Ob.

[181] Cf. D. Kaufmann, *Die Sinne*, p. 133/34, n. 18.

[182] As in the Arabic texts, we find in the Hebrew sources coming from Spain the Latin form *"musica,"* while the Greek form *"musike"* prevails in the texts which come from the East. Cf. Wolfson, *"The classification of sciences," HUCA*, Jubilee vol., 1925, 302/03; also Farmer, *Facts etc.*, p. 66. also *Encyklopaedie des Islam*, article "musiqi."

HEBREW		GREEK	LATIN	ARAB	ENGLISH
(G) מנעימות(ן)		μέλος	vox, melodia	*laḥn*	melody, tune
(B1) נענוע		τόνος, κίνησις, byz. νεῦμα	tonus, neuma, ictus, sonus	*nagham, ṭanīn*	tone, beat, (rhythmical) mode
(B2) נענוע(ן)	(נגינה, נענע)	byz. νεαννοή[183]	neuma, tonus, vox tremula		shake, trill, tremolo-mode
	קול	φωνή, φθόγγος, byz. ἦχος	vox, sonitus, modus	*ṣawt, ghinā'*	voice, sound, tone
	שיר	ὕμνος, ᾠδή	hymnus, carmen	*shi'r*	poem, hymn, song.

[183] The Hebrew *ninnua* was unquestionably the source for the Byzantine *νεαννοῆ*, which in turn made its way into the early European theory. Neither the Byzantines nor the Western theorists understood the term *neannoe*, or *neannoeane* — they took it as a mnemonic cue-word. More about *neannoe* will be said in the writer's forthcoming article on this matter. (Musical Quarterly 1942).

B. AUXILIARY TERMS

(Usually connected with one or more terms of the A-class).

HEBREW	GREEK	LATIN	ARAB	ENGLISH
נגבה, נבה, (B1) הגבהה	ἐπίτασις, ὀξύτης	vox acuta, alta, elevatio	(pers.) zīr	heigh, height
(G) הקפהכב	σύστημα, κύκλος byz. τρόχος	ordo, cyclus	dā'ira	cycle, system
(B2) הגבה, הגבהה	ὀξύτης	acuitas, elevatio		height
(E) הבגה	διαστολή	elongatio		dilatation
(G) התפשטותהבגה	διαστολή			
(E, G) הקבצה	συστολή	diminutio, contractio		contraction
(B1) זמן	χρόνος	tempus, tactus	īqā'	time, measure
זמן בנה אחת	χρόνος πρῶτος	tempus primum	īqā'	unit of measurement
(AXX) הלחן	ποίησις, σύνθεσις, μελοποιία	compositio, ordo	ta'līf	composition, order
הלחן הלחנים	μελοποιία			composition of tunes
הלחן הבגנים				composition of tunes
הלחן הנעימות				composition of modes
הקבלה הלחן				combination of sounds
A XVIII) המחבר	σύνθετος	coniunctus	mutaqārib	combined

193

HEBREW	GREEK	LATIN	ARAB	ENGLISH
חדה, חדוד	ἀραίωσις	acuitas, altitudo	ḥādd,	sharp, sharpness
חכמה, החכמה	ἐπιστήμη	scientia musicae	mūsīqī	science of music
חכמת הדבור	τέχνη θεωρητική	theoria musicae	mūsīqī	science of music
חכמת המוסיקה		theoria musicae	mūsīqī	science of music
החכמה הלמודית		theoria musicae	mūsīqī	science of music
חכמת הניגון		theoria musicae	mūsīqī	science of music
חכמת השיר		theoria musicae	mūsīqī	science of music
חכמת הזמר		theoria musicae	mūsīqī	science of music
חכמת ההלחן		theoria acustica	mūsīqī	acoustics
יחס	λόγος	ratio, proportio	nisba	relation, proportion
(F, G) יחס אשר בכל	διὰ πασῶν	octava, diapason	bi-l-kull, al-kull, taḍʿīf	octave, diapason
(F, G) חמש	διὰ πέντε	quintus tonus		fifth
(F, G) ארבעה חמש	διὰ τέσσαρον	quartus tonus		fourth
(F, G) חמש הכל	διὰ πασῶν καὶ διαπέντε	diapason et diapente		fifth over the octave
(F, G) הכל, הכפל, כפל	διὰ πασῶν	octava	al-kull	octave
(F, G) כובד, כבדה	πύκνωσις	gravitas, pondus	thaqīl	heaviness, weight
(B, F) מחבר, מורכב	σύνθετος	coniunctus	anwāʿ, ajnās	combined, tempered
מין	γένος, τρόπος	species, genus		species, mode

HEBREW	GREEK	LATIN	ARAB	ENGLISH
(E) נגון, זמר, נגינה) לחן, נגן	τόνοι, νόμοι, μέλη	modi, toni	laḥn, naghamā	modes, tunes, melodies
(B1, 2) מנגנת, תנועה, גל	ἄνω, ἄρσις	arsis, elatio mobilis	nabra	moved, moving
(G) מסכים	σύμφωνος	concors, consonans	muwāfaqa	consonan, concordant
בלתי מסכים, מלאכה, המלאכה הזאת, זנות	διάφωνος / τέχνη	dissonans / ars, usus / ars musica		discordant / art, profession / art of music
(B1, 2) מפרד, נבדל	ἀσύνθετος	separatus, disiunctus	mufraqa	isolated, disjoined
מעשי	πρακτικός	musica activa, practica	'amalī	practical (music)
(D1, 2) החכמה המלאכת המעשית	πρᾶξις μουσικῆς, ἐπιστήμη τῆς μουσικῆς τέχνης	musica activa		science of practical music
(A) מתוקן, נגן מתוקן	μουσικὴ τεχνική	musica artificialis		arranged, artistic music
(B1) נח, נחת	κάτω, θέσις	gravis, humilis immobilis	sākin	resting, low
(E) נמכה, נמיכה	βαρύς, βαρύτης	gravitas,		low, lowness

195

HEBREW	GREEK	LATIN	ARAB	ENGLISH
נבג, נגיעה—מנגינים נגינה, נגינות בנבאה	ἄνω, ἄρσις, κίνησις	mobilis, elatus tonorum sequentia	*nabra*	moving, high successive tones
מכבה, מכבר—הדר קפל	κύκλος, σύστημα, byz. τρόχος	cyclus, systema	*dā'ira*	cycle, system
מכבה קלהל (XVIII	byz. κύλισμα	quilisma tremula vocis		trilling of the voice
מכבד (B1)	κατὰ περίοδον, σύνθετος	coniunctus	*mutaqārib*	contiguous, tied together
עיון	θεωρητικός	speculativa, theorica	*al-'ilm al-nazarī*	theoretical
ההכמה המוסיקת העיונית (2,	ἐπιστήμη μουσικῆς θεωρητικῆς	musica speculativa		science of theoretical music
עדך, ל, חם	λόγος	ratio	*nisba*	relation, proportion
עדך אשר בכל	διὰ πασῶν	diapason	*al-kull*	octave
שבירה, רעבה, הרקה (B2)	διάστημα	intervallum	*bu'd*	interval, musical unit
שבירה, רעדה, הרקה (XVIII	byz. κύλισμα	quilisma, tremula		trill, vibration, break
שוה, חוש, הבדל (D2)	ἁρμονικός	harmonicus	*muwāfaqa*	harmonic
שחחה, שחחות—שפל, הן	βαρύτης	gravitas		low, lowness

HEBREW	GREEK	LATIN	ARAB	ENGLISH
(B2) נחת, שוחחת	βαρύς, κάτω	gravis, immobilis	sākin	resting, low
שעיר	λόγος, μέγεθος	modulus, longitudo		measure, size
שעיר מחזן	ῥυθμός, μέτρον	rhythmus, metrum	baḥr	measure of time, rhythm
(B1) שפל, השפל, השפלה	βαρύς	gravis		low, lowness
(A XXI) הבכה, מספר, מכפר (B2/3) מחנה תנועה	σύνθετος, κατὰ περίοδον κίνησις	coniunctus motus	mutaqārib ḥaraka	tied together, joined movement, mode
כלי	ὄργανον	instrumentum	āla	instrument
כלי, נבל, כמר, שיר.		instrum. musicae		musical instrument

APPENDIX

TRANSLATION OF THE HEBREW PASSAGES QUOTED IN THE TEXT
OF THE ARTICLE

The numbers refer to the notes respectively of which the Hebrew is here translated.

47. He also said: "reasoning leads knowledge to known objects (of the corporeal world); but Music leads to spiritual knowledge."

48 and 58. Finally, he said: "There are three categories of professions: (1) professions in which speech preponderates over action; (2) others in which there is more action than speech; (3) others again in which both speech and action are of equal importance. To the first category belongs the telling of stories and fables, which is accomplished by words and not by actions. The profession in which there is more action than speech is represented by the physician whose deeds outweigh his speech. It is in the profession of Music that action is of equal importance to speech. Music, therefore, is the best profession, provided that its words coincide with its action, as in the case of a lute-player, whose melody corresponds to his motions."

52. You should know that something of a musical nature is found in the pulse-beat; for just as the perfection of musical art consists of the production of tones according to a certain proportion between them with respect to their acuteness and heaviness, and with respect to melodic cycles and intervals between the individual beats, so do the same proportions apply to the human pulse.

54. Euclid said: "Music is an art which connects every melodic species with its own type; it makes use of the temperaments; it stirs up that which is at rest, and brings to rest that which is restless."

57. Favorinus, the sage, said: "He who is able to harmonize the motions of the soul and nature, until they vibrate together like four harmonious strings of a musical instrument, for him

the joy of the world and its pleasures will be in harmony with his own pleasure. When he wants to be joyful, his memory encompasses the pleasures of the world, as he ponders by which of them he may obtain his desire.

"Music is such a sublime subject that the dialectic faculty is inadequate to its presentation, leaving the philosophers powerless. But the soul perceives Music through the medium of melody. As soon as the joy of the soul evoked by Music became manifest, people yearned for that joy, paid attention to the soul and, forsaking the contemplation of the affairs of the transient world, hearkened to the soul.

"The significance of Music consists in the fact that it accompanies every profession, just as an intelligent man can find an associate in every person."

72 and 75. Third question: "Why did the musicians say that a *Kinor*, if it is of good proportion, has to have four strings, each of them thicker than the other?"

Answer: "They did it to the end, that the tones of each of the four strings might strengthen one of the four humors. One of the four strings called *Al-Bam*, consists of 64 threads of silk. Its tone, on account of the string's thickness, invigorates the black humor. The second string, called *Mathna*, consists of 48 threads. Its tone invigorates the white humor. The third string, called *Mathlath*, consists of 36 threads. Its tone strengthens the blood. The fourth string consists of 27 threads, and is called *Zir*. Its tone, because of its fineness, invigorates the yellow bile."

85. Another said: "A singer has to show by his song the mood of his soul; and a lute has to be attuned to its appropriate melody."

88 and 89. Maimonides, Responsum on music, *MGWJ* 1873, pp. 174–180. (Goldziher.)

Question: Is it permissible to listen to the Arabic *Muwassahat* and to music in general?[a]

---

[a] *Muwashah* is a lyrical poem or song, very popular in Arabic literature from the 11th century on. Originally an Arabo-Spanish form of poetry, it later spread also to North Africa. Cf. Ribera, *op. cit.* pp. 119, 128-34, *et passim*.

Answer: It is known that music in general and rhythmic music[b] in particular ('iqa'at איקאעאת) is forbidden, even if it is not joined with words; for the Rabbis say: אדנא דשמעא זמרה תעקר (Soṭ. 58a). The Talmud teaches expressly (Giṭ. 7a) that there is no difference between the hearing of vocal or instrumental music, and music in general. Such music is forbidden, except when it belongs to prayer which moves the soul either to joy or to sorrow. The Rabbis support this by the words of the prophet: אל תשמח ישראל אל-גיל כעמים (Hos. 9.1). We explained the reason for this prohibition elsewhere as follows: The power of desire must be restrained and not stimulated. We need not pause for the exceptional individual whose soul might be saved by these impressions and whose comprehension of intelligible things might be facilitated, enhancing his submission to things Divine. Legislative wisdom shapes its statutes with regard to the majority, i. e. the common run of people. The prophets have already expressed their disapproval of the use of musical instruments in the following passage: הפרטים על-פי הנבל כדויד חשבו להם כלי-שיר (Am. 6.5). Moreover, as we stated in our commentary on Abot (I., 17), there is no difference between the singing of Hebrew or of Arabic words. Permission or prohibition depend exclusively upon the content of the words. The listening to any licentious utterance is forbidden, even if it is only spoken. If it is accompanied by instrumental music, it would involve three prohibited acts: (1) The listening to licentious utterances, (2) listening to vocal music, (3) and listening to musical instruments.

If this happens in a tavern, there is a fourth prohibition involved, for it is said: (Is. 5.12) והיה כנור ונבל תף וחליל ויין משתיהם If the singer is a woman, there is a fifth prohibition, according to the dictum of the Talmud. (Ber. 24a) . . . קול באשה ערוה; the more so, if she sings at a banquet.

It is the intention of Divine providence that we be a holy nation, so that we should not speak or do anything which is not perfection or would not lead us to perfection. We must not per-

---

[b] Goldziher overlooked here the significant musical term *'iqa'at* which emphasizes the rhythmical quality of a mode; actually *'iqa* corresponds to our *rhythm*. See also Farmer's interpretation of this responsum in the *Journal of the Royal Asiatic Society*, Oct. 1933, pp. 866-884.

form anything which stimulates those mental forces which deter us from the good, or do anything whereby we neglect (our better ego) by vanity or dalliance . . . The songs mentioned by the Gaonim are permitted because they are hymns and songs of exultation, as is explained by Alfasi . . . e To extend the prohibition to songs which are perfectly decent is a thing never heard of either by Gaon or by layman . . . d

Maimonides, *The Eight Chapters*, (שמנה פרקים) ed. Gorfinkle, p. 30. There are, indeed, times when the pleasant may be used for a curative purpose as, for instance, when one suffers from loss of appetite, it may be stirred up by highly seasoned delicacies and agreeable palatable food. Similarly, one who suffers from melancholia may rid himself thereof by listening to songs and to all kinds of instrumental music, by strolling through beautiful gardens and splendid buildings or by gazing upon beautiful forms . . .

99. The fifth said: "Living in solitude, the soul sings plaintive melodies, (emphasizing the vanity of this world), whereby it reminds itself of its own superior world. As soon as Nature sees this, and becomes aware of it, Nature presents herself with all sorts of images (sensory beauties) introduced, one by one, to the soul, until finally Nature succeeds in recapturing the soul. The latter, busy with the affairs of the transitory world, will soon forsake that which constitutes its own essence. It will abandon sublime compositions and the rhythm of artistic melodies and, ceaselessly allured by wordly pleasures, will become, with all of its faculties, utterly submerged in Nature's ocean."

114. He (Plato) used to say to the musician: "Show us the harmony of trees in their blossoms, and the harmony of flower-beds in their various perfumes."

e This passage is entirely misunderstood in Schmiedl's Hebrew translation of the responsum; cf. *Mishne Torah Ta'anit* V., §14. *See also* the corroborative statements in A. Freimann's edition of Maimonides' responsa, Jerusalem 1934, p. 338 ff. Extensive rabbinic material on this question is also offered in Boaz Cohen's study *The responsum of Maimonides concerning Music*, New York 1935.

d Cf. תשובות הגאונים באסף Nr. 21, (Moses Gaon); Harkavy, תשובות הגאונים Nr. 60, (Hay Gaon); Alfasi, *Ber.* 25b. *See also* Farmer's interpretation, with which we do not entirely agree, and Boaz Cohen, *op. cit.*, pp. 12–19.

116. Ephorus mentioned a general principle derived from the experience of war, and said: "A warrior has to drink a strong drink when he reaches the battle line. If he has done so, he will be fit, otherwise the fire in him will be extinguished, motion will stop, and the body will become cold to such an extent that he will appear like a man trembling and shivering. The channels, (i. e. the blood-vessels) will be destroyed and the warmth blocked. But if he drinks, kindling his ardor, his ardor will move by musical rhythm. And when musical rhythm has inflamed his ardor in turn, then appears the form (i. e. the Platonic *eidos*) of courage. For the movement of war is determined by the rhythm of Music. This is a statement well known to the heroes of war, although not every brave warrior is able to explain it, unless he is keen and intelligent with regard to military secrets. Many of the courageous men, therefore, used to drink a little wine when they came into the ranks, in order to stir up movement, and to get rid of fear and sorrow which they may have to meet, so that right at the outset, when reaching the battle line they will by virtue of the ardor resulting from wine, be provided with the heat of the elements. Wine, therefore, is only an occasional device, making it possible for the musical rhythms, produced by the musicians, to move the warrior toward courage. It is courage (not wine) that moves courageous men. For when musical rhythm is generated and maintained to the end, the sublime form (i. e. the virtue *andreia*) becomes manifest."

He also said: "A small quantity of wine stimulates the mind, (i. e. its rhythmical functions), and causes pleasantness of speech as an effect of the mind's rhythmic structure. For everything which is measured (rhythmically) is pleasant. But it may be that the pleasantness of speech derives from the excellence of the spirits of those assembled."

138 and 146. The science of Music envisages eight modes of melodies, which differ from one another because of expansion and contraction, height and depth, and other differences in their musical structure. The eighth mode functions as a genus which comprehends the other seven modes: and this is the meaning of: "To the chief musician upon *Šeminit*." (Ps. 12.)

The Psalmist has alluded to this cryptically, that is, by means of the number seven in the repetition of the word *kol* in the Psalm: "Give unto the Lord, O ye mighty," (Ps. 29), while the phrase: "All say: 'glory'," (v. 9) alludes to the eighth mode comprehending all of the others. I cannot explain any further.

140. Furthermore, since the entire line AB consists of 3 imaginative lines TB; for TB makes 2/3 of CB, the half of AB, and that which constitutes 2/3 of a half makes 1/3 of the whole. The proportion of the tone AB will therefore equal three tones TB. This proportion is called that of the octave and the fifth, because it is combined from the proportion of the Octave, (namely the double, as explained already), and the proportion of an increase by one half, called the fifth, the explanation of which follows here immediately: For AB equals 1½ ZB, since ½ ZB equals 1/3 of AB; it follows that AB equals 1½ZB. The tone of AB is, therefore, equal to 1½ of the tone ZB, and is called the proportion of the Fifth, because the same proportion exists in the number five. The number 5, indeed consists of 3 1/3 (= 10/3), the proportion of which to 5 equals the proportion of ZB to AB. (10/3:5/ = ZB:AB), and a third (of 5) which makes 1, ½, 1/6, the proportion of which to 5 equals the proportion of ¼TB:AB.

141. The fifth proportion is called that of a double or triple plus two portions, as for instance the proportion of 8 to 3, for 8 is a double of 3 plus two thirds (8/3 = 2 + 2/3); or as the proportion of 11 to 3, because 11 is a triple of 3 plus two thirds (11/3 = 3 + 2/3). They are also called combined proportions, when the preceding terms of the proportions (the numerators) are multiplied by one another, and then the following terms (the denominators) are also multiplied by one another.

154. Saadia Gaon, *'Emunot We-De'ot*, X, end. (Ibn Tibbon's translation.) Likewise an isolated sound, an isolated melodic unit, or an isolated melody or mode moves but one of the dispositions of the soul, so that through them the soul may sometimes be endangered. However, a mixture of them will harmonize the manifestations of the soul's dispositions and powers. It is necessary to know the effects of the isolated modes in order that they may be combined accordingly. We say that the melodies (modes-*niggunim*) are of eight patterns, each of them having

a certain number of tones (beats-*ne'imot*). The first mode consists of three beats tied together, one in motion and one at rest. The second mode consists, likewise, of three beats tied together; one resting and another moving. These two modes stir up the ardor of the blood, and consequently the passion for rulership and domination.

The third mode consists of two beats tied together, between which there is no time for another beat while one beat rests. But between every low, high, and low tone there is time for one beat. This mode alone stimulates the yellow bile, and consequently the virtues of fortitude, courage and their like.

The fourth mode consists of three beats tied together, between which there is no time for a single beat; but between every three beats, there is time for one beat. This mode alone stimulates the white humor (phlegm), and consequently makes manifest the dispositions of vileness, servility, cowardice, and their like.

The fifth mode consists of one single tone, and two different tones between which there is no time for one beat; but between the rising inflection (*arsis*) and falling inflection (*thesis*) there is time for one beat.

The sixth mode consists of three tones in motion.

The seventh mode consists of two contiguous beats between which there is no interval of a beat; but with an interval of two beats between every two tones.

The eighth mode consists of two contiguous beats, between which there is no interval of a tone; but with an interval of two tones between every two tones.

The last four modes affect the black bile, and lead to the manifestation of various dispositions of the soul, at times to joy, for example, and at other times to sorrow.

It is, therefore, the custom of kings to intermingle the modes in such manner, that their souls come to a harmonious balance, wherein these melodies may stimulate such dispositions as help the kings in directing their kingdom, so that they may be neither too merciful, nor too cruel, neither too mighty, nor too timid, neither too much nor too little given to joy.

162. Tones, furthermore, are divided into categories of intervals, so that some of them increase or diminish in size by com-

parison with others. Everyone of these parts again can be reduced to the smallest fractions possible where all further subdivision is precluded.

176. The association of tones (*ne'imot*) determines their impression upon the hearer. It is either one of succession as, for instance, when we strike one string and then, at the termination of this sound, strike another string, producing another tone; or it is a combination of tones as, for instance, when we vibrate two strings simultaneously so that from both together comes forth a composite tone, as is produced by the musical instrument, called *'Abub*.

As a summing up, the following theses are propounded:

1) The principle of *ethos* is common to Greek, Jewish, and Arabic music theory.
2) It is applied to melodic modes and to meter by the Greeks; to rhythm, word, and meter by the Jews; and mainly to the instruments and their parts by the Arabs.
3) Both allopathic and homeopathic effects of music on a mentally ill person are postulated by Greek and Jewish thinkers.
4) The principle of eight modes has been erroneously transferred from melodic to rhythmic modes in Judaeo-Arabic music theory.

ERRATA IN

THE PHILOSOPHY AND THEORY OF MUSIC IN JUDAEO-ARABIC LITERATURE

ERIC WERNER and ISAIAH SONNE

in Volume XVI of the Hebrew Union College Annual

p. 255, line 6, *for* המות *read* המלות

p. 255, line 7, *for* הנהוגית *read* הנהוגות

p. 258, note 27, *for* עילו *read* עליו

p. 258, note 27, *for* ל"אבד *read* לאב"ד

p. 260, note 36, *for* ארך *read* ערך

p. 294, line 17, *for* בכול *read* בכל

p. 297, note 151, *for* עליעזר *read* אליעזר

p. 298, line 3, *for* Astonomy *read* Astronomy

p. 307, line 2, *for* הגבחה *read* הגבהה

p. 307, last line, *for* מחומר *read* מחובר

p. 309, lines 7 and 8, *for* מלאה *read* מלאכת

Greek Ideas on
Music in Judeo-Arabic
Literature

Reprinted with permission of The Free Press, a division of Macmillan Publishing Co., Inc. *The Commonwealth of Music—In Honor of Curt Sachs*, ed. G. Reese and R. Brandel, (New York, 1965), pp. 71-96.

I. Definition and Classification of Music

$\mathcal{T}$he expression "Hellas in the Orient's embrace," coined by the art historian Strzygowski, well describes the pseudomorphosis of cultures in the Near East from the rise of Hellenism to the decline of the Arabic caliphate. Oswald Spengler has labored the point to its extreme consequences; and his less original but more careful confrère, Arnold Toynbee, has once more stressed the importance of this pseudomorphosis.[1] Thus the historian is now prepared to accept ancient Greek ideas in Islamic disguise. Toynbee's scrutiny of this intellectual superimposition merits citation for his discernment of the two antagonistic trends involved in it:

> The Islamic state, in the first chapter of its history, was up in arms against the political ascendancy of Hellenism in Southwest Asia and Egypt—an ascendancy that had been upheld there by Roman power since the last century B.C. On the cultural plane, on the other hand, Islam eventually equipped itself for playing its part as a universal religion by drawing on Hellenistic intellectual resources.

71

Thus its attitude towards Hellenism was the ambivalent one of attraction towards it on the cultural plane coexisting with hostility towards it on the political plane. . . .[2]

Toynbee, however, neglects all Jewish elements in Arabic philosophy, although he is quite familiar with some of its Christian components.

In the Arabic literature on music, confluent Biblical, Hellenic, Hellenistic, and Islamic ideas form an impressive synthesis. The Jewish authors, writing under the spell of both Hellenic thought and its Arabic interpretation, attempted a reconciliation of this composite philosophy with Biblical and Rabbinic concepts. It is mainly in this respect that they deviate from their Arabic confrères and teachers. This is already evident in the definition and classification of music.

Here a word of caution may be appropriate. The following pages deal chiefly with the *concept of music* as expressed in Judeo-Arabic literature; they are less concerned with the actual performance or structure of Jewish or Arabic music. This kind of music was occasionally contrived at the courts of the caliphs and was mainly cultivated there.[3] In general, the musical culture of the Arabs reflects, in a different spectrum, another synthesis of Greek and Mesopotamian civilization—i.e., of the old Aramaean and Hebrew—just as early Christian songs represent a synthesis of Hellenistic and the newer Jewish-Syrian ideas and practices. Thus, for example, the mythical father of all music, called Yubal in the Bible, becomes Tubal in Islamic tradition; his sister, the Biblical *Na'amah*, is the Arabic Ḍilal (possible Delilah?).[4]

The older musical culture of Judaism did not develop in a steady, unbroken course: with the destruction of the Second Temple the further evolution of art music ceased for the next 1400 years. Still, the musical glories of the Temple cast a sunset glow over subsequent discussions of music among the Jews. Islam, on the other hand, could only look forward to attaining new heights and was less handicapped by either prohibitions or nostalgias.[5]

Yet even in the Islamic orbit the status of musical scholarship was by no means undisputed. The secular sciences (to which the study of music belonged), including all philosophical propedeutics, flourished under the Fatimide and Spanish caliphs, whereas they encountered considerable opposition in the northwest of Asia Minor. In fact, the influence of Hellenic thought on Islam was not equally distributed at any time or in any region.[6] The Hellenic component in Arabic musical speculation came to the fore only after a fierce battle with the puritans; it took place about the very same time as, in Judaism, a similar battle—out of which emerged the professional precentor (*hazan*) of the synagogue— was being fought for and against the newfangled metrical hymns or *piyyutim*. These initial disputes began in the 7th century and lasted until the 10th.

In examining the ways in which the Greeks, Arabs, and Jews *defined* music, we are at the outset confronted with a paradoxical situation. It is well known that the chief domain of the musical culture of the three nations was *vocal* practice, usually connected with a text. Yet the definitions that we shall quote show a remarkable neglect of music as a communication linked with words. Of the four Hellenistic definitions, namely those of Ptolemy, Aristides Quintilianus, Cleonides, and the Anonymus Bellermann, not one mentions the connection between tones and words. Ptolemy: Μουσική ἐστιν δύναμις καταλεπτικὴ τῶν ἐν τοῖς ψόφοις περὶ τὸ ὀξὺ καὶ τὸ βαρὺ διαφορῶν —a definition that stresses the scientific aspect of distinguishing between high and low pitches. Aristides Quintilianus: Μουσική ἐστιν ἐπιστήμη μέλους καὶ τῶν περὶ μέλος συμβαινόντων —a definition that presents music as the science of melody and of matters pertaining to it. Cleonides: Μουσική ἐστιν ἐπιστήμη τῆς τοῦ ἡρμοσμένου φύσεως —a definition that regards music as the science of the nature of harmonic structure. Anonymus Bellermann: Μουσική ἐστιν ἐπιστήμη μέλους τελείου καὶ ὀργανικοῦ—a definition that treats of music as the science of perfect melody, including instrumental tunes.[7] Three of the four definitions term music a science, and one calls it a faculty (δύναμις). Three stress the melodic component in general, and only Ptolemy is concerned with intervals and pitches. Here already we encounter the distinction between music as science (ἐπιστήμη) and as skill, applied in performance (τέχνη), a distinction that later, in Arabic and Jewish literature, was stressed constantly.

The Greek ideas found their way into the Arabic realm through translations and paraphrases by Syrian scholars. Such texts were accessible to Muslims as well as to Jews. From the period when this transition from Hellenistic to Syro-Arabic culture was in progress, we encounter a fifth important definition, attributed to Euclid: "Music is a science [or profession] which connects every species [genus] with a thing pertaining to the same species [genus]. Subduing the nature (temperaments), music stirs up that which is at rest and brings to rest that which is restless." [8] The first part of this statement, transmitted to us by Ibn Honein, is not quite clear; the second part, however, combines elements of the "ethos-doctrine" with a kinetic approach.

In contrast with this speculative description, Al-Farabi's statement is pragmatic and straightforward: "Music is a science (theory) that occupies itself with melodies, not only with their arrangement and composition, but also with their practical performance.[9] This definition exceeds in its second part the scope of any of the statements quoted above: it refers also to the *interpretation* of melodies. Such a practical approach is not far from the Aristoxenian concept, which judges music almost exclusively according to acoustical and sensual criteria, relying upon the ear and its perception rather than upon mathematics. It was accepted by the Arabs rather than by the Jews. The latest classic theorists of Arabic civilization, such as Safiyu-D-Din (late 13th century) and his contemporaries, attempted a synthesis of the strictly mathematical approach of the Pythagoreans and the "practical" and phenomenological ideas of the Aristoxenians.[10]

Although the texts of Al-Kindi's definitions "are so sadly maimed by copyists that even a tentative reconstruction is unsatisfactory," [11] it is clear that this great Arabic theorist (c. 800-875?) was the first philosopher in the history of music to make an exact distinction between a sound, the result of a system of non-periodic vibrations (Arabic *saut*), and a note or tone, caused by periodic vibrations (Arabic *naghma*).[12] This distinction, generally neglected in musical theory (except in treatises on acoustics), has recently become very important; it represents the watershed between "traditional" or "conventional" music and "electronic music" or *"musique concrète."*[13]

On the Jewish side, the first straightforward definition of music occurs in Spain in the writings of R. Moses Botarel (end of the 14th century). There we read: "The science of song and melody—this is music; the science of melody, i.e., of the motion of ascending and descending tones, as well as the study of intervals." [14] The late occurrence of the definition in Hebrew is somewhat puzzling; it does not, however, indicate a lack of interest in the subject, as we shall see. If anything, it betokens a certain reluctance to define an art, the value and religious importance of which was fully recognized by earlier Hebrew authors, even in Scripture. Those authors were more concerned with speculations on the psychological influence of music and its multi-valued functions, to borrow a mathematical expression, than with semantic problems.

The "science of music" has two aspects in Judeo-Arabic literature: applied music theory and esthetic-ethical speculation on the moral influence of music. This bipartition corresponds to a similar dichotomy within the general discussion of music.

Practical music
↓
calculation of pitches
and intervals

Theoretical Music
↓
theory applied to ethics
and esthetics

Turning to classifications of music, we encounter Greek ideas in profusion; the ones most frequently elaborated in the Arabic and Jewish orbit were those of Aristoxenos, Plutarch, Aristides Quintilianus, and Aristotle. In the subsequent tabulation we shall juxtapose each of the Greek systems with at least one Arabic and one Jewish counterpart, thus demonstrating the gradual metamorphosis of Hellenic ideas.[15]

The tabulation, on pp. 76-77, shows quite tangibly that the Greeks were the music-teachers of both Arabs and Jews; this much is well known.[16] But it is also evident that our Judeo-Arabic authors were not content with simply paraphrasing their Hellenic sources. In almost every case they elaborated upon the Greek ideas. In these elaborations, Arabs and Jews usually parted company. While we find that in the field of definition and in the division of the octave, etc., the Jewish authors clearly depend upon Arab sources, especially on Al-Farabi and Ibn Sina (Avicenna), the situation changes as soon as we examine ideas on the philosophy of music, i.e., its moral influence. Here we encounter sharp differences between Islamic and Jewish thought.

II. The Ethos Doctrine

Whatever the status of Greek speculations on the *ethos* of musical composition may have been—and it changed considerably from the Pythagoreans to Aristoxenos, Philodemus, and Ptolemy—neither the place nor the function of the *ethos* doctrine within the classic Greek system of musical thinking is comparable to the place and function of the fully developed doctrine as expressed by Arabic and Jewish authors. We encounter here a curious vacillation in the nature of the doctrine. The fact that music was embedded in the Quadrivium next to arithmetic, geometry, and astronomy, makes evident the recognition of its *rational* character as a science.[17] Yet all during the Middle Ages rational astronomy served as handmaid to superstition-ridden astrology; and speculation about the moral influence of music was tinged with astrological and alchemistic conceptions. The Arabs managed to link them even with physiological principles, following some of Galen's suggestions.

Where, finally, cabbalistic thought emerged powerfully in Judaism, it was applied to the philosophy of music. Cabbala, ethos-doctrine, alchemy, astrology, the therapeutic value of music, and the axiom of the harmony of the spheres formed an ideological compound, which it is difficult for anybody to unravel who is not familiar with late Gnosticism and Neo-Pythagoreanism.[18]

According to the Pythagoreans, the human soul is in constant motion. This motion is defined by certain numerical proportions that

DEFINITION

Greeks

1. Aristoxenos:
Movement of Tones
2. (Pseudo)-Plutarch:
Science pertaining to voice and tone [19]
3. Aristides Quintilianus: [20]
Science of melody and of all things pertaining to it

Arabs

1. Al-Farabi: [21]
Science of understanding harmony and harmonic species; also of melodies and their composition
2. Safiyu-D-Din: [22]
Science of tones, whose height or lowness can be measured exactly; also of all compositions of such tones

Jews

R. Moses Botarel:
Science of song and melody; science of ascending and descending tones, also of intervals

CLASSIFICATION

Greeks

1. Aristoxenos:
a) *Theoretical*
Study of Intervals
Harmony
Melopoeia
b) *Practical*
Rhythmics
(1) in speech (λέξις)
(2) in melody (μέλος)
(3) in bodily motion (κίνησις σωματική)

Arabs

1. Al-Farabi:
a) *Speculative*
(1) Principles
(2) Intervals
(3) Tone-word relationship
(4) Rhythms
(5) Melopoeia
b) *Practical*
Invention of harmonic species
(1) in natural media (voice)
(2) in artificial media (instruments)

Jews

1. Shemtob Ibn Falaquera: [24]
a) *Theory*
(1) Principles
(2) Intervals
(3) Consonances, instruments
(4) Rhythms
(5) Melopoeia of metrical texts
b) *Practice*
(1) Production and performance of tones
(α) by natural means (vocal)
(β) by instruments
(2) Practical composition

2. Aristotle:
Ethical (ἠθικαί)
Expressing action (πρακτικαί)
Evoking enthusiasm (ἐνθουσιαστικαί)
3. (Pseudo)-Plutarch:
Harmonic-melodic (ἁρμονική)
Rhythmic (ῥυθμική)
Metric (μετρική)
4. Aristides Quintilianus:
a) *Theoretical*
Acoustics
Arithmetic
Harmonic-melodic
Rhythmic
Metric
b) *Practical*
Melopoeia
Rhythmopoeia
Poetry
Vocal Training
Instrumental Training
Acting
Informative (ἐξαγγελτικόν)
Pedagogic

2. Al-Kindi:
Melody
Rhythm
Philosophy
Ethos of rhythmic melody:
(1) creating grief
(2) exciting delight
(3) producing veneration, honor, and praise (*mu'tadie*) [23]
3. Safiyu-D-Din:
a) *Theory*
Acoustics
Intervals
Groups, scales
Rhythms
b) *Practice*
Melopoeia
Compositions
c) *Performance*
Interpretation
Ornaments (vocal or instrumental)
Moral effects

2. Ibn Aknin: [25]
a) *Theory*
(1) Principles
(2) Numerical relations of intervals
(3) Harmonic-melodic composition
(4) Theory of rhythms and meters
b) *Practice*
(1) Melopoeia; practical composition
(2) Performance and interpretation
(3) Moral effects

attend the harmonic relations of the tones.[26] Therefore, certain tunes evoke corresponding motions of the listener's soul. The mathematical analogy linking the ratios of the soul's motion, the vibration of strings, and finally the movements of the heavenly bodies, constitutes the basis upon which rests the principle of ethical power—in Greek philosophy, the ἐπανόρθωσις τῶνἠθῶν. The idea of the moral *katharsis* of the emotions,[27] as proclaimed by Aristotle and his followers, is closely related to the older Pythagorean ideology. The connection between body and soul is improved and "harmonized" by properly selected tunes, and this involves also the idea of music as effective medical treatment. The motions of the celestial bodies, of the macrocosmos, are supposed to be paralleled by those of the soul.[28] Thus a complicated numerical calculation in musical astrology begins to take shape.[29]

Turning from the physical to the physiological, we meet the somewhat strange conception that music affects the "humors" or the human body. Here the Arabs and the Jews went far beyond the original Greek idea. The Greeks, as we have seen, asserted a close relationship between music and medicine, ascribing to music a distinctly therapeutic effect upon both body and soul. But while Plato, Aristotle, and the Neo-Platonists were content to state the fact, explaining it by the cathartic and sedative influence of the musical art, the Arabic and Jewish philosophers went boldly and almost materialistically into physiological details. They emphasized the effect of music on the humors, blood, phlegm, yellow bile, and black bile. Let us compare some of the most significant statements on these points. Leaving aside the many legends of the Greeks, Arabs, and Jews, telling how music cured some highly fantastic ailments, we turn to the ideas that lie behind these stories.

The Greeks linked medicine and music in two different ways:

1. The Pythagoreans consider number and proportion as instruments of the imitative principle (μίμησις), which prevails in all of the arts. This is somewhat similar to the thought of the Aristotelians.[30] Thus music, medicine, and mathematics employ the same fundamentals; music does so in rhythms, intervals, and proportions, and medicine does so in the proportion of the humors and medicaments and, particularly, in the mysterious ratios of human pulsation,[31] whereas, in mathematics, number and proportion are the working material itself. Plato expresses similar ideas in his *Timaeus*.

2. The other link between music and medicine is more physiological. It is based chiefly on the term *katharsis* in a medical sense. Aristotle as well as Galen uses this word with the connotation of "purgation." Considering how Jacob Bernays has exhibited the predominantly medical background of the entire cathartic idea, we could characterize this principle as that of a treatment basically homoeopathic.[32] The Neo-Pla-

tonists Proclos and Jamblichos accepted Aristotle's explanation. Cure was accomplished, according to the Aristotelian prescription, by playing, before the insane corybantes, frantic melodies on the orgiastic instrument, the Phyrgian aulos. Thus *katharsis* was brought about homoeopathically. The Pythagoreans, however, preferred the playing of solemn, soothing melodies for the maniacal listeners in order to impress upon their disorganized souls the magically numerical and cosmic order, attuning them, as it were, to the proportions of the universe. This is the type of *katharsis* that is allopathic.[33]

The literature of the Arabs and the Jews discusses only the allopathic form of treatment, although in their philosophy cathartic elements still play a part. But for therapeutic purposes Arabs and Jews seem to have relied entirely on Pythagorean principles, which they stressed to the limits of the absurd. Being good physicians, keen observers, and consistent logicians, the Arabs zealously embodied everything in their Pythagorean concept. Accordingly, each musical mode, even each string of their chief instrument, the *'ud*, had to be seen *sub specie mundi*. The four seasons, the four humors, the four cardinal virtues, and the four elements had to be embodied in their music theory.[34]

We find in Honein-Alharizi's *Maxims of the Philosophers* a characteristic statement: "The reason for our making four strings is their correspondence to the four temperaments of which man is composed." [35] The author goes on to associate with every string of the *'ud* a special effect upon some special humor. No less specific is Falaquera, and also Saadya who, in his *Emunot wede'ot* (Beliefs and Opinions), Chap. 10 (end), connects every rhythmical mode (Arab. *naghama*, Hebr. *ne'imā*) with one humor and one virtue respectively. A highly important source for our subject is also the *Ikhvan es-Safa* ("Brethren of Purity"), from which Saadya may possibly have borrowed.[36]

We quote now a few sentences from the *Ikhvan es-Safa* by way of illustration:

> The musicians restrict the number of the strings of the lute to four,[37] neither more nor less, in order that their work might resemble the things of sublunar nature in imitation of God's wisdom.
> The treble string is like the element of fire, its tone being hot and violent.
> The second string is like the element of air; its tone corresponds to the humidity of air and to its softness.
> The third string is like the element of water; its tone suggests water-like moisture and coolness.
> The bass string is like the heaviness and thickness of the element earth.

Subsequently the *Ikvan es-Safa* explains that the treble string cor-

responds to the yellow bile, the second string to the blood, the third
to the saliva, and the bass string to the black bile, as elaborately
explained.

Our source continues: "If one employs these tones in appropriate
melodies and uses these melodies at those times of the night or day,
the nature of which is opposed to the nature of a virulent disease . . . ,
they assuage the sickness, breaking up its force and relieving the sick
ones of their pains." [38]

Thus music was generally considered a strictly allopathic, pain-
relieving, or invigorating medicine, corresponding to the mixtures of
the humors or of the elements. Ibn-Sina refers to these matters
frequently in his al-Kanun.[39] Throughout Arabic literature, the Pythagorean relationship between astronomy, music, and medicine is consistently maintained.

Falaquera's *Mebhakkesh* ("The Searcher") closely follows these
ideas. This work is a poetic revision of an earlier work, *Beginning of
Wisdom*, with a stronger emphasis on the Pythagorean point of view.[40]

From here on it is only a short step, in fact an imperceptible gradation, to a detailed and elaborate theory of the influence of music upon
the individual emotions. It seems, however, that in this field the
Oriental nations preferred less of system and more of detail, fewer explanations and more plain statements. There are even more significant
differences, which we shall consider presently.

We are confronted now with a perennial problem of philosophy
and esthetics, a problem that concerns us today as much as it did the
people of three thousand years ago, a problem that is unlikely ever
to be solved objectively. It cannot be our task to discuss that problem
itself, and we shall only describe the different attitudes toward it found
in Greek, Arabic, and Hebrew Literature.

The problem to which we refer poses two chief questions, which
we shall formulate cursorily:

1. Does music express emotions and, if so, how?
2. Does music evoke emotions and, if so, how?

We may, again in a cursory way, classify the first question as one
relating to the expressive powers of music and the other as one relating
to the impressive powers. The very approach to these problems differs
among the Greek, Jewish, and Arabic authors and shows their unique
characteristics, although the answers frequently sound similar. But we
must not allow these apparently similar answers to deceive us about
the fundamentally different attitudes assumed. The Greeks consider
the issue either from the psychological-ethical side, exemplified by the
Pythagoreans, Platonists, and Aristotelians, or from the purely esthetic-

formalistic side, as exemplified by the Sceptics and the Sophists. Both questions are answered in the affirmative by the first group, while the Sophists give a negative answer to at least the first question and restrict their affirmative answer to the second one to a few cases. They explain the influence of music upon the emotions by a materialistic theory of the association of words and ideas.[41] Furthermore, the Greeks are far more interested in the second question than in the first. Both questions were answered in the affirmative by Aristotle. To the first he applied the principle of *mimesis*, i.e., imitation of the emotions. In dealing with the second, he modified and even contradicted Plato's explicit evaluation or disapproval of certain modes and their ethos.[42]

Very clear in this respect is the doctrine of Aristoxenos, a disciple of Aristotle, who probably gave the first characterization of the three τρόποι (styles), viz., the systaltic, the diastaltic, and the hesychastic. The first is described as paralyzing human energy. It includes love-songs as well as funeral lamentations. The second is strong and virile, spurs to action, and thus becomes the heroic style employed in tragedy. The last is in between. It indicates and at the same time stimulates balance of mind and feeling.[43] We notice here, as a decisive criterion, the effect that music allegedly has upon human will-power. *A priori*, Aristoxenos assumes that music expresses the same ethos that it is supposed to evoke in the listener. In all cases, only such music is considered good that arouses ethical powers and eventually dissipates emotions that are harmful or evil.[44] In short, the Greeks aim not to evoke stormy or violent feelings but to banish them, thus creating a happy philosophical balance of the soul.

Quite different is the Arabic approach, and different again the Jewish approach. It is here that we find perhaps the only really important departure of the Jewish attitude from Arabic influence in the entire realm of musical thought. The Arabic writers either consider music in its psycho-physiological, even in its materialistic aspect, or view it from the lofty tower of their metaphysical or mystical speculations.[45] If we ask which attitude in Arabia was not that of the esoteric scholars but that of the people in general, there can be no doubt that the materialistic concept represented the common outlook.[46] The Arabs in general prefer emotional excitement to eudemonic pacification. The philosophers discarded the sentiment of the masses and adopted much of the Greek ideology, even if with some change of emphasis. However, the question of expression in music is deemed important by Al-Farabi, though all but disregarded by the Greeks, whose distinction between "expressive" and "impressive" Al-Farabi adopted.[47]

Arabic thinkers raised no issue about harmful and unpleasant emotions: "Other good melodies evoke such emotions as satisfaction, ire, clemency, cruelty, fear, sadness, regret, and other passions." [48] The Jewish authors try to avoid anything violent, excessive, or even licentious.

While Arabic literature contains some genuinely esthetic speculations on music, Hebrew thinkers were all but indifferent to esthetics of any kind. This apparent disregard is well established in Scripture, and hence is not only traditional, but authoritative.

To Biblical literature the idea that music is beautiful is evidently alien; music had its place in the ritual of the Temple, or it served as a spontaneous expression of any individual or a group, but it did not have any direct connection with the "esthetically beautiful." That conception is linked to visual sensations only, as the Song of Songs and similar poems seem to indicate. Even so late a book as Ecclesiasticus, which describes in the most glowing terms the cult of the Temple, uses the word "beautiful" only where a visual sensation is involved.[49]

Otherwise the epithet "beautiful," when employed in Scripture, is always on the borderline between the esthetic and the ethical. A few examples will illustrate the point: "For it is a pleasant thing [the Hebrew word *na'im* indicates the pleasant, the agreeable, and the morally good simultaneously] if thou keep them [the words of the wise] within thee" (Proverbs 22:18); or: "Behold how good and how pleasant [*na'im*] it is, when brethren dwell together in unity" (Psalm 133:1). Here the Hebrew terms are *tob* (morally good) and *na'im* (pleasant, agreeable). A similar combination is found in the following verse: "The Lord is good [*tob*]; sing praises to His name; for it is lovely [*na'im*]" (Psalm 135:3). The juxtaposition of the "good Lord" and the fitting praises that are "lovely" is perfect.

In the entire lengthy description of the first Temple (I Kings, Chap. 5-8) the word "beautiful" does not occur; it does occur, however, in Proverbs 31:30, where it has a derogatory sense: "Favour is deceitful, and beauty [*yofi*, sensual prettiness] is vain."

The acoustical beauty of a voice or of an instrument is usually described as "sweet," "agreeable," "strong." Hence, the purely esthetic element in musical matters is not fully represented in Old Testament and early Rabbinic literature; these sources either stress the social point of view ("agreeable"), or the sensual ("sweet"), or the majestic. This type of description is found in Sirach and Josephus, perhaps under the influence of Hellenism.

Quite unlike the classic Greek estheticism with its sharp distinction —beautiful or ugly—Judaism poses another antithesis: sacred-secular. Two characteristic passages will clarify this. In the beautiful Psalm 23, the Psalmist concludes:

Thou anointest my head with oil;
My cup runneth over.
Surely, goodness and mercy
Shall follow me all the days of my life;
And I will dwell
In the house of the Lord for ever.

To the Jewish singer, the last prediction of the psalm promises happiness, bliss, and beauty all together. Similarly, with sharper emphasis, the concept is expressed in the following: "And they [my priests] shall teach my people the difference between the Holy and the Common and cause them to discern between the unclean and the clean" (Ezekiel 44:23).

From this passage the standard prayer has been derived that is recited at the end of every Sabbath: "Praised be Thou, O Lord our God, King of the Universe, who makest a distinction between the Holy and the Profane, as between light and darkness . . ."

In one respect, however, Jewish and Greek conceptions of the esthetically valuable are very much akin; just as in Platonic philosophy the truly Good is also the truly Beautiful, so in Judaism the genuinely Holy is also the Beautiful and the Good. Thus a resemblance to the concept of Plato's *kalokagathia* (the beautiful and good) is in evidence in Jewish thinking. We encounter it, for example, if we compare Plato's remarks about Socrates' ugliness with the Talmudic anecdote of R. Joshua ben Hananya and the king's daughter:

R. Joshua ben Hananya was an ugly hunchback. Once a king's daughter ridiculed him because of his ugliness and marvelled, rather dubiously, that a treasury of wisdom should be sheltered in so unattractive an abode. Whereupon R. Joshua asked her in what kind of vessels people preserve their best wines: in silver, gold, or clay. She replied that the best wines are kept in containers of simple clay. Then he asked her why she was so astounded that beauty of learning and wisdom should be sheltered in his—physically unattractive—person.

The core of the comparison of Socrates and R. Joshua may be expressed in the following statement: mere external pleasantness is, on the highest level of Greek and Jewish philosophy, spurned in preference to a "beautiful soul." In Scripture, the identity of beauty and holiness is best expressed in Psalm 29:2; 96:9 ("beauty of holiness").

This antinomy between the Arabic and the Jewish conceptions of music becomes most perceptible in Maimonides. What we have said about the state of Arabic music sheds a new light on his *Responsum* concerning music. It becomes clear that Maimonides had in mind chiefly the exciting and sensual songs of the Arabs and the Arabian Jews.[50]

Maimonides makes three distinctions: 1) He admits that there are some few connoisseurs who study music as a suitable means of reaching a higher wisdom (the Greek διανόησις). But, he continues, one must not base one's conclusions on these individual cases. The laws of the Torah were written not for exceptional people, but for the majority. 2) The prohibition of secular music is based on Hosea 9:1; Isaiah 5:12; Amos 6:5; and Babylonian Talmud, Tractate Berachot 24a, emphasizing that, in most instances, music does nothing but excite lust. It makes no difference whether the texts of the songs are in Arabic or in Hebrew; for not the language, but only the content of an utterance matters. The Jewish people must become a holy nation and must avoid everything that does not lead to perfection. 3) The music that is mentioned and even recommended by the proper spiritual leaders is of a purely religious character and consists of psalms, hymns, and songs of exultation. Secular music ought not to be tolerated; surely not when performed by a singing female. Elsewhere, however, music as a therapeutic measure [51] receives Maimonides' commendation.

All that separates the ideology of Jewish philosophers from the Arabic view is clearly recognizable in this *Responsum*. Maimonides endorses religious music. He wishes to eliminate all secular music, regardless of the few individuals who study such music in order to achieve a higher wisdom. He stresses the Biblical and Talmudic tradition and opposes the fashion of his time. In his preoccupation with the religio-ethical effects, Maimonides completely ignores esthetic appreciation. (The same is true, as we know, of his attitude toward poetry.) [52] On the whole, Maimonides faithfully reflects the Platonic and not the Aristotelian point of view. Like Plato he gives an ethical evaluation rather than an esthetic classification. [53] Still there are also some deviations. The highest aim of the Greek philosopher-artist is the world of ideas. Music is only an instrument for ethical education [54] and has all but lost its religious function. The highest goal of Maimonides, on the other hand, is the intellectual and ethical perfection that leads to the prophetic perception of the Divine. Music may, in some cases, conduct one to this goal. Nonetheless, music has no place in ethical training. Thus there are two different levels on which music appears as a spiritual force. It is hard to avoid associating the position of Maimonides with the function of music among the troops of ancient prophets, in whom it aroused the *nebuah*, the prophetic inspiration. [55] Maimonides refers, in fact, to the story of the prophet Elisha: "But now bring me a minstrel. And it came to pass, when the minstrel played, that the hand of the Lord came upon him." [56] This incident is mentioned in the philosophies of music throughout the ages, together with references to David, Miriam, and Asaph. The Church Fathers took over the story and passed it on to the philosophers as an irrefutable proof that music has divine potentialities.[57] Jewish literature also refers to this frequently.

We may regard the *doctrine of virtue* as an extension of the ethos-doctrine. Here the interrelationship between philosophy and music becomes even more articulate.

An almost mystical realm opens up before us when we consider the Neo-Platonic philosophy of the movements of the soul as affected by music. Here Greek, Arabic, and Jewish views converge. We confront an eclectic combination of ideas derived from Plato, Aristotle, Porphyry, and Plotinus. In one and the same Syro-Hebraic work,[58] we may find the views of all four philosophers reposing peacefully side by side. We give but one example: "Living in solitude, the soul sings plaintive melodies [emphasizing the vanity of the world] whereby it reminds itself of its own superior world. As soon as nature (the physical world) sees this . . . she presents herself in various forms, introduced one by one to the soul, until she finally succeeds in recapturing the soul. The latter, busy with worldly affairs, soon forsakes its own true essence and abandons that which is sublime in composition and in the rhythm of artistic melodies. At last . . . , the soul is entirely submerged in Nature's ocean." [59]

Very similar ideas may be found in Aristides Quintilianus, who describes the soul's solitude, the cathartic influence of music upon it, and the temptations, such as those offered by tawdry pleasures,[60] that keep it from perfection.

Alongside this grand and lofty vision, we find in Honein-Alharizi's work strictly Platonic theories, of which we quote only two examples:

> Plato once said to a guitar-player who accompanied the music with his voice, "This voice is material, we do not need it." "Master," asked his disciples, "are you not material?" "Yes," replied Plato, "but my body is a servant of my intellect." [61]

This idea is directly borrowed from *Timaeus* 67; another thought, which has found its most articulate expression in the *Republic* III, 398 C, and also in *Laws* II, 669 C, is incorporated in the following as a legend of Alexander the Great, Aristotle's most celebrated disciple:

> Alexander, when he was a young man, once sat with his father and his courtiers in a tavern. A musician sang a song of love and cohabitation between a courtier and a maid servant of the king. The king was angry and said to the musician: "Do you not know that it is written: 'Bodies of free men shall not be coupled with bodies of slaves, lest their offspring be bad ones'? And it is also written: 'You shall not drink wine, lest it alter your character and corrupt your mind.' "

Views more materialistic than those expressed in this story seem
to have been characteristic of the Arabs.[62] In the Hebrew sources such
views are almost totally missing.[63] Besides details about the individual
virtues, so extensively pondered by the Greeks, are rarely found in
Jewish literature. The Arabs, on the other hand, reared a considerable
hierarchy of virtues that music was believed to evoke.[64] Al-Farabi and
Ghazzali, in particular, stressed these speculations. Once more it is Saadya
who followed the Arabic way. The virtues according to Saadya are
power to reign, fortitude, humility, joy, and sorrow (!). In general,
he follows the lines of Honein's work and shows striking resemblances
to the *Ikhvan*.[65] He does not, however, refer to those virtues which
Plato "standardized": [66] wisdom, moderation, justice, and courage. As
for the Hebrews, their literature prefers to stress the virtues that are
dianoetic or prophetic, apparently assuming that the practical virtues,
the ordinary or civic ones, were already achieved by the performance
of the Biblical commands.

If we ask which element of music was supposed to possess the greater
ethical power, melody or rhythm, we must answer without hesitation:
rhythm. On this point, Arabs, Greeks, and Jews agree completely.
That this view was generally accepted, we can see from all of the later
Greek and Arabic writers.[67] Saadya's entire theory is based on rhythmical constructions common in Arabic theory.[68]

III. The Harmony of the Spheres

Closely related to the ethos doctrine is the venerable principle of the
harmony of the spheres.[69] This ancient and beautiful conception was,
as we know, one of the keystones of Pythagorean cosmology. But today
it has begun to appear that the idea of sounding spheres originated much
earlier, in Egyptian and perhaps also in Babylonian culture. Apparently,
it belonged to the esoteric doctrines of the priestly classes. Only in Greek
philosophy does this conception emerge into the light of public and
systematic discussion. The Greeks incorporated the idea into the general
principle of harmony within the universe and within the human soul.

For Plato's cosmogony, harmony in its widest sense is an indispensable element.[70] Plato's allusion to the dance of the stars and to their
perfect proportions represents a distinctly Pythagorean trend of thought.
Aristotle was the only great philosopher of his time who energetically
combated the idea, although he did acknowledge its fascinating beauty.[71]
Of the later thinkers, the Neo-Platonists and the Pythagoreans again
stressed this conception. Thence it found its way into the theories
of astronomy and music of the dying ancient world.[72] Ptolemy and

Aristides Quintilianus fashioned very concrete and mathematically elaborate systems of cosmic harmony, developing some of the ideas of Nicomachus of Gerasa.[73] The last mentioned was one of the many Syrian writers who formed the bridge between Greece and Arabia over which Pythagorean doctrines traveled.[74]

The theory of cosmic harmony was not as popular with the Arabs or the Jews as it had been with the Greeks. Hence the concept of harmony of the spheres, which fitted so beautifully into the general ἁρμονία κόσμου of the Greek philosophers, while accepted and mentioned by the Arabs, was not greeted by them with much enthusiasm.[75] Al-Farabi, for one, opposed it. He vents his feelings against this doctrine in the words: "The opinion of the Pythagoreans that the planets and stars produce harmonious sounds in their courses is erroneous." [76] Nevertheless, most of the Arabic authors adhered to the ancient idea, notwithstanding Al-Farabi's great prestige. It became a cherished tradition, abandoned unwillingly even when not accorded much weight.

A different attitude is to be found in Hebrew literature. Allusions to the harmony of the spheres already appear in the Bible. The Talmud also accepts the theory, though not in a straightforward unequivocal way.[77] Jewish literature, accordingly, links the harmony of the spheres to Biblical and Talmudical authorities rather than to astronomical observation of the universe. If a Jewish writer was, in addition, inclined toward Pythagorean ideas, he could naturally support them with the available Biblical statements. Philo is the most vigorous advocate of the Pythagorean idea among the earlier Jewish philosophers. To him, the heavens are the archetype for all musical instruments. The purpose of the musical structure of the cosmos is to provide the accompaniment for hymns of praise. The seven planets are compared to the seven strings of the lyre.[78]

Among the Hebrew writers considered in this article, only Falaquera (in his *Mebakkesh*) and minor authors insist on the harmony of the spheres, though most of them support the theory by Biblical citations.[79] In his earlier work, *Beginning of Wisdom*, Falaquera follows Ibn 'Aknin almost verbatim, or rather Ibn 'Aknin's source, Al-Farabi's *De scientiis*, and does not even mention cosmic harmony.[80] It appears that Falaquera later became more friendly toward the old Pythagorean theory. As for Isaac Ben Abraham Ibn Latif, one of the lesser writers, it is characteristic that he constantly emphasizes the esoteric nature of his ruminations: "The psalmist has spoken cryptically . . . I can explain no more . . . This speculation can be grasped only by those who are initiated into both sciences." [81] The Neo-Platonists, Moses ibn Ezra and Abraham ibn Ezra, both accepted the doctrine. The former acclaims it in his poems; [82] the latter, less ardent, is content with one or two references to it. Strangely

223

enough, of all Biblical passages alluding to cosmic harmony, Abraham ibn Ezra chooses Psalm 93:4, but misses such inviting opportunities as those offered by Job 38:7 or 38:37.[83] Simon Duran also broaches the ancient idea in the same connection.[84]

The most consistent and significant opponent of the entire doctrine is Maimonides; in his *Guide* he unequivocally expresses his antagonism.[85] Thus we arrive at the surprising conclusion that philosophers of the greatest consequence in their respective lands, viz., Aristotle, Al-Farabi, and Maimonides, were sceptical of or even inimical to the theory of cosmic harmony. To what extent the latter two did or did not follow Aristotle on that question is a problem with which we shall not deal. Yet the attitude of these thinkers did not deter later generations from returning to the old Pythagorean track. In Hebrew literature, however, Maimonides almost set a standard on this issue, so that the principle of spheric harmony was abandoned by most of his followers.[86] It appeared instead in the camp of his antagonists, i.e., in the literature of the Cabbalists. There it received the utmost elaboration throughout the following centuries. We cannot discuss these sources here, for the position of music in the esoteric literature of the Jews would require a special study.

A comparison of the Greek theories on the calculation of intervals, or even on the structure of melodies, with the Arabic and Jewish systems is a more difficult task than the examination of philosophical ideas. The crux here is the Arabic terminology employed in these writings. H. G. Farmer has shed a good deal of light on these problems, and d'Erlanger's editions of the main sources of Arabic applied theory of music has made available the most important writings.[87] Yet, until the Greek terms *tropos, nomos, eidos,* and *tasis,* which were used most perplexingly and perhaps promiscuously, are elucidated beyond any possible doubt, and until some Arabic terms, such as *lahn, 'usul, ghina,* are also clearly explained, we must content ourselves with the words of Curt Sachs: "It would be a mistake to imagine that the intellectual processes of combining, permutating, and coupling [intervals, modes, tetrachords, etc.] were actually responsible for the motley diversity of Mohammedan music; in other words, that lifeless theory created living melody." [88] We are able to trace Greek ideas in the *literature* on music of Arabs and Jews; nor is it hard to find Aristoxenian methods in the calculation of intervals and the division of the octave as practiced in Islamic civilization: yet living music does not depend on philosophical or even mathematical ideas. They may serve as foundations, but the musical superstructure—composition and performance—, while partly determined by abstract conceptions, is in principal autonomous; the morphology and structure of Arabic or Jewish music draws its most characteristic traits from psychological and linguistic forces. Their interrelation with music and its theory forms a chapter hitherto neglected but fascinating nonetheless.

Notes

1. Arnold J. Toynbee, *A Study of History*, Vol. XII, "Reconsiderations," (New York: Oxford University Press, 1961), p. 450.

2. Toynbee, *op. cit.*, p. 466.

3. Cf. Julián Ribera, *Music in Ancient Arabia and Spain* (Stanford: Stanford Unversity Press, 1929), Chaps. III (end) and VI (end), p. 72, *et passim;* also Higini Anglès, "Hispanic Musical Culture from the 6th to the 14th century," *The Musical Quarterly*, XXVI (1940), pp. 503 f, where one reads: "The religious musical Christian culture of the 9th and 10th centuries could not compete with the musical culture of the Arabic courts."

4. H. G. Farmer, "The Music of Islam," in *New Oxford History of Music*, Vol. I, "Ancient and Oriental Music," ed. by Egon Wellesz (London: Oxford University Press, 1957), p. 423.

5. It should not pass unnoticed (and unreprehended) that H. G. Farmer in his fine essay on the music of Islam puts Ishtar and Yahwe on the same footing. This betrays an attitude which, as Martin Buber has pointed out repeatedly, is tinged with the Protestant prejudice that the God of the Hebrew Bible is a pre-monotheistic, tribal deity, who is best disposed of by referring to him by a name on a par with the names of other pagan divinities. Such remnants of the Lagarde-Wellhausen saga should no longer be seriously maintained.

6. Cf. H. G. Farmer in *New Oxford History of Music*, pp. 428 ff.

7. Cf. Eric Werner and Isaiah Sonne, "The Philosophy and Theory of Music in Judaeo-Arabic Literature," *Hebrew Union College Annual*, XVI (1941), pp. 251-319, and XVII (1943), pp. 511-573, Chap. I; also *Die Musik in Geschichte und Gegenwart*, ed. by Friedrich Blume (Kassel: Bärenreiter Verlag, 1949-   ), Vol. IX, col. 976-977.

8. Cf. Werner-Sonne, "The Philosophy and Theory of Music in Judaeo-Arabic Literature," XVII, p. 531.

9. Al-Farabi's definition is given in Rodolphe d'Erlanger, *La Musique arabe*, Vol. I (Paris: P. Geuthner, 1930), pp. 6-7, and Vol. III (1938), p. 191 (as quoted by Safiyu-D-Din); see also H. G. Farmer's edition of Al-Farabi's *Isha Al 'Ulum (De scientiis)* in Farmer's *Al-Farabi's Arabic-Latin Writings on Music* (Glasgow: The Civic Press, 1934).

10. Of early authors, only St. Augustine comes near this attitude in his celebrated definition "Musica est scientia bene modulandi" (if we are permitted to interpret *modulari* as referring to the production of tones). The assumption that Al-Farabi knew Augustine's definition is hardly tenable.

11. Cf. H. G. Farmer, *Sa'adyah Gaon on the Influence of Music* (London: A. Probsthain, 1943), p. 23.

12. *Ibid.*

13. The periodicity of vibration, which gives birth to tone, is a *necessary* condition for music in the traditional sense; the question of its being also a *sufficient* condition constitutes today a crucial problem of musical esthetics.

14. Cf. Moses Botarel, *Commentary on the Sefer Yetzira* (Mantua, 1562); see also Werner-Sonne, "The Philosophy and Theory of Music in Judaeo-Arabic Literature," XVI, p. 264, note 50.

15. A careful examination of the main sources shows the prevalence of a general ideological trend only in the realm of the applied and moralizing theory of, or speculation on, music; in the field of performance we encounter, of course, all sorts of regionally and temporally limited ideas, trends, fashions, and fads. The greatest authority in the field of Islamic music, Prof. H. G. Farmer, while fully familiar with this pluralism of musical customs, is perhaps sometimes inclined to overlook the pluralism for the sake of a clearer general picture. A characteristic symptom of this regionally "plural tradition" in the Islamic orbit is the muezzin's invitatory to prayer—a chanted passage from the Kor'an. Even this sacred call to worship irked the Islamic puritans and elicited a theological controversy. Finally, after the victory of the "populists" over the legalistic purists, "the cantillation [of the invitatory] itself was not confined to any fixed melodic contour, and so, from the shores of Morocco to the Oxus, one may hear this cantillation today in almost as many patterns as there are mosques." (H. G. Farmer in *New Oxford History of Music*, I, p. 439.) Again, there is a Jewish counterpart to this development: the Masoretic accents of the Bible were being introduced between the 6th and the 10th centuries, but they and their cantillation became a hotbed of theological controversy—a long and tedious struggle between puritanic legalists and a more democratically inclined group of scholars. Here the term "democratic" has no direct political significance, but has been chosen to indicate the rule of the majority, which *in this case* proved to be wholesome and wise.

16. We need only to quote the preface of Al-Farabi's second (lost) volume on musical instruments, in order to demonstrate that both Arabs and Jews were themselves aware of the Greek patrimony. There we read: "We treat here whatever came down to us of the writings of the celebrated Greek theoreticians. . . ."

17. Cf. Werner-Sonne, "The Philosophy and Theory of Music in Judaeo-Arabic Literature," XVI, p. 257 (Honein-Alharizi's ideas on the place and function of music).

18. Ibn Aknin finds a place for music after the study of Writing, Torah, Mishna, Grammar, Poetry, Talmud, Theology, Logic, Mathematics, Optics, and Astronomy. He remarks: "The practice of music precedes the theory. The former must come first, because its healing power cannot show itself except by actual performance . . ." (Werner-Sonne, "The Philosophy and Theory of Music in Judaeo-Arabic Literature," p. 255).

19. Cf. (Pseudo)-Plutarch, *De musica*, ed. by Robert Volkmann (Leipzig, 1856), p. 57.

20. Cf. Aristides Quintilianus, *De musica*, German transl. by Rudolf Schaefke (Berlin-Schöneberg: M. Hesse, 1937), p. 167.

21. Cf. Al-Farabi, *Isha Al'Ulum (De scientiis)* in H. G. Farmer, *Al-Farabi's Arabic-Latin Writings on Music*, pp. 21-31.

22. Cf. Rodolphe d'Erlanger, *La Musique arabe*, III, p. 192.

23. Cf. H. G. Farmer, *Sa'adyah Gaon on the Influence of Music*, p. 15.

24. Cf. Werner-Sonne, "The Philosophy and Theory of Music in Judaeo-Arabic Literature," XVI, pp. 269-270.

25. Cf. *ibid.*, p. 265.

26. Cf. Ptolemaeus, *Harmonica*, III, Chap. IV.

27. We are using in this study the term "emotion" in place of the more correct, but unusual, "affectus." The terms are not quite identical, however, and we apologize for this lack of precision.

28. Cf. Plato, *Timaeus*, 34B.

29. If Hermann Abert in his *Lehre vom Ethos in der griechischen Musik* (Leipzig: Breitkopf & Härtel, 1899) disposes of this entire system with the words "gelehrte Tifteleien" (learned hairsplitting), then let us remember the enormous influence of this great conception upon philosophy, esthetics, music, and astronomy up to Newton. Even in such sober books as those of the astronomer Eddington we may find speculations that are closely related to Pythagorean ideas. At any rate, Abert's rash statement could hardly be sustained in our times.

30. Cf. Aristotle, *Metaphysics*, I, 6, 987 b, 11.

31. Aristides Quintilianus elaborates upon the theory of pulsation in true Pythagorean spirit: "The pulsation that corresponds to normal circumstances—analogous to the octave 1:2, or to the fifth 2:3, or to the fourth 3:4—does not necessarily endanger life. . . . Those pulsations, however, that present themselves in an entirely non-consonant ratio . . . are dangerous and may bring death." (See *De musica* in Marcus Meibom, *Antiquae musicae auctores septem*, Vol. II, Amsterdam, 1652, p. 127.) The entire medieval theory is full of similar statements. Cf. Boethius, *De institutione musica* in J. P. Migne, *Patrologiae cursus completus. Series latina* (Paris, 1844-55), Vol. LXIII, 1170; Boethius is the chief source for all further speculation.

32. Aristotle, *Politics*, VIII, 1341 b 32. We give here part of his report: "We see that if those insane persons (ἐνθουσιαστικοί) listen to enthusiastic melodies which intoxicate their souls, they are brought back to themselves again, so that their catharsis takes place exactly like a medical treatment." He relates how corybantes were cured by listening to corybantic tunes. (*Ibid.*, 1340 b 8.)

33. Aristides Quintilianus, ed. by Marcus Meibom, pp. 103-107.

34. Although Greek literature offered the basis for the scheme, it was the more radical Arabs and Jews who tried to link anything and everything to their musical system. Whatever the Christian writers wrote in this fashion was always borrowed from the Arabs, even with the help of Arabic words. Thus, in Odo of Cluny's and in Hucbald's writings there occur words like *scembs, kaphe, neth,* and *caemar,* clearly recognizable as Arabic terms. Yet the Christian authors do not know their origin or their meanings. Cf. Martin Gerbert, *Scriptores ecclesiastici de musica sacra potissimum*, Vol. I (1784; facsimile ed., Berlin, 1905, also Milan: Bollettino bibliografico musicale, 1931), p. 249. Even in our day it has been possible for a scholar like G. Lange (in his article on solmization, *Sammelbände der Internationalen Musikgesellschaft*, I, 1899-1900, pp. 539 ff.) not to recognize the Arabic origin of Odo's syllables. See especially H. G. Farmer, *Historical Facts for the Arabian Musical Influence* (London: W. Reeves, Ltd., 1930).

35. Cf. Werner-Sonne, "The Philosophy and Theory of Music in Judaeo-Arabic Literature," XVII, p. 530 (Honein, Chap. 20).

36. Cf. Jacob Guttmann, *Die Religionsphilosophie des Saadya Gaon* (Göttingen: Vandenhoeck & Ruprecht, 1882), pp. 287 ff, which stresses the almost verbal similarity of the *Ikhvan* with Saadya's text in the musical portion. Since Honein is older than both Saadya and the *Ikhvan*, we have to look for

a common (probably Syrian) source, from which all the three authors drew. Cf. Anton Baumstark, *Aristoteles bei den Syrern*, Vol. I (Leipzig: B. G. Teubner, 1900), pp. x-xii.

37. Cf. H. G. Farmer, *An old Moorish Lute Tutor* (Glasgow: The Civic Press, 1933), p. 38: "Ziryab claimed to have added a fifth string to the lute. . . . Naturally, he had to connect it with the cosmic scheme and hence associate it with a fifth nature—the soul. What would have prompted this association? In the Pseudo-Aristotelian *De mundo* (393a) we find a fifth element—ether, which occurs in the *De musica* of Aristides Quintilianus."

38. *Ikhvan es-Safa*, ed. by F. H. Dieterici, Vol. VI, *Die Propädeutik der Araber* (Leipzig: J. C. Hinrichs, 1872), pp. 126-128.

39. The medico-musical system, as accepted by Arabs and Jews, admits of this tabulation:

String	Element	Humor	Quality	Season
Zir (treble)	fire	yellow bile	hot	summer
Mathna (2nd)	air	blood	humid	spring
Mathlath (3rd)	water	phlegm	cold	winter
Bam (bass)	earth	black bile	dry	autumn

40. On the relation between Falaquera, Ibn 'Aknin and Al-Farabi, see H. G. Farmer, *Al-Farabi's Arabic-Latin Writings on Music* (cf. note 9 *supra*), pp. 6, 57, where a very clear picture is given; also Moritz Steinschneider, *Die hebräischen Übersetzungen des Mittelalters und die Juden als Dolmetscher* (Berlin: Bibliographisches Bureau, 1893), par. 12. Thus, Güdemann's assertion of an alleged Averroes influence is no longer tenable.

41. Cf. Hermann Abert, *op. cit.*, par. 4, 5, 9, 11. The problem itself has created an enormous literature, of which we cannot give a comprehensive bibliography here. We mention only the works in which such bibliographies may be found: Adolf Aber, *Handbuch der Musikliteratur* (Leipzig: Breitkopf & Härtel, 1922), pp. 470-490; Ernst Kurth, *Musikpsychologie* (Berlin: M. Hesse, 1931; Bern, 1947), Index. It was this perennial problem that created the famous struggle for and against Richard Wagner.

42. Cf. Plato, *Politics*, III, 398C-402; Aristotle, *Politics*, VIII, 7, 1342a, b.

43. Hermann Abert, *op. cit.*, pp. 67-69.

44. Cf. Plutarch, *Quaestiones conviviales* III, 8th question, c. 2. "The wailing-song and the funeral-flute excite pain and bring about tears, but afterwards attune the soul to compassion, gradually mitigating and annihilating the painful emotion."

45. Cf. *Arabian Nights*, ed. by E. W. Lane, p. 400: "Ibn Sina hath asserted that the lover's remedy consisteth in melodious sounds, and the company of one like his beloved . . ." *Ibid.*, pp. 129, 302, *et passim*. Compare with this Shakespeare, *Twelfth Night*, Act. I, Scene 1: "If music be the food of love, play on!"

46. Cf. Charles Montagu Doughty's statement, in his *Travels in Arabia Deserta* (London: J. Cape, 1936), about the polar nature of Arabic culture, which is both rude and refined, containing materialistic and mystic elements at the same time; also: "Music is in constant connection with everything intoxicating: wine, love, and ecstasy . . ." (Robert Lachmann, *Musik des Orients*, Breslau: F. Hirt, 1929, pp. 98-101.)

47. Al-Farabi, *Kitab* I, p. 13.

48. Al-Farabi, *Kitab* II, pp. 89 ff.

49. Ecclesiasticus, Chap. 48-50.

50. I. Goldziher, in "Das Gutachten des Maimonides über Gesang und

Musik," *Monatschrift für Geschichte und Wissenschaft des Judentums*, XXIII (1875), pp. 174-180, omits consideration of the tendency of Arabic music at the time of Maimonides.

51. Here it is the physician Maimonides who speaks, the faithful disciple of the great Arabic tradition of medicine. Cf. Maimonides, *Shmone Perakim*, in Joseph I. Gorfinkle, *The Eight Chapters of Maimonides on Ethics* (*Schmone Perakim*) (New York: Columbia University Press, 1912), p. 30.

52. Many centuries later, a truly Christian philosopher, a stranger to his own contemporaries, displayed a somewhat similar attitude toward music. In Kierkegaard's *Entweder Oder* we meet striking resemblances to Maimonides. But the Danish thinker grants us a choice only between the beautiful and the good, which makes it not a little difficult to lean in favor of the good when Kierkegaard makes Mozart his champion of beauty.

53. We set the typical statements of both Plato and Maimonides side by side:

Plato, *Laws*, II 668 A, *Politics*, III 398 C, *Politics*, II 376 E, *Laws*, II 669, etc.: Then, when anyone says that Music is to be judged by pleasure this cannot be admitted; and if there be any Music of which pleasure is the criterion, such Music is not to be sought out or deemed to have any real excellence but only that other kind of Music, which is an imitation of the good. The chief place of Music is in the *paideia* (transl. by B. Jowett, IV, p. 197).

Maimonides, *Responsum on Music*: Secular Music is to be prohibited, because it arouses lust and wickedness. Music of a religious character and Music leading to ethical wisdom are permitted. The only decisive criterion of Music's value is its religious-ethical essence. The chief place of Music is in the Synagogue, and generally, in worship.

54. At bottom, Plato seems to have cherished the same ideas as Maimonides regarding the religious functions of music, although he is not quite as outspoken on this issue and clothes his conception in the form of a historical report. He says: "Among us and our forefathers . . . Music was divided into various classes and styles; one class of song was that of prayers to the gods, which bore the name of hymns; contrasted with this was another class, best called dirges; paeans formed another; and yet another was the dithyramb, named, I fancy, after Dionysos . . ." (Plato, *Laws*, III, transl. by Bury, Vol. I, p. 245.)

55. Maimonides mentions the story of Elisha while discussing the nature of prophecy. Cf. *Guide of the Perplexed*, II, 32. Cf. also Plotinus' great conception of the chanted prayer: "The tune of an incantation, a significant cry . . . These two have a power over the soul . . . similarly with regard to prayers; the prayer is answered by the mere fact that one part and the other part (of the All) are wrought into one tone like a musical string which, plucked at one end, vibrates at the other also. . . ." (Stephen Mackenna, *Plotinus on the Nature of the Soul*, Oxford: P. L. Warner, 1924, p. 96.)

56. Dr. Morgenstern, in his illuminating "Amos-Studies III," looks upon the Elisha story from quite a different angle: "And in order to divine for them as requested Elisha proceeded to work himself into a state of ecstasy, in accordance with the customary technique of the professional prophets, by having a musician play in his presence. The significance of this procedure is unmistakable. Within two years after the death of Elijah Elisha had fallen from the high level of prophetic standards and technique of his great master

to the much lower level of the professional prophets . . ." (*Hebrew Union College Annual*, XV, 1940, p. 228.)

57. Of the innumerable references to the stories of David or Elisha, we mention here only three of the most characteristic ones from Christian sources:

(1) *Joanni Damasceni vita a Joanne Hierosolymitano conscripta* (J. P. Migne, *Patrologiae cursus completus. Series graeca*, Paris, 1857-66, Vol. XCIV, 473).

(2) Regino Prumiensis (d. 915) in J. P. Migne, *Patr. lat.*, Vol. CXXXII, 490.

(3) Roger Bacon in Robert Belle Burke, *The Opus Majum of Roger Bacon*, Vol. I (Philadelphia: University of Pennsylvania Press, 1928), pp. 259 ff. Here the philosopher confuses the name Elisha with Elijah!

58. Honein-Alharizi's *Maxims of the Philosophers* in Werner-Sonne, "The Philosophy and Theory of Music in Judaeo-Arabic Literature," XVII (cf. note 7 *supra*), pp. 513 ff.

59. This thought might in a more general form occur in Schopenhauer's *Welt als Wille und Vorstellung*. Cf. F. Rosenthal in *Hebrew Union College Annual*, XV (1940), p. 468.

60. Cf. *De musica* in Marcus Meibom, *Antiquae musicae auctores septem*, p. 184.

61. Honein-Alharizi, *Maxims of the Philosophers*, 19:15.

62. Cf. Friedrich Albert Lange, *The History of Materialism*, transl. by Ernest Chester Thomas, 3rd ed. (New York: Harcourt, Brace & Co., 1925), p. 177: "Mohammedanism is more favorable to materialism than Christianity or Judaism"; also, p. 181: "The Arabs set to work with an independent feeling for exact observation, and developed especially the doctrine of life, which stands in so close a relation to the problems of materialism."

63. The inklings of materialistic reasoning, which may be found in Falaquera and Saadya, are more than counterbalanced by a strong emphasis upon religious and theological principles.

64. Cf. Julián Ribera, *Music in Ancient Arabia and Spain*, 3rd ed., pp. 90 ff.

65. Cf. note 36 *supra*.

66. Cf. Plato, *Politics*, IV, 441 C.

67. Aristotle, *Poetics*, Chap. i; also, very clearly evident in Aristides Quintilianus' *De musica*, ed. by Marcus Meibom, p. 31.

68. This fact has been overlooked by all writers on Saadya except H G. Farmer; perhaps because the passage about music is a "rather dark one" (Steinschneider), "offers difficulties" (Guttmann), "has not been properly explained," Henry Malter, *Saadia Gaon, his Life and Works* (Philadelphia: The Jewish Publication Society of America, 1921). In view of Saadya's emphasis upon rhythm, the statement of P. Gradenwitz (in *Monatschrift für Geschichte und Wissenschaft des Judentums*, 1936, p. 463) that the rabbis unanimously objected to rhythmical music, cannot be upheld. Here Gradenwitz, or the rabbis, or both, confuse rhythm and meter.

69. How inseparably these two conceptions are connected may be seen in the following juxtaposition of sentences: "Coelum ipsum sub harmoniae modulatione revolvitur. Musica movet affectus." (Isadore of Seville in Gerbert, *Scriptores*, I, 20 b.)

70. Cf. Plato, *Timaeus*, 34 B ff; *Politics*, VII, 530. The word χορεῖον,

used in *Timaeus*, 40 c, can be understood only as the rhythmic motion of the heavenly bodies.

71. Cf. Aristotle, *De caelo*, Chap. ix, 290 b 12.

72. Cf. Sir Thomas Little Heath, *The Copernicus of Antiquity, Aristarchus of Samos* (New York: Clarendon Press, 1913), pp. 105-115.

73. Cf. Ptolemy, *Harmonics*, in Ingemar Düring, *Die Harmonielehre des Klaudios Ptolemaios*, III (Göteborg: Elanders Boktryckeri Aktiebolag, 1930), Chap. XVI-XIX, Aristides Quintilianus, *De musica*, ed. by Marcus Meibom, pp. 145-155; Nicomachus of Gerasa in Karl von Jan, *Musici scriptores graeci et melodiarum veterum quidquid exstat* (Leipzig: B. G. Teubner, 1895), pp. 230-43, 272, 276-80, *et passim*. A survey of the entire ideology is given in K. W. F. Piper, *Mythologie und Symbolik der christlichen Kunst*, I, pp. 245-75.

74. It is significant that three of the most important authors who wrote on music in Greek were Syrians, viz., Nicomachus of Gerasa (c. 100 A.D.), Porphyrius of Tyre (c. 260 A.D.), and Jamblichus of Coelesyria (Palestine, c. 310 A.D.).

75. Except in the *Ikhvan* which, being fervently Pythagorean, stresses to the utmost the conception of spheric harmony. Cf. *Ikhvan es-Safa*, ed. by F. H. Dieterici (see note 38 *supra*), pp. 162 ff. On Al-Kindi's attitude, see Moritz Steinschneider, *Al-Farabi* (St. Petersburg: Académie Impériale des Sciences de St. Petersbourg, Mémoires, Série 7, Tome 13, No. 4, 1869), p. 80.

76. Cf. *Kitab*, I, p. 28.

77. Psalms 19:1, 93:4, 96:11, 97:6; Job 38:7, 38:37; Ezekiel 1:4, 1:22; Babylonian Talmud, Tractate Joma 20b, 21a.

78. Ὁ τοίνυν οὐρανός, τὸ μουσικῆς ἀρχέτυπον ὄργανον ἄκρως ἡρμόσθαι δοκεῖ δι' οὐδὲν ἕτερον ἢ ἵνα οἳ ἐπὶ τιμῇ τοῦ τῶν ὅλων πατρὸς ᾀθόμενοι ὑμνοὶ μουσικῶς ἐπιψάλλωνται. (*De somniis*, I., 37, in *Philo's Works*, ed. by Colson and Whitaker, Vol. V., p. 314 [Loeb Classics]). Elsewhere he states that the idea of cosmic harmony has been developed by the Chaldeans. See also Hermann Abert, *Die Musikanschauung des Mittelalters* (Halle: M. Niemeyer, 1905), pp. 39 ff. Also, I. Heinemann's article, "Philo," in August Friedrich von Pauly-Wissowa, *Realencyclopädie des classischen Altertumswissenschaft* (Stuttgart: J. B. Metzler, 1839-52).

79. Chiefly Psalm 19:1 and Job 38:7.

80. The decisive word on Al-Farabi's negative attitude toward the theory of spheric harmony has been written by H. G. Farmer in *Al-Farabi's Arabic-Latin Writings on Music* (see note 9 *supra*).

81. Here the esoteric influence of cabbalistic thought is clearly noticeable.

82. Moses ibn Ezra in a *piyut* for the New Year writes glowingly about the "sounding, revolving vaults of the heavens, their inaudible harmony . . ."

83. Cf. Abraham ibn Ezra's Commentary on Psalm 93:4. " 'The sound of great waters': More than the sound of great waters is the Great Name in the heights, and that in turn is surrounded by the orbits of the spheres and their sounds." Cf. also Abraham ibn Ezra's Commentary on Job 38:7. " 'Who can tell': Nothing in the celestial world is comparable to the power of the spheres and their sound and their mathematical relation." (Paraphrase.)

84. Cf. Simon Duran, *Magen Abot*, 52 ff.

85. Maimonides, *Guide of the Perplexed*, II, #8 (Chap. XXXII). We may realize here to what an extent the different translations of a single Scriptural verse have influenced philosophy. The passage, Job 38:37 says: "Who can number the clouds by wisdom . . . ?" Vulgate: "Quis enarrabit coelorum

rationem, et concentum coeli quis dormire faciat?" Authorized version: "Who can number the clouds in wisdom?"—or "Who can stay the bottles of heaven?" The interpretation of the Vulgate may be found also in Hebrew literature; cf. Abraham ibn Daud, Commentary on *Sefer Yezirah*, Chap. I, f. 27, col. 3. The Christian philosophers refer to the Vulgate version, which is their chief basis for the doctrine of spheric harmony. Cf Boethius, *De institutione musica*, in J. P. Migne, *Patr. lat.* LXIII, 1171. Also Aurelianus Reomensis, in M. Gerbert, *Scriptores* I, 32, who refers to the passage from Job and to the seven voices of the planets, linking them to the eight musical modes of the Church. This idea occurs also in cabbalistic literature in connection with Psalm 29:2-9, where the seven voices of God are interpreted in quite the same manner. Allusions to the astro-musical idea are very frequent. Kepler himself defended this theory in his *De harmonice mundi*, and Shakespeare refers to it in the beautiful passage, *The Merchant of Venice*, Act V, Sc. 1.

86. Cf. Moritz Steinschneider, *Al-Farabi*, p. 244 (note to p. 80).

87. H. G. Farmer, "Islamic Music" in *New Oxford History of Music* (see note 4 *supra*), I; *Historical Facts for the Arabian Musical Influence* (see note 34 *supra*); *A History of Arabian Music to the XIIIth Century* (London: Luzac & Co., 1929); *Al-Farabi's Arabic-Latin Writings on Music* (see note 9 *supra*); *The Sources of Arabian Music* (issued privately by the author, Bearsden, Scotland, 1940). Also, Rodolphe Baron d'Erlanger, *La Musique arabe*, 5 vols. 1930-49) (see note 9 *supra*).

88. Curt Sachs, *The Rise of Music in the Ancient World, East and West* (New York: W. W. Norton & Co., 1943), p. 281.

The Psalmodic Formula
Neannoe and its Origin

Reprinted with permission of *Musical Quarterly*, 28, 1942, pp. 93-99.

THE FORMULAE *neannoe, noeagis,* etc., well known from Byzantine theory and from the writings of Aurelian of Réomé, Hucbald, John Cotton and others, have caused many speculations as to their origin and meaning. Three generations of musicologists, from Ambros to Tillyard and Ursprung, have endeavored to discover the origin of these mysterious words. However, none of them has succeeded in reaching any final conclusion. The opinion which prevails today is that the formulae, whose meaning was unknown even to the old Byzantines, are just another type of the many mnemonic solmization-syllables. A nursery rhyme, as it were, at the cradle of Music.

Let us consider for a moment the most reliable sources in which these apparently meaningless formulae occur.

I

Aurelian of Réomé (*Musica Disciplina,* in Gerbert, *Scriptores* I, 39ff, especially Chaps. 8 and 19) relates that he once asked a Greek for the real meaning of the words *neannoe* or *noeagis,* etc. The answer he received was that they had no specific meaning, but were merely expressions of joy and delight. This is much the same explanation that St. Augustine gives of the words of the *jubilationes.*[1]

Hucbald, in his *Commemoratio Brevis,* gives us, together with these syllables, the melodic formulae of the eight *toni,* notated in the so-called *Dasia* notation. He is unable, however, to explain the meaning of the syllables themselves. The same is true of John Cot-

---

[1] Augustinus ennarr. in Ps. 99 (Migne, *Patrologiae cursus completus. Series Latina* XXXVII, 1272): "Qui jubilat, non verba dicit, sed sonus quidam est laetitiae sine verbis: vox est enim animi diffusi laetitia, quantum potest exprimentis affectum, non sensum comprehendentis. Gaudens homo in exultatione sua ex verbis quibusdam, quae non possunt dici et intellegi, erumpit in vocem quandam exultationis sine verbis; . . ." Cf. also Hieronymus (St. Jerome), in Ps. 32: "Jubilus dicitur, quod nec verbis nec syllabis nec litteris nec voce potest—erumpere aut comprehendere quantum homo Deum debeat laudare."

ton, who uses them in his *Tonarius*.[2] In Bernard of Clairvaux's *De correctione Antiphonarii* (Mabillon, *Opera*, Paris, 1719, I, 691 ff., s.a. Gerbert) the words are explained as meaningless mnemonic syllables.[3]

Odo of Cluny, Berno of Reichenau, Hucbald's *De Musica*, and Regino, all use the formulae without being much concerned about their etymology. It is apparent that their origin was forgotten even by the Byzantine teachers of the Western theorists. Riemann labored painstakingly to establish some connection with the Greek syllables τε, τα, τη, τω. While he succeeded in tracing the function of the formulae in the tetrachords back to Aristides Quintilianus,[4] he has not satisfied us with the explanation that the formulae are only corrupted Greek solmization-terms, the originals of which were meaningless in themselves.[5]

We do not intend to discuss here the underlying musical system of the eight *toni*, or the connected theory of the scales. This has already been done by such outstanding scholars as Fleischer, Riemann, Thibaut, Gastoué, and others. This study is limited to the problem of the real origin of the words in question and an attempt to explain their meaning.

There was never a doubt that these formulae came to us *via* Byzantium. Both Aurelian and Hucbald emphasize this fact. By way of explanation, the latter adds: "As for *noannoeane, noeagis*, etc., we do not believe that they have any more meaning than mere syllables which accompany musical modulation."[6] Other than this, no explanation is even attempted.

The disputed formulae occur in variant forms, viz.: *Noannoeane, Noeanne, Noeagis, Nenano, Nana*. They are corruptions of the Byzantine ἐπηχήματα, and are mnemonic, or perhaps ecstatic, words for the intonation of the *octoechos*. Their function in the Latin theory was to serve the singers as cue-words for the solmization, and at the same time as mnemonic aids. In this respect, they

---

2 Gerbert, *Scriptores* I, 214ff.

3 Oskar Fleischer, *Neumen-Studien* I, 112.

4 *Zeitschrift der Internationalen Musikgesellschaft* XIV, pp. 273ff.

5 In Aristides' system, the syllables represent the masculine and feminine vowels, which serve for the intonation of the tunes. (Ed. Meibom. p. 92.)

6 Gerbert, *Scriptores* I, p. 216: "Utpote Noannoeane et Noeagis et caetera, quae putamus non tam significativa esse verba, quam syllabus modulatione attributas." Also: "Noane vero non sunt verba aliquid significantia, sed syllabae ad investigandam melodiam aptae."

are like the well known *ut re mi*. There is this important difference, however: the *ut re mi* became the names of individual tones in the scale, whereas *neannoe, noeagis,* etc., kept their function of symbolizing whole *pneumata*. In fact, the latter were the first paradigms for the psalm-tones. It was only after the 11th century that they yielded to the ordinary "passwords", *Alleluia* or *Evovae* (*Seculorum, a*men), the latter representing the end of the lesser doxology. In other words, *noannoeane* and its variant forms were paradigms used in the teaching and studying of psalm-intonations, sometimes called *pneuma* or *neuma*.[7]

We know today, and the evidence of this fact becomes more imposing every year, that, at the time of Charlemagne, Byzantium had an extremely strong influence on the Church music of Western Europe, and that this lasted up to the 10th century. However, since the Greek priests themselves could not explain the meaning of their own syllables (as we are told by Aurelian and others[8]), no one seemed to be further concerned with the problem until the very beginning of modern musicology. We have already mentioned Riemann's attempt to solve the riddle by going back to the sound formulae of Aristides Quintilianus[9], but beyond that he could not proceed. Such men as Peter Wagner, Amédée Gastoué, Jean-Baptiste Thibaut, and Robert Lach, do not even make an attempt to explain the linguistic root of the formulae.

In Fleischer, however, we do find an analogy which throws some light on our problem. He says: "The same tonic formula of the *noannoeane* [musically quoted by Fleischer] serves for the Alleluia as well. The *Musica Enchiriadis* refers constantly to this tonic formula in presenting the modes. This formula, in reality, is a musical paradigm for the author of the *Musica Enchiriadis*, employing as underlying texts both *Alleluia* and *Noannoeane* without distinction. Obviously, this tonic formula possesses a particular authenticity for the author. In this practice we see a late vestige of the original psalmody, in which the group-*neuma* was executed on the Hebrew word *Alleluia*, in the same way as the group-*neuma*

---

[7] Johannes Tinctoris, *Diffinitorium:* "Neoma [sic] est cantus fini verborum sine verbis annexus." (Chrysander, *Jahrbuch für Musikwissenschaft* I, 97.)

[8] Gerbert, *Scriptores* I, 42ff.: "Etenim quemdam interrogavi Graecum, in Latina quid interpretarentur lingua? respondit, se nihil interpretari, sed esse apud eos laetantis adverbia."

[9] Aristides Quintilianus, ed. Meibom. pp. 92f.

of the Lamentations are executed today on the letter-names of the Hebrew alphabet."[10]

This analogy with the group-*neuma* in the *Lamentationes Jeremiae*, sung upon the Hebrew letter-names *Aleph, Beth, Gimel,* etc., is remarkable indeed. (The practice still exists in the Roman Catholic Church during Holy Week.) However, unless we find Hebrew words or terms which may be the potential origin of the *Neannoe,* it leads us nowhere.

Dom Jeannin, the noted French scholar, first suggested the possibility of Syrian origin.[11] Almost a century ago, Villotteau proposed that the form and structure of the syllables indicated a Chaldean influence. Neither of these two men, however, was able to name a Syrian or a Chaldean word as the possible root from which *Neannoe* might have been derived. Rebours, therefore, was justified in concluding: "The efforts which have been made to find in them the ancient Greek notes, originally borrowed from the Chaldees, are very laudable. But, the matter has not been clarified very much. Yet we restrain ourselves from refuting this theory *a priori.* As for the Greeks themselves, they were unable to render any account of the significance (meaning) of those terms."[12]

II

In the remaining pages of this paper, we shall attempt to trace the origin of *Neannoe* and its variant forms to a certain term in early medieval Hebrew, where it had a definite musical connotation. We know that there was considerable cultural interchange between Jews and European Byzantines in early medieval times. Many Greek terms were in use in the standard Jewish prayer-book of Southeastern Europe, the so-called *Mahsor Romania.*[13] Likewise, in many other Hebrew works we encounter Greek words which were adopted and adapted by the Jews. This is especially true of Hebrew philosophical literature, in which the theory of music and metrics finds its modest place among the *septem artes liberales.*

The dominant cultural influence was Arabian, and through the Arabian philosophers and Encyclopaedists of the day, the Jews received the last glimpse of ancient Hellenism. Conversely, we

10 Fleischer: *Neumen-Studien* II, 60.
11 Jeannin-Puyade, *L'Octoëchos syrien,* in *Oriens Christianus,* New Series III, 1913.
12 Rebours, *Traité de psaltique,* p. 77f.
13 S. Krauss, *Studien zur Byzantinisch-jüdischen Geschichte,* pp. 114-137. Cf. J. Perles, in *Byzantinische Zeitschrift* II, 3-4, 1893.

have many instances in which both Arabic and Byzantine culture borrowed from the Hebrew. Let us cite a few examples.
Among other musical terms borrowed from the Byzantines, we
find in Hebrew literature such words as: ἀντιφώνη, ὕμνός, ποιήτης,
κοντάκιον, etc.[14] On the other hand, in Byzantine literature we find
such Hebrew terms as *Haikal* (Hebr. *ḥekhal*, sanctuary), desig-
nating a part of a monastery chapel; *Amanate* (Hebr. *emmunat*,
certainty, truth); *Sabakathion* (Aramaic *Sabkhatha*, wicker-work,
wicker-basket.)[15]

In the Talmudic vocabulary, and later in medieval philosophical works, we discover the words *ninnua* or *nana*, sometimes
nanua. The root meaning is originally "to move", "to shake"
(*movere, motus*). Subsequently it acquired the derived meaning
"to move the voice"; and it finally came to mean "melodic movement". I found it used in this latter sense by four well known
medieval authors.[16]

Of particular significance is the use of the word *ninnua* in the
musical theory of Saadya Gaon's *Emunot V'deot*, Chap. 10. This
work was written originally in Arabic, but we possess no less than
three Hebrew translations. In two of them, the term *ninnua* appears unmistakably as a musical term. Let us consider some of the
most important passages from Hebrew works, in which *ninnua*
or *nana* occurs.

1) He quavers [*ninnua*] with his voice. Yalkut, Prov. 953.
2) Sings with tremulous voice [*ninnua*]. Talmud, Tr. Sanhedrin, 101a.
3) The first mode has three [melodic or rhythmic] patterns
   [*neanuot*]. Saadya, *Emunot V'deot*, Chap. 10, transl. Ibn
   Tibbon.
4) The science of music knows of eight [rhythmic or me-
   lodic] modes [*ninnuot*]. Saadya, ibid. Transl. by an anonymous writer, possibly Berakhya Hanakdan. In this translation the term *ninnua* or *nana* appears fifteen times.
5) The word occurs with the same connotation in a fragment
   of Moses Abulafia, published by Steinschneider in *Otzar
   ha-s'pharot* IV, 30.

[14] J. Perles, *ibidem*.
[15] Hebraisms in the *Koine*, cf. *Byz. Zeitschrift* III, 155; IV, 185; XI, 190, 599;
XII, 442. See also *Zeitschrift für alttestamentliche Wissenschaft* XXII, 83-113.
[16] Yehuda ibn Tibbon, Berakhya Hanakdan, Abr. ibn Chiya, Moses Abulafia.

It is remarkable, indeed, that the three translations of Saadya's work, when expressing the phrase "melodic or rhythmic pattern", employed either *ninnua* or *ne'ima* (mode—Arabic, *naghama*). *Ne'ima* is well known in the European theory. It is the origin of the term *neuma*.[17] Both *neume* and *pneume* were used to designate the same thing, viz. the modes of psalmody, particularly for the melismatic *caudae*.[18] (However, in that sense, *neuma* is erroneously used for *pneuma*.)

It is difficult to give an exact translation of *ninnua*. Perhaps it is best to define it as "quivering melodic movement", or "fluctuating mode". This description seems to fit well the richly embellished psalmodic formulae of Berno, Cotton, or Hartker.[19] Their melismatic-periheletic practice obviously contains that "fluctuation" of the melodic line which was later abandoned in favor of the more rigid system.[20]

Our theory, which proposes that the origin of the *neannoe* formula is to be found in the Hebrew word *ninnua*, gains even more probability when we consider that almost all the terms used in Church music to designate melismatic movement originate in the Bible—or, at least, in the Hebrew language. *Alleluia*,[21] *Sela*, *Amen*, were diacritical cue-words in ancient as well as in medieval times.[22] The term *Jubilus*, very familiar to the Church Fathers and theorists, is derived from the Hebrew *yobel*, which means *sound*, *clangor*, *flourish*.[23] *Sela* has been understood and translated as the *Diapsalma*, the instrumental interlude of several Psalms.

Thus, our *noannoe-ninnua* hypothesis not only is supported by

[17] About the Hebrew *ne'ima-neuma*, cf. Fleischer, *Neumen-Studien* I, 31, 111. See also Riemann, *Handbuch* I², p. 82. Also Hommel, *Untersuchungen zur hebräischen Lautlehre*, p. 75.

[18] The entire chapter about the musical modes, particularly in Saadya's work, is highly interesting for the history of musical theory. The author of this paper intends to interpret this heretofore obscure passage in a subsequent article.

[19] Riemann, *Handbuch* I², pp. 57ff.

[20] Note well Hucbald's statement (*De Musica*, in Gerbert, *Scriptores*, I, p. 118): "Hae autem consuetudinariae notae non omnino habentur non necessariae; quippe cum et tarditatem cantilenae, et ubi tremulam sonus contineat vocem, vel qualiter ipsi soni iungantur in unum. . . ."See also P. Wagner, *Einführung in die gregorianischen Melodien* III, 320ff.

[21] In the *tonarii* of the 12th-14th centuries, the *Alleluia* lost its meaning and became a mere paradigm for psalm-intonations, a "vox exultationis et laetitiae" (St. Augustine).

[22] Cf. my article "Morphological Notes on Catholic and Jewish Musical Punctuation," in "Annual of the Hebrew Union College", Cincinnati, 1940, p. 353.

[23] Ex. XIX, 13, Lev. XXV, 13, Num. XXXVI, 4, etc.

certain pieces of linguistic evidence in Hebrew literature, but also fits well into the picture of constant cultural interchange between the Orient and the Occident. How great a change took place with regard to the musical function of our formulae, is a subject we leave for another occasion. It is sufficient here and now to have unriddled the problem of the origin and meaning of the terms themselves.

Manuscripts of Jewish Music in the Eduard Birnbaum Collection of the Hebrew Union College Library

Reprinted with permission of *Hebrew Union College Annual*, 18, 1944, pp. 397-428.

I N HIS illuminating essay "Songs and Singers of the Synagogue in the Eighteenth Century," the late A. Z. Idelsohn, ל'צ'ז, drew public attention, for the first time, to that unique collection of Jewish musical writings, which we know by the name of its learned collector, the late Eduard Birnbaum.[1] Since the volume which contains Idelsohn's splendid contribution is by now out of print, it might not be amiss to quote those passages from it which appraise the significance of this great treasury of synagogal music.

"They (the singers and cantors) share the same lot as most of the Jewish poets of the Synagogue, in regard to the data of their life-record; but, while the poets frequently incorporated their names in acrostics, the musicians had no such tool, and therefore their names were forgotten while their songs delighted the souls of thousands and thousands. It is only sheer accident that their creations were preserved in writing and (still more extraordinary!) in their own handwriting. There remains yet to be acquired a considerable quantity of fairly rich material in the valuable manuscripts of those Jewish singers and musicians who first started using European means to express their musical thoughts.

"Indeed it demanded great energy and patience and endurance and devotion on the part of that person who would gather those remainders of yellow music sheets of the eighteenth century, poorly written, scattered throughout the world in

---

[1] *HUCA* I, Jubilee Vol. 1925, p. 398.

397

obscure corners, with the rubbish of dusty archives of the old communities in Central Europe, or in the hands of the descendants of old hazzanic families who had not the slightest idea of their historical value. And such a person — indeed a personality — the Synagogue song found in the late Eduard Birnbaum (1855–1920), cantor of Koenigsberg Germany — a man who devoted forty-five years of his life, until his death, to that tedious task — a man who collected singlehanded more material than an entire institution with a staff of employees would have gathered. Due to this unique devotion to and love for his ideal, *The History of Jewish Music*, the Jewish people is now in possession of a collection of its songs. And due to the bibliographical foresight of Mr. A. Oko, librarian of the Hebrew Union College Library, who sensed the far-reaching import of the unique collection, we are able to become acquainted with the distinctive Jewish song of the eighteenth century."[2]

Idelsohn then goes on to discuss in particular the manuscripts written by *hazanim* of the eighteenth century, which form a major part of the Birnbaum Collection.

It is the present writer's intention to give, in the following pages, a survey of this entire collection, but without going into excessive detail. Indeed, a minute report could easily fill a full sized book and an additional catalogue. Having catalogued most of these manuscripts himself, the writer feels entitled to the statement that the Birnbaum Collection contains the most copious and authentic material extant, both in manuscript and in print, on the development of synagogal music.

Apart from the merit of having initiated and accumu'ated this splendid collection by his own very modest means and with indefatigable patience and perseverance, Birnbaum, also as the pioneer and first lexicographer of Jewish music, deserves our special and grateful consideration. For it was he who took the study of Jewish Music which, till then, had been the hobby of a few dilettant *hazanim* and raised it to the level of a legitimate and recognized branch of the Science of Judaism.

[2] *Ibid.*

EDUARD BIRNBAUM

A MEMORIAL

The family from which Birnbaum came, the home in which he grew up, the period during which he reached his manhood were all unmistakably determining factors in his career. Born in Cracow in 1855, the son of a distinguished talmudic scholar, he became familiar with Hebrew literature and Jewish lore in his earliest youth. Yet it was the beautiful, pure voice of the eleven year old boy which made his teachers on the Yeshiva at Szobotisch decide: "He must become a *ḥazan*." Had it not been for his striking musical talent, he might have become one among the other Rabbis in Eastern Europe. It was his ardent interest in Jewish Music that led him instead to the field of musical scholarship and to close scholarly contacts with A. Berliner, H. Vogelstein, L. Loew, D. Kaufmann, and others. In order to become a good *ḥazan*, he first had to be a good musician: This dictum was originally proclaimed by Salomon Sulzer and was generally accepted during the latter half of the nineteenth century.

Accordingly Birnbaum went to Vienna and studied under Sulzer, attending at the same time, Jellinek's classes at the Beth Hamidrash. This marked the beginning of his intimate and devoted friendship with the admired Sulzer, more than fifty years his senior. After intensive study with the great Viennese cantor, Birnbaum went to Breslau where he studied at the cantorial school of the chief *ḥazan*, Moritz Deutsch. At the same time he attended some classes of Prof. Heinrich Graetz who took a warm interest in the promising young student. At the age of sixteen, Birnbaum was appointed by Prof. Graetz to serve as regular cantor at the Breslau Theological Seminary. His services, however, lasted only one year, for he accepted a position as full time cantor in Magdeburg under the Rabbi, Dr. Rahmer, scholar and editor. Two years later, the promising young singer was called to a fine position in Beuthen, Silesia, after a short period of advanced study under his fatherly friend, Sulzer, in Vienna; and from 1874–79 he was the beloved cantor of the large Beuthen congregation. During these five years he frequently went to Vienna to work with Sulzer and to Koenigsberg to study with the old master of Eastern *ḥazanut*, Hirsch Weintraub. In Vienna, Birnbaum sat at the feet of such famous scholars as Guedemann and Jellinek, and made the acquaintance of Steinschneider and David Kaufmann. Weintraub was so convinced of Birnbaum's extraordinary ability that he designated him as his successor. When Weintraub retired, Birnbaum did indeed succeed him. The community in Koenigsberg, well knowing how to respect the shining light in its midst, raised Birnbaum's salary several times and, by appointing him for life, secured his services permanently. This proved necessary in order to counteract the many enticing calls which came from Vienna and other large cities. From this time on, Birnbaum's life ran a smooth course, interrupted only by frequent journeys in connection with his ceaseless studies.

Birnbaum's literary and scholarly endeavors started at Koenigsberg. His work presents, on the whole, a rare combination of talmudic, rabbinic, and musical pursuits, always reflecting the spirit of the Science of Judaism. Since Birnbaum was equally conversant with all three of these fields, he was apparently destined to become the Zunz, the Steinschneider, or the Geiger of Jewish Music. Although he did not attain that stature, he developed nonetheless into a great and unique scholar.

From the very outset Birnbaum was confronted with all of the difficulties connected with the Science of Judaism which, in his special case, entailed a maze of additional obstacles. Did not any liberal work in the — then young — field of Jewish Science demand the utmost tact and caution? Particularly in the domain of Rabbinics, is not the balance, between fundamentals on the one hand, and their reinterpretation on the other, a most delicate one?

But the study of Jewish Music is even more intricate. In the first place we must consider that it occupies a common area in which Music, Liturgy, Philology, and Rabbinics overlap. It is subject to all the vulnerabilities of these fields without enjoying any of their advantages. Unlike these, it deals to a great extent with purely oral tradition. There are no phonographic records, comparatively few manuscripts, and very little printed music to furnish authentic, historical material. Our Hebrew literature contains no clear unequivocal musical terminology,[3] nor was there, prior to Birnbaum, any systematic spadework in this branch of science. Indeed, to this very day, a real bibliography of Jewish music does not exist.

Thus, when Birnbaum set out to investigate the vast uncultivated domain of Jewish Music, a ground replete with splendid ruins, he had three aims toward which to work:

1. A systematic history of Jewish Music.
2. The incorporation of Jewish Music within general musicology as well as within the Science of Judaism.
3. Gradual examination of our musical heritage aimed at a scientific distinction between genuine tradition and pseudo-tradition.

To reach these goals, Birnbaum had to forge his own tools and devices. They were (a) the application of the exact musicological (i. e., historic-philological) method to his realm of study; (b) the collection of as many authentic sources as possible; and (c) constant comparison between liturgical and musical developments.

The very first of Birnbaum's scholarly essays, a review of Baer's *Baal T'filla*, demonstrated that he was well aware of the problems confronting him.[4] Investigating the origin and the existence of our musical tradition, he endeavoured to isolate and to reestablish what he deemed its individual constituent elements. He then compared them, where comparisons would be fruitful, with traditions of other related cultures, e. g. with the Gregorian music of the Catholic Church. He was, in addition, always alert to consider his material under the aspect of the manifold trends within Judaism, contemporary with his sources. This methodical principle imparts to his studies lasting value, integrating history, musicology, and liturgics into an accurate picture. Among his

---

[3] My colleague, Dr. I. Sonne and I have given a tabulation of musical terms in medieval literature, comparing Hebrew, Arabic, Latin, Greek, and English terms. (*HUCA*, 1941.)

[4] *Juedisches Literaturblatt* 1898, Nrs. 24, 27.

most important essays are "Briefe aus Koenigsberg"[5] (*Der Juedische Cantor* 1883–4) written at the request of Mr. Francis Cohen, London, when the latter wished to deliver a learned address on the music of the Synagogue.[6] In these essays, we note Birnbaum's earliest attempts to set up certain criteria for determining the age of synagogal melodies, although he did not always reach definite conclusions. In his review of Joseph Singer's book *Die Tonarten des traditionellen Synagogengesanges, ihr Verhaeltnis zu den Tonarten der christlichen und vorchristlichen Musikperiode* (Vienna 1886), Birnbaum goes much beyond Singer's theses. He ends with the prophetic and arresting demand: "Wenn wir trotzdem noch manche Psalmodie wiedererkennen . . . ., so mag das ein Fingerzeig sein, dass wir bei der Erforschung unserer Melodien immer den Gregorianischen Gesang zu Rate zu ziehen haben."[7] This has since become a generally accepted maxim.

An excellent liturgico-musical study that reveals the thoroughness of his method is his series of articles on "Musikalische Tradition bei Vorlesung der Megilla."[8] This constitutes an initial attempt to find the first links in the chain of musical tradition based upon talmudic-midrashic investigation. At the same time it represents a valuable contribution to the controversial problem of the development of *Ḥazanut*. It also enters the scarcely explored filed of the early history of the מנהגים. Here is where Birnbaum expounds his theory of the formal structure of the synagogal chant. As a whole, the study contains excellent spadework and deserves to be translated and expanded. Though little known, it is a classic in its realm.

Our scholar's full scientific capacity is exhibited in the essay, "Juedische Musiker am Hofe von Mantua von 1542–1628."[9]

---

[5] A Bibliography of Birnbaum's writings scattered through many different magazines and stretching over a long span of time will be found in appendix I.

[6] Mr. Cohen was the expert on Jewish Music for the *Jewish Encyclopedia*. Many of his articles make use of Birnbaum's original material without always referring to Birnbaum. Indeed, the latter had to accuse Mr. Cohen openly of plagiarizing him. (Cf. *Israelit. Wochenschrift*, 1904, p. 246).

[7] *Jued. Literaturblatt* 1886, Nrs. 24–25.

[8] *Allgemeine Zeitung des Judentums*, 1891, Nrs. 12–14.

[9] *Kalender fuer Israeliten*, Vienna 1893.

Here Birnbaum, not content to discuss sources already known, brought new material to light and exhausted his subject. Jewish cultural history and general music history are linked in a masterly way. The article remains definitive to the present hour and merits translation into English. Particular attention is given to Salomone Rossi, thus supplementing D'Indy's and Naumbourg's fragmentary and unsatisfactory edition of Rossi's Hebrew compositions.[10]

Returning to his favorite subject, the origin of musical tradition, Birnbaum examines the Sephardic נוסח in his review of F. Consolo's famous collection ספר שירי ישראל "Libro dei canti d'Israele."[11] But his outstanding contribution to this problem is the essay "Ueber den Ursprung der Traditionen im Synagogengesang."[12] The law of love breathes throughout this work. With tender care, our musical heritage is analysed and, in many cases, vindicated before the tribunal of history. The musical rendition of the *Ķeroba*, together with psalmody and scriptural cantillation, is considered the foundation stone of our musical tradition. Examining the tune of the *Minḥa 'Amida* for the Sabbath, Birnbaum demonstrates, by an excellent piece of sagacious reasoning, that this tradition goes back to the time of Saadya Gaon. The melody of the *Kedusha de-Sidra* is found to have originated even earlier, in the time of the first Gaonim. The influence of the school upon the music of the synagogue is well explained, and the relationship between *ḥazan* and *paitan* is extensively discussed. Finally, Birnbaum reveals that a personality of outstanding reputation and commanding stature — to all appearances R. Yehudaj Gaon — supported the early *ḥazanim* with his authority.[13] This discovery is one of the most important historical results of Birnbaum's study. Thereafter,

---

[10] Paris, 1877.

[11] *Jued. Literaturblatt* 1893, Nr. 19.

[12] *Jued. Literaturblatt* 1899, Nrs. 39, 40.

[13] Cf. ספר האשכול I., Ch. 25, ed. Auerbach. (Halberstadt 1867) p. 55: ורב צמח כתב מנהג אצלנו החזנים . . . והחזנים הראשונים קבלו ממר רב יהודאי, והוא מרבו עד רבו . . . . Also ספר האשכול ed. Sch. Albeck, Jerusalem 1935, p. 104–5. ואמרים כי קבלה היא בידם מחזנים הראשונים שקבלו ממר רב יהודאי ורב יהודאי מרבו עד ד'. Cf. also Ginzberg, Geonica II., p. 53.

the Gaonic period attracted the attention of Jewish scholars
more and more. Our author made a fine contribution to that
province of study. His essay "Ueber die Verdienste der Gaonen
um die juedische Liturgie und den Synagogengesang" attempts
to reconstruct the history of our traditional chant from the time
of the Amoraim down to Natronai Gaon and later.[14] It is regrettable that both of these last mentioned articles were published in little known periodicals; otherwise Birnbaum's results
would soon have become an established part of the Science of
Judaism. Small wonder that some recent writers in the field of
Geonics proved unfamiliar with those important essays.

The article on "Polen und der polnische Ritus" deals again
with the problem, so fascinating for Birnbaum, of how traditions came into being.[15] Here he follows Zunz, who long before
had surmised that the Polish and South-Russian traditions have
a common Byzantian origin. Zunz did not discuss musical tradition, although he mentioned it. Birnbaum's article, concentrat-
ing on music, now closed this gap.

Meanwhile, Birnbaum had become in the sphere of Jewish
music, the leading authority, and his correspondence with
scholars was steadily expanding. Twice he was called upon to
conduct postgraduate courses for the alumni of the Jewish
teachers' colleges in Germany. We possess the two manuals of
the lectures which he delivered on these occasions.

Modestly Birnbaum called these profound studies *Liturgische
Uebungen*, (I and II).[16] They establish a wholly new method of
comparing the development of certain prayers with their tunes,
investigating the latter from the point of view of style, and the
former from that of historic Rabbinism. Unfortunately, these
exercises deal with their subject in such a condensed and concise
manner (in order to save space and money) that it is sometimes
necessary to transcribe certain passages into longhand language,
as it were. These studies, though offering priceless new material

---

[14] *Israel. Wochenschrift* 1903, Nr. 4.

[15] *Oesterreichisch-Ungarische Kantorenzeitung*, 1909.

[16] Verband der Juedischen Lehrer im Deutschen Reich. In Commission
bei M. Popelauer, Berlin, 1900, 1902.

both for the musician and for the historian of liturgy, have not as yet been fully evaluated.

As a final tribute to the memory of his great teacher, Salomon Sulzer, Birnbaum wrote a series of ten articles for Sulzer's centennial. This affectionately tendered homage "Zum Gedaechtnis Salomon Sulzer's"[17] displays our author not only as a conscientious and diligent scholar but also as a spirited and tactful chronicler with a gift for elegant literary style.

When we consider Birnbaum's position in the history of Jewish Science today, almost a generation after his death, we must admire the great versatility of his scholarship; liturgy, musicology, Jewish lore, rabbinics, all of these were subjects with which he was equally familiar. Methodologically, he follows Zunz's system of collecting and comparing. Intellectually, he was a fine product of Central European *Haskala*. His was a universal interest in all phases of Judaism, and the carefully arranged alphabetical indices of his innumerable books would constitute material for a learned encyclopedia. Some of his ideas were ingenious and original; all of them were logical. And yet we must ask ourselves whether he really achieved the aims which he had set.

It is true, he did not write a systematic history of Jewish Music, but he successfully incorporated Jewish Music into the Science of Judaism and into General Musicology. For the scientific examination of tradition and for the distinction between genuine tradition and pseudo-tradition, Birnbaum has given us the tools and has shown us the method of further research.

Except for a comprehensive system of Jewish Music so fervently desired by him, yet never achieved, Birnbaum came very near to the realization of his principle ideas. The cause of his shortcomings was chiefly his deep entanglement with the sheer material which fascinated him to such a degree that, to gain the indispensable detachement, required the utmost effort. Nonetheless, Birnbaum has left us a solid foundation upon which to build and a set of effective tools with which to work.

[17] *Israel. Wochenschrift* 1904.

Outstanding among these implements is his collection of musical manuscripts and books. Considering his very modest financial means we must admit that the fruit of his labours, this collection, amounts almost to a miracle. But even more astonishing than the accumulation of books and manuscripts is his own thematic catalogue of traditional Jewish melodies. We shall describe and evaluate this hitherto unknown *magnum opus systematicum* in some of the following pages.

Before parting from this lovable and admirable personality, I should like to add a few remarks about his abilities as a cantor.

A gentleman from Koenigsberg who knew Birnbaum personally was kind enough to relate to me a few observations. "Birnbaum's musical taste was excellent; never did he permit theatrical music or virtuoso pieces in the service. His warm feeling, his thorough understanding of every detail of the liturgy, made the service truthfully a divine one. As his ideal aim was the complete integration of sacred word, cultic event and liturgical music, so he personally represented an integration of the scholar, the creative artist, and the hazanic minister: in every respect an ideal *Shliakh Tzibbur*."

THE EDUARD BIRNBAUM COLLECTION

The Eduard Birnbaum Collection (E. B. C.) consists of four sections, namely: (1) general Hebraica, printed and written, (2) books and periodicals, chiefly on synagogal music, and printed synagogal or Jewish compositions, (3) musical manuscripts, indices for his books, and a few letters, and (4) last in order but in many respects first in importance, Birnbaum's own handwritten thematic catalogue of melodies, tunes, cantillations, recitatives, etc., alphabetically arranged according to the Hebrew texts. To give a detailed description of that magnificent collection can not here be our task. We must content ourselves with pointing to a few outstanding items at present unknown to the public. Even so, one is loath to chose one manuscript to the exclusion of others hardly less interesting.

I.

Ms. 4   F 71

This manuscript consists now of sixteen quarto leaves of which the ninth is almost wholly torn out. On 24 of the 30 pages, we find writing of which the initial portion is missing. As my colleague Dr. Sonne tells me, the paper is good and contains an Italian watermark used in the second half of the sixteenth century.[18] The manuscript was formerly the property of the late Rabbi, Dr. Moise Ehrenreich of Rome, who bequeathed it to Birnbaum. The 24 written pages are furnished with note staffs, drawn with a so-called rastral, then the customary apparatus for musical staving. Obviously we have a written choir part before us. The hand shows a neat intelligent Italian, Hebrew, and musical script. The music of this manuscript is explicitly intended for two choirs, each of which consists of soprano, alto, tenor, and bass. Everything is written exclusively in the treble clef, and accordingly our manuscript seems to be for the first part of the second choir. It contains not the leading part but probably the part next to it. The 21 complete pieces contain unique material, both from the liturgical and musical point of view. In the following we give a survey of the contents:[19]

Fragment of an unidentified *piyut*.   (1)
Inscription: *Canto 2 Chore a 8.*
                          .ואמרין   until   .... ובא לציון   (2)
Inscription: *Canto 2 a 8*
                          [20]. . . זכור ברית   (3)
(Cf. Davidson אוצר II, p. 212, Nr. 115.)

[18] I am indebted to my colleague, Dr. Sonne, for his assistance in connection with the manuscript. My sincere gratitude belongs also to my friend, Dr. S. Atlas, for some interesting suggestions and to my student, Rabbi M. Machenbaum, for his thoughtful aid.

[19] For the full text of the five *piyyutim*, hitherto unknown, see in Appendix II. Cf. also our illustrations Nrs. 1 and 2.

[20] A poem for circumcision Cf. also F. Consolo, *Canti d'Israele*, p. 75, Nr. 163.

(For the same occasion; unknown *piyut*) ... דע לך   (4)

Inscription: *Canto 2° Chore a 8.*

(For שמחת תורה)   ²¹... תשיש חתן   (5)

Inscription: *2 Core*

²²... כתר יתנו לך   (6)

up to the end of the קדושה.

Inscription: *Canto 2 Core*

²³.עושה פלה   until   ..... ראו בנים   (7)

Inscription: *Canto 2° Core*

²⁴.אמן הללויה   .... ברוך ה'   (8)

.ברכו את ה'   .... ועד   (9)

Inscription: *Canto 2° Core*

²⁵.עד העולם   .... אלוהים השיבנו   (10)

Inscription: *Canto*

²⁶.מי חכם וישמור .... ויתבוננו. עד העולם   (11)

Inscription: *Canto 2° Core*

²⁶ᵃ.... אין כאלהינו   (12)

added Ps. 102.14, transliterated in Latin
letters.

Inscription: *Canto 2° Core.*

(fragment of   ... אלהים ה' בהקריב לסיני לעם   (13)
an unknown *piyut*; the rest of the leaf
is torn out)

Inscription: *Canto 2° Chore.*

... שישו דודים הנחמדים   (14)

(Unknown *piyut* for שמחת תורה)

Inscription: ח' קולות שיר לשמחת תורה

.... אל חי תמים צוה   (15)

Inscription: פסוק לאמר קודם ברכו לשמחת
תורה

²¹ A poem for שמחת תורה with allusions to the names of the חתן תורה and
חתן בראשית.
²² The Sephardic preamble of the *Kedusha.*
²³ The usual Italian and Sephardic preamble of מי כמוכה.
²⁴ Ps. 106: 48.
²⁵ Cf. *Maḥzor Rome* ק'נ'; לשבועות; (Ps. 80.4; 80.8; 80.20. Ps. 28.9.)
²⁶ Ps. 107.43.   ²⁶ᵃ See photograph # 1.

(16)

(a) אתה ה' תשמרם . . . [27]

(b) שמע ה' תחנתי . . . [28]

(c) סביב רשעים יתהלכון . . . [29]

Inscription: *Cto 1mo Choro a 8.*

(See Appendix II.)   (17)   בורא עולם, יחיד נעלם . . .

Inscription: ק ד ש

(18) *Cheder* (sic!) יתנו לך . . . .   לדור ודור הללויה.

added "*Alleluia*"   (כתר)

(Transliteration of the scribe)   (19)

　　Jachad culam cheduscia leca iescialesciu
　　chema scieneemar nal iad nevieca.
　　Ecad hu eloenu hu avinu hu malchenu umoscinenu
　　hu iasminenu beracamav scienid lene(!) col cai.

Inscription: *Cto 2do Choro à 8.*

Sign: ○ 3|1   (20) שירו נא שבחי יה אותם . . . טעונים[30]

　　3 ○   הנחילם תושיא עם מצות
　　1   השבים פסחי יה עם מצות

Inscription: *Canto 2do Chore a 8.*

(21)   יגדל אלוקים (!) חי . . . . קדשתו.

Inscription: *Cadmon Basso Alto*

Inscription: *Basso capo.*

C   הנו אדון עולם . . . . ומלכותו   שפע נבואתו . . .
C   נאמן ביתו.

Inscription: *Basso capo.*

C   לא יחליף . . . . כרשעתו . . ישלח . . . ישועתו
　　מתים יחיה . . . . שם תהלתו.

The man who wrote the manuscript must have been a fine
musician no less than a person well educated generally; his Italian transliteration of the Hebrew is almost faultless. His musical
ductus shows the trained musician in every detail, although he

---

[27] Ps. 12.8.
[28] Ps. 6.10.
[29] Ps. 12.9.
[30] See photograph # 2.

wrote the manuscript apparently in great haste. While his
cursive Hebrew script shows a hand obviously familiar with
such tasks, there occur, nonetheless, certain ortographic blunders
which exclude the possibility that a real Hebrew scholar could
have been the writer.[31] Two of the *piyyutim* (#15 and #17)
hitherto unknown, are vocalized; yet the vocalization is strictly
phonetic, following the Italian-Hebrew pronounciation without
regard for grammatical minutiae. No distinction is made between
Tzere and *Segol* or between *Patach* and *Kametz*.

Concerning the musical script, the following facts are obvious:
(1) The *ductus*, while flighty, is clear and intelligible. The
manner of notation, especially the writing of quavers and of
accidentals, suggests a date between 1630–1650. We shall see
later that all other features of the music correspond to that era.
(2) Occasionally the writer uses old-fashioned devices; yet in
general he shows a progressive mind. To cite just a few instances:
He sometimes makes use of the bar-stroke new at that time.
On the other hand, we find the outdated *signum perfectionis*
twice, to indicate a triple tact. The quavers are modern, yet in
some places old-fashioned signs for rests occur. (3) The Hebrew text is well placed beneath the notes. Each word is spelt
from right to left, but the sentences are set from left to right
in order to correspond to the normal course of music. When it
comes to the distribution of words to music, the scribe follows,
in general, the rules of Zacconi.[32]

Having examined the exterior of the manuscript, we shall
now proceed to consider its content, both as to music and as to
text.

Of the 21 pieces, 10 are well known scriptural verses or
familiar quotations from the liturgy for weekdays or holidays.
Of the 11 *piyyutim*, the numbers 3, זכור ברית 12, אין כאלהינו
and 21 יגדל belong to the ritual common to world Jewry. # 4
דע לך seems to be an addition to זכור ברית, for it likewise cele-
brates the ברית מילה. Four poems, (# 5, 14, 15, 17) glorify the

---

[31] E. g., שבטי for שבחי, or וישלך for וישלח; ברה for ברא etc.

[32] *Prattica di musica* (Venice 1596) Prima parte. Libro primo c. 63. Cf.
also Joh. Wolf, *Handbuch der Notationskunde*, I., p. 443.

festival of שמחת תורה or the חתן תורה, two even in their super-scription; #20 seems to refer to Shabuot. To my knowledge, none of these last mentioned *piyyutim* has been previously known or published. At least nrs. 15 and 17 deserve to be publicized beyond the sphere of learned studies.[33]

When we turn now to the music, our attention is immediately drawn to its most striking feature, viz. the arrangement for two antiphonal choirs. This kind of choir-setting was a famous specialty of Venice where it originated.[34] Giovanni Gabrieli, the musical director of San Marco in Venice, was the *spiritus rector* of that new and effective practice, the *cori spezzati*. It did not take long until Rome followed suit and Nanini, Allegri, Legrenzi and others became the representatives of what we call — not with perfect exactness — the Venetian-Roman School. Characteristic of this style is its rigid purity and intransigence in the face of the most revolutionary changes, brought about by the rise of opera and its monodic diction. The strict observance of the "classic" *a cappella* style was but slightly mitigated by the introduction of settings for double choruses (*Stile osservato*). Our manuscript shows the prevailing influence of that school in every detail, with only one exception (#19). This instance is a typical melody in the fashion of the monodic arias, at that time, brand new, as we find them in the dramatic *"stile rappresentativo."* We quote:

Ja — chad cu-lam   che-du-scia,   le-ca

---

[33] For the full text of these *piyyutim*, see Appendix II.

[34] It has been said that the two organ lofts opposite one another in the Cathedral of S. Marco in Venice were the immediate occasion for the invention of double-choirs by Adriaen Willaert, famous musical director of S. Marco until 1562. However, we know today that, long before Willaert, that practice prevailed in certain towns of Northern Italy, for instance, in Modena. It was Willaert's disciples, Andrea and Giovani Gabrieli, who developed the mannerism of double choirs into a legitimate feature of the baroque.

ie - scia - le scia che - mo scie - ne - e - mar nal iad ne — vi — e - ca.

A comparison with a typical recitative of a Roman opera shows close proximity to our example:[35]

Although it is not easy to ascertain all of the mannerisms of an 8-part-choir composition from one middle part, and certainly not conclusive, we shall endeavour to guess at the fundamental stylistic elements of the work. It was probably not very polyphonic, though our part is rather lively. Yet the range of our extant part is very small, hardly one octave, with seldom any occasion to carry a prominent tune. Rhythmically, it shows the free attitude of the early 17th century. Changes between double and triple tact are frequently indicated. In general, the compositions seem to prefer a rather isorhythmic diction. The tonality, while not yet our major, is also no longer strictly modal. Cross relations seem not to have disturbed our composer. The choruses appear to be well planned; the formtype ABB is occasionally indicated. In some places we find sharp alternation of choirs. This feature becomes very clear when parts of Hebrew sentences are missing and rests appear in their place. The refrain form is represented in nrs. 15, 17, and 21. Nrs. 15 and 17 seem to have the same or a very similar melody. #21 suggests a free rondeau form. Most startling is the remark at the end of nrs. 15 and 17 *"ritornello fine"* and *"ritornello."* This is intelligible only if we assume instrumental accompaniment, since it is to this that the term is usually applied. Such a practice in the synagogue would

---

[35] S. Landi: *San Alessio, Prologo.* (Cf. Buecken's *Handbuch der Musikwissenschaft;* R. Haas, *Das Barock,* p. 71.)

Eduard Birnbaum

No 1.

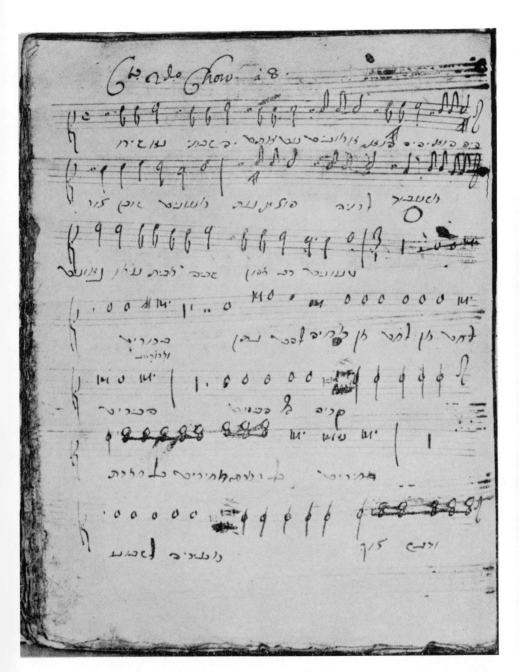

No. 2

MINISTÈRE
DU COMMERCE
DE L'INDUSTRIE
DES POSTES
ET DES TÉLÉGRAPHES

EXPOSITION UNIVERSELLE
DE 1900

CONGRÈS INTERNATIONAUX

Paris, le 10 Juin 1900

Monsieur

M. le Dr Hugo Riemann m'écrit
que vous avez l'intention de vous joindre
une communication pour le Congrès d'histoire
de la musique, qui se tiendra à Paris du
23 au 30 Juillet prochain. Croyez que
vous en serez très honoré, et que nous
vous remercions de votre aimable adhésion.

Je vous envoie ci-avant le programme
du Congrès, et un bulletin d'adhésion. Veuillez
vous avoir la bonté, en me le renvoyant
signé, de m'indiquer exactement le sujet

de votre communication ("De l'orchestration
wagnérienne", je crois ?), et me dire si
vous avez l'intention de la présenter vous-
même au Congrès. (Et dans ce cas,
quelle en sera la durée approximative ? Il
communication de 15 minutes renouvelable,
en conférence plus étendue.) Ou bien
s'agit-il d'un Mémoire manuscrit que
vous nous envoyez ? Pour savoir dire
que nous souhaitons vivement que
vous veniez personnellement à Paris.

Veuillez croire, Monsieur,
à notre considération très distinguée

Romain Rolland

26 rue Notre Dame des Champs.

not be incompatible with contemporary custom, as both compositions mentioned are epithalamia for the (בראשית 'ח), חתן תורה on שמחת תורה which was not considered a יום טוב so strict as to preclude the playing of musical instruments.[36]

Here the question arises whether the manuscript contains traditional Jewish material. But that question cannot be answered at all, since we are not in possession of those parts which carry the leading melody. The fact, however, that all other traits are strictly à la mode and in typical Roman-Venetian style excludes the probability of inherently traditional elements. Let us not forget that Salomone Rossi, presumably a contemporary of our composer, employs very few, if any, Jewish traditional motives in his liturgical compositions.

Turning now to the question of the manuscript's provenance, we realize at once that it originated in Italy. To define its birth-place more accurately, it must have come from a community with Minhag Sephardi. The preamble (כתר) of the *Kedushah*, the *invitatorium* of the (ראו בנים) מי כמוכה are distinctive criteria of the Sephardic ritual. Thus far we are lead by the text. The music is more revealing. Both in Rome and in Venice, in fact in all Northern Italy, compositions for two choirs were in vogue during the seventeenth century; but the Sephardic ritual was more common in northeastern Italy, especially in the Venetian republic. Moreover, we know that many Jewish musicians frequented the court of the Gonzagas in Mantua and that there was a lively traffic between the Jewish communities of Mantua, Ferrara, and Venice.[37]

During the first third of the seventeenth century, a dynamic personality of dominating authority and artistic temperament enriched Jewish life in Venice: Rabbi Leon da Modena, a most versatile figure, an author who says of himself that he mastered (or at least dabbled in) twenty six different avocations.[38] Among them he counts music, play-writing, and *Ḥazanut*. He founded a musical academy "בזכרני את-ציון" which gave weekly concerts

[36] Dr. Sonne directed my attention to this fact.

[37] Cf. E. Birnbaum, "Die juedischen Musiker am Hofe von Mantua." (*Kalender fuer Israeliten*, Vienna 1893.)

[38] Cf. Leon da Modena, חיי יהודה, ed. Kahane, Kieff 1911-12, p. 64.

in the Ghetto.[39] However, this splendor did not last very long. "The devastation caused by the plague of 1630 wrought havoc in this as in every other form of local activity; and though the musical society continued to exist for at least nine or ten years more, it never fully recovered from the blow."[40]

Here also we may mention Modena's active interest in the Hebrew compositions of Salomone Rossi. It was due to the incessant initiative and encouragement of the Rabbi that Rossi was commissioned to write his synagogal compositions for choirs of three to eight parts — pieces which have kept their appeal and beauty down to the present day.

We possess an enthusiastic report about that "Accademia Musicale" and its performances on שמחת תורה under the leadership of Leon da Modena. The writer is his former disciple, the apostate Giulio Morosini, (alias Samuel Nachmias del Salonicco). He says: "I remember well that at the time of my successes in Venice during 1628 or thereabouts, if I am not mistaken, the Jews fled from Mantua because of the war, and some came to Venice. At that juncture Mantua flourished in many fields of study. Also the Jews applied themselves to music and to the playing of instruments. Upon their arrival in Venice, they organized an academy of music in the Ghetto where I was living, and sang there twice a week in the evenings. It was chiefly certain leading personalities and the rich men of the Ghetto who supported that institution. I also was to be found among those there assembled. My teacher, R. Leon da Modena, was the *maestro di cappella*.

"In that year, two rich and brilliant personalities were elected bridegrooms of the Law — as explained above — one of whom was a member of the academy. With the help of the musicians, there had been arranged for our benefit two choirs in the Spanish Synagogue which was beautifully decorated and

[39] Cf. A. Ottolenghi, R. Leon da Modena. *Rivista di Venezia*, Luglio 1929.), also C. Roth: "Academia musicale del Ghetto veneziano" in *Israel*, Vol. II., and H. Zoller: "Theater und Tanz in den italienischen Ghetti." (*Mitteilungen zur juedischen Volkskunde*, vol. 39.)

[40] Cecil Roth: *Venice*, p. 201. (*Jewish Communities Series* of the JPS), Philadelphia 1930.

adorned with silverware and jewels. On the two evenings, i. e.
on the "Octave" (sic) of the feast *Sh'mini Atzeret* and *Simḥat
Tora*, these choirs sang figural music (that is, music in artistic
settings; note of the translator) in the Hebrew language, also a
part of *Arvith*, several psalms, and the *Minḥa*: that is to say,
also the afternoon service of the last holiday was solemnized
by music. Thus, during some hours of the evening, a throng of
noblemen and ladies gathered amid such great applause that
many officers and policemen had to guard the gates to secure
quiet and safe passage. Among the instruments, an organ also
was brought into the synagogue, which is not permitted by the
Rabbis, because it is the instrument usually played in our
churches . . . ."[41]

Elsewhere Morosini emphasizes the great part choral singing
played on שמחת תורה. He reports that rhymed *piyyutim* with
references to Jerusalem and the coming of Elijah and of the
Messiah were sung; sometimes in Spanish or Turkish.[42] In the
center of the festivity are the חתן בראשית and חתן תורה in whose
praise are rendered hymns, encomia, and eulogies.[43] Their names
are celebrated in poems created *ad hoc*, and all the arts (above
all, music) have to contribute to their glorification. When reading
such reports, we need not be surprised that the strict orthodoxy
of Venice tolerated such secularistic activities.[44] We learn that
שמחת תורה was not considered a full holiday, inasmuch as the
prohibition of work on that day was somewhat flexible.[45] Already
in the early sixteenth century, the Rabbis had permitted dancing
in the synagogue on that occasion.

And now we return to the five *piyyutim* in our musical
manuscript. In them can be found all of the features mentioned
by Morosini, rhymed poetry, double choir, typical processionals,
poems celebrating the names of the "bridegrooms of the Law,"

[41] Guilio Morosini, *Via della Fede*, Rome 1683, p. 793. (Vol. II.) Translation by Eric Werner.
[42] *Ibid.*, p. 789. Cf. also D. Simonsen, G. Morosini's "Mitteilungen ueber
seinen Lehrer Leon da Modena," in the *A. Berliner Festschrift*, Berlin 1903.
[43] *Ibid.*, p. 788.
[44] *Ibid.*, p. 793.
[45] Cf. *Jewish Encyclopedia*, article "Simḥat Tora."

"*musica figurata*" (a novelty in an orthodox synagogue), the rite of the "*Scuola Spagnuola.*" All of this minutely confirms Morosini's description. It does not seem a very bold hypothesis, therefore, to assume that our manuscript originated between 1628 and 1650, in or around Venice, influenced by the circle of Modena's musical academy. 1628 is a *terminus a quo* since, in that year, the academy was founded by the gifted Jewish musicians fleeing from Mantua. 1650 is apparently a *terminus ad quem* since thereafter the academy no longer existed and since Modena had died a short time before. It is very improbable that Salomone Rossi was the composer; certainly we would have heard about it. Nor can I suggest any other name. Much depends upon the interpretation of the term "*maestro di cappella*" used by Morosini. If it denotes merely or exclusively the conductor, then the assumption of Modena's authorship is not warranted. But, in those times, a *maestro di cappella* was usually much more then merely a musical director. He had to officiate as his own composer, director, accompanist, and conductor. If we understand the term in so broad a manner, it would be possible to assume that Leon da Modena, that versatile, artistic personality, was himself the composer of our manuscript.[46] Be that as it may, this much we can assert: our fragment is a unique anthology of liturgical compositions, chiefly for double choir in the musical style then most fashionable, written by a highly skilled musician, probably by a master. It originated in or around Venice, between 1628 and 1650. Probably soon afterward the orthodox reaction against artistic music got the upper hand and became so strong that all "figural music" in the Synagogue was abandoned and forgotten. At least Benedetto Marcello, the Venetian *Nobile* who recorded eleven ḥazanic melodies of the Sephardic and German Jews of Venice around 1700, does not say a word about artistic Jewish endeavours in music, although he expatiates freely upon the musical standards of Venetian Jewry.[47] He states moreover that nowhere did he find notated

[46] Not, however, the scribe! The numerous orthographic blunders in the Hebrew text make this hypothesis entirely untenable.

[47] Cf. E. Werner, "Die hebraeischen Intonationen des B. Marcello," (in *MGWJ*, Breslau, 1937, November-issue.) Modena's responsum permitting

music in the synagogues of Venice or elsewhere, although he had been searching for it.[48] This can have only one meaning: artistic music was, in his time, no longer fostered in the synagogue. Another *argumentum ex silentio* is offered by the traveller Abraham Levy of Amsterdam who, in his travelogue, speaks of the fine traditional music heard in the great Levantine synagogue of Venice. Not a word about artistic efforts which at that time, in the beginning of the eighteenth century, would certainly have been a feat well worth mentioning.[49]

All of these facts seem to verify the exultant descriptions of the musical ability of the Venetian Jews in the period of Modena, and our manuscript adds proof to those reports.

II

By far most of the manuscripts of the Birnbaum collection stem from the latter half of the eighteenth and the first half of the nineteenth century. These have been discussed extensively in Idelsohn's article mentioned in the beginning of this study. Certain items, however, not specified there, deserve at least a brief word of appreciation. It is well known, for instance, that the famous Louis Lewandowski was, for a number of years, the assistant of the cantor Abraham Lichtenstein in Berlin; and Idelsohn has, perhaps for the first time, realized how deeply Lewandowski was indebted to and influenced by his superior. As Idelsohn puts it, "Lichtenstein's hazanut became so much a part of him that he considered it as his (Lewandowski's) own . . . . And in publishing that hazanut in his work *Kol Rinnah Utfilla*, Lewandowski did not mention even the name of Lichtenstein, apparently believing that his music was or had become *His*. Only by means of Lichtenstein's own manuscript do we recognize the origin."[50] Indeed, it is fascinating to watch the transition

---

the use of artistic music in the synagogue is included (in French translation)in Naumbourg's edition of Salomone Rossi's Hebrew compositions, Paris 1876-7.

[48] Cf. E. Werner, *op. cit.*, p. 402.

[49] Cf. A. Z. Idelsohn, *Jewish Music in its Historical Development*, p. 202, and 507, n. 22.

[50] *Ibid.*, p. 276.

from Lichtenstein's unorganized but really ingenious and splendidly melodious style to Lewandowski's skilled and classic arrangement of the same tunes. As an original inventor of melodies along traditional lines, Lichtenstein even surpasses Lewandowski. Our collection contains, among numerous other manuscripts of Lichtenstein, a *"Tal-Kaddish"* of enchanting beauty, a veritable gem which well deserves a new setting worthy of its splendor. Among other pearls, we mention here some fine originals from Sulzer's hand, today perhaps unique in the world, since the Germans burnt the old synagogue in the Seitenstettengasse of Vienna, where the bulk of Sulzer's manuscripts had been preserved. All the writings of Hirsch Weintraub, the third great reformer of synagogal music, are contained in our collection, among them his famous "Tempelgesaenge" in their first and second versions. Besides, we have a rare opportunity to look into Weintraub's workshop, since all of his sketches, notes, and the like are here accessible. Worth mentioning are also his unprinted orchestral compositions which show him to have been a gifted and serious follower of Mendelssohn. It is touching to observe, in these scores, Weintraub's unyielding struggle with problems of orchestral technique.

Of great historic importance are the complete handwritten vocal scores of the liturgies for the whole year, arranged according to communities. Birnbaum collected all of the liturgical music of Hamburg, Braunschweig, Prague, Copenhagen, Hannover, Magdeburg, Breslau, Stettin, Koenigsberg, and many other cities. Usually these scores start about 1825 and are continued into the sixties. They constitute priceless authentic material for the future historiographer of the music of Jewish Liberalism. Approximately three hundred folio volumes give a virtually complete picture of liturgical as well as musical developments in Central Europe during these formative years. A specialty *sui generis* is also the complete score of the temple music of the ancient community of Leghorn (Livorno) in three bulky volumes. However, it must be added that the traditional material contained in these compositions is frequently effaced through the carelessness, the clumsiness, and the irresponsibility of the arrangers who were, in the main, non-Jewish musicians.

A great number of manuscripts of *ḥazanim* from Russia, Poland, the Baltic states, France, England, the Netherlands, and Scandinavia make the collection really all European. Added to it are a considerable number of explanatory or reference notes which await resuscitation and evaluation. Excellent help for such work is offered through numerous sets of liturgical and cantorial periodicals, likewise a part of our collection. Most of these are very rare since few libraries in this country took the trouble to collect them.

Birnbaum's scholarly interests brought him into contact with many musicologists and many students of the related arts. Several of the letters document his intensive and manifold discussion of all topics connected with the musical history of ancient and mediaeval times. Although most of that correspondence is now outdated, some of the letters deserve mention either on account of the writer's personality or because of the subject under discussion.

A regular correspondent of Birnbaum's was the famous musical scholar, Prof. Hugo Riemann, who held Birnbaum's judgement in high regard and quoted him occasionally in his work. Upon Riemann's suggestion, Romain Rolland, in his function as general secretary of the musical section of the world's fair of France in the year 1900, invited Birnbaum to deliver a learned address on the subject of ancient Jewish music before an international audience of scholars and artists. Everything was arranged for Birnbaum's trip to Paris when a sudden illness in his family prevented his fulfilment of that flattering invitation.[51]

Peaceable as Birnbaum usually was, some of his letters show traces of sharp polemics. In all of these cases, without exception, musicology has vindicated Birnbaum's views. One instance should be quoted here, since Birnbaum took the issue out of the sphere of private correspondence and placed it before the public.[52] This occurred when he turned sharply against Professor Emil Breslaur who, in a shallow and ignorant pamphlet, had denied

---

[51] See photograph # 3.

[52] "Unsere erste Musikbeilage" in *Juedische Presse*, (*Lehrer und Kantor* 1899, Nr. 3. A reprint in A. Friedmann's *Birnbaum-Festschrift*, Berlin 1922, p. 158–163.

the authenticity of traditional Jewish music.[53] Birnbaum replies: "Well, I can inform the gentleman that the Jews possess elements of the most ancient music in their synagogal chants, elements of which all Churches must be envious and, for that matter indeed, are envious. The Churches will never fully understand the medieval *neumes* unless they take the trouble to study the medieval Jewish grammarians and their system of musical notation, in order to apply these principles to their *neumes*."

"It is both curious and wonderful that a Christian professor (having the advantage of being a historian) must tell a Jewish professor that he went much too far when he disputed the originality of synagogal chant (E. Vogel, Jahrbuch 1899, p. 54). When a Jesuit, Father Dechevrens of Paris, reaches the conclusion that 'the Gregorian Chant is the music of the Hebrews and that there is for every one of the Roman Catholic melodies but one modal system, not that of the Greeks but that of the *sacred Hebrew nation*,'[54] then it is very disgraceful for a Jewish professor to resort to such extremely foul means in order to wrap himself in a historic cloak. (The end of the quotation on page 65 of his pamphlet is taken from my study *Juedische Musiker am Hofe von Mantua*.)"

All of his life Birnbaum dreamed of writing, indeed intended to write, a comprehensive history of the music of the Synagogue. All of his studies and articles, his collecting, searching, travelling, and copying were to serve that one final aim, a systematic history of Jewish liturgical music. That book, alas, was never written. Another *magnum opus* was finished, however, which constituted his most important bequest and was destined to become a challenge to future Jewish musicologists.

III

This great work is a musico-liturgical catalogue listing all melodies of synagogal songs printed or written in Europe between 1700 and 1910, to which are added many bibliographical

---

[53] Emil Breslaur: *Sind originale Synagogen- und Volksmelodien bei den Juden geschichtlich nachweisbar?* Leipzig 1898.

[54] X. Haberl, *Kirchenmusikalisches Jahrbuch* 1899, p. 119 a.

references. Such a catalogue amounts to a complete thesaurus of all synagogal melodies of Europe and is an exact instrument by which to test the authenticity of any given traditional tune. The catalogue contains about seven thousand cards, arranged alphabetically according to the first words of the Hebrew texts. Each card is furnished with a musical quotation of the initial motive of the melody referred to. The Hebrew text is carefully underlaid, and the first two or three sources of each tune are traced. I may be permitted to point out briefly the great value of this remarkable work.

The catalogue serves both practical and scientific purposes and constitutes a reference work by which to find, for any given text, the tune and its source, or inversely, if the melody of a known or unknown text is to be identified, our catalogue will list it, provided the melody has ever been published or was frequently sung in a synagogue between 1700 and 1910. Should this catalogue ever be published — and it most assuredly deserves to become generally available — it would be indispensable for any *ḥazan* who takes his duties seriously or for any good choir leader of a temple and certainly for all students of Jewish liturgy and music. Indeed, its scientific value even surpasses its practical utility.

Better than any textbook, it illustrates the development of our liturgical music along certain lines and styles. Today we know fairly well how strongly the music of the Christian environment determined the course of the synagogal music in the last three-hundred years. Thanks to this catalogue, every change can now be followed closely from one version of a melody to the next, from each decade to the decade following. We can observe something that has so often proved a fascinating riddle for the musicologist, namely, the migration of certain tunes from one corner of Europe to the other. The precise tracing of these itinerant tunes will undoubtedly shed much light on the mystery of the birth and the propagation of folksong in general, a subject most controversial among students.

Moreover, we are now in a position to examine and to check the authenticity of any individual melody which is asserted to

be "traditional." All too often has this term been used and mis-
used, and it was always a complicated process to distinguish
between genuine tradition and pseudo-tradition. Now we can
state that, if the "traditional" melody to be examined is of
European derivation, it will be found in Birnbaum's catalogue.
If we fail to locate it there or if we fail to find there a version or
a variant ever so distantly related to it, then it is not genuinely
traditional. I have made a series of tests the results of which
have fully confirmed this statement. Furthermore, the exact
bibliographical implementation of the catalogue facilitates research into the genesis of art music within the Synagogue. It can
be said, without undue simplification, that we created a liturgical art music only when our leading ḥazanim became familiar
with musical notation. As soon as they took to writing or copying music, artistic songs began to flourish in the Synagogue. The
trend of the ḥazanim in Europe ran from East to West, musical
education from South to Northeast. It is only natural that our
religious art music, reaching its first peak in South Central
Europe, proceeded rapidly westward and then slowly but inten-
sively eastward.[55] We need not be surprised, then, to find widely
differing grades and nuances of traditional elements blended
with secular artistic features throughout the development of
synagogal art music. Similarly the traits of individual ḥazanim
are at times curiously touched, in spots, by the personal style of
composers who lived possibly a century earlier. All of these
characteristics of our cult music can now be studied with ease,
thanks to the catalogue and to the Eduard Birnbaum Collection
and to the help of an exact scientific apparatus.

In order to illustrate the structure of the catalogue and
to explain it concretely, we give two examples picked out at
random:

[55] The writer is aware of the fact that the trends and directions mentioned
above are due to certain general conditions which exerted a determining influence over the entire material and spiritual life of European Jewry. The question
of the musical education of the Jews or of the migration of the ḥazanim is but
secondary. Those conditions followed from the general status of the Jew and
its varied consequences.

שאו שערים

Chor. מלכיות לראש השנה

Se — u she-o-rim ro —— —— shay-chem.

Lewandowski, קול רנה p. 124.
Idem תודה וזמרה vol. II., p. 214.
Ms. 124 vol. III, p. 122.
Ms. 91, (שירי מקהלת) p. 44.
Lichtenstein, (A. J.) Ms. 125, Heft 18, p. 37.

שאו שערים

Samuel Nr.6, p. 4.
Erssler, מנינות, Nr. 6, p. 11. (Choir.)
Rosenstein, Nr. 12, p. 11. (cf. note.)
Ms. 82, Psalm-Responses, שאו שערים — סלה

We gave two examples of the arrangement of the catalogue.
There are 33 more cards listed under the שאו שערים offering as
many musical quotations and respective bibliographical references.

———————

These pages were written with the intent of directing the attention of Jewish scholars to the work of Eduard Birnbaum. At the
same time we seek to arouse scholarly interest in his magnificent
collection. Today it is inevitable that we ask ourselves: where
would this treasury of tradition have been, had not Dr. Oko,
former librarian of the Hebrew Union College, possessed the
foresight to secure it for our library? Dr. Oko's remark "Thus

the acquisition of the Birnbaum Collection was not an accident,"[56] we consider a modest understatement. Dr. Oko may
be assured of the gratitude of all students of Jewish lore. This
writer is deeply indebted to Dr. Oko for his personal interest in
the Birnbaum collection. Acknowledgments are likewise due
Dr. Walter Rothman, librarian of the H. U. C., and Mr. Moses
Marx, the head-cataloguer, for their kind assistance.

An old proverb says: *Habent sua fata libelli.* To the Birnbaum
catalogue, as yet unpublished and unknown, may fate show
itself propitious!

APPENDIX I.

BIBLIOGRAPHY OF EDUARD BIRNBAUM'S ESSAYS ON JEWISH MUSIC

This is a first attempt at a bibliography of the musical articles
of Birnbaum, all of them widely scattered through various
periodicals appearing over a long stretch of time. I am almost
certain that the present bibliography is not complete. But even
so, it may serve as a starting point for further research. Many
valuable references may also be found in A. Friedmann's Birnbaum Memorial, *Dem Andenken Eduard Birnbaum*, Berlin 1922.

1. "Voranzeige der Breslauer Synagogengesaenge von M.
   Deutsch." (*Juedischer Cantor*, 1880, Nr. 1)
2. "Ueber Salomon Sulzer." (*Jued. Cantor* 1881)
3. Necrology on Hirsch Weintraub. (*Jued. Cantor* 1882, Nr. 1)
4. 'Briefe aus Koenigsberg." (*Jued. Cantor*, 1883, Nr. 3, 5)
5. "Adolf Schoenfelds Haggada Ausgabe." (*Jued. Literaturblatt* 1885)
6. "Byron's Hebraeische Melodien." (*Jued. Cantor* 1886,
   Nr. 46).
7. Review of the *Sephardische Gesaenge* by Bauer and Loewit.
   (*Jued. Literaturblatt* 1889)

[56] Dr. A. S. Oko: "Jewish Book Collections in the U. S. A." (*American Jewish Year Book*, Vol. 45, p. 78.)

8. "Musikalische Traditionen bei der Vorlesung der Megilla."
(*Allgem. Zeitung des Judentums* 1891, Nrs. 12, 13, 15.)

9. Review of Hirsch Weintraub's *Tempelgesaenge*. (*Wiener Kantorenzeitung, Wahrheit*, 1891, series of ten articles.)

10. Review of S. Sulzer's *Sikoron, Gabe der Erinnerung*. (*Jued. Literaturblatt* 1891.)

11. "Kritische Blaetter." (*Koenigsberger Jeschurun* 1892, Nr. 1.)

12. "Juedische Musiker am Hofe von Mantua." (Singer's *Kalender fuer Oesterreichische Israeliten*, Vienna 1893.)

13. Review of F. Consolo's *Libro dei canti d'Israele* (*Jued. Literaturblatt*, Nrs. 18, 19.)

14. Necrology on Louis Lewandowski. (*Jeschurun* 1894, Nr. 8.)

15. Necrology on Jaques Rosenhain. (*Jeschurun* 1894, Nr. 36.)

16. Michael Sachs' Responsum about the *ḥazan*. (*Jeschurun* 1895, Nr. 38.)

17. "Franz Schubert als Synagogenkomponist." (*Allgem. Zeitung des Judentums*, Nrs. 5, 6, 7.)

18. Review of A. Baer's *Baal Tefilla* (*Der praktische Vorbeter*) in (*Jued. Literaturblatt* 1898, Nrs. 24, 27.)

19. "Ueber den Ursprung der Traditionen in Synagogengesang." (*Jued. Literaturblatt* 1891, Nr. 9.)

20. "Ueber die liturgische und kantorale Vorbildung des Kultusbeamten." (*Israelitische Wochenschrift* 1899, Nr. 9.)

21. "Unsere erste Musikbeilage." (*Juedische Presse*, in supplement "Lehrer und Kantor," 1899, Nr. 3.)

22. *Liturgische Uebungen* I, (Verband der juedischen Lehrer im Deutschen Reich; in Commission bei M. Popelauer, Berlin 1900.)

23. "Ueber *Yehi Rotzon*" (*Israelitische Wochenschrift*, 1902, Nr. 26.)

24. *Liturgische Uebungen II*. (Verband der juedische Lehrer im Deutschen Reich, Berlin 1902.)

25. "Ueber die Verdienste der Gaonen um die juedische Liturgie" etc. (*Israelitische Wochenschrift*, 1903, Nr. 4.)

26. "Zum Gedaechtnis Salomon Sulzers." (Biography of Sulzer on the occasion of his centennial. A series of ten articles in *Israelitische Wochenschrift*, 1904.)

27. "Polen und der polnische Ritus." (*Oesterreichisch-Ungarische Kantorenzeitung*, 1909.)
28. "Wolf Bass aus Prossnitz." (*Oesterreichische Wochenschrift*, ?)
29. "Ueber den Ursprung der Kol-Nidre-Melodie." (*Hamburger Israelitisches Familienblatt*, 1909.)

APPENDIX II.

TEXT OF THE PIYYUTIM OF THE ITALIAN MANUSCRIPT M 4 F 71, NOT CONTAINED IN DAVIDSOHN'S "OZAR"

Nr. 5.

תשיש חתן כמשוש איתן מה זה יום זה רב. שמחתך חתן ת ו ר ה |:מלא אורה:|
(twice) טובה באה זיווג בחר האל בחר האל היקימו לך אל תוך נחתן ר א ש י ת
|: עטרת שית (twice) |: ביתיך תודה לשמו |:נגד עמו |: תָתָן (!) נא פה, הוא הדרתך
לקרוא תורה לָבָך עורה (כדבורה) דת תושיה, היא תובתך אורך
ימים ושנות חיים יוסיף אל חי במעון שבֻחָך ברוך אתה בבואך |: וברוך אתה
בצאתך |:

———————

Nr. 14.

שישו דודים הנחמדים יצליח אל את שמחתכם גילה רינה |: ישמיעו נא |: מכל
פינה תודה לכם נבחרים הם |: כל טוב בהם |: טובים שוים הוא הדרתכם חתן
נעים הוא נצמד עם תורה כלה נאה מה טובתכם, ברכת שדי נא לידידי ובני בנים
יפרו מכם| תזכו לראות כל נראות
עת יפליא |:אל עת יפליא אל בישועתכם :| עת יפליא :|

———————

Nr. 15.

(Vocalization is here omitted, since it is often misleading.)

ג י ל

אל חי תמים צוה אומים כל איש יחיד ישלים נפשו בחר האל עם ישראל נין תם
חתם על לנשוא, ג י ל שואבה, שמחה רבה, |:רומז טוב העולם הבא :|

Above it, in different ink:

תזכו לְיֵראות כל נוראות
(1)   תזכו לְיֵראות כל נ(ה)וראון (?)

Continuing the first text:

עת יפליא אל בישועתכם.
יזכו עם דין אל נן עדן יָשוב חֻשוב. ג י ל

———

[1] The Italian Jews barely pronounce the ה. They are consequently inclined to omit it altogether or to replace it occasionally by an א. To them ה and א are easily interchangeable.

לְמַעַן שׁרְשׁוּ שבעה חופות נאות יָפוֹת יה כֵּן תִּיקֵן במקום קָדְשׁוּ. שמחה נָאָה מִי
לֹא ראה מה נוֹרָאָה שמחת תורה. שׁוּב לא ירָאָה מָשׂוֹשׂ נָאָה גם כִּי יחיה מכל נברא.
גִיל.

מכל מינים שיר ניגונים כינור נבל תוף עם זמרה שם סוּלָמוֹת נרות רמות רמז
ודמות עולם אוֹרָה. גִיל

מורה שמן כי כאוֹמן ישא יונק ישאו שרים, אל ישראל עת בא גואל מָעָלָה מַעֲלָה
כאבירים. גִיל

מחול סובב איש יה חוֹבֵב עוֹשֶׂה לרמח אל יום נורה יומֵין עתיק אל כל צדיק
יראה תוכו זיו תפארה. גִיל

‖: ינחיל תמים שי עולמים מור ובשמים הרבה מָשָׂרָה. ישיש אותן כמשוש חתן דָּן
לְוַיְחַן לסעוֹד ברה.(א) ‖[2]   ''ritornello fine''

Nr. 17.

בּוֹרֵא עוֹלָם, יָחִיד נַעְלָם, חָתַם הַכָּל עִם חוֹתָמוֹ.
סוֹף אוֹתוֹתָיו, וּפְעוּלוֹתָיו, יָצַר אָדָם בְּדְמוּת צַלְמוֹ:‖
דוֹדִי זה בא ברוך הבא עם רוב חבה שמחה רבה
דּוֹדֵנוּ בָּא עִם רוֹב חִיבָה ‖:שְׂמְחָה רַבָּה נָשִׂישׂ עָמוֹ:‖
הַמְשִׁיל אוֹתוֹ, עַל כָּל בֵּיתוֹ, הִגְדִּיל לוֹ שֵׁם עַל עוֹלָמוֹ.   (2)
אַרְמוֹן שָׁבְתּוֹ וּמְנוּחָתוֹ, תּוֹךְ גַּן עֵדֶן שָׁם הֱקִימוֹ.   דּוֹדֵנוּ
בֵּין עֶלְיוֹנִים. נַם אוֹפָנִים, לְכְבוֹד הָאֵל יוֹדָה לִשְׁמוֹ.   (3)
הֵכִין לוֹ זֵר אֵלָיו עָזְרִי מִצַּלְעוֹתָיו וּבְשַׂר עַצְמוֹ. דּוֹדֵנוּ
בַּת זוּג נָאָה אַצְלוֹ יֵרָאָה יִשְׂמַח עָמָה נַם הִיא עָמוֹ.   (4)
יוֹדָה לָאֵל נָא יִשְׁמָעֵאלִי לִקְרוֹא חוֹרָה יִתֵּן שְׁכְמוֹ.   דּוֹדֵנוּ
חָתָן רֵאשִׁית אֵל חַי יָשִׁית אֶת בִּרְכָתוֹ לוֹ בִּמְקוֹמוֹ.   (5)
בָּרֵךְ חֵילוֹ כֹּל טוּב רַב לוֹ צוּר עוֹלָמִים יַטִּיב טַעֲמוֹ. דּוֹדֵנוּ
יִשָּׂא דִגְלוֹ זִיו גּוֹרָלוֹ יָצִיץ פֵּרְחוֹ תּוֹךְ אוּלָמוֹ.   (6)
זַרְעוֹ יָכְשָׁר תָּמִים יָשָׁר מֵעוֹלָם לֹא יַחְסַר לַחְמוֹ.   דּוֹדֵנוּ
חַיִּים טוֹבִים שָׁנָיו רַבִּים יִרָאָה כָּל טוּב עֵת בָּא יוֹמוֹ.   (7)
אָז יָרִים אֵל עַם יִשְׂרָאֵל יִשְׁלַח גּוֹאֵל יִפְדֶּה עָמּוֹ.   דּוֹדֵנוּ   ''ritornello''

[2] See *supra* the previous note!

[3] Dr. Sonne presumes that אליו עזר and ישמאל are respectively allusions
to the names of the חתן תורה and of the חתן בראשית. Perhaps they were uncle
and nephew.

[4] See the previous note. In general, this poem is full of hints and allusions.
This, however, is not the place for analyzing the manifold quotations and the
presumably personal references.

Nr. 20.

שירו נא שבחי יה אתם עם אמונים, הוא יהיה הוא היה צור שוכן מעונים, עת
הוציא לרויה משעבוד גאונים, עמו מבית שביה מהון רב טעונים, ברורים נתן
להם מחיר |: מן לחם :| ה(א)בירים, הביאם אל קְרְיָה, |: חמדת כל מחירים :|,
לשבוע מפיריה |: צוף ודבש יערים, :| חמול נא ישעה יה, ישלך(ח) את אליה, עם
גואל בחירים, תבנה בית אורה גם תוליך יְשָׁרִים, מְצִיָה אל צביה, על כנפי נשרים.
הנחילם תושיה עם מצות, הַשְּׁבִיעָם פִּסְחֵי יָה עִם מַצּוֹת.

The Role of Tradition in the Music of the Synagogue

Reprinted with permission of *Judaism*, 13, 1964, pp. 156-163.

I

ALTHOUGH THE TERM "TRADITION" APPEARS IN the title of this article, its author is obliged to start with an honest admission: the term "musical tradition" is meaningless to him, unless it is strictly defined and limited. For we have many traditions, differentiated regionally, historically, and stylistically; genuine ones and spurious ones, traditions conveyed by anonymous collectivities, and others which can be traced to one or several individuals. Yet, we generally start from two assumptions which are widely taken for granted: 1) that each tradition contains certain authentic elements: 2) that all musical traditions are reducible to one "Platonic" *Ur*-tradition, to an ontological *prima essentia,* from which they all emerged in the course of time.

I do not see how such assumptions can be tested, let alone proved. Therefore, we must not start with such axiomatic assumptions but with the phenomenology of the musical repertoire of the Synagogue as it stands today. Judaism has not recognized a central authority on ritual since the end of the Gaonate. In order to provide a historical *point d'appui* for our phenomenological quest, we should search for the last *authoritative* statement dealing in any way whatsoever with the music of the synagogue.

We find it in the responsum of R. Natronai Gaon concerning the chant of Scripture. This reference is available in the *Mahzor Vitry*. Its contents do not interest us here; it is sufficient to note that in this decree the Gaon stated certain principles of musical performance in the Synagogue, just as today the Pope establishes—*mutatis mutandis*—and legally fixes the musical practice of the Roman Catholic Church: he determines and authenticates the tradition.

Shortly thereafter the status of musical tradition in the Synagogue became controversial, not to say chaotic: we encounter in Yehuda Halevi's *Kuzari* certain remarks and opinions about the suitability or unsuitability of certain musical forms for the Synagogue; but his arguments are subjective, however theological they may appear. Nor did they remain undisputed—and thus commenced the ongoing debate concerning the status of music in the Synagogue. Frankly speaking, I fail to find a continuous thread in the plethora of rabbinic responsa or utterances on this subject, except in one respect: the general dislike of the *hazan,* his office, his position, his musical taste. Still, out of the many negative reactions we can abstract, by an *argumentum e silentio,* what the Rabbis did *not* oppose: the simple psalmodic recitation. In fact, this silent approval approaches, amidst the sardonic and often unfair attacks on the *hazan,* the famous praise which St. Augustine had bestowed upon the musical practice he found in the diocese of St. Athanasius: that the cantor's chant was nearer to recitation than to actual singing.

In 1622 Juda Leon da Modena, chief rabbi of the Republic of Venice and president of its rabbinic court, sanctioned the use of art-music for the synagogue in a learned and authoritative responsum. Some copies of this legal opinion, printed in the first edition of Salomone de' Rossi's Hebrew compositions, have come to our attention recently: they were studied and discussed in Polish and Russian Talmudic academies. From the marginal notes we see that his decision was generally recognized. Yet in his *t'shuva* musical tradition is not even mentioned.

Contradicting each other are two interesting responsa by R. Joel Syrkes and R. Elchanan Henle Kirchhan; the former approved of Christian choristers (in the synagogue) even if they sang ecclesiastical chant, provided Jewish singers were not available. The latter pours out his most mordant sarcasm and bitter irony on such indifference. It is important to observe that Rabbi Syrkes lived and taught in Poland, whereas Kirchhan served Bavarian communities. May we conclude from this single case that the Eastern rabbis were more indifferent to the cause of Jewish musical tradition? I leave the question unanswered; but the learned and knowing Thebans who now concern themselves, however superficially, with the question of Jewish musical tradition should bear such and similar cases in mind, *before* they form their so-called theories. For similar discrepancies and contradictions are not rare in other regions and centuries. It seems that the theologians never reached a consensus on this question; we cannot depend upon the opinion of just one or two of them, however learned. And much less upon those self-appointed "guardians of tradition" who in our days—and in their ignorance—fervently champion a "tradition" which, at closer analysis, emerges as corrupted German, Polish, or American folk- or hit-songs, rendered in *hazanic* style.

And yet: there is sufficient and cogent evidence, both historical and morphological, of continuous musical traditions in Judaism, although they are regionally variegated. Some of them reach back to the first centuries of our era. This is not the place to discuss the pertinent

274

facts and documents which demonstrate this statement beyond perad-venture of a doubt; suffice it to say that today all musicologists have agreed on this point. Whether or not we shall be able to prove the existence of one common *Ur*-tradition of all synagogal chant is a dif-ferent question, to which we shall return later, however briefly.

EVEN WITHIN THE BOUNDARIES OF SUCH regional traditions there appear certain nuances and typical variants, which shed a good deal of light on the *sociological* factors that determine both the preservation and the development of the oral tradition. Thus, to cite but one example for many, we can well distinguish during the 18th century sharp dif-ferences between the chant in small communities and in the great cen-ters of Germany. I am referring to a number of manuscripts which clearly show that the basic, or, to be cautious, the older, tradition was better preserved in the small rural communities than in the big cities. In these small places older German folk-songs, and especially elements of military music, have made considerable inroads, but these alien ele-ments are noticeable only in the *piyyutim* and rarely in the prose texts of our liturgy. Closely connected with this stratification of syna-gogal music was the social status of the cantor: in smaller places he served often as teacher, butcher, or secretary to the community; this integrated him and his family fully in the congregation. Indeed, very often he was born in it or in its neighborhood. The case was essentially different in the larger Jewish centers: there the cantor was but a transient singer, a "concertizing" soloist, and often enough a show-man and *primo uomo*. As a rule, he was not permanently appointed and functioned chiefly as a "religious entertainer" of the masses and their taste, to which the Synagogue during the 17th and 18th centuries stooped all too often.

Another case in point is the status of the cantor in the Polish and Russian Hasidic centers. There he and his "tradition" were almost totally eclipsed by the choir-singing of that remarkable male society which was centered about the person of the *tzaddik*; it was the latter and his musical preferences, often radically deviating from any estab-lished synagogue-tradition, which set the tone and style of Hasidic song. In general, it was the Yiddish-Slavonic dancing or meditating song which the Hasidim cultivated. Thus the cantor was neglected—and with him the older tradition.

Among the tradents we have to consider three main categories, or rather their archetypes, of which there are many diversified and indi-vidualized forms: 1) The honorary precentor. This *ba'al tefilla*, usu-ally a layman and integrated member of the community, often an inde-pendent "gentleman of leisure" (*batlan*), is commonly the most reliable conveyor of synagogal tradition, although, or rather because, he is often unable to read music. 2) The professional, appointed cantor. As his livelihood depends upon his ability to please the congregation, he cannot afford to be too critical in his choice of material, traditional or not; he must appeal to the majority's taste, which is usually the lowest common denominator. 3) Finally, we should not overlook the significant part of the women in Oriental communities, where they have established—or rather preserved—some ancient traditions as wailing-women, as singers of secular "romances," of old dancing-songs, of wedding- or birth-songs. Their topics being love, courtship, birth, and death, their songs truly encompass all the highlights of human life. As the professional cantor is much less commonplace in Oriental communities than in the West, it is not surprising that these communities have retained the inherited tradition more faithfully than the Western centers, which are served by the *hazan*; the *hazan's* Oriental counterpart, be he a layman or a *hacham*, is certainly less exposed to the tradition-destroying temptations of virtuoso-style.

II

ANY SERIOUS STUDY OF JEWISH MUSICAL TRADITION—or any other tradition, for that matter—must take into consideration the facts of Jewish dispersion for 2,000 years, the lack of a central authority for more than a millenium, and their corollary: the peculiar status of pseudomorphosis (in Spengler's sense of that term), in which tradition has existed and grown in Judaism. This phenomenon, first stressed by Spengler and his followers, has been observed in many cultures, where an old stratum is overlaid and "coated" by others of more recent origin. This coating-over must not be understood in a mechanistic sense; it alters not only the surface but enters into deeper-lying compounds of civilizations, creating interrelations and complex results of symbioses.

It is a commonplace lament to deplore the loss of so-called "pure" racial or national elements in high civilizations. Certainly Polonius' homely maxim, "Neither borrower nor lender be," is not applicable to the history of cultures. Quite to the contrary! All high civilizations thrive by borrowing and lending, by interdependence, by the process of assimilation and absorption. The anthropologist in search of "pure," one-dimensional cultures and traditions must go to the Bushmen or to the Papuans, who still today live under Neolithic conditions.

There are, of course, degrees within the scale of the cultural interdependence. Modern physical science differentiates between events in "closed" and "open" systems. Applying this distinction to the history of culture, it is easy to see that Jewry has lived and produced in a generally open system for at least 1200 years. Exceptions, such as the communities of Cochin, Yemen, Djerba, or Kurdistan, show in their traditions a vastly different picture than the majority of Jews in the world. While their traditions are much more stabilized and often older, they are, by the same token, also much more stagnant, not to say petrified. For they lacked the opportunity, indeed the life-giving chance of active assimilation.

I avail myself here of a penetrating and important distinction pertaining to the phenomenon of assimilation, so generally (and foolishly) decried by our "guardians of tradition." First proposed by the philosopher Hermann Cohen many years ago, its fundamental character and deep insight have been frequently tested. The main point of it is the categorical distinction between active and passive assimilation.

Active assimilation is good, necessary, and wholesome. Every living creature maintains its life by constant assimilation: it actively assimilates light, air, water, and elements of nutrition into its system; it absorbs and digests them. Conversely, when a living organism dies, powerful forces from the outside assimilate the creature's compounds, thus causing its decomposition: the once active, living creature is *being* assimilated. Applying this categorical distinction to the cultural life of nations and groups, we may say that in the Jewish people, due to its dispersion, we may sometimes find active and passive assimilation *at the same time*. Thus, e.g., while Central European Jewry *was* assimilated, Israeli Jewry performed an active process of assimilation; while Italian Jewry *was* slowly assimilated during the age of the Renaissance, the movements of Sabbatai Zvi and, earlier, those of R. Yitzchak Luria provided the positive forces of *active* assimilation.

It was long believed, ever since J. G. Herder and the 19th-century romanticists, that in closed systems traditions remain practically immutable. Modern anthropology and ethnomusicology have demonstrated the fallacy of this naive belief. As a matter of fact, we have sufficient data at hand to suggest a mathematical law of change within an oral tradition even in "closed" systems, provided that the time-intervals are sufficiently large.

INTIMATELY LINKED TO THE ROMANTIC NOTION of the basic immutability of national tradition was the concomitant belief that true folk-song represents the pure, distilled spirit of a national group; furthermore, that it organically grow out of the spirit of an *anonymous* multitude, and was handed down, generation after generation, in unchanged form. The existence of individual creators of folk-songs was denied by the romantics, although today quite a few names of "first poets" or "first singers" are known. This complex of the essentially "pure" national spirit of tradition is still *the* stock-in-trade merchandise of many lay-organizations, which claim, not only in the Jewish field, to be fostering and cultivating the guaranteed *prima essentia* of their respective national civilizations. Thirty or forty years ago, many scholars still adhered to these tenets of a romantic creed in the spontaneous creativity of the anonymous collective; among them we encounter, in the Jewish field, names such as A. Z. Idelsohn, S. Marek, S. Rosowsky, and J. Engel. The entire Haskalah ideology adhered to this concept; even Ahad Ha-am was not very far from it.

After such preliminary observations, the following theses, however paradoxical they may sound, will not come as a shock. I suggest:

1) An orthodox, that is, a tradition-minded group or authority does not shape tradition; at best it maintains it.

2) Conversely, a reforming group or authority first destroys, then creates tradition.

3) While the foregoing two principles are historically demonstrable and can be so proved, the third principle is a result of purely empiric observations. It says: an *oral* tradition is in general better preserved at the periphery of a given cultural orbit than at its center. There are some historical instances showing this thesis in action: it can be seen, e.g., in the history of Jewish calendars, in the development of Byzantine liturgy, or, to cite an American example, in the ballads of the hill-billies and mountaineers in Kentucky and Tennessee. While the truth of this thesis cannot be proved with sufficient exactness, it has a good probability in the mathematical sense.

The suggested theories would explain, *inter alia,* the decay of oral tradition in Central and West European Jewry, where the forces of rigid rabbinic authority and of passive assimilation worked against each other and brought Jewish musical tradition perilously close to complete collapse at the end of the 18th century. The Hasidic revolt, on the other hand, shaped a new system of customs and traditions; in music, it destroyed the cantor's legacy and instead borrowed a great deal of substance from the secular folk-song of its non-Jewish environment. Still, it was able to integrate these foreign elements, that is, to assimilate them actively.

Our hypothetical principles also explain the strange fact that the study and the conscious utilization of musical tradition has always fared better under a liberal conception of Judaism than under an orthodox régime. After all, Leon de Modena was the last orthodox rabbi to display sincere and active interest in synagogal music—but then, he was, perhaps, not "strictly" orthodox. That the Jewish center of the world, Jerusalem, pays little heed to either the study or the preservation of tradition, in comparison to, say, New York City or Paris, can be understood by the application of the norm, according to which peripheral sections are more tradition-minded than the centers, which at best maintain but hardly ever create tradition. To be fully operative and appreciated, a scholar such as Idelsohn had to come from Israel to America.

After these many mental reservations and cogitations we should be ready, perhaps not fully entitled, but equipped to canvass the two assumptions at the beginning of the essay.

III

WHAT ARE, THEN, THE MOST SIGNIFICANT results of the researches in Jewish musical tradition? In answering this question I am bound to commit certain simplifications as I must avoid all too technical jargon. The facts which will be related and discussed are true, but only statistically so; i.e., in every instance 70 per cent or more of the investigated items agreed with it.

1) All over the world, Jewish musical tradition consists of three or four categories of formal structures. These formal archetypes are: psalmodies and simple prayer-chant, Scriptural cantillation, melodies of *piyyutim,* and florid, melismatic chants. This categorical distinction of structures is common to all synagogue music, but, while the archetypes are common, their tonal substance is vastly variegated. A comparison of the tunes of an archetypical structure shows common elements only in coherent regions, that is, in the Ashkenazic, Western Sephardic, Eastern Sephardic, Yemenite, Babylonian *minhagim* respectively. They show little or no similarity between each other.

2) The influence of the non-Jewish environment is felt mostly in the chant of *piyyutim* and of recitatives; it is less noticeable in closed regions, more in open systems. The corollary of this norm lies in the fact that the closed regions show little musical development, the open ones more.

3) In three of the four categories the relationship between text and chant plays a decisive role: in psalmodic structures the words and their parallelistic order dominate the chant absolutely; in Scriptural cantillation the syntactic accents and their arrangement according to the Masoretic punctuation determine the course of the melodic rendition; in the *piyyutim* it is either the metrical scheme or the strophic structure (rhyme refrain) which regulates the tune. Only in the florid coloratura melodies musical forces reign autonomously; in these pieces the text becomes a pretext for elaborate vocal showpieces. These "wordless hymns," which were looked upon with suspicion and disfavor by the Rabbis, emerged fairly early, were driven underground, were banished by R. Solomon Adret, and finally sanctioned by the Hasidic *tzaddikim* in the form of the *niggun,* an almost wordless song lying between meditation, dance, and religious frenzy. Neither they nor their Jewish (and Arabic) forerunners show any similarity to their Christian counterpart, the famous *Jubilationes* (Alleluja chants), which enthused faithful Christians ever since St. Augustine.

4) Of all forms, the simple psalmodies and orations have the highest age in every tradition. Yet in their tonal material they exhibit

very few, if any, common elements. Thus, e.g., in Ashkenazic tradition a melody is usually in *major* for praise and thanksgiving, in *minor* for penitence and supplication. In the Yemenite tradition the "major" mode stands for mourning and lament; the Western "minor" mode is hardly used. In the tradition of Jews from Kurdistan the organization of the tonal scale is still primitive; in Moroccan-Jewish chant it is highly developed; etc.

5) Finally, we reach the main problem: Is the assumption of a basic *Ur*-tradition justified or, at least, tenable in the light of modern research? The answer to this question is conditional: if there are any common elements beyond the common structure, they may possibly exist only in strict psalmodic forms, not in cantillations, melismatic chants, and least of all in melodies of *piyyutim*. Yet, the strictly *musical* investigation of psalmodic forms meets an obstacle inherent in their frequent *sprech-gesang* performance, in which speech-like articulation of the text constantly interrupts musical pitches. Modern acoustical technology will probably help to overcome these difficulties, and we should be able to give a definitive answer to this last question within the next ten or fifteen years.

HOWEVER THIS PROBLEM WILL BE SOLVED, it is already obvious that there exists a continuity of the musical tradition of the Synagogue. Even if a common *tonal* substratum should not be demonstrable, two essential facts stand out which leave no doubt on this question: as is now generally known, the Yemenite, Babylonian, and Kurdistani traditions display so many common elements, not only in their forms but also in their tonal substance, with the oldest strata of ecclesiastical chant (Roman, Byzantine, Armenian) that only the assumption of a common Palestinian source would account for these identities. The more so, as neither the Yemenite nor the Kurdistan Jews have had any direct contact with Christianity. The second argument relates to the fact that in these old Jewish centers a sharp and categorical distinction was, and is, made between secular and liturgical chant, and within the latter, between the performance of *piyyutim* and that of psalms and Scriptural cantillation. Secular songs and often *piyyutim* reflect the musical style of the respective Arabic environments, mostly of the 15th and 16th centuries. The psalmodies, however, have retained their rigidly archaic character, a totally different modal structure, and an obviously archetypical unity.

Thus, it is *au fond* the immutable word of Scripture which has guarded and preserved the genuine elements of Jewish musical tradition.

RENAISSANCE

The Mathematical Foundation of *Ars Nova*

Reprinted with permission of *Hebrew Union College Annual,* 17, 1942-1943, pp. 564-572.

A

Coussemaker and Riemann still use the name Leo Hebraeus as that of the author of that work. Into the matter of identifying the author, neither of these scholars probed very far, although reference to a Jewish encyclopedia would fully have cleared up the question.[1] Their remarks, moreover, betray woefully inadequate ideas regarding the treatise's contents. Both scholars labor under the impression that the work discusses the calculation of intervals; but such is, by no means, the case.

These misconceptions were eventually dispelled by Joseph Carlebach in his book *Levi ben Gerson als Mathematiker* (Berlin 1910). This work, which presents the text of the treatise in the original Latin, identifies anew and beyond peradventure of a doubt, Leo Hebraeus with Gersonides.[2] The Carlebach edition is based on the manuscript *"De Numeris Harmonicis"* in Cod. Basiliensis F II. 33. In a brief introduction (p. 127) Carlebach advances the view that the author undoubtedly composed his work in Hebrew and then had it translated into Latin for Bishop Philipp de Vitry. Carlebach was further of the opinion that Gersonides was too scantily conversant with Latin to bestow upon the translation any kind of supervision.[3]

While Riemann, like other scholars who were misled by the title and by lack of intimate knowledge, supposed the work to be one dealing with the calculation of musical intervals, Carlebach

[1] E. v. Coussemaker, Scriptores medii aevi etc., III., X. H. Riemann, *Geschichte der Musiktheorie,* pp. 235 ff.

[2] Cf. Renan-Neubauer, *Les ecrivains juifs francaises,* p. 296. Steinschneider, *Hebraeische Uebersetzungen,* p. 66. Gross, *Gallia Judaica,* p. 94, furthermore Joseph Carlebach, *Levi ben Gerson als Mathematiker,* p. 96 ff.

[3] Cf. Carlebach op. cit. p. 97. Against this assumption it must be stated, that Gersonides seems to have known a good many works of his contemporary fellow-scholars.

candidly admits: "I am unable to conjecture the bearing of the thesis (which follows) upon mediaeval musical theory."[4] The more recent of the major publications that concern themselves, even if cursorily, with Leo Hebraeus, (for instance Besseler's *Studien zur Musik des Mittelalters* or Reese's *Music in the Middle Ages*) likewise say nothing about the significance of his work for mediaeval musical theory in general or about its importance for Philipp of Vitry in particular.[5]

And yet, to Philipp, the treatise of Gersonides must have been of great consequence. The treatise opens with the statement:[6] "In Christi incarnationis anno 1342 nostro opere mathematico iam completo fui requisitus a quodam eximio magistrorum in scientia musicali, sc. a magistro Philippo de Bitriaco de regno francie, ut *demonstrarem unum suppositum in predicta scientia* sc: omnium numerorum armonicorum quilibet 2 numero distinguntur praeter istos 1 et 2,2 et 3,3 et 4,8 et 9. Armonicum autem numerum sic describit: armonicus numerus est, qui et quelibet eius pars praeter unitatem per equa 2 vel 3 continuo vel vice versa usque ad ipsam unitatem findi potest" . . . "Sunt igitur continui: 1, 2, 4, 8, et 1, 3, 9, 27, et vice versa 6, 12, 18, 24 etc."

Translation: "In the year 1342 of the incarnation of Christ, my work on Mathematics having been completed, I was requested by the noted master of musical theory, Master Philipp de Vitry, to demonstrate a certain postulate of that science. The postulate is this: All pairs of harmonic numbers are mathematically distinguishable except the following: 1 and 2, 2 and 3, 3 and 4, 8 and 9. We mean, by a harmonic number, every number which is itself divisible and subdivisible down to unity not only by 1 but also by either 2 or 3 or by any combination of 2 and 3, (and whose factors are similarly divisible and subdivisible down to unity). Examples of harmonic numbers are: 2, 4, 8, 9, 12, 27, 18, 24 etc."

---

[4] Carlebach, op. cit., p. 142, n. 3.

[5] Besseler, *Studien zur Musik des Mittelalters*, I. II, in *Archiv fuer Musikwissenschaft* VII, p. 181 ff. and VIII p. 196 ff. Also G. Reese, *Music in the Middle Ages*, p. 346, not mentioning Leo Hebraeus.

[6] Carlebach, op. cit., p. 129.

Thus it is clearly stated (1) that Gersonides was requested by Philipp de Vitry to provide a certain desired proof, (2) that the thesis to be demonstrated was a *suppositum in predicta scientia* (musical theory), and (3) that *numerus harmonicus* is, in this presentation, a mathematical concept which has nothing to do with the calculation of musical intervals although, from that calculation, the phrase itself may originally have been derived.[7]

The following questions accordingly arise: What is the connection between the work of Gersonides and the projects of Philipp? To what extent is the thesis of Gersonides a *suppositum* of mediaeval musical theory? For this thesis with its mathematical formulation, what is the musical background? Was Gersonides acquainted with contemporary works which similarly handled musical problems *more mathematico*?

To disentangle this snarl, it is essential that we first understand something about Philipp's aims and achievements. A comparison of Philipp's musical theories with the exposition of Gersonides will furnish us the clue.

B

Of Philipp de Vitry's theoretical works, we possess only one whose authenticity is undisputed, namely his *Ars Nova*. This is confirmed by Anonymus VII (Coussemaker, Script. III, 408 a) and by a treatise emanating from the school of John de Muris (ibid. 107a), one of the leading musical theorists of his time. This treatise, incidentally, mentions only *one* tract as attributable

---

[7] About the term *numerus harmonicus* see Carlebach, op. cit. p. 142, n. 4., referring to the expression ערך הנגינות with Abr. Ibn Ezra. Cf. also *HUCA* XVI, p. 260, n. 36. Prof. Barnett, of the University of Cincinnati, to whom I am indebted for several interesting ideas in connection with this problem, points out that the term *numerus harmonicus* in our sense is created either by Philipp or Gersonides and does not occur elsewhere in mathematics. He is convinced, furthermore, that the restriction of the theorem to the characteristic numbers of musical division, 2 and 3, indicates clearly its purely musical implication. I venture, therefore, the hypothesis, that *numerus harmonicus* is nothing but a wrong translation of the Hebrew ערך הנגינות — meaning *numerus musicae*.

to Philipp of Vitry.[8] The novelty about Philipp's work was
the reform he affected in the domain of musical notation, especially by his revolutionary systematization of time divisions
(*mensura*). Though technical details might lead us too far
afield, it might not be amiss to dwell briefly here upon the
problem and Philipp's solution.

    Philipp systematized the musical notation of his time in
accordance with two principles which he consistently observes.
(1) While the preceding period treated the various note-values,
maxima, longa, brevis, semibrevis, minima, etc., as diversified and
exceedingly individualized, Philipp insisted upon a homogenous
treatment and upon subdivision of the note-values down to the
minima. His age recognized rythms of two beats and rythms
of three beats. In contrast with modern practice, all note-
values could be two-beat and three-beat at one and the same
time. Thus a *longa*, according to Philipp could be subdivided
in the following manner:

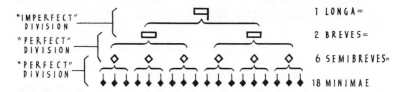

also *longa* = 2 *breves* = 4 *semibreves* = 12 *minimae*
or *longa* = 3 *breves* = 9 *semibreves* = 27 *minimae* etc.
On ecclesiastical dogmatic grounds, a threefold division of a

---

[8] Besseler, *op. cit.*, p. 181. The problem of the personality and the work
of John de Muris can finally be considered as solved since Besseler's studies·
Without any doubt, we know that the musical theorist John de Muris was
identical with the mathematician of the same name. This fact became evident
through the MS f lat. 72811, f 159¹ of the Bibl. Nat., Paris. In his brief review
of the personality of John de Muris, Besseler writes: "He belonged to the same
generation as Pierre Roger, afterward Pope Clement VI, who is said to have
been a friend of his youth; to the same generation as Philipp de Vitry together
with whom he is twice mentioned in the motets; and to the same generation
as Leo Hebraeus (born 1288) his mathematical colleague." He is not identical,
however, with Julianus de Muris, a chancellor of the Sorbonne about 1350,
as formerly assumed.

note-value is "perfect," while a twofold division is "imperfect." Conversely, "perfectio" is applied to an aggregation of three notes of equal value, and "imperfectio" to an aggregation of two notes of equal value which, by their combination, produce a superior value. Philipp lets the two-part time take its place on an equal footing alongside of the older three-beat time which had thus far been the only one deemed acceptable.[9] One can readily see that the largest possible number of *minimae* (as subdivisions of a *maxima*) is $81 = 3^4$; the smallest number is $16 = 2^4$; between them lie numbers like 18, 24, 27, 36, 54, etc., *multiples of the basic numbers 2 and 3 and their powers*. (For instance $36 = 2^2 \cdot 3^2$, $54 = 2^1 \cdot 3^3$ etc.)

(2) A second notable innovation was the use of points as attachments to the notes. While the Ars Antiqua employs points only to indicate the limits of bars or measures, points now acquire, as *puncti divisionis, perfectionis, imperfectionis, alterationis*, and *syncopationis*, manifold and confusingly varied functions. For the problem before us, the only note-points which are of importance are the *puncti perfectionis* and the *puncti alterationis*.

The *punctus perfectionis* originally had the effect of transmuting a note of two beats into one of three beats. This is the only use that has persisted to our own time. We can perceive how the use of the *punctus perfectionis* or *additionis* permits the derivation of the above mentioned numbers. (For instance $54 = 36 + \frac{36}{2}$, $81 = 54 + \frac{54}{2}$, $36 = 24 + \frac{24}{2}$, etc.)

Alteration is, in certain cases, a possible doubling of a briefer note-length because of its position between two greater note-lengths, for instance:

The second semibrevis is here extended to a doubling of its length so that the sum-total of the basic units is, because of the alteration, increased by 1.

We now recall the thesis which Gersonides was to demon-

---

[9] Cf. J. Wolf, *Handbuch der Notationskunde*, pp. 331–342.

287

strate at Philipp's request. It had to be shown that, with the exception of the pairs 1 and 2, ($= 3^0$ and 2^1), 2 and 3, ($= 2^1$ and 3^1), 3 and 4, ($= 3^1$ and 2^2), 8 and 9, ($= 2^3$ and 3^2) that is, the several powers of two and three and their corresponding products, the so-called harmonic numbers, differ from one another by more than unity.

If Philipp wished to place his system upon a solid foundation, his theory was obliged, by the demands of his age, to observe the following conditions: 1.) The perfect or the imperfect mode of division had to be extended quite generally over the entire number system, (i.·e. beyond the previously accepted limit $3^4 = 81$), without modification or confusion; 2.) Those differences in the modes of division might not be canceled by such division changes as *perfectio*, or *punctus additionis* or *alterationis*; 3.) If the ultimate sum of the tiniest units differed by so much as 1 — as in 1 and 2,2 and 3,3 and 4,8 and 9 — that final sum had to be related to *differing modes of division* as their resultant. For instance:

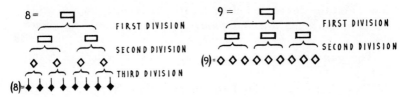

Philipp, to generalize his system of division completely, needed proof that *except for the pairs of numbers instanced, no pair of multiples or of powers of 2 and 3 differed by so much as 1*. For Philipp's purpose, this mathematical presupposition was indispensable, the reason being this: One could readily perceive that, up to 9, confusion of the modes of division was, by no means, possible; that, in other words, the pairs of numbers which differed only by 1 must, up to 9, belong to divergent modes of division. But it would have been stupendously difficult to demonstrate this as a *general theorem*. Such demonstration, however, becomes superfluous if all we need is proof that, in no other case, do multiples of the powers of 2 and 3 differ by so much as 1.

Such proof meanwhile satisfies all of the above mentioned conditions: _

1. By and large, Gersonides' demonstration that, beyond the numbers 8 and 9, all multiples of the powers of 2 and 3 differ by more than 1 removes all limits to the possibilities of generalizing the divisions and the subdivisions; as John de Muris had still maintained, when he said: *"non est autem multum possibile voci ulterius pertransire"* (*beyond the minima*). This was likewise because of practical considerations involved in the technique of singing, where the smaller the time values, the greater the required degree of skill.[10]

2. Division changes like *alteratio*, *perfectio*, or *Punctus additionis* invariably change the number of minimae by *more than unity*. For instance the alteration:

A. (ALTERATED) = + | = 27 MINIMAE
(NOT ALTERATED) = + | = 12 OR 18 MINIMAE

B. (ALTERATED) = + | = 21 MINIMAE
(NOT ALTERATED) = + | = 14 OR 18 MINIMAE

C. PUNCTUS ADDITIONIS
   a) IN 2 BEATS: = 12 SEMIBREVES
   b) IN 3 BEATS: = 18 SEMIBREVES

The final results of our division changes are, in our necessarily simple examples, 27, 12, (18), 21, 14, (18), 12, 18. In a more extensive series of examples, the differences become appreciably broader.

3. Up to the number 9, the sum-totals differing by 1 are always the outcome of *different modes of division*. The need of examining every subsequent case separately ceases after it has been demonstrated that multiples of the powers of 2 and 3 differ from one another by more than unity. That is, speaking mathematically: the inequality

$$3^m + 1 \neq 2^n, \text{ whereby } m, n \neq 1, 2.$$

---

[10] Actually, the later development, by introducing Semiminimae, Fusae, and Semifusae, went beyond the old boundaries.

is valid.[11] Precisely this is what Gersonides proves, thereby
supplying Philipp with the desired *suppositum* of musical theory.
Gersonides demonstrates that the results of ever so many divisions and subdivisions can not be confused; which yields the
consequence in each case that, from the sum-total of the smallest
units, *one and only one* basic mode of division can be mathematically deduced.

C

If Gersonides, in order to familiarize himself with the *suppositum*, consulted the works of contemporary musical theorists —
which was, by the way, neither necessary nor very probable —
the only author that comes into consideration would be his
mathematical colleague, John de Muris, who had expounded
the entire of the musical theory of his time in strictly mathematical style. Among John's writings, the second part of his
Ars Novae Musicae approaches nearest to Gersonides' problem.
From a purely mathematical standpoint, John determines the
relations of note values to one another. Accepting the traditional "perfect" division, he obtains, by raising to powers his
basic number 3, the limiting value of $1:3^4 = 1:81$, i. e. the relationship of the *minima* to the *triplex longa* (*maxima*). Quite unmistakable is John's opposition to the *Ars Antiqua* in an un-
usually striking passage which may have afforded the immediate occasion of Philipp's assignment to Gersonides: "It is
necessary to take caution against the example adduced by those
with whom we take issue in this work. There are those who
believe that, since the point is the sign of perfection, they can
easily, by means of the point, change all imperfect notes into
perfect notes. Nonetheless, when the point of the imperfect
longa is appended in the form of a *semibrevis*, it remains by no
means clear whether the arrangement involves a perfect *longa*
of three *breves* or of two *breves*. If now the *Ars Antiqua* to which
we stand opposed insists nonetheless that the resultant is a
perfect *longa* of three *breves*, it would then also have been possible

[11] The exact mathematical discussion of the problem in Carlebach, op.
cit., p. 62 ff.

to deduce this perfect *longa* from the *prolatio* of two *breves*. Before the addition of the point, the *longa* was doubly imperfect; it contained a total of 5 *semibreves*. By the addition of the point, the *longa* becomes doubly perfect, containing 9 where it should contain but 6 *semibreves* . . . But this chain of reasoning is invalid."[12]

If Philipp would achieve real clarification and unification, as he undoubtedly intended, this ambiguity of the *Ars Antiqua* had to be unconditionally removed. It was Gersonides who, in this situation, accomplished the final step thereby deciding the question in favor of the *Ars Nova*.

Through all of these illustrations, we sense the rational mathematical spirit of the *Ars Nova* which must have exerted a powerful appeal upon such a mathematician and naturalist as Gersonides. The data are dissected into rigidly bounded units and these are then linked with one another by logical abstractions.[13] This new, mathematically grounded theory of musical measurement proved serviceable to the hitherto blocked development of musical notation.

[12] "Cavendum tamen ab instantia tam solemni, quam faciant, contra quos in hoc opere disputamus: omnia imperfecta perfici per punctum, cum punctus sit signum perfectionis, infallibiliter existimantes. Si enim addatur punctus notulae per semibrevem imperfectae, quae longa est, an sit perfecta trium aut duarum brevium ignoratur. Cum tamen dicat ars antiqua cui volumus obviare, quod perfecta trium erit, licet fuisse possibile eam ex valore duarum brevium protulisse. Ante additionem puncti prima erat imperfecte imperfecta, valens quinque semibreves; per additionem vero puncti redditur perfecta perfecte, valens novem semibreves, cum non deberet valere nisi 6." (Johannes de Muris, *Musica practica*, in Gerbert, *Scriptores* II, p. 299)

[13] Cf. Besseler, op. cit. (*Archiv fuer Musikwissenschaft* VIII, pp. 197 ff.)

The Last Pythagorean Musician: Johannes Kepler

Reprinted with permission of W.W. Norton & Co., Inc. *Aspects of Medieval and Renaissance Music: a Birthday Offering to Gustave Reese*, ed. J. LaRue, (New York, 1966), pp. 867-882.

SINCE HINDEMITH'S opera *The Harmony of the World* (Munich 1957), musicians have been made aware again of the conception pronounced in the title, and championed by the hero of the work: the astronomer, mathematician, or, according to his own preference, the "natural philosopher" Johannes Kepler. Through a modern opera the musician and musicologist of today learns of Kepler's profound knowledge of ancient and Renaissance music theory. For except the solid article in *MGG*, the reference books will tell him little, if anything, touching on Kepler and music. Otherwise his name means practically nothing to the musical scholar. This was not always so. Aside from the astronomer-composer Sir William Herschel, whose astronomical occupations had made him thoroughly familiar with Kepler's writings, many students of music theory, from Mersenne to Euler, Padre Martini, and Marpurg, were cognizant of his musical learning. When his astronomical discoveries, epoch-making in every sense, were thrown into the limelight of fame by Newton, the significance of his musical thinking fell into oblivion. A few outsiders, such as A. von Thimus [1] and R. Hasenclever,[2] tried to keep his name alive in the history of music theory—in vain! For the quadrivium, once the fertile soil of many great ideas, including Kepler's, had collapsed with the onset of particularization. Thus, mathematics, music, and astronomy, formerly closely linked sister disciplines, were separated from each other.

In Kepler's own time, however, the quadrivial elements were still

[1] A. von Thimus, *Die harmonicale Symbolik des Altertums* (Cologne 1876).
[2] R. Hasenclever, *Die Grundzüge der esoterischen Harmonik* (Cologne 1870).

sufficiently close to each other to be studied together. The artificial distinction between the humanities and the sciences, of which modern culture has no reason to be proud, did not exist as yet. In particular, the concept of a philosophy of nature encompassed, as a matter of course, all cosmological speculations that had emerged in Western thought ever since Pythagoras. And many of them concerned themselves with the harmony of the spheres. It is one of history's ironical quirks that the greatest astronomer and music-theorist of antiquity, Ptolemy, was definitely refuted by Kepler, who had utilized ideas of Ptolemy. Indeed, when he studied for the first time the original Greek text of the ancient astronomer, he felt gratitude for Divine Providence, which "had the same thought about the harmonic formation turned up in the minds of two men who (though lying so far apart in time) also had devoted themselves entirely to contemplating nature." [3] These are, of course, the words of a devout and faithful Christian, and they display the distance between him and the Greek Pythagoreans better than any commentary.

This seems to be of the highest significance: without his obsession with a demonstrable harmony within the solar system, *expressible in musical notation*, Kepler would never have discovered his celebrated Third Law, the law out of which emerged Newton's concept of gravity. What makes Kepler's ideas unique is their seeming anachronism. While the Third Law was far ahead of its time—Galileo pronounced it false still in 1632, and only Newton proved it—in his way of thought Kepler harked back more than two millennia, to the Pythagoreans. Yet he demanded strictly *empirical proofs*, not speculative arguments. This Janus-faced attitude is characteristic of most pioneers of science during the late Renaissance.

We shall understand this antinomy better if we observe the status and reputation of Pythagorean thinking during the 15th and 16th centuries. Copernicus had followed certain of these conceptions, but Luther called him "the fool who went against Holy Writ," and the Holy Office of the Curia condemned his theory as heretical. Moreover, the new though self-appointed preceptor of all science, Bacon, considered the theories of Copernicus, Kepler, and Galileo all false, because they were, to him, Platonic or Pythagorean. He would have nothing of speculative or imaginative science, and the less so, the more systematic it was. "In Baconian science the bird-watcher comes into his own, while genius, ever theorizing in far places, is suspect." [4] Indeed, he had little faith in intuition—the course he proposed "leaves but little to the acuteness or

[3] Cf. Max Caspar, *Kepler*, transl. Doris Hellman (New York 1962), p. 276 ff.
[4] Cf. C. C. Gillispie, *The Edge of Objectivity* (Princeton 1960), p. 77.

strength of wits, but places all wits and understandings nearly on a level." [5] This sounds democratic and fair indeed, but such doctrine will never succeed in science. Yet there was reason enough for taking such a vigorous stance: the humanists of the time leaned too much toward a purely speculative cosmology, which often enough stooped to a set of esoteric, utterly uncritical fantasies. Such enlightened thinkers as the humanists Pico Della Mirandola and Johannes Reuchlin dabbled in Cabbala and Hermetics; and Kepler had to defend himself against a mixture of Cabbala, Numerology, and Rosicrucianism, represented by the Scottish nobleman Sir Robert Fludd (de Fluctibus), in the penetrating words: "I hate all cabbalists . . . Fludd takes his chief pleasure in incomprehensible picture puzzles of the reality, whereas I go forth from there, precisely to move into the bright light of knowledge the facts of nature which are veiled in darkness. The former is the subject of the chemist [here meaning an occult alchemist], followers of Hermes and Paracelsus; the latter, on the contrary, the task of the mathematician." [6] Those humanists who remained rationalistic enough to resist either Aristotelian dogmatism or Baconian pragmatism were "skeptical about the value of science, which, as they said, helped in no way toward a happy life." [7] And yet, the first definite announcement of Kepler's aim and his findings, written in a letter to his friend Wackher von Wackenfels one year before finishing the *Harmonice mundi*, has a curious ring after all: "We and the entire choir of planets revolve around the sun, subservient to him, as it were, as his own family and possession . . . As for the heavenly tones, they are to be reproduced in the usual manner of notation. The lowest note [in each case] is always the aphelion, the highest the perihelion . . . Indeed, the tones of the individual [bodies] are thus distinct, of course, with respect to the pitches, varying in height, of the musical scale." [8] (transl. E. W.)

Were it not for two references of this letter, it might be dismissed as one of the thousands of fantasies, which in past ages one scholastic divine copied from another. But these two items are novel and revolutionary indeed: Kepler promises to set down the exact notation of the tones of the planets; moreover, he identifies as the lowest tone of each

[5] *Ibid.*, p. 74.
[6] Cf. Caspar, *op. cit.*, p. 303.
[7] Cf. T. S. Kuhn, *The Copernican Revolution* (Cambridge, Mass. 1957).
[8] Johannes Kepler, *Gesammelte Werke*, ed. W. von Dyck, M. Caspar & F. Hammer, VI: *Briefe* (Munich 1940–41): "At solem et nos et omnis planetarum chorus circumimus, ei veluti famulantes, eius propria familia et peculium . . . Nam toni coelestes sunt exprimendi schematibus usitatis. Prima nota est motus aphelius, summa perihelius . . . Suntque revera sic distincti singulorum toni, diversis scilicet altitudine clavibus in scala musica" (pp. 254–55).

planet its aphelion, as the highest, its perihelion. Obviously, he meant to test and prove his amazingly concrete thesis of the celestial harmonies.

II

So FREQUENTLY has the term "harmony" been misunderstood, and so manifold are its possible applications, that we must ask quite seriously: what did "harmony" mean to Kepler? It had for him at least three different meanings, and it will be useful as well as necessary to distinguish among them: (1) Musical harmony, i.e. any interval which according to Kepler's music theory is harmonious-consonant. (2) Mathematical harmony, i.e. the division of quantities in two or more parts according to the so-called "harmonic" section. If there are two quantities, a and b, their harmonic mean or division is obtained by the formula

$$\frac{2ab}{a+b}.$$

A special case of the harmonic division is the "golden section" (*sectio aurea*) which plays an important part in classic sculpture, architecture, and music, but also in modern technology. It is represented by the equation

$$a : b = b : a + b, \quad \text{whence} \quad a = \frac{b}{2}(\sqrt{5}-1).$$

The Pythagorean numbers of the first divisions of the monochord were also sometimes called harmonic. Finally, a sequence of numbers whose reciprocals form an arithmetic series is called a harmonic progression. Thus 1, 1/2, 1/3, 1/4, 1/5, etc. form a harmonic progression. This is a remnant of Ptolemy's theory of harmony, and has often been misunderstood.[9] (3) Occasionally the term "harmony" is used by Kepler in a sense closer to the ancient Greek meaning of that word. Then it had the general significance of something fitting, suitable, well proportioned, be it a piece of carpentry or the orbit of a planet. In this sense it was later used by Leibnitz.

Early in life Kepler intuitively but erroneously sensed the astronomical harmony of the world. Taking quite literally Copernicus's remark, "We find in this arrangement a marvelous symmetry of the

[9] Cf. C. v. Jan, *Die Harmonie der Sphaeren*, in: *Philologus*, LII (Goettingen 1894); also the article *Ptolemaios*, in: Pauly-Wissowa, *Real-Enzyklopaedie des klassischen Altertums*. Especially the harmonic division has been misunderstood, even by Riemann, *Geschichte der Musiktheorie* (2nd ed. Berlin 1920); see *infra*, text adjacent to fns. 35–36.

world and a harmony in the relationship of the motion and size of the
orbits, such as one cannot find elsewhere," [10] Kepler set to work as early
as 1599 to prove the harmonic character of the cosmos. He described
that first brainstorm, by which he envisaged—faultily—the law of the
planets, in all of its pristine enthusiasm: "The delight that I took in my
discovery I shall never be able to describe in words." [11] That fundamental
idea was false; yet it led, after 25 years of searching and checking, trying
and rechecking, to the three laws that bear his name and made it immortal. At his time only six planets were known: Mercury, Venus,
Earth, Mars, Jupiter, and Saturn. Following the Copernican theory,
which envisaged the Earth as one of the planets, Kepler made the bold
attempt to apply the proportions of the five so-called Platonic regular
bodies to the distances between the planets. This fundamentally Pythagorean conception was first divined—though not clearly pronounced—
in Plato's *Timaeus*. There it was already linked with the idea of the harmony of the spheres.[12] Kepler's first vision of geometrical proportions
within the orbits of the planets was quite erroneous; and 22 years later,
when he had found the correct solution, he wrote: "If my false figures
came near the facts, it happened merely by chance. . . ." [13] For Kepler
was never satisfied with vaguely approximate solutions, and certainly
not with the ancient Platonic phantasmagorias of the cosmos: he insisted
on exactitude, on proof, on numerical laws, while Plato was opposed to
any kind of experimental science. Thus, in this categorical demand
Kepler goes far beyond the ancients, and even more did he deny
Aristotle's disclaimer of cosmic harmony: "Hence it follows: the claim
that through the motions of celestial bodies harmony comes into being,
in which the tones form *symphoniai*, is, though noble and original, by
no means true." [14] How concretely the mature Kepler understood the
phrase "cosmic harmony" may be seen from a few lines quoted from the
table of contents opening the fifth book of *Harmonice mundi*:

I. De quinque solidis figuris regularibus
II. De cognitione cum iis, proportione harmonicarum
III. Summa doctrina astronomicae, necessaria ad contemplationem har-
moniarum coelestium
IV. Quibus in rebus ad planetarum motus pertinentibus expressae sint

[10] Copernicus, *De revolutionibus*, I, Chap. 10.
[11] Cf. Caspar, *op. cit.*, p. 276.
[12] Cf. Plato, *Timaeus*, Loeb Classical Library (New York 1929), pp. 109ff, 126ff, 137ff.
[13] Kepler, *Mysterium cosmographicum*, Cap. 21, notes 8 and 11.
[14] Cf. Aristotle, *De coelo*, 290b (transl. E.W.). This attitude was shared by two great scholastic philosophers, Maimonides and Al-Farabi.

harmoniae simplices, et quod omnes illae in coelo reperiantur, quae in cantu insunt.[15]

V. Claves scalae musicae, seu loca systematis, et genera harmoniarum, durum et molle, a certis motibus expressa esse.

VI. Tonos seu modos musicos, singulos quodammodo a singulis planetis exprimi

VII. Contrapuncta, seu harmonias universales omnium planetarum. Easque diversas, aliam scilicet ex alia, existere posse, etc., etc.

Every astronomer or philosopher could have set forth the titles of the first four chapters. It is only thereafter that Kepler took the decisive step: he refers to *concrete musical scales* to be encountered in the movements of the planets; he speaks, later on, of the new-fangled genders of harmony, major and minor. He promises to show at least the possibility of a contrapuntal harmony among the planets, clearly notated and by no means an intellectual fantasy. Later on he will provide (Chap. IX) *a demonstratio*, an empirical and scientific proof of his thesis. And how humbly, yet proudly, does the last passage read: "Notes to this [Ptolemy's] part of the Harmonics, wherein I explain and refute the author [Ptolemy] and wherein I compare his findings and conjectures with my results." [16] Alas, this part of the appendix, so magnificently outlined, had mainly for technical, i.e. financial, reasons, to be reduced to a brief summary.

What did Kepler know about music? In sharp contrast to the vague ruminations of the Neo-Pythagoreans among the humanists, Kepler had familiarized himself with both the ancient and contemporary theory of musical harmony.

His letters contain a good many concrete musical examples, references, and questions. Through Boethius's work, which was still very much read, Kepler gained entrance to the older Greek sources, both in music and mathematics. Yet, where the Neo-Pythagoreans of his own time indulged in an esoteric numerology, Kepler wrote: "I do not wish to prove anything by the mysticism of numbers, nor do I consider it possible to do so." [17] Quite to the contrary! He wanted to encounter the "true nature of *musical* harmonics" in the world. Thus he analyzes the structure of the scale in accordance with Zarlino and Glareanus, whose

[15] How Kepler would have rejoiced over the discovery of the orbits of certain stars, e.g. 61 Cygni! It is sinusoidal, corresponding with the vibration of strings and tone-waves. Cf. H. Shapley, *The View from a Distant Star* (New York 1963), p. 60.

[16] J. Kepler, *Gesammelte Werke*, VI, 290: "Notas ad hanc partem harmonicarum, quibus authorem explico, refuto, eiusque vel inventa vel attentata cum meis comparo."

[17] Quoted after Caspar, *op. cit.*, p. 97 (letter, 14 September 1599, to Herward von Hohenburg).

works he had studied.[18] In a letter he gave a technical musical analysis of the sequence *Victimae paschali laudes*.[19] When he rushed to the defense of his old mother, who was accused as a witch by the Inquisition, he took with him, as reading matter, Vincenzo Galilei's *Dialogo*.[20]

III

THIS IS NOT the place to explain Kepler's line of astronomical thinking. We shall limit ourselves to demonstrating how his concern with musical harmonies aided and guided him toward his aim. Utilizing ideas and rules of music theory, Kepler attained his objective in four steps; and like a true Pythagorean, he juxtaposed mathematical and musical conceptions. Frankly, this method was not without occasional handicaps, arbitrary statements, and the like. The most difficult problem arose in identifying harmonic relations with consonant intervals. Thus the pure fourth is more harmonic, from the mathematical point of view, than the major third. But Odington and Johannes de Muris, to mention two great music theorists of the Middle Ages, considered the proportion of the Pythagorean major third, 5 : 4, as irrelevant for the musician, who would prefer the less simple but more consonant proportion $\frac{81}{64}$.[21] Moreover, misunderstandings arose concerning the harmonic progression (1, 1/2, 1/3, 1/4, 1/5, 1/6), which Zarlino considered the mathematical model of the minor scale.

Kepler dealt with six planets, including the earth, plus sun and moon, that is, with eight celestial bodies. (Uranus, Neptune, and Pluto had not been discovered at this time.) Convinced that this identity with the number of tones of the diatonic scale was not accidental, he began to search for identical properties between mathematical and musical harmonies. Under such circumstances the seventh overtone caused just as much trouble to him as to a conservative music theorist. He had to eliminate the number 7 as a member of his harmonic relations. Yet why should he stop at 6? (Octave 2, fifth 3/2, fourth 4/3, major third 5/4, minor third 6/5.) He could refer to Zarlino, whose work he knew; yet he was searching for musical as well as mathematical reasons for his self-imposed limitation. He started with a geometrical analogy: the regular polygons that can

---

[18] In *Harmonice mundi*, III, and esp. V, Chap. 5.
[19] Letter to Heydonus (May 1605), *Gesammelte Werke*, VI.
[20] *Gesammelte Werke*, VI, 479.
[21] Nonetheless, Odington is inclined to take 5 : 4 as the correct proportion of the major third. Cf. Riemann, *Geschichte der Musiktheorie* (2d ed. Berlin 1920), pp. 119–20. The Arabs knew the 5 : 4 proportion as consonant even before Odington. Cf. Riemann, *op. cit.*, p. 394.

be inscribed in a circle. He had to show that the division of a circle into equal parts by a line, a triangle, square, pentagon, and hexagon each was possible, not by a regular heptagon, which cannot be constructed by using only straight-edge and compass. This condition was and still is an inherent principle of Euclidian geometry. Kepler justifies his exclusion of the heptagon by stressing that this polygon would lead to irrational numbers ("numeri ineffabiles").[22] Yet he had to exclude other regular polygons, e.g. that of 15 sides, which can easily be constructed and does not lead to "numeri ineffabiles." We shall skip here the ingenious sophistries by which Kepler excluded such polygons; nor shall we speculate on how he might have reacted, had he known of Gauss's construction of the regular polygon of 17 sides! Thus he satisfied himself that the hexagon and octagon corresponding to the minor third and third octave are valuable and necessary, while the other polygons which exceed eight sides are not. Or in other words: "What may be constructed in geometry, is consonant in music," which in this form is absolutely untenable both from the mathematical and musical point of view.[23] And yet, even so critical a theorist as Salinas (1577) took more or less the same position as Kepler, i.e. he operated with similar sophistries as did Kepler in order to eliminate 7 from his harmonic relations.[24] It was only Mersenne (*Harmonie universelle*, 1636—after Kepler), who boldly suggested that habit might lead to considering the intervals corresponding to 6/7, 7/8, and even 5/7 as consonances.[25] Thus far all harmonics were understood as pure mathematical proportions. Yet Kepler himself turns against this very same one-sidedness in Plato, calling it a tyranny, because it violates the natural instinct of hearing.

We realize that Kepler's first step was erroneous; and yet it led him to the final correct solution. This situation repeats itself in the course of his researches. *Ducunt fata volentem . . .*

The mathematical results gained by Kepler were in full agreement with Zarlino's dictum (as Kepler had meant them to be): "Within the numbers 1: 2: 3: 4: 5: 6: all consonant harmonies are determined." [26]

[22] Kepler's "ineffabiles" is a Latinization of the Greek term *alogos*. This is pure Pythagoreanism, for he studiously avoids the word "irrational" since he had to deal with other irrational numbers rather than with quantities that could be constructed geometrically but not arithmetically, e.g. $\sqrt{2}, \sqrt{3}, \sqrt{5}$, etc.

[23] Cf. Kepler's letter to H. von Hohenburg of 14 September 1599, *Gesammelte Werke*, VI.

[24] Cf. F. Salinas, *De musica*, II (Salamanca 1577), Cap. 24, here quoted after Riemann, *op. cit.*, p. 397.

[25] Riemann, *op. cit.*, pp. 398-99, footnote.

[26] Cf. G. Zarlino, *Istitutioni harmoniche* (Venice 1558), I, Cap. 15: "Della proprietà del numero Senario et delle sue parti et come tra loro si ritrova la forma d'ogni consonanze musicale." See also *infra*, text adjacent to fns. 35-36.

Also the "harmonic" division of the fifth into the major and minor third, to be found in Zarlino, is accepted by Kepler, although he seems to have had some trifling misgivings about this division: [27]

Ex. 1

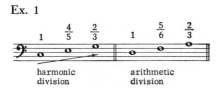

harmonic   arithmetic
division   division

Riemann has demonstrated in his *Geschichte der Musiktheorie* that Walter Odington already knew the harmonic division of the fifth into major and minor thirds.[28] Kepler's main premise consisted in excluding —both in music and mathematics—all proportions that involve the numbers 7, 11, 13, and similar primes. These proportions would (according to Kepler and all his contemporaries) produce only discordant intervals and harmonies.

Having established the mathematical "purity" of the major scale, Kepler proceeds to deduce the "melodic" intervals (*intervalla concinna*) from the principal harmonies, i.e. the whole tone (major and minor) and the two types of semitone. Then he develops out of the diatonic the chromatic scale *more mathematico*. Finally he attempts to formulate the principles of a *melopoeia* and a critique of polyphonic music; here we encounter ideas of Glareanus, S. Calvisius (*Melopoeia* 1582), A. Reinhard (*Monochordum* 1604), and G. M. Artusi (esp. his *L'Arte del contrappunto* 1586). The entire second part of Book III of the *Harmonice mundi* is yet to be evaluated by a competent musicologist; it offers ample food for thought. For here Kepler goes into musical details, quotes Josquin and Lasso, discusses various types of cadences, syncopes, good part-writing, and other problems of *musica practica*.

In his second step, Kepler finds the very same harmonic proportions that he had established in the regular polygons and in the musical scale also in the observable behavior of the planets. He lets the reader accompany him in his heuristic attempts to discover such celestial proportions;

[27] A modern mathematician would shrug his shoulders when considering Zarlino's harmonic and arithmetic division of the fifth and its resulting major and minor triads. For these results depend on the *direction* of the operation, upward or downward, respectively.

$$\text{Harmonic mean: } \frac{2.1.\frac{2}{3}}{1+\frac{2}{3}} = \frac{4}{5}\,; \quad \text{arithmetic mean: } \frac{1+\frac{2}{3}}{2} = \frac{5}{6}$$

[28] Riemann, *op. cit.*, p. 119.

nor is he ashamed to display his groping through a series of erroneous assumptions. Since he had constantly to resort to Tycho Brahe's and his own tables, which antedate the telescope, it is a profoundly moving spectacle to watch this honest and tenacious seeker of truth in his laborious quest. His task was now to find an equivalent for the proportion of the octave in the orbits of the planets; and after some experiments, he comes to the conclusion: "There is a distinction between the harmonies conveyed to us by the senses . . . and harmony *per se*, as abstracted from all sensuous entities . . . but in principle it is the same kind of harmony, which is defined by the proportion of $2 : 1$, whether it is audible in tones, and then called octave, or visible in the beams of planets standing in opposition . . ." [29] Thereafter Kepler compares the proportions of the major axes of two planetary orbits; but in vain. Then he investigates the times of revolutions—with negative results—as well as the relations between the velocities of two planets—again without result. Then he compares the times during which two planets move the same length of an arc; here the results were inconclusive, but Kepler sensed that he had come near the solution. Finally he projects his ideal observer into the sun and calculates the extreme values of the planet's angular velocities, as seen from the sun, i.e. the planet's movement at perihelion and aphelion. And here he finds the required proportions and with them his celebrated Third Law, in modern terminology: the squares of the periods of revolution of any two planets are as the cubes of their mean distances from the sun. He proceeds to the distinction between the harmony of a planet's movement and the proportions established by a pair of planets. Immediately there occurs to him a vivid comparison with living music: "Just as the simple chant or monody which we call chorale, and which alone was known to the ancients, relates to the polyphonic, so-called figural chant, invented during the last few centuries: so also are the harmonies of a single, individual planet related to the harmonies of a pair of planets, if contemplated simultaneously [*ad harmonias junctorum*]." [30]

Such an analogy appeared natural to a man who, like Kepler, distinguished between harmonies of the senses and pure harmonies. If the soul, which recognizes and, indeed, *creates* harmony, were missing, the sensual things continue as before, but their harmony has disappeared. Why? Because harmony is a thing of reason. Hence to find and realize hidden

[29] This is not an exact translation of the rather intricate Latin text, but rather my paraphrase of the passage in *Harmonice mundi*, IV, Chap. 1 (*On harmonic proportions*).

[30] J. Kepler, *Gesammelte Werke*, VI, 316.

harmonics is a creative act of the soul. This train of thought is based upon an old concept that Kepler had found in Proclus's Neo-Platonic commentary on Euclid's elements. For Kepler, the celestial harmony, proof of God's transcendence, is an intellectual harmony; its finest sensual and intelligible counterpart is to be found in music and its proportions.

Following his table of contents, Kepler relates the harmonies found in the planet's elements to the proportions of the scale and to polyphonic music. He begins with the scale, placing the aphelions and perihelions in numerical sequence by a mathematical transposition of all relations into one single octave; he thus obtains (a) the major scale of G with C and C♯; and (b) a minor scale on G with E♭ and E♮:

Ex. 2   (after Kepler, *Gesammelte Werke*, VI, 319)

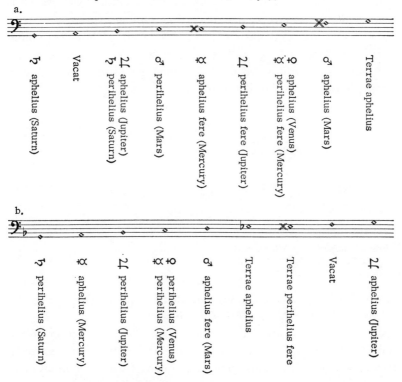

Thereto he boldly adds: "It follows that the musical scale (or the system of one octave), is doubly expressed in the sky, even according to the two *genera* of melody . . ." [31] From here he proceeds to the analysis of the scales that he just encountered "in motibus coelorum" according

---

[31] *Ibid.*, p. 320: "Est igitur in coelo duplici via, et in duobus quasi generibus cantus, expressa scala Musica, seu systema unius Octavae."

to the usual arrangement "per sectiones harmonicas." It is here that we meet a variety of implied assumptions pertaining to the music theory of Kepler's generation: he refers to the melodic-intervallic as well as to the polyphonic consonant relations of two or more voices, and in principle he does not make a categorical distinction between the two types of harmony—the simultaneous (vertical) and the subsequent (horizontal) one. He seems to have known the standard descriptions of harmony, especially those of Gafurius and Glareanus. Although he follows Zarlino in all essential points, he sees nothing illogical in the coexistence of the two *genera* of major and minor with the traditional octave species of the Middle Ages, for he tries to provide the necessary intervals for the *modi*. This was by no means easy; in fact, no clear *modus* is really recognizable in Kedler's attempt. Quite to the contrary, the reader is treated to a collection of melodic phrases pertaining either to the major or minor. This does not prevent Kepler from stating: "sunt ergo modi Musici inter Planetas dispertiti." He adds, in all fairness, that other and more modal distinctions are needed, which he cannot adduce. The melodic phrases assigned to the planets are:

Ex. 3

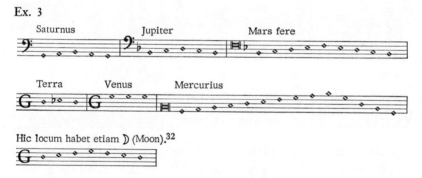

Hic locum habet etiam ☽ (Moon).[32]

In melancholic humor, he observes that the phrase assigned to the earth reads Mi—Fa—Mi, for *Miseria et Fames*.

Now Kepler is ready for the third step: the construction of the "Universal Harmony" of all planets, sounding together. He was really carried away by this conception, and opens Chapter 7 in hymnic language: "Nunc opus, Uranie, sonitu majore!" ("Now, Urania, greater sound is required!") In the subsequent paragraphs he challenges the contemporary composers to follow his lead by utilizing the specific har-

---

[32] He proceeds in the following manner: when assigning to Saturn, the most remote planet (in aphelion) the subcontra G, the most rapid motion of Mercury (at its perihelion) corresponds numerically to e^5; reducing all proportions to one single octave, almost all notes of the diatonic major scale emerge quite naturally.

monies that he had found in the sky: "Sequimini Musici moderni remque vestris artibus, antiquitate non cogniti, causate!" [33] In the margin Kepler suggests the composition of a "celestial" motet based upon his data: "I wonder if I am not committing a turpitude by demanding from the composers of this age an artfully contrived motet for this eulogy? The Royal Psalter and other sacred books could easily provide an apt text. But hark ye, there are no more than six parts in the heavenly symphony! For the moon chants her own monody, belonging to the earth as an infant in its cradle. Assemble your notes, so that it may become a book of music for six parts, and I promise to be its diligent sponsor. For whoever will express the music of the heavens most fittingly, as described in this book, to him Clio grants the crown and Urania will give him Venus as his wife." I do not know if a composition has actually been elicited by Kepler's vision or his extravagant promises. As his laws were not generally recognized before their interpretation by Newton—even Galileo had considered them erroneous—the chances seem slim. Perhaps a Mersenne or Kircher could have written such a "cosmic motet" for six parts, but both were members of Catholic orders and had therefore to bridle their tongues and pens.

Yet Kepler was bent on demonstrating that "theoretically" the "Supreme Harmonist" himself had created the conditions necessary for a true celestial harmony of six parts. He insisted: "The heavenly motions are nothing but a continuous song for several voices . . . a music, which, through discordant tensions, through syncopes and cadences . . . progresses toward certain designated quasi six-voiced clausulae, and thereby sets landmarks in the immeasurable flow of time . . . Man wanted to reproduce the continuity of cosmic time within a short hour by an artful symphony for several voices, to obtain a sample of the delight of the Divine Creator in His works, and to partake of His joy by making music in the image of God." [34]

Yet he insisted that such a cosmic symphony is of purely intellectual, not sensual nature. In contradistinction to Galileo, for whom the physical world was an exact realization of geometrical principles, Kepler retained the ontological distinction between the ideal form as represented by mathematics, and its material realization. For him the essence of the world was spiritual, yet he maintained that it could and should be demonstrable through human senses and sciences. Thus he was aware of the slight numerical discrepancies—he calls them vices—in the planetary motions; he knew full well that a four-part harmony would occur only

[33] *Ibid.*, p. 323.
[34] *Harmonice mundi*, V, Chap. 7.

once in many centuries, because the moments when the planets stand to each other harmoniously are very rare: a six-part harmony might have occurred at the beginning of time! And here the indefatigable calculator begins to wonder if it would be possible, under such an assumption, to determine the age of the world.[35]

Kepler does not follow this tempting idea but presents at this stage a table that gives, both mathematically and musically, the values "Harmoniae Planetarum omnium seu Universales Generis Duri." Again we must ask ourselves what kind of harmony he was seeking and finding, for he speaks of *harmonia, sectio harmonica,* and the like, when he contemplates sequences such as 1, 2, 3, 5, 10, 15, 16, 20, 32, etc. It seems that he uses here a terminology, known to mathematicians and music theorists, that originated with Jamblichus's *Commentary on the Nicomachian Arithmetics.*[36] This author states that a "musical proportion" exists between two quantities a and b when the following equation is satisfied:

$$a : \frac{a+b}{2} = \frac{2ab}{a+b} : b$$

It is this equation, not the one quoted by Riemann (for Zarlino), which yields the *sectio harmonica.* Representing the c by 1, the g by 3/2, we obtain, in accordance with the above equation:

$$1 : \frac{1 + \frac{3}{2}}{2} = \frac{2.1.\frac{3}{2}}{\frac{5}{2}} : \frac{3}{2}, \text{ or } 1 : \frac{5}{4} = \frac{6}{5} : \frac{3}{2}$$

in accordance with Zarlino's and Odington's definition of the major third as the harmonic division of the fifth.

These proportions occur between planets, as Kepler admits, only under certain optimal conditions. Yet mortal man, "imitating his creator, finally invented the art of polyphonic music, unknown to antiquity; he wanted . . . to sense, as far as possible, the delight of the Divine Master in His works; he strives to experience the very same delight that such music [*imitatione Dei*] affords." [37] Here speaks not a Pythagorean, but a devout Christian.

---

[35] *Ibid.,* p. 324. Shortly before he shows that his old idea of the exact relationship between the regular bodies and the interplanetary spaces could not work.

[36] Jamblichus, *Commentaries ad Nicomach. Arithm.,* ed. Temml (Leipzig 1871), p. 168. See also F. Cajori, *History of Elementary Mathematics* (New York 1917), p. 30ff. This division seems to have originated in Babylonian astronomy.

[37] *Ibid.,* p. 328.

IV

Now LEAVING behind him all cosmological fantasies, Kepler returns to this earth and to his science. In his fourth step, he gives the rigidly observational and empirical proof of his theory, especially of his Third Law and its fundamental harmonic proportions. The numerical harmonies between the planets' angular velocities at their orbital extremes (aphelion and perihelion) were correlated with the observed mean velocities and with the time of a complete orbital revolution. Between these time values and the mean distances of the planets from the sun, the Third Law had, by induction, established a simple mathematical relation. Hence, the actual comparison of the theoretical distances with those resulting from observation constitutes the empirical test of Kepler's theories. As by-products of these calculations there emerge, again by the postulate of harmonic proportions, the correct values of the individual eccentricities for each planet. The aim that Kepler had envisaged 25 years earlier, the harmonic-geometrical laws of the solar system, had been reached, and the many bypaths, sometimes mystic, often fantastic, opened great new vistas for the genius who completed what Kepler had begun: Isaac Newton. His discernment—singling out from a jungle of hundreds of theorems and statements the Three Laws as definitive and decisive—must not be underestimated. For nowhere in Kepler's own writings do they appear together in the same treatise.[38] Yet it would not be quite fair to underrate their significance for Kepler himself, as a modern author does: "The three laws are the pillars on which the edifice of modern cosmology rests; but to Kepler they meant no more than bricks among other bricks for the construction of his baroque temple, designed by a moonstruck architect." [39]

A different judgment comes from a sober-minded historian of mathematics, the late E. T. Bell, who described the significance of the Three Laws in these words: "Kepler's laws were the climax of thousands of years of an empirical geometry of the heavens. They were discovered as the result of about 22 years of incessant calculation, *without logarithms*, one promising guess after another being ruthlessly discarded as it failed to meet the exacting demands of observational accuracy. *Only Kepler's Pythagorean faith in a discoverable mathematical harmony in nature sustained him . . .*" [40]

[38] It has been rightly stated that the Three Laws were "for Kepler simply snatches of melody in search of a symphony." (C. C. Gillispie, *op. cit.*, p. 37.)

[39] Cf. A. Koestler, *The Sleepwalkers* (New York 1959), p. 396. This book contains a magnificent biography and evaluation of Kepler, but tends too much to rhetorical hyperbole.

[40] E. T. Bell, *The Development of Mathematics* (New York 1945), p. 161; the italics are mine.

Kepler was by no means the only scholar of his time who speculated and theorized on the solar system; many others, such as Osiander, Fludd, or the Leipzig theologian Paul Nagel, had similar ambitions and even similar ideas. Yet both their methods and their aims were quite different: they wanted to prove Scripture, or to predict the future, or to interpret the numbers in the Books of Daniel and Revelation; they were not first-class mathematicians like Kepler, nor did they worry about exact empirical tests of their hypotheses; nor had any of them the bold idea of searching for numerical and musical harmonics in the Universe, although they all raved about it.[41]

In retracing Kepler's long and tortuous path, we might now single out his musical ideas. He begins by modifying Greek music theory, as expressed in Platonic doctrine and by Ptolemy: for Kepler sixths and thirds are consonances, and he endeavored to prove this unprovable axiom geometrically. He searches for harmonic progressions in the heavens; he improves Zarlino's conception of the major third as a harmonic division of the fifth; he builds his musical knowledge into his astronomical view of the world, and seeking a numerical harmony valid for *all* planets, he hits upon his Third Law. In his Faust-like urge, Kepler even starts to search for theological reasons behind the celestial harmonies. The devout Lutheran Christian, albeit a little tinged with pantheistic dreams—how could it be otherwise?—combines concepts of the Pythagoreans, of Boethius, of the great music theoreticians of the Middle Ages and the Renaissance; and he has experienced more than just a waft of the new era of empirical, not speculative, science.

And yet, his attitude toward astronomy, mathematics, music theory, and theology is still that of a great humanist: the fatal gulf between science and humanities had not opened as yet; he is much more of an artist than a mere "accountant of phenomena." [42] "We still share his belief in a mathematical harmony of the universe. It has withstood the test of ever-widening experience." [43] Thus writes a celebrated contemporary scientist. As for us, Kepler's profound understanding of musical laws and their application to the world of predictable phenomena will ever constitute a vindication of our discipline.

[41] Cf. G. Loria, *Storia della matematiche* (Milano 1950), p. 415f: "His Third Law might have been written by some superstitious fellow of the Pythagorean School . . . yet it is a proof of an extraordinary power of imagination, which would have led others to nothing but lunatic ruminations, but which guided Kepler to his great results . . ." (transl. E. W.)

[42] This striking phrase was coined by the late Lecomte de Nouy in his *Road to Reason.*

[43] H. Weyl, *Symmetry*, in: *The World of Mathematics*, ed. J. R. Newman (New York 1956), I, 720.

Two Obscure Sources of Reuchlin's "De Accentibus ...Linguae Hebraicae"

Reprinted with permission of *Historica Judaica*, 16, 1954, pp. 39-54.

I

THE spiritual climate in which Reuchlin boldly ventured to publish his Hebrew studies was a mixture of theosophy-cabbala, genuine humanistic zeal, and, last but not least, belief in the divinely revealing nature of the Hebrew language. If, perchance, Hebrew served the younger Reuchlin as a mere tool to unriddle the secrets of the cabbala and thereby to demonstrate the truth of certain Christian dogmas,[1] the older Reuchlin approached the study of the Hebrew tongue more in the spirit of his fellow-humanists, in conformity with their watchword, "Ad fontes!"

The intellectual curiosity of the Renaissance was a feature much more characteristic of Italy than of Germany. When the Florentine nobleman Gianozzo Manetti began to study Hebrew systematically with a Jew (about 1450), he set a pattern that was followed by almost all Christian scholars for the next century.[2] It seems that the nucleus

---

1 Cf. Ludwig Geiger, *Johann Reuchlin* (Leipzig, 1871), pp. 172-176, where the main sources are given. Also S. A. Hirsch, "Reuchlin, Father of the Study of Hebrew among the Christians." *Jewish Quarterly Review*, O. S., VIII (London, 1896), 451 ff.

2 Cf. Jakob Burckhardt, *Die Kultur der Renaissance in Italien*, ed. Goetz (1925), pp. 198 ff. See also Vita Manetti in Ludovicus Ant. Muratori, *Rerum Italicarum Scriptores*, XX (Milan 1723 ff.), Col. 552 f.; Vogelstein-Rieger, *Geschichte der Juden in Rom*, II, (Berlin, 1895-96), p. 73, where Manetti is tentatively identified as the opponent of Moshe ben Yizchak de Rieti in a public religious disputation.

of the world-famous collection of Hebrew manuscripts in
the Vatican was provided by Manetti, who also succeeded
in interesting Popes Nicholas V and Sixtus IV in the pursuit
of Hebrew studies.

Different was the situation in Germany and Central
Europe. The paradoxical attitude of intelligentsia and
nobility, who took up Hebrew studies abroad while expelling
the Jews from their own homeland, is definitely *sui generis,*
or rather *Germaniae generis.* Friend of the Jews, as Reuchlin
certainly was, he stated simply that from his own homeland
of Swabia the Jews were expelled and he, Reuchlin, had to
go abroad to study the proper pronunciation and cantillation
of Hebrew texts. But not a word of regret, no plea for
the Jews![3]

It is well known, and Reuchlin himself asserted it more
than once, that the ultimate goal of his Hebrew studies was
to convince the world, and most of all the Jews, of the
validity of the fundamental dogmas of the Roman Catholic
Church.[4] It was for this purpose that he wanted to use his
knowledge of Hebrew, and it is this purpose which accounts
for his insatiable curiosity to learn everything concerning
the cabbala and the Jewish customs connected therewith.[5]
Yet it would be neither fair nor correct to ascribe the fine
Hebrew background that Reuchlin painstakingly acquired
over a period of almost thirty years, solely to his desire to
proselytize the Jews. Reuchlin was a true child of his time,
a man of manifold interests, that ran the gamut from music
to classical studies, from cabbala and Hebrew philology to
learned Latin comedies.[6]

---

[3] *Reuchlin, De accentibus,* fol. LXXI: "cui plane nulla Judaeorum
relicta est conversatio quippe cum fuerint prope toto vitae meae tamque a mea
patria exacti et extorres judaei, nec in ullo ducis Suevorum territorio habitare
audeant." See also C. G. Wächter, *Württembergisches Privatrecht,* I (Stuttgart, 1839-42), p. 100 f.

[4] Cf. Reuchlin, *De verbo mirifico,* third book; also A. Geiger, in *Jüdische
Zeitschrift für Wissenschaft und Leben,* VIII (1870), 255 f. Even the popes
searched for christological material to be gleaned from the Talmud; see
Johannes Reuchlins Briefwechsel, ed. Ludwig Geiger (Stuttgart, 1876), No.
CCCI, p. 331 (Bamberg).

[5] See in this connection the highly interesting letter of Fra Ellenbog
ibid., No. CCLXXV, p. 310.

[6] Cf. L. Geiger, *Johannes Reuchlin,* pp. 8, 69, 165 ff. etc.

In this study we shall examine only a small section of Reuchlin's work, namely, the third book of his *De accentibus linguae hebraicae* (Hagenau, 1518). In this book, which he entitled *Negina* (chant, melody), we witness a syndrome of Reuchlin's grammatical, classical, and musical interests.

As every reader of Reuchlin's books knows, that famous humanist, in this respect different from most of his contemporaries, gave credit where credit was due. From Jews he had acquired his Hebrew knowledge, and these teachers, personally known to him, and the Hebrew authors, from whose works he had profited, he always remembered faithfully.[7] He did not hesitate to acknowledge that they remained his masters.[8]

Since he mentions them by name, there is no need here to discuss their merits; almost all of them are very well known. Yet there are two among them of whom we know relatively little. Indeed, one of them has remained a mysterious personality to this day. They were Flavius (Raymundus) Mithridates Romanus and Johannes Bossosthenius, *vulgo* Boeschenstein. The following pages are devoted to their respective contributions to Reuchlin's third book of *De accentibus linguae hebraicae*.

II

Reuchlin refers to Flavius Mithridates Romanus in the third book, fol. LXXXi a, b and on fol. LXXXiii b to Johannes Boeschenstein. The first mentioned passage reads in translation:

. . . we have set down everything according to the teachings of the Hebrews, in the same way in which they treated this matter in their grammatical and musical books. It was, however, hard work for us to invent examples, apt for general instruction; and every student will confirm the veracity of this remark.

It is true, we once heard Raimund Mithridates the Roman, when he was making the rounds of the French and German universities and

[7] Cf. Reuchlin, *De accentibus*, fol. LXXX b and LX a: "Ac simul id quidquid est quod in hebraicis sum consecutus (Hercle quod comparatione doctissimorum Judaeorum exile nimium iudico) amicos caelare non possum..."
[8] *Ibid.*

gymnasia, a man well versed in Hebrew, Greek, Arabic, and Latin. He attempted to systematize Hebrew prosody as a parallel of the Greek pattern, in this way:

As the *tonoi, chronoi, pneumata, pathemata* of the Greeks were used, so were they also employed in the mode of the Hebrews. For the Hebrews, too, classified the *tonoi*, i.e. the accents.

The *Acutus* corresponds with *Cadma* and *Maarich*.[8a]

The *Gravis* corresponds with *Tarha* and likewise with a preceding *Cadma, Segula, Zarka,* and *Azla.*

The *Circumflex* corresponds with *Shofar yasar* [*munach*] and *Yareach ben yomo.*

The *Tempora* likewise:

Longum corresponds in the beginning of a sentence to *Tharsa*, in the middle of a sentence to *Rebia*, in the end of a sentence to *super* A to *Karne para*, with preceding *Yareach ben yomo; super* E to *Pazer gadol; super* I it is passed, otherwise sometimes in the last letter *Zarka* [?]. In the praepenult letter (after a preceding *Darga*) merely to *Thebir*, and indifferently in all cases to *Zakeph gadol.*

Breve has nothing, except in the last syllable *Thalsa.*

Media Quantitas [middle length] is ambivalent [*anceps*]. At the beginning stands *Sophar Mahapach,* in the middle *Threnhuttrin,* at the end and sometimes in the middle *Salseleth.* In the last and penult trochaic syllable stands *Threpastin,* and also for the last (if in the following word there occurs *Thebir*), *Darga.*

Passiones: As for the *passiones* [affects] of prosody, he taught that the suspensions [breaks] of the sentences are represented at the beginning [of the sentence] by *zakeph katon;* in the middle by *Athnahtha,* in the end by *Soph pasuk.* Likewise there might be a hyphen *Samich* [*sic* for *S'micha*], and a hypodiastole *pasek.*

When Mithridates in this way ended his course of teaching and instruction, the students swore that they had not understood him at all. Therefore, after the fee agreed upon had been fully paid, the students left the teacher and his teachings as if it had been the dogma Scotinon [probably an allusion to the doctrine of will, as expressed by Duns Scotus, a principle not recognized by the Church] and he, Mithridates, returned with heavily swollen purse to Italy.[9]

[8a] Here I follow exactly Reuchlin's spelling and orthography.

[9] This completely misunderstood theory of Hebrew accentuation was blindly taken over by Sebastian Münster and others. Cf. Josef Perles, *Beiträge zur Geschichte der hebräischen und aramäischen Studien* (Munich, 1884), pp. 195 ff. This old interpretation was, to my great amazement, reprinted and seriously presented by A. Z. Idelsohn, *Jewish Music in Its Historical Development,* (New York, 1929), pp. 69-70, who paraphrased Reuchlin and Mithridates without mentioning either of them.

Who was this Mithridates? Most of the documentary vestiges lead us to the court of Pico della Mirandola, where Mithridates first appears. He was one of Pico's Hebrew teachers, together with a certain Datylo Hebraeus, "huius obtrectator [erat] Mithridates Romanus," as we read in a letter of Widmanstadt-Oesiander to Seripandus, the disciple of Cardinal Aegidius of Viterbo.[10] There was a time when Jules Dukas' identification of Mithridates with R. Jochanan Alemanno was accepted.[11] But after Steinschneider's penetrating refutation, the conjecture can no longer be maintained seriously.[12] The reason for Dukas' identification was the fact that both men in question had translated a number of cabbalistic treatises into Latin.[13] Steinschneider lists thirty-eight of the supposed translations of Mithridates, contained in the Cod.Vat., Nos. 189-191. Obviously, only a highly learned Jew could have had the ability to translate such intricate texts into Latin.

If Mithridates was a native Roman, as was assumed by his contemporaries Sebastian Münster and Widmanstadt on the sheer evidence of his sobriquet, "Romanus," he must have been the son of a Byzantine Jew. Reuchlin emphasizes his extensive Hebrew, *Greek*, and Arabic knowledge, a combination unheard of among occidental Jewry. Moreover, he gives himself the Greek-sounding name *Mithridates*, but takes care that this name occurs in the Bible.[14] Still, all this is mere conjecture. The crucial point, however, is his theory of the accents, the manuscript of which, entitled *De tropis hebraicis*, seems to be lost. Reuchlin and Münster still knew it, and especially the latter praised it highly.[15] An other-

[10] Full text of Widmanstadt's letter in Perles, *op. cit.*, pp. 181 f.

[11] Cf. Jules Dukas, *Recherches sur l'histoire litteraire du quinzieme siècle* (Paris, 1876); see also N. Brüll's *Jahrbücher für Geschichte und Literatur*, III, (1877), 196 f.

[12] Cf. M. Steinschneider in *Hebräische Bibliographie*, XXI (1881-2), 109-115 etc. Perles, *loc. cit.*, identifies Datylo with Jochanan Alemanno.

[13] Steinschneider, *loc. cit.*, and pp. 130-32; also Stephanus et Josephus Assemani, *Bibliothecae Apostolicae Vaticanae Codicum Manuscriptorum Catalogus* I, (Rome, 1756), Nos. 189-191, pp. 155-163.

[14] Ezra 1:8; 4:7.

[15] Seb. Münster, *Opus Grammaticum* (Basle, 1549), pp. 383-387.

wise unknown Imbonatus still recommends it in Wolff, *Bibliotheca Hebraea.*[16]

Mithridates' theory of the Hebrew tropes, as far as we know it from its brief description quoted above, is in every respect a product and a legacy of Byzantine music theorists. However, their works were not published or translated in the western world before the eighteenth century. Whether the Byzantines, in their turn, had borrowed elements of their theories from the Arabs is still a controversial question.[17] At any rate, the division of the musical functions of the accents of the Greek prosody stems directly from Byzantine writers. A small part of the Arabic theory concerning the classification of music had been translated by Dom Gundissalinus (twelfth cent.), who made Al-Farabi's *Ihsa 'al-'ulum* accessible under the title *De Scientiis.*[18]

However that may be, the fact that Reuchlin quotes (in Greek letters) the *Greek* terminology of Mithridates makes it obvious that Mithridates' source was Greek, not Arabic. The famous Byzantine theorists Pachymeres, Bryennious, and Koukouzeles had evolved a system which at each point shines through Mithridates' Hebrew application.[19]

The most interesting term of the Byzantine system, as presented by Mithridates, is the *pneuma;* there it signified the logical reading of a text with special reference to syntactically correct punctuation.[20] Reuchlin did not fully understand Mithridates' use of the Byzantine terms, for he lumped together the *pneumata* and *pathemata* in one single

[16] Wolff, *Bibliotheca Hebraea* (Hamburg, 1733-45), II, 612.

[17] Cf. H. G. Farmer, *Historical Facts for the Arabian Musical Influence* (London, 1929), pp. 48 ff, 54 ff.

[18] Cf. Werner-Sonne, "The Theory and Philosophy of Music in Judaeo-Arabic Literature," *Hebrew Union College Annual,* XVI (1941), 266-72, where all sources are given.

[19] It should be mentioned that Al-Mas'udi, quoting an older author, knew of the same divisions into modes (*tonoi*), beats (*chronoi*), caesurae (*pneumata*), and of the emotional affects (*pathemata*). Cf. Al-Mas'udi. *Prairies d'or (Mrurj al dhahab)* VIII, p. 90. See also H. G. Farmer, "The Old Persian Music Modes," *Journal of the Royal Asiatic Society* (January, 1926).

[20] Cf. P. Wagner, *Gregorianische Melodien,* II, (Leipzig, 1912), 15, 52, and passim; also O. Fleischer, *Neumenstudien,* I, (Leipzig, 1895), 92.

rubric. Obviously, not only the ordinary students of Mithridates could have sworn "se non intellexisse." Nonetheless, that much remained in Reuchlin's memory for him to associate the "affective" (*pathemata*) qualities of the accents with their punctuating function.

Another misunderstanding of Mithridates' theory, perpetuated by Reuchlin, may be cleared up here. The former speaks of the *accentus acutus*, the Byzantine *neume oxeia*, of the *gravis*, the Byzantine *neume bareia*. It was but natural for the Latinist Reuchlin to add the prosodic-phonetic accent circumflex, although it does not exist as a Byzantine *neume*, neither under this nor under any other name.

After these comparisons it appears evident that Mithridates applied Byzantine systems and terms to the interpretation of the masoretic accents.

Let us now evaluate again the facts concerning Mithridates. He taught Hebrew at the court of Pico della Mirandola, where Greek Jews seem to have found a refuge. He was familiar with Hebrew, Aramaic, Arabic, Greek, and Latin. He applied the Byzantine theory of ecphonetic neumes to the masoretic accents, as we know from Reuchlin's and Münster's descriptions. Certainly he was a Jew, since he stipulated that nobody else but Pico should be present when he was teaching Aramaic, the language of the Cabbala.[21]

The notion that Mithridates came from Byzantine stock emerges as a distinct possibility to be considered. It is known that after the conquest of Constantinople in 1453 many Jewish scholars fled to Italy and made their appearance in the circles of the humanists and at the courts of the humanistic-minded aristocracy. Among these princes Pico certainly held a prominent position.[22] Possibly Mithridates was still reared in Constantinople; at any rate, his knowledge

---

[21] Cf. Joann. Pici Mirandulae *Opera* II, (Bologna, 1496), 386; also Dukas, *op. cit.*, p. 72.

[22] Cf. Cecil Roth, *History of the Jews of Italy* (Philadelphia, 1946), pp. 204-5.

not only of the Greek language, but of the then current
Byzantine theory of musical neumes, leads us to believe that
he was not an occidental Jew, but a scholar who had lived
in Byzantine as well as in Arabic environments. Unfortunately, his work *De tropis hebraicis* is lost. If it should be
discovered, we probably shall be able to trace his identity.
Although Reuchlin did not fully grasp the scope of Mithridates' application of the Byzantine system to Hebrew accentuation, he felt instinctively, and perhaps rightly, that
Mithridates offered an artificially contrived construction,
not an organically grown system.

III

Only a little more transparent than Mithridates is the
character and personality of Johann Boeschenstein, who
provided for Reuchlin the musical notation and arrangement of the Torah-cantillation at the end of the third book
of *De accentibus linguae hebraicae*. There Reuchlin calls
him *Bossosthenius sacerdos*.[23] This priesthood was doubted
quite early, and even during his lifetime voices were heard
claiming that he was a Jewish convert, calling him an op-
portunist, a swindler, a scoundrel, and the like. We shall
later examine these statements. First, however, we shall
investigate Boeschenstein's "priesthood."

Boeschenstein himself has, with one rather enigmatic
exception, never used this title, not even in his apology, *Ain
diemietige Versprechung* [An Humble Statement] (no
place given, 1519 or 1523). Usually, he signed himself
"Johannes Boeschenstein, Kaiserlich Majestaet Kapellan"
(Chaplain to His Imperial Majesty).[24] The only exception

---

[23] The passage (fol. LXXXIII) is not without a quaint charm. Reuchlin
writes: "Like Orpheus . . . in Thrace, sic nos a jugum Hercynium atque
Bacenas in Suevia, Pythagoreo more cithara nostra docemus divina Hebraeorum
carmina resonare, quorum symphoniam his subjungimus. Diatonicum autem
modulamen nobis attulit Bossosthenius sacerdos. Harmoniam fecit Christo-
phorus Sillingus Lucernensis . . ."

[24] Thus in Perles, *op. cit.*, p. 32, notes; also Steinschneider, *Katalog der*

(written in Judaeo-German) reads: *"Ani Yochanan Boeschenstein, Cohen Keysser kathavti."*[25]

If *Cohen* is understood as priest in the Catholic sense, then a sharp discrepancy emerges, since Boeschenstein in his apology and elsewhere speaks of his "nachkumenden gepluet" (succeeding blood, i.e., children) and "meinen nachkommen zu gut" (for the sake of my descendants), which is, of course, impossible for a priest.[26] There are two ways to resolve this contradiction. He may have already left the Catholic Church and become a Protestant, which is not impossible, since in 1518 he was teaching Hebrew at the University of Wittenberg under the close supervision of Martin Luther. There, however, he signed himself in the *Album Academiae Vittebergensis* (ed. Förstemann) as "Johannes Boeschenstein de Esslingen Privilegiatus Cesaree Maiestatis Pbr. [pro bona re?] Hebraice ligue [sic] interpres Dioc. Constancien."[27] In other words, he still insisted on his official position with the diocese of Constanz. This seems incompatible with our first explanation, although it does not rule it out completely. Yet in 1518 Luther had by no means severed his relations with the Catholic Church. Another explanation might accept *capellanus, privilegiatus,* and *cohen* as free paraphrases of *subdiaconus*. Before the Council of Trent a subdeacon was not strictly under the vow of celibacy, and even the question whether a subdeacon belonged to the *ordo major* or *minor* was not unequivocally answered by the Church. If we accept this explanation, Reuchlin's calling him *sacerdos* might be traced to the title *capellanus*, which may mean anything and everything.

There is yet another interpretation of *capellanus*. Boeschenstein was a very able musician, and there are at least two substantial proofs of his musical prowess extent:

---

hebräischen Handschriften in der Kgl. Hofbibliothek München (2nd ed. Munich, 1895), No. 401, k, 1 (p. 222-3), No. 259, 3 (p. 124).

[25] Cf. Perles, *op. cit.,* p. 32, note.

[26] L. Geiger, *Das Studium der hebräischen Sprache in Deutschland* (Breslau, 1870), p. 49, notes.

[27] *Ibid.,* p. 51, 2.

(1) the transcription of the oral Bible cantillation to musical notation; and (2) at least three musical manuscripts and compositions.[28] In his time the choristers of a royal chapel had the privilege of calling themselves *capellani;* the head of the choir was *magister* or *regens capellanorum.*[28a] This would justify the description, "Kaiserlich Maiestaet Capellan," but it would not fully cover the puzzling *Cohen Keysser.* However that may be, if Boeschenstein was ordained at all, it was no higher than a subdeacon.

Joseph Perles, in his excellent *Beiträge zur Geschichte der hebräischen und aramäischen Studien,* apodictically and without convincing proof calls Boeschenstein "a baptized Jew, although a very ignorant one." He echoes the often uttered accusation that Boeschenstein was an opportunistic convert, who "acted the Jew among Jews, and professed Christianity among Christians."[29] The only evidence offered by Perles are a few letters in Hebrew and Judaeo-German and a "sigh over his apostasy," to be found in Steinschneider's Catalogue of Hebrew Manuscripts in Munich. I was utterly unable to find this deploration of his apostasy. Instead— and perhaps Perles had this in mind—I came across praise of and prayer for the Jewish community of Regensburg, wherein he mentions a few names. I quote the passage in transcription and translation:

Das Tehillim hab ich Jochanan Boeschenstein kauft zu Tubingen bishnas [1518 in Hebrew letters] aus Rabie [?] Sohov Moshe Aurbach. Tovoth raboth osso li vekol hakehilo be-Regenspurg. Adonoi yagen [?] yiten alehem. R. Meir, Moshe Schulhof, Boruch Hacohen Wird, solt ein Meschumad in emuna heoli' [corrupt?], als wil leiden, als bei Jehudi' man werd kein Meschumad, im aulom das glab ich genzlich.[30]

[The book of Psalms I, Yochanan Boeschenstein, have purchased in Tübingen in the year 1518 from Rabbi Sohov Moshe Aurbach. He has done me much good, he and the whole community of Regensburg. God

---

[28]   Cf. Reuchlin, *op. cit.,* after fol. LXXXIII (not paginated); Steinschneider, *op. cit.,* No. 401, 1; 401. c; 401, k 227.

[28a]   Cf. M. Praëtorius, *Syntagma musicum* (Wittenberg and Wolfenbüttel, 1615-20), II, ch. 2.

[29]   Cf. Perles, *op. cit.,* p. 27.

[30]   Cf. Steinschneider, *op. cit.,* No. 400, p. 220.

may protect and reward them, R. Meir, Moshe Schulhof, Boruch Hocohen Wird. If a convert to [Christian] faith came here, he would suffer, as among Jews one does not become a convert in ages, so I am absolutely convinced.]

I am unable to read into this hodge-podge of legal and personal notes a sigh over his "apostasy," even less since he signs the letter "Kapellan." This shows clearly that he was not acting the "Jew among Jews," but exactly the opposite: he was acting the Gentile among Jews. There is no doubt, however, that he liked the Regensburg community, which he could not have done had he been a convert. We have two more statements to evaluate his position. Melanchthon, who first had warmly received Boeschenstein in Wittenberg, tells, after Boeschenstein's death, and maliciously enough, the following anecdote:

We had a professor of Hebrew here [in Wittenberg], who used to say: "What shall I do? I can live elsewhere much better." I asked him, in which place. He answered: "I could live nicely among the Jews of Regensburg. Once, [when I was there] I took a stroll in the court of their temple. An old woman came, gave me a *Batzen* [silver-coin] and asked me to read a mass for her; then a second and a third came with the same request; thus I can make six *Batzen* during the week.[31]

Luther's epithets are not too complimentary, either. He called Boeschenstein "by name a Christian, actually an arch-Jew."[32] In the same vein wrote Seb. Münster.[33] An entirely different suspicion against him was levelled—more than two centuries after his death—by J. S. Baumgarten. He makes the following conjecture:

It would almost appear, concluding from this translation [of the Lord's Prayer and the *Ave Maria* into Hebrew] and in consideration of the place of publication [Cologne (1539), the bulwark of Pfefferkorn, Hogstraten, et. al.] that its author, Johann Boeschenstein, at last had turned to Cologne and solemnly rejoined the Roman Church.

---

[31] Cf. Geiger, *Das Studium der hebräischeu Sprache in Deutschland*, p. 51; the quotation from Melanchton's *Narrationes jucundae*, in J. G. Schelhorn's *Ergötzlichkeiten aus der Kirchenhistorie und Literatur* (Ulm and Leipzig, 1762-1764), II, 737.

[32] Cf. Geiger, *op. cit.*, p. 52.

[33] *Ibid.*, p. 50.

. . . Maybe he had uttered such intentions previously, and was hence called by Luther an apostate. This is more likely than that he should have been so accused because of an alleged conversion to Judaism, in which sense his [Luther's] expression has often been understood; thus the unfounded rumor was confirmed that Boeschenstein was born a Jew. . . .[34]

In view of this little anthology of bad names which Boeschenstein was called during and after his lifetime, it is necessary from the historical as well as from the moral point of view to study the actual evidence critically, *sine ira et studio.* In doing so the following data are available:

(1) Boeschenstein, also Boschenstein was, according to his own statement, born in Esslingen in 1472; he always signed himself as *Esslingensis,* and was so addressed by his contemporaries. He tells us in his apology[35] that his family came from Stein am Rhein, and it is easily conceivable that the name Boeschenstein had been formed as a compound name from "Bosch in Stein."

(2) He studied Hebrew with R. Moshe Möllin of Weyssenburg, whom he calls "praeceptorem meum" and to whom he set up a grateful memorial in these words: ". . . A similar fate [as Reuchlin's] afflicted me for many years, when I was attacked—of course by rabid adversaries—and put into jail. I was bitterly hated by the Jews, because I had learned their language, and by Christians, because I had conversations with Jews. One man I except here, my first teacher in the elements of the Hebrew language, Moshe Möllin of Weyssenburg, whom no forgetfulness will ever erase from my memory, since he alone, free of any perfidy, remained faithful to me."[36]

(3) He went in 1505 to Ingolstadt, in 1513 to Augsburg, in 1518 to Wittenberg, in 1521 to Heidelberg, then to Antwerp and Zürich, where he seems to have taught Zwingli. In 1525 we find him for a short time in Nürnberg, which he left abruptly, despite a fine recommendation by

---

[34] Cf. J. S. Baumgarten, *Nachrichten von merkwürdigen Büchern,* III (Halle, 1753), 118-9.

[35] See *supra,* note 24.

[36] Cf. *Reuchlin's Briefwechsel,* ed. L. Geiger, No. CLXXXVI, p. 216.

Melanchthon,[37] and he died in 1540 in Nördlingen, a pauper.[38] In between he must have lived in Tübingen, Regensburg, and Munich.

(4) Among his contemporaries he was known for his greediness; and we have at least two advertisements by Boeschenstein himself, in which he addresses himself to Jews, soliciting them to study Hebrew-German with him; there also are testimonies of his eagerness to teach Hebrew to Christians.[39] There cannot be any doubt but that he was keen to sell his Hebrew knowledge to the highest bidder.[40]

(5) A very rare pamphlet of Boeschenstein (*Ain getreuwe ermannung zu allem volk . . . der Christlichen Kirchen aufrur und zwytracht zu verhueten*) ("A Faithful Admonition to Everyone . . . to Save the Christian Church from Riot and Discord") (Augsburg, no date given) clearly takes the Protestant side; and the fact that he was called to Wittenberg and accepted the call confirms his Protestant sympathies. However, of his disciples, whom he lists in his letter to Reuchlin, one was Johannes Eck, the theological opponent of Luther; another was Sebastian Sperantius (Sprentz), bishop of Brixen in the Tyrol; some of the others were more inclined to the Protestant side. At the same time we must not forget that between 1500 and 1520 a legal, open schism or secession from the Catholic Church had not yet taken place. Matters were still fluctuant, persons still flexible.

(6) As has been mentioned above, Boeschenstein was an accomplished musician. To transcribe from oral tradition the Torah cantillation in exact musical notation for each accent, as he had done at least twice, was an achievement of the first order.[41] He composed psalms and four

---

[37] Cf. Geiger, *Das Studium der Hebräischen Sprache*, p. 52: "Joh. Boeschenstein, egregie doctum in hebraicis meo privatim, dein et publico Universitatis nomine, tibi recommendo. Bonus vir est."

[38] Cf. *Allgemeine Deutsche Biographie*, art. "Boeschenstein."

[39] Cf. Perles, *op. cit.*, p. 32, where the Judaeo-German text is quoted.

[40] "Um ein ziemlich Gelt" (for a considerable fee). Cf.: Perles, *loc. cit.*

[41] Aside from the transcription printed in Reuchlin's *De accentibus,*

German sacred songs, probably for Protestant assemblies, of which "Da Jesus an dem Kreuze stund" (When Jesus Stood Before the Cross) is the best-known.[42]

(7) Boeschenstein was never able to hold a position for more than a few years. This learned vagabond was driven —not by external, but by inner forces—from one university to another, from one environment to another, and possibly from one Church to another, and back. His mercurial personality could not resist material inducements, wherever they came from, be it the Jewish side or the Christian— *non olet!* In one respect, however, he remained steadfast and faithful to his very highest ideal: to study, to teach, and to propagandize the Hebrew language to as many persons as possible.

The presentation of these facts should make it not too difficult to appraise this strange man with detached judgment. And yet it is not easy, for so many elements of his "human equation" are unknown to us, that we should be guided by great caution. He was a man disliked by many. Aside from certain personal qualities, such as restlessness and greed, the reason that he himself gives in his letter to Reuchlin for being generally disliked sounds plausible enough: He was suspect to the Jews because of his familiarity with their customs; and he was despised by the Christians for the very same reason. Did not the illustrious Reuchlin himself share somewhat the same fate with Boeschenstein? Some of Reuchlin's opponents betray exactly the same attitude.[43]

Boeschenstein *was not a baptized Jew;* this fact can be clearly established, since Jews were not permitted in the duchy of Swabia during his lifetime, except in "free [inde-

Boeschenstein had transcribed the cantillation in another manuscript, cf. Steinschneider, *op. cit.,* No. 401, k, p. 223.

[42] Cf. Zahn, *Melodien der deutschen evangelischen Kirchenlieder,* I, (Gütersloh. 1889-93), No. 1706, p. 455; also Julian, *Dictionary of Hymnology,* art. "Boeschenstein": "After taking Holy Orders as a priest" . . . (without documentation); the full history of his hymns in Philipp Wackernagel, *Das Deutsche Kirchenlied, von den ältesten Zeiten bis zum Anfang des 17. Jahrhunderts* (Leipzig, 1863-77), II, 109 f.

[43] Cf. the letter of the theological faculty of Cologne to Reuchlin in his conflict with Pfefferkorn, in *Reuchlins Briefwechsel,* No. CXXXIII (2 Jan-

pendent] cities." His birthplace, Esslingen, was not one of those privileged cities, at least not in his time. Reuchlin himself testifies to this fact.[44] On the other hand, there is no doubt that he tried to gain, repeatedly and stubbornly, material profit in his dealings with Jews. He was, as a scholar, almost generally respected, at least during his life. The only fellow-student who thought little of him was Seb. Münster.[45] But the latter's judgment seems to be considerably colored by envy and resentment. It is, moreover, undisputable that Boeschenstein had a number of important persons among his disciples.

He was, in all probability, originally a partisan of Luther, who, in a mild humor, termed him once "veteranus."[46] He took great pride in his status at the Imperial Court, which seems to have been that of a chorister at the emperor's chapel. His ability and interest in the musical field might have increased his personal prestige, although he lived in an intensely musical-minded era and milieu, when some of his most prominent contemporaries, such as Emperor Maximilian I, Martin Luther, and Pico had attained a musical skill far beyond that of an ordinary dilettant.

Boeschenstein must have had friends among the Jews of Regensburg; and it is quite conceivable that there he occasionally played the part of a faithful Jew. Had he been a convert, he certainly would not have written in Hebrew script, "A convert will suffer among Jews, since among Jews one does not become a convert."

Towards the end of his life Boeschenstein probably came to terms again with the Roman Church in some form of reconciliation, or he would not have translated the *Ave Maria* into Hebrew, to be published in Cologne.

In spite of all these rather strange and disturbing facts,

---

uary 1512); see also the *Defensio Joannis Reuchlin* (Tübingen, 1513), fol. H 4 a, b.

[44] See *supra*, note 3.

[45] In Münster's *Opus Grammaticum* (Basle, 1542), *Praefatio*.

[46] Cf. L. Geiger, *Das Studium der hebräischen Sprache*, p. 94, note 1.

his love for the Hebrew language was genuine and sincere. Together with Reuchlin and Seb. Münster, we have to recognize Boeschenstein, adventurer and vagabond that he was, as one of the foremost pioneers in the Hebrew language, customs and music among the turbulent Gentile world of the Renaissance and the Reformation.

MENDELSSOHN

New Light on the Family of
Felix Mendelssohn

Reprinted with permission of *Hebrew Union College Annual,* 26, 1955, pp. 543-565.

IT needs no telling that history often carries an admixture of myth and that the origin of such myths is often hard to trace. But in the case of the noted composer, Felix Mendelssohn Bartholdy, it is otherwise. The legend of a sweet tempered, happy Felix and of an ideally harmonious Mendelssohn family is a legend of known origin. Its source is none other than Felix Mendelssohn's nephew, Sebastian Hensel, author of *Die Familie Mendelssohn,* a widely read work. Nor is it difficult to espy the motives for this retouching, a retouching which often approximates distortion and misrepresentation.

In the preface to the first edition of *Die Familie Mendelssohn,* Hensel writes:

> . . . Soviel als moeglich habe ich die urspruengliche Form bewahrt, und in diesem Sinne, als Chronik einer guten deutschen Buergerfamilie, moechte ich das Buch betrachtet und gelesen wissen.
>
> Allerdings musste eine tief eingreifende Umarbeitung vorgenommen werden. Nicht dass irgend etwas zu verheimlichen gewesen waere: was ich fortgelassen habe, war entweder fuer das groessere Publikum nicht interessant genug, oder so Intimes und Heiliges, (wie zum Beispiel die Brautbriefe meiner Mutter . . .) dass ich es nicht veroeffentlichen wollte und durfte. . . . . Eine reiche Sammlung von Familienbriefen an Felix, welche eine Fuelle schoener und interessanter Mitteilungen enthaelt . . . . , war mir leider nicht gestattet zu verwerten; es ist so eine beklagenswerte Luecke entstanden.
>
> . . . ich glaubte zwar schon ziemlich streng in der Kritik des Aufzunehmenden und Wegzulassenden gewesen zu sein; indes auch hierin merkte ich bald, dass noch mehr geschehen muesse . . . auch die schon veroeffentlichten und von mir wieder aufzunehmenden Briefe von Felix wurden einer noch strengeren Sichtung unterworfen. . .

Though sympathizing with Hensel, we note that he mentions two types of omission: those of self-censorship and those pressed upon him by members of the family. We must recall that *Die Familie Mendelssohn* was published at a time when Wagner's virulent attacks on Felix Mendelssohn (*Das Judenthum in der Musik*) were being echoed by many a German writer and were receiving the endorsement of the German public. Hensel — to be fair to him — had reasons for omitting whatever might have raised any doubts as to a "typically good German bourgeois family."

Hensel's portrait rests upon a cautiously sifted collection of Felix Mendelssohn's letters. These letters had already been carefully edited by Carl, the son of Felix, and Paul, the brother of Felix (1861). Subsequent memoirs and biographies were adjusted to the stereotype which the 1861 and the 1879 editions of those letters had created. Exceptions were the correspondence with Carl Klingemann, Mendelssohn's most intimate friend (Essen 1909), Edward Devrient's *Reminiscenzen* (Leipzig 1869), and the *Memoiren* of A. B. Marx (Berlin 1865). These, however, tell us little about the inner life of the Mendelssohn family or about their religious and social perplexities. That dearth of first hand sources will explain why, down to the present day, no authentic biography of the composer has appeared. While there have been popular accounts of Felix Mendelssohn's life, writers intent upon a genuine grasp of the subject have found themselves thwarted by the inaccessibility of the original documents. An authoritative biography of Felix Mendelssohn came to be regarded as well nigh impossible.

Until members of the Mendelssohn family put the family papers at my disposal, no outsider had ever been thus favored. I am indebted to Prof. Felix Gilbert of Bryn Mawr College, to Prof. Joachim Wach of the University of Chicago, and to his sister, Mme. Susie Heigl Wach of Locarno, as well as to Miss Margaret Deneke of Oxford, England, for their gracious cooperation and the help without which neither this nor the coming studies could have been attempted.

From the five thousand letters and other sources examined, some surprising revelations ensued. The man as well as the artist, his family, and his work began to show features previously unsurmised or suppressed. Revision was indicated even for points of genealogy. That Felix Mendelssohn was the son of Abraham Mendelssohn and the grandson of Moses Mendelssohn is generally known. But never do we learn of his ancestors on the side of his mother. Leah Mendelssohn, *née* Salomon, was also the scion of a noted house. She was descended from Daniel Itzig, court-Jew of Frederick the Great. It will profit us to look into that strand of Felix Mendelssohn's lineage. An amazing sequence thereupon comes to light.

Daniel Itzig (1722–1799), the court Jew, and his wife Miriam *née* Wulff, had sixteen children — five sons and eleven daughters. The daughters, in accordance with custom, obtained husbands who were either learned Rabbis or wealthy financiers.

One of the daughters, Franziska (Fanny) married the Austrian banker, Baron Nathan von Arnstein. Felix Mendelssohn's favorite sister Fanny was named after this Franziska.

Another daughter of Daniel Itzig was Caecilie (Zipporah). Caecilie married Baron Eskeles, von Arnstein's business partner.

Yet another daughter of Daniel Itzig was Henriette. Henriette was married to Moses Mendelssohn's son, Nathan. Her sister, Bluemchen, married David Friedlander, Moses Mendelssohn's favorite disciple.

Still another daughter of Daniel Itzig was Babette (Bella) (1749–1824). Babette's husband was the court jeweler, Levi Salomon. Babette and Levi Salomon had a son, Jacob Salomon Bartholdy. They also had a daughter Leah. Leah became the wife of Moses Mendelssohn's second son, Abraham, and the mother of the great composer.

We present these relationships graphically:

Daniel Itzig — Miriam Wulff
　　　　|
　　　Franziska — Nathan Adam von Arnstein
　　　Caecilie — Baron Eskeles
　　　Henriette — Nathan Mendelssohn
　　　Bluemchen — David Friedlander

Sarah — Samuel Levy Chalfan
Babette — Levin Salomon
|

Jacob Salomon Bartholdy
    Leah Salomon — Abraham Mendelssohn
        |

    Felix Mendelssohn Bartholdy

We must avoid the supposition that either the Itzig Family or the Mendelssohn family acquired its distinction not until the eighteenth century. Both families were of noted descent. Both traced their ancestry to the renowned Rabbi Moses Isserles of Cracow (1520–1572), famed as philosopher and glossator. Both families had kinship with the families of Heine, Ephraim, Oppenheimer, Beer, Mayerbeer, the Counts Wimpffen and Fries, the Barons Pereira, Rothschild, and Pirquet. Abraham and Felix Mendelssohn mention Isserles in their correspondence.

All of Daniel Itzig's male grandchildren, upon their conversion to Christianity, assumed different names. Best known of these was the prominent jurist and criminologist, Julius Eduard Itzig, who, having altered his name to Hitzig, became the butt of ridicule by his distant kinsman, Heinrich Heine:

> ... Alsbald nahm ich
> Eine Droschke und ich rollte
> Zu dem Kriminalrat Hitzig,
> Welcher ehmahls Itzig hiess —
>
> Als er noch ein Itzig war,
> Traeumte ihm, er seh' geschrieben
> An dem Himmel seinen Namen
> Und davor den Buchstab H.
>
> "Was bedeutet dieses H?"
> Frug er sich — "etwa Herr Itzig
> Oder Heil'ger Itzig? Heil'ger
> Ist ein schoener Titel — aber
>
> In Berlin nicht passend" — Endlich
> Gruebelnsmued nannt' er sich Hitzig,
> Und nur die Getreuen wussten
> In dem Hitzig steckt ein Heil'ger.

This piece of deliberate insult hardly enhanced Heine's popularity with the Hitzig or with the Mendelssohn family, Julius

Eduard Hitzig being Leah Mendelssohn's cousin as well as Nathan Mendelssohn's nephew. A ludicrous spectacle indeed, one convert deriding another! Thirty years earlier, Leah Mendelssohn, then a young woman of twenty-two and still a Jewess, had penned the following comment on young Hitzig's conversion:

Berlin, 26. August 1799

. . . . Itzig hat seine Studien in Wittenberg beendet und ist seit einigen Wochen hier. Was werden Sie aber sagen, wenn ich Sie mit seinem Ueber-gang zur christlichen Religion bekannt mache? Luthers Geburtsort und die heilige Staette seiner Lehren hat auf ihn gewirkt, er konnte der Be-gierde, unter dem Bilde dieses grossen Mannes getauft und gleichsam dadurch von ihm beschuetzt zu werden, nicht widerstehen, und hat vermittelst dieses Schrittes zum Seelenheil dann nebenher den weltlichen Vorteil erlangt, naechstens in seinem Fache angestellt zu werden.

. . . ich zweifle beinahe, ob eine beschwerliche Amtsfuehrung in diesem Lande (Polen) ihm Beharrlichkeit und Geduld genug lassen wird, dem erwaehlten Stande treu zu bleiben. Wie sehr ich dies wuensche, kann ich Ihnen nicht beschreiben; die meisten Abtruennigen haben bisher durch schlechtes, oder doch inkonsequentes Betragen eine Art von Veraecht-lichkeit auf diesen Schritt geworfen, der auch die Besseren brandmarkt. Traete jemand auf, der durch untadelhaften Charakter, durch Ausdauer in seinen Vorsaetzen und Weltklugheit in seinem Benehmen (nach welcher die meisten Urteile ja, traurig genug, gefaellt werden) ein achtungswertes Muster darstellte, so wuerde ein grosser Teil dieser nur zu begruendeten Behauptung verschwinden. Erfreulich waers, wenn man dieser Heuchelei entbehren koennte; aber der Drang nach hoeherem Wirken, als dem eines Kaufmanns, oder tausend zarte Verhaeltnisse, in denen der nahe Umgang mit andern Religionsverwandten junge Gemueter verwickeln kann, lassen doch in der Tat keinen anderen Ausweg. . . .

Thus was the situation realistically analyzed by a young woman who, in the very same letter, waxes enthusiastic over the poems of Goethe and applauds Schiller for his "lofty ideals."

All of Daniel Itzig's daughters were good looking and gifted. From many accounts we know that music and literature were fostered in Daniel Itzig's home. Hennings, a contemporary, ap-prises us that, with the Itzigs, the music of Sebastian Bach and Philip Emanuel Bach had become a cult. This occurred fifty years before 1829 when the "St. Matthew's Passion" of Bach was revived through the memorable performance by Felix Mendelssohn Bartholdy. On the lists of those subscribing to the works of the Bach family, the names of at least four different Itzigs never fail to appear.

The most colorful and, by all means, the most gifted of the Itzig daughters was Zorel (Sarah) born in 1763 and, in 1783, married to Samuel ben Salomon Levy Chalfan ("money-changer"). Against the background of a Jewry which prayed for emancipation yet, despairing of emancipation, sought refuge in Christianity, Sarah Levy stands forth as a woman of character and accomplishment. Sarah had received an excellent French education; she was well versed in French literature. The ambassador of Napoleon was one of her frequent callers. She and her "evenings at home" have been described by various writers. The following is an excerpt:

> In her salon the old lady (she was then 80 years old) was sitting, the sweet spiritualized face framed by an old-fashioned lace cap. With her two companions she was reading 'The Midsummer Night's Dream' with distributed parts. Mendelssohn's composition of this drama enchanted all hearts at the time. (The author of this report, a young woman writer, obviously was not aware that Felix Mendelssohn was Sara's grand nephew).

> Her musical soirees were famous, although at that time no longer as popular as 50 years before, when she and her family championed the music of Sebastian and Philip Emanuel Bach.

> She was deeply grieved by the apostasy of some of her near relatives. 'I am like a tree without leaves (Hier steh ich, ein entlaubter Stamm, a quotation from Schiller), so many of my relatives are estranged to me by their conversion,' she wrote to her friend, the famous Protestant theologian Schleiermacher, who had done his level best to proselytize as many intelligent and attractive Jewesses as possible.

> She used to say, referring to the then general fashion of conversion: 'As the Jewish belief is, even according to Christian doctrine, the foundation upon which the whole structure of Christianity is erected, how can I be expected to break down the basement of my house in order to live in its first floor?'

Sarah Levy read the Bible regularly and with a scholar's understanding. While her distant cousin and close friend, Henrietta Herz, became a favorite proselyte of Schleiermacher, Sarah, in spite of her admiration for the theologian, remained true to Judaism. Among recipients of her charities was the Jewish

Orphan Asylum in Berlin to which she donated the sum of 90,000 Thalers, today the equivalent of $500,000.

This remarkable woman had, already in her youth, cultivated the music of the Bachs, particularly that of Phillip Emanuel Bach and Wilhelm Friedemann Bach. She was, in fact, Wilhelm Friedemann Bach's star pupil and generous patroness. After the death of Phillip Emanuel Bach, Sarah supported the widow. She even had a bust made of the master. Many years later this bust was placed in the concert hall of the royal *Schauspielhaus* in Berlin.

Sarah's deep interest in the music of the Bachs brought her the acquaintance of Karl Friedrich Zelter, conductor of the Berlin *Sing-Akademie*. Zelter became Felix Mendelssohn's teacher. It seems that Sarah had recommended him to Leah, her niece. Of Sarah Levy's musicianship, Zelter must have thought highly, for we find her, between 1806 and 1808, performing at the ultra-conservative *Sing-Akademie* as a soloist on the harpsichord. At the *Sing-Akademie* Sarah was, if not the first to perform as soloist, at least among the first. She remained always on excellent terms with that institution and donated to it her famed musical library.

The early correspondence of the Mendelssohn family contains frequent reference to Sarah Levy but, after the year 1822, mention of her fades. The proud old lady may have felt inclined to withdraw from her relatives after their conversions. It is recorded, nonetheless, that Fanny, the sister of Felix Mendelssohn, together with "Aunt Levy" and with President Steffens of the Berlin University, attended the performance of her brother's music to "Midsummer Night's Dream." On one occasion, Rebecca, the younger sister of Felix Mendelssohn, saw a resemblance between Aunt Levy and the grand-duchess of Medici, by reason of Aunt Levy's "Saturdays-at-home amid frescos, marble, and profundity of spirit." Sarah Levy survived most of her near relatives, including Felix. She died in 1854, childless, at the age of ninety-one.

A nephew of Sarah Levy was Jacob Levin Salomon, Leah Mendelssohn's brother. It was through Jacob Levin Salomon that the name Bartholdy came into this branch of the family. He had inherited from his grandfather, Daniel Itzig, a sumptuous mansion and garden which the family humorously named "Little Sans Souci" but which the Berlin populace called "Der Judengarten." Its first owner, more than a hundred years earlier, had been a Mayor Bartholdy of the suburb Neukoelln. When Jacob Levin Salomon, to the chagrin of his orthodox mother, decided to embrace Christianity, he substituted "Bartholdy" for the Jewish "Salomon." He went so far as to persuade his brother-in-law to append the name "Bartholdy" to the Jewish "Mendelssohn." Jacob Levin's letter of persuasion has been published. This letter, together with its hitherto unpublished preamble exhibits the *sauve-qui-peut* attitude which prevailed in that day among the Jewish upper classes:

> ... Ich bin keineswegs ueberzeugt von der Richtigkeit Deiner Argumente fuer Loyalitaet gegenueber Deinem Namen und Glauben. Du sagst, Du seiest es dem Andenken Deines Vaters schuldig — glaubst Du denn etwas Uebles getan zu haben, Deinen Kindern diejenige Religion zu geben, die Du fuer die bessere haeltst? Es ist geradezu eine Huldigung, die Du und wir alle den Bemuehungen Deines Vaters um die wahre Aufklaerung im allgemeinen zollen, und er haette wie Du fuer Deine Kinder, vielleicht wie ich fuer meine Person gehandelt. Man kann einer gedrueckten, verfolgten Religion treu bleiben; man kann sie seinen Kindern als eine Anwartschaft auf ein sich das Leben hindurch verlaengerndes Maertyrertum aufzwingen — solange man sie fuer die alleinseligmachende haelt. Aber sowie man dies nicht mehr glaubt, ist es eine Barbarei.— Ich wuerde raten, dass Du den Namen Mendelssohn Bartholdy zur Unterscheidung von den uebrigen Mendelssohns annimmst, was mir umso angenehmer sein wird, da es die Art ist, auch mein Andenken bei ihnen zu erhalten und worueber ich mich herzlich freue. . . .

This letter reflected the personality of its writer. Whether or not we commend its reasoning, we must recognize that the opportunism of this letter shows at least consideration for the writer's family. That the Jewish *intelligentsia* of that time, dazed by their craving for emancipation, lacked a historical understanding of Judaism, has been noted by students of that epoch. In that regard Jacob Bartholdy was no better than his contemporaries, despite his capability as a historian of the art of Greece and of the Renaissance. His study of Mycenae (1805) and the diligence, with which he collected the sculpture and the ceramics of the family Della Robbia, secured for him an honored place among nineteenth century archaeologists and art historians.

Notwithstanding these accomplishments, Bartholdy was despised by influential people of his acquaintance. Men of such divergent backgrounds as Baron Gentz, the confidant of Prince Metternich, and Von Niebuhr, the Prussian envoy to the Vatican, branded Bartholdy as a "demagogic rascal," charging that "by reason of his slyness, often bordering the unscrupulous," Bartholdy was "a veritable misfortune for Chancellor Hardenberg."

Cardinal Ercole Consalvi, who felt under obligation to Bartholdy, obtained for him the position of Prussian Consul General in Rome. It was the task of Bartholdy to report first-hand observations of the political crises and tensions which, at that time, pervaded the entire of Italy. Bartholdy discharged his duties with sagacity and courage. His book, *The Carbonaria*, dealing with the Neapolitan revolution, showed him, the opponent of all political conspiracy, to be a clear-sighted, almost prophetic statesman. Perhaps the best characterization of him is that contained in his obituary which appeared in the *Algemeine Deutsche Zeitung* in 1825:

> ... Bartholdy's Kopf war rein morgenlaendisch, die juedische Abkunft auf den ersten Blick unverkennbar.... Anstrengungen aller Art ertrug er leicht, aber die Ruhe nicht. Diese liebte er durch Spiel, zuweilen durch sehr hohes, zu unterbrechen. Sein Gedaechtnis war trefflich.... Sein Witz war schlagend, seine Antworten behend. Er fuehlte sich zu groesseren Verhaeltnissen berufen, als vielleicht seine Geburt, seine nicht einnehmende Gestalt, seine mehr ins Breite als Tiefe gehenden Studien zu gestatten schienen. Er musste nicht nur die alten Edelleute, sondern auch die alten Christen zwingen, ihn unter sich zu dulden, er musste sich beliebt, gefuerchtet, unentbehrlich machen, allen alles, bestaendig in aufsteigender Bewegung sein, um da geduldet zu werden, wo ein Andrer Platz nimmt, ohne besonders daran zu denken.

To us such words are painfully familiar. They give the gentile portrait of the Jewish self-made man and snob. Bartholdy was jeered at even by the daughter of Moses Mendelssohn, Henriette, who had gone over to Catholicism. Of Bartholdy, Henriette said: "He ought to become Pope! Bartholdy I or Leo X who deeply loved everything beautiful but never reckoned with the cost!"

Three sharply worded letters addressed to his brother-in-law, Abraham Mendelssohn, indicate the attempt of Bartholdy to keep his nephew, Felix, from becoming a professional musician. Naturally Felix resented these moves. We shall see how Felix, in reprisal, strove to lessen Bartholdy's name and influence.

At first glance it would seem that, with regard to Judaism as well as on other issues, Abraham Mendelssohn shared his brother-in-law's views. Such however, was far from being the case. One can hardly imagine two persons differing from one another more than these two men. Leah Mendelssohn writes to Felix, her son:

4. Juni 1830.

... Ich habe mir abermals ein Herz gefasst und deinem Vater cicero-nianisch ins Gewissen geredet ... es hat wenig geholfen. So verdirbt er sich und uns das schoene Leben und tut zu Hause wie ein von Gram ge-beugter und verzweifelter Mann. Gott, wie gluecklich koennte der Mann seyn und machen! Er aber, die Seele von einem Gatten und Vater, be-findet sich stets im Zweifel ueber irgendetwas, tief in seinem Herzen. Ich weiss nicht, was ihm diese Zweifel schafft. . . . .

In these words a wife describes her husband at a time when the fame of their son was rapidly expanding, when the husband's business was prospering, and when everything appeared to be at its best.

Like her brother, Bartholdy, Leah Mendelssohn aspired to receive into her salon all types of celebrities, all kinds of persons notable by birth or by repute. Her husband disliked such pre-tensions. He teased his wife about her "aristocratic inclinations." To himself he applied the words which have become famous: "Formerly I was the son of a father; now I am the father of a son." This apparently harmless quip was in reality tinged with bitterness. The name Mendelssohn imposed upon its bearer a burdensome responsibility. Abraham Mendelssohn felt this bur-den. He was also one of the very few Jewish persons who sensed the dilemma of the time.

To his wife and daughters, Judaism signified little. To them it was something decrepit and outworn, hardly worth mentioning, at most a theme for jokes. With Abraham it was otherwise. While he did not favor the Orthodox Jewish forms of observance, he never indulged in Jewish jests or in facetious turns of Yiddish phrase such as those with which his wife and daughters spice their letters.

In a letter on the hundredth anniversary of his father's birth Abraham expresses himself thus:

> 12. August 1829.
>
> Am 10. September wird meines Vaters 100 jaehriger Geburtstag eingesegnet, und die juedische Gemeinde will dazu ein Waisenhaus fondieren und ihm seinen Namen beilegen. Letzteres gefaellt mir wohl, und ich werde nach meinen Kraeften dazu beytragen. Aber ich werde mit jedem Tag ein abgesagterer Feind aller Feyerlichkeit und Form. Und so werde ich es auch vielleicht dem Zufall zu verdanken haben, dass eine Reise, welche ich in einiger Zeit vielleicht machen muss, auch diese ceremonie vertraegt. .

Abraham Mendelssohn hoped that his reverence for his father would form a pattern which his children would follow with respect to himself. Consciously and unconsciously he did all he could to imbue the minds of his children with a family saga in which their father and Moses Mendelssohn, their grandfather, would merge into an image of a "great father." He succeeded in his endeavor.

As to matters Jewish, Moses Mendelssohn had, in a unique way, contrived to bridge the gap between life and thought. But, with Abraham, that disparity created an insoluble conflict. Abraham regarded conversion as a sheer formality to which he had to submit because of the Christianity adopted by his children. In a well-known letter to his daughter Fanny upon her Protestant confirmation, Abraham wrote:

> Paris, Pfingsten 1820.
>
> ..... Die Form unter der es Dir Dein Religionslehrer gesagt, ist geschichtlich und wie alle Menschensatzungen veraenderlich. Vor einigen tausend Jahren war die juedische Form die herrschende, dann die heidnische, jetzt ist es die christliche. Wir, Deine Mutter und ich, sind von unsern Eltern im Judentum geboren und erzogen worden und haben, ohne diese Form veraendern zu muessen, dem Gott in uns und unserem Gewissen zu folgen gewusst. Wir haben Euch, Dich und Deine Geschwister, im Christentum erzogen, weil es die Glaubensform der meisten gesitteten Menschen ist und nichts enthaelt, was Euch von Guten ableitet, vielmehr manches, was Euch zur Liebe, zum Gehorsam, zur Duldung und zur Resignation hinweist, sei es auch nur das Beispiel des Urhebers, von so wenigen erkannt und noch wenigeren befolgt.

Years after Abraham Mendelssohn was baptized, in letters which he exchanged with another convert, Ignace Moscheles, pianist and composer and Felix's friend, there appear quotations from Talmud.

Abraham's approach to Judaism was entirely philosophical; it lacked all appreciation of history. Yet he spared neither his own feelings nor those of his son. Proud though he was of the name Mendelssohn, he demanded that, for the sake of consistency and integrity, Felix drop the name altogether. If the name Mendelssohn is famous in the world of music, it is due not to Abraham but to the insistence of Felix himself. We give, in its entirety, our English translation of Abraham's letter in this connection (here published for the first time):

Berlin July 8, 1829.

Dear Felix:-

Today's family sheet will run full without my contribution . . . I will therefore write you separately because I have to discuss with you a most serious matter.

The suspicion has come to me that you have suppressed or neglected or allowed others to suppress or neglect the name which I have taken as the name of our family, the name Bartholdy. In the concert programs you have sent me, likewise in newspaper articles, your name is given as Mendelssohn. I can account for this only on the supposition that you have been the cause.

Now, I am greatly dissatisfied about this. If you are to blame, you have committed a huge wrong.

After all, a name is only a name, neither more nor less. Still, so long as you are under your father's jurisdiction, you have the plain and indisputable duty to be called by your father's name. Moreover it is your ineffaceable, as well as reasonable, duty to take for granted that, whatever your father does, he does on valid grounds and with due deliberation.

On our journey to Paris after that neck-breaking night,[1] you asked me the reasons why our name was changed. I gave you those reasons at length. If you have forgotten them, you could have asked me about them again. If my reasons seemed unconvincing, you should have countered with better reasons. I prefer to believe the former, because I am unable to think of any reasons countervailing. I will here repeat my arguments and my views.

My grandfather was named Mendel Dessau. When my father, his son, went forth into the world and began to win notice and when he

[1] In the year 1825 when Felix was 16 years old.

undertook the project which can not be too highly praised, that noble project of lifting his brethren out of the vast degradation into which they had sunk, and to do this by disseminating among them a better education, my father felt that the name, Moses ben Mendel Dessau, would handicap him in gaining the needed access to those who had the better education at their disposal. Without any fear that his own father would take offense, my father assumed the name Mendelssohn.[2] The change, though a small one, was decisive. As Mendelssohn, he became irrevocably detached from an entire class, the best of whom he raised to his own level. By that name he identified himself with a different group. Through the influence which wisely and worthily he exerted by word and pen and deed,— an influence which, ever growing, persists to this day,— that name Mendelssohn acquired a Messianic import[3] and a significance which defies extinction. This, considering that you were reared a Christian, you can hardly understand. A Christian Mendelssohn is an impossibility. A Christian Mendelssohn the world would never recognize. Nor should there be a Christian Mendelssohn; for my father himself did not want to be a Christian. "Mendelssohn" does and always will stand for a Judaism in transition, when Judaism, just because it is seeking to transmute itself spiritually, clings to its ancient form all the more stubbornly and tenaciously, by way of protest against the novel form[4] that so arrogantly and tyrannically declared itself to be the one and only path to the good.

The viewpoint, to which my father and then my own generation committed me, imposes on me other duties toward you, my children, and puts other means of discharging them into my hands. I have learnt and will not, until my dying breath, forget that, while truth is one and eternal, its forms are many and transient. That is why, as long as it was permitted by the government under which we lived,[5] I reared you without religion in any form. I wanted you to profess whatever your convictions might favor or, if you prefer, whatever expediency might dictate. But it was not so to be. I was obligated to do the choosing for you.[6] Naturally, when you consider what scant value I placed on any form in particular, I felt no urge to choose the form known as Judaism, that most antiquated,

[2] Abraham Mendelssohn seems to have forgotten or not to have known that his father, to the end of his life, used a seal with the Hebrew inscription: "Moses, the Stranger (Ger) from Dessau."

[3] This alludes to the Hebrew Ben Menaḥem, an appellative for the Messiah.

[4] What Abraham Mendelssohn means by "die neue Form" is not clear. He may have had in mind Israel Jacobson's Reform movement which he happened to dislike.

[5] This refers to the time when the Mendelssohns were living in Hamburg under the French authorities of occupation.

[6] After the Prussian laws of emancipation of 1812. Abraham had by then returned to Berlin.

distorted, and self-defeating form of all. Therefore I reared you as Christians, Christianity being the more purified form and the one most accepted by the majority of civilized people. Eventually, I myself adopted Christianity, because I felt it my duty to do for myself that which I recognized as best for you. Even as my father found it necessary to adjust his name to conditions, filial devotion, as well as discretion, impelled me to adjust similarly.

Here I must reproach myself for a weakness, even if a pardonable one. I should have done decisively and thoroughly that which I deemed right. I should have discarded the name Mendelssohn completely. I should have adhered to the new name exclusively. I owed that to my father. My reason for not doing so was my long established habit of sparing those near to me and of forestalling perverted and venomous judgments. I did wrong. My purpose was merely to prepare for you a path of transition, making it easier for you that have no one to spare and nothing to care about. In Paris, when you, Felix, were about to step into the world and make a name for yourself, I deliberately had your cards engraved: Felix M. Bartholdy. You did not accept my way of thinking. Weakly enough I failed to persist. Now I only wish, though I neither expect nor deserve it, that my present intervention may not have arrived too late.

You can not, you must not carry the name Mendelssohn. Felix Mendelssohn Bartholdy is too long; it is unsuited for daily use. You must go by the name of Felix Bartholdy. A name is like a garment; it has to be appropriate for the time, the use, and the rank, if it is not to become a hindrance and a laughing-stock. Englishmen, otherwise a most formal lot, change their names frequently. Seldom is anyone renowned under the name conferred at baptism. And that is as it should be. I repeat: There can no more be a Christian Mendelssohn than there can be a Jewish Confucius. If Mendelssohn is your name, you are *ipso facto* a Jew. And this, if for no other reason than because it is contrary to fact, can be to you of no benefit.

Dear Felix, take this to heart and act accordingly.

Your Father and Friend.

This letter, while meticulously honest, was at the same time unrealistic. Its minimizing of "form," a philosophic notion borrowed from the philosophy of the enlightenment, was inapplicable to life's actualities.

Though I was unable to find the reply of Felix to this letter, the facts speak for themselves. In the four concerts conducted by Felix after that letter was sent, his name appears as Mendelssohn, in open contradiction to his father's wishes. Felix's entire outlook differed from that of Abraham. Felix actually toyed with the idea of dropping the name Bartholdy altogether. In this regard Felix was not alone. His sister Rebecca often signed her letters: Rebecca Mendelssohn *meden* Bartholdy — *meden*, Greek for "never."

Abraham was a tragic figure. Of unusual intelligence, fine education, and wide reading, he was the most gifted of Moses Mendelssohn's sons. But, as a radical rationalist and a Kantian, he failed to understand Judaism in its emotional and historical phases. While lacking the devoutness of his father or his son, he was capable of acute philosophical and critical speculation. He saw the problems of the present, but he saw them only in their contemporary bearings. He was obtuse to the import of the past and the possibilities of the future.

His sense of responsibility is obvious in every one of his longer missives. These divulge an austere consciousness of duty. When Felix jubilantly sent home a beautiful letter from the aged Goethe, the father replied sternly (June 13, 1830): "That letter from Goethe made me realize anew the onerous duty which it will be your life's task to fulfill."

That was by no means how Goethe's letter impressed Felix. But, as Felix matured, he came, more and more, to accept his father's ethical views, views which were deepened by Felix's own religious bent. A study of the relationship between that father and that son would yield some significant insights.

What was it that brought Abraham Mendelssohn to rear his children as Christians? Inasmuch as the above quoted letter of Jacob Bartholdy is undated, our best clue to the year of Abraham Mendelssohn's decision emerges from letters addressed by him to Fanny, his daughter.

Amsterdam, 5. April 1819.
.... Lass es vor allem die Wirkung haben, dass Du stets eifriger be-mueht seiest, der nie genug zu liebenden und zu ehrenden Mutter zu Gefallen zu leben, durch Gehorsam zur Liebe, durch Ordnung zur Frei-heit und Heiterkeit zu gelangen. Es ist die wuerdigste Art, dem Schoepfer zu danken und ihn zu ehren. Unser *aller* Schoepfer. Es gibt — die Religion sei wie sie wolle — nur *einen* Gott, nur *eine* Tugend, nur *eine* Wahrheit, nur *ein* Glueck.

The very same letter carries the first intimation that Fanny was being instructed by a Protestant pastor. Fanny was con-firmed on the Christian Pentecost of 1820. Deeply sceptical is

341

a letter which Abraham Mendelssohn wrote to Fanny on that occasion. From that letter we quoted above (p. 553). The following is another excerpt from the same:

> Ob Gott ist? Was Gott sey? Ob ein Teil unseres Selbst ewig sey, und, nachdem der andere Teil vergangen, fortlebe? und wo? und wie? — Alles das weiss ich nicht und habe Dich deswegen nie etwas darueber gelehrt. Allein ich weiss, dass es in mir, in Dir und in allen Menschen einen ewigen Hang zu allem Guten, Wahren und Rechten, und ein Gewissen gibt, welches uns mahnt und leitet, wenn wir uns davon entfernen. Ich weiss es, glaube daran, lebe in diesem Glauben, und er ist meine Religion.

From these letters it appears that, at least so far as his children were concerned, Abraham Mendelssohn had, as early as 1819, decided to abandon Judaism. What surprises us is that, as late as 1817, his letters bespeak an interest in the ideas of his wife's uncle, David Friedlander, Moses Mendelssohn's disciple. Abraham expressed the hope for what he called "the emancipation of the Jews *in toto* — something preferable to the emancipation of individuals." What caused Abraham Mendelssohn to change his mind? It may have been the "*Judensturm*," a minor pogrom in which some Jews underwent looting, hooting, and beating. The outbreak caused him to despair of collective emancipation and to hope instead for the emancipation of individuals through baptism. An additional reason, a personal one, may also have played a part. Felix, his son, the apple of his eye, had at the age of ten, during the *Judensturm*, suffered a shocking experience. A royal prince, meeting the boy on the street, had spat at Felix's feet and exclaimed "Hep, hep, Judenjung." The incident, generally unknown, is described in the *Denkwuerdigkeiten* of Varnhagen von Ense. That humiliation was too much for Abraham. In his philosophy, religions differed only as to form, and no form was of any great consequence. Why then should he expose his children to martyrdom for the sake of one of those forms?

His father's influence remained with Felix throughout life. Most of his father's ideas proved to Felix's advantage with, however, one important exception. The father's minimizing of form in religion did not appeal to the devout-minded son. Nor did the father's philosophy immunize the son against some bitter experiences typical of any intelligent convert who, during his formative years, while no longer rooted in Judaism, was not yet established in Christianity. These experiences brought Felix some unpleasant lessons. Thus he became approachable only to his relatives or to the small coterie which had frequented "his father's house" in Berlin. This reserve is puzzling. How it contrasts with the expansiveness of his personality in other respects! Especially baffling are the deviations. In England Felix went out of his way to win friends: and he succeeded in that aim. Why this double standard, one for England and one for the Continent? Why this reserve toward men, coupled with an attractiveness for women? This artist with keen eye, radiant mind, warm heart, and witty temperament, why did he restrict himself to the narrow circle of relatives and of friends acquired in youth?

Felix's penchant for exclusiveness was no secret. While his father warned against it, his mother sympathized and condoned. Felix's robust old teacher, Zelter, writing to his friend Goethe, offers this comment:

> 29. October bis 2. November 1830.
> .... Felix wird jetzt wahrscheinlich in Rom sein, worueber ich sehr froh bin, da seine Mutter immer gegen Italien gewesen ist. Ihn hier und im Lande in dem verderblichen Familiengetraetsch wie einen Gallert zusammenrinnen zu sehen, war meine Furcht, da ich ihn wirklich fuer den besten Spieler halte, weil er alles spielt und aller Arten maechtig ist.

The brother-in-law of Felix, Hensel, the painter, hinted at this in his caricature of "the wheel." Hensel depicted the entire Mendelssohn group as a wheel, the hub of which was Felix, making music like Arion. The spokes were the sisters and various family friends. The wheel was firmly closed. Sufficient unto itself, it excluded the rest of the world.

It would be correct perhaps to describe Felix as being on the defensive. During his youth and early manhood he underwent some upsetting experiences. These may have caused him to resemble the proverbial burnt child. We recall some of these:

Reared at the dawn of emancipation, in a family whose practices were still in some respects Jewish, he met, in the salons of his parents and their friends, Jews and non-Jews consorting as equals. After ten years of these idyllic conditions, he was rudely awakened by the insults of the prince at the time of the *"Juden-sturm."*

Another incident happened in 1824 when Felix was fifteen years old. The family was vacationing at Dobberan, then a much frequented resort on the Baltic. Felix and his beloved sister Fanny were insulted by rowdies who flung stones at them and who shouted "Jew-boy" and similar invectives. Felix bravely defended his sister, but collapsed afterward. The tutor of Felix, K. L. Heyse, father of the novelist Paul Heyse, tersely describes the occurence:

> August 1824
> Dobberan.
>
> ... Felix benahm sich wie ein Mann, aber nach unserer Rueckkehr war ausser Stande seine Wut und Indignation ueber die Demuetigung, die ihm widerfahren, zu unterdruecken. Am Abend brach sie in einem Strom von Traenen und wilden Beschuldigungen allgemeiner Art aus. . .

His tranquility was again shattered when, in 1832, his family prevailed upon him, against his own wishes, to become a candidate for the directorship of the Berlin *Sing-Akademie*. Old Zelter, who had just died, had expressly designated Felix, his star pupil, as his choice for his successor. Felix was already celebrated in most European cities as pianist, composer, and conductor. He and his family had been members of the *Sing-Akademie* for years. His great-aunt, Sarah Levy, and her brothers had been patrons of the society since its founding. Felix had made the *Sing-Akademie* famous by his memorable performance of Bach's "St. Matthew's Passion" rendered for the first time since the death of Bach in 1750. Despite all this, Felix was rebuffed. The *Sing-Akademie* refused to elect a "Jew-boy," no matter how able. It preferred the mediocrity, Herr Rungenhagen, to whose incumbency was largely due the stagnation of Berlin's musical life between 1830 and 1850.[7] The prominent musical critic, L. Rellstab, a friend of Felix, in words less of indignation than of regret, voices himself thus:

[7] "The cantatas (of Bach) still remained forgotten. . . It would have been otherwise if Mendelssohn, as he had hoped, had become Zelter's successor. . ." (Cf. A. Schweitzer, *J. S. Bach*, English edition, I, 246.)

16.

d. ... sehe d der ... ... und immer
... Mose, indem d Gott arbeitet ihm
...

~~striked out line~~

Ich bin der Herr dein Gott, der ich dich aus
Ägyptenland und dem Dienst[hause] geführt
habe. Du sollst keine andern Götter neben
mir haben. Du sollst dir kein Bildnis machen.
~~...~~ du sollst den Namen des
Herrn nicht missbrauchen. Gedenke des Sabbath-
tages, dass du ihn heiligest. Du sollst deinen
Vater u deine Mutter ehren. Du sollst nicht
tödten. Du sollst nicht ehebrechen. Du sollst
nicht stehlen. Du sollst kein falsch Zeugniss
reden. Lass dich nicht gelüsten!

                    Chr.

Dass ich dich liebe, mein Gott, lass mir deine
Gebote halten. Amen!

                    F. M. D 21 Aug
                              1825

Mose

ein Oratorium

... moege er (Mendelssohn) durch die vielfachen Unannehmlichkeiten, die er bey seinem warmen Eifer fuer das Gute und die Kunst erfahren musste, nicht so abgeschreckt sein, dass er die Lust zu einem erneuten Versuch verloren haette! Moegen ihn alle diese Widrigkeiten nur zu hoeherem Streben anspornen!

Notwithstanding many consolations, that setback blighted, for Felix, everything associated with Berlin, and fixed upon him an inclination to avoid new acquaintanceships.[7a]

Unlike his skeptical father, Felix was profoundly religious. His compositions — Psalms, motets, oratorios — attest to his devoutness. God meant something to Felix, as his letters amply demonstrate. His thinking was influenced by Schleiermacher whom he knew and admired. For Felix, his father's colorless philosophy hardly sufficed, a philosophy which almost anticipated the Ethical Culture of a century later. Like Schleiermacher, Felix would be "responsive to the Infinite." As with Schleiermacher, so with Felix, the personality of Jesus was of no prime importance. In the letters of Felix, the name of Jesus never occurs. Felix prefers such substitutes as "heaven," "the eternal," and the like. His religious sentiments embrace a sincere regard for Judaism on which Felix, unlike his father, held a positive stand. Was it mere coincidence that, in the year 1832, the year of his reverse, Felix wrote for his friend, A. B. Marx, the entire libretto of an oratorio "Moses"? Marx rejected the libretto, as is understandable, considering that Marx was an eager convert to Christianity, loath to identify himself with anything that had an Old Testament flavor and no tinges of Christology. To this day, the manuscript of the "Moses" has remained unknown to all except to members of the Mendelssohn family and to the present writer.[8] References by which Felix identifies himself with Judaism abound in his correspondence. We quote a few:

[7a] The unpublished letters of Doris, old Zelter's daughter, who all during her life had experienced only kindness and benevolence from the Mendelssohns, are replete with vicious and anti-Semitic remarks about Felix's immediate relatives.

[8] See, on the page opposite, the photograph of the first page and the last page of the libretto in Felix's own handwriting.

London, May 29, 1829.
... ich kann Euch auf solche Entfernung nicht alle kleinen Schritte,
Ruecksichten und Verhaeltnisse mittheilen... Aber wie Vater sagt: Wer
sich im Studium der Lehre *per se* recht vertiefe, zu dem kaeme alles:
Glueck, Erfolg, die Liebe seiner Mitmenschen und die seines Schoepfers
— und just das ist geschehen... Im Grunde sind Gott, Kunst und Leben
nur Eins.

Felix did not know that his father's remark was a literal quotation from a chapter commonly appended to the Jewish *Sayings
of the Fathers*. The passage reads: "Whosoever labors in the
Torah for its own sake merits many things;... He is called
friend, beloved, a lover of the All-present, a lover of mankind ...
and it gives him sovereignty and dominion and discerning judgment ... and it magnifies and exalts him above all things"
(Abot VI. 1). His sympathy for the Jewish people was infused
with religious ardor:

London, 23 July, 1833.
... Heut frueh haben sie die Juden emanzipiert, das macht mich stolz,
zumal da vor ein paar Tagen Eure lumpigen Posener Ordnungen hier
runtergemacht worden sind, nach Recht und Billigkeit.[9] Die Times fuehlte
sich vornehm und meinte, in England sey es doch besser (fuer uns) und
nachdem gestern eine Menge Judenhasser: Mr. Finn, Mr. Bruce, und der
Rohsche Inglis gesalbadert haben, schloss Robert Grant, der die bill ein-
bringt, indem er fragte, ob sie glaubten, dass sie da seyen, um die Pro-
phezeiungen zu erfuellen (denn darauf stuetzen sie sich) und sagte, er
hielte sich an das Wort "Glory to God, and good will to men", and darauf
waren ayes 187 und noes 52. Das ist ganz nobel und schoen und erfuellt
mich mit Dankbarkeit gegen den Himmel....

Correspondingly Felix did not mince words when repudiating
an ill-advised remark of his sister Rebecca. Rebecca had written
to him how a relative of Moses Mendelssohn, a certain observant
Jew, was, to Rebecca's displeasure, being introduced into the
best of Berlin society. Rebecca wrote:

23 ? 1829.
... Ich bitte Dich aber, lass salva venia H. Dessauer aus dem Spiele,
(Felix had asked about him) ueber den ist schon mehr Gerede gewesen als

---

[9] The edicts of Posen provided, as preliminary to the emancipation of the
Jews, the recognition of two different classes. The privileges of emancipation
were for the upper class only.

er es verdient, und Gott sey Dank, er ist abgeschoben worden; aber nicht, ohne seine Schwester praesentiert zu haben. Ich bin kein Juden-feind, es geht mir aber ueber den Spass. . .

Felix replied:

London, 17 July 1829

Du, l. Beckchen, musst Rueffel besehen. Was meinst Du damit, dass Du schreibst, Du seiest keine Judenfeindin? Ich nehme an das sey nur ein Scherz; denn sonst wuerde ich ganz andere Saiten aufziehen. Es ist wirk-lich sehr liebenswuerdig von Dir, dass Du nicht Deine gesamte Familie verachtest, nicht wahr? Ich erwarte von Dir uebrigens eine volle Erklae-rung der Affaire Dessauer im naechsten Brief. . .

And yet, diligently though he strove to be in accord with himself and his fellowmen, Felix did not succeed. He was keenly aware of the conflict between his ancestral Judaism and the German culture in which he was steeped. In addition to this, he confronted a dilemma which lurked at the very core of his being, a dilemma involving his music. He was neither a true romanticist nor a pure classicist. Many musicologists have tried to circumvent the difficulty by calling Mendelssohn a "romantic classicist" (Alfred Einstein) or "a composer with a strong streak of romanticism but with also much that is akin to the eighteenth century" (Philip Radcliffe.)

Being a man of keen intelligence and good education, Felix Mendelssohn understood his predicament. He often expressed impatience with his "cataloguers" and "categorizers," but in vain. The issue was, after all, a vital one. He was attacked by the conservatives for his romanticism and by the romanticists for his reactionism. To those criticisms he paid scant attention, since men for whose judgment he cared, men like Schumann, Hiller, Chopin, Cherubini, and Berlioz acknowledged him for what he was. With all of these, Felix Mendelssohn, though some-what reserved, was on excellent terms.

Felix Mendelssohn did not possess what today would be called peace of mind. He did not even deem it desirable. In all events, the notion of a pleasant, harmonious, angelically patient Mendelssohn is a legend. This tradition must be supplanted by the truth, which is less blithe in the victorian sense. Felix Mendelssohn was autocratic, irascible, hyper-sensitive, proud, and dignified. He was possessed of an eternal restlessness, probably the result of his stern parental upbringing which permitted him as a child never a half-hour of idleness or relaxation. For this persisting discontent, there were also deeper reasons, psychological reasons, but into these we will not here enter.

Felix Mendelssohn was, at the same time, a person of self-effacing generosity, of intriguing charm, of warm feeling, of perfect integrity, and of large magnanimity. No artist was ever less vain. His letters betray never a trace of smugness, egotism, or conceit. On the contrary, letters to his kinfolk and intimate friends abound in self-dissatisfaction and in antipathy to recognition or praise. His mother's snobbishness did not reappear in him. He was a true aristocrat.

The University of Leipzig conferred on him the honorary doctorate, a distinction much higher than that implied by the same degree in the United States. But he never availed himself of that title. The king of Prussia appointed him *Generalmusik-direktor*, but he joked about that appellative. He was decorated with the highest civilian order *"Pour le Mérite"* which vested him with the title *"Excellenz."* Yet, of this, he never made use. Once he called it *"Piepmatz,"* (peekaboo birdie), in banter about the insignium worn beneath the collar.

For all that, Wagner, who hated Mendelssohn, regarded him as a snob. Wagner may have been partly right, but right in a sense beyond Wagner's own comprehension. Felix Mendelssohn was an aristocrat in every fiber. He knew his origin. He was conscious "of the stable where he was bred." Always assured of a livelihood, he depended upon no galleries for applause. Success pursued him; he did not pursue success, at least not for its own sake. To Richard Wagner, a worshiper of success, such an attitude was as incomprehensible as the *"noli me tangere"* manner of one who, like Mendelssohn, could not be brought to his knees by any slinging of mud.

None but an aristocrat could respond as Felix Mendelssohn responded when his teacher, Zelter, granted him and his friend Devrient permission to render the first performance of Bach's "St. Matthew's Passion" since 1750. In bitter pride, Felix Mendelssohn exclaimed: "To think that it took a comedian and a Jew-boy to create anew the greatest of Christian music!" That sardonic retort, of which *"spernere sperni,"* "the spurner spurned," is the feudal counterpart, sums up young Mendelssohn and his conflicts. To retrieve his true contours, many layers of legend, of Victorian priggishness, and of false tradition have to be chipped away.

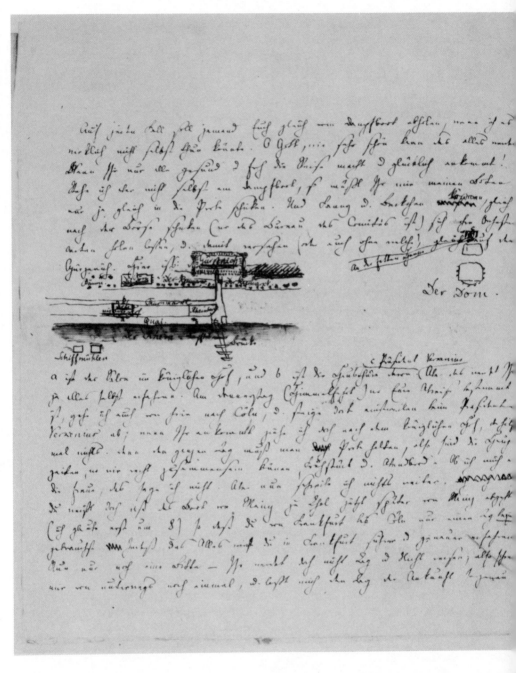

Sketch of Cologne, in a letter from Mendelssohn to his father; Dusseldorf, May 23, 1835 (somewhat reduced)

The Family Letters of
Felix Mendelssohn Bartholdy

Reprinted with permission of *Bulletin of the New York Public Library*, 65, 1960, pp. 5-20.

IN MUSICAL history we encounter a series of first-rate letter writers, beginning with Mozart, continuing through the nineteenth century (Hector Berlioz, Robert Schumann, Felix Mendelssohn, Franz Liszt, Richard Wagner) and into our own times (Gustav Mahler, Richard Strauss, Arnold Schoenberg, and others). The letters of most of these composers deal, however, almost solely with their personal activities and problems. Only two wrote letters that transcend narrow personal interests: Mozart and Mendelssohn. The family letters of these great musicians describe not only their intimate thoughts and the events of their careers but contain an abundance of more or less objective observations and critical judgments, expressed in continuous, lively dialogue with the recipients, and reflecting widely the customs, ideas, prejudices of the whole age in which they flourished. Not that the two men's letters are at all similar. Whereas Mozart writes a German strongly flavored by his native Salzburg patois, Mendelssohn's epistolary diction is, much of the time, impeccable and almost consciously literary. Yet though his style is finely wrought, it loses no iota of liveliness whether he is describing a landscape, an organ, a city, a festivity, a comic incident, or a visit with Goethe. Later we shall sample a few of these artistic passages.

In view of the recent purchase of the collected family letters of Mendelssohn by The New York Public Library, it may be interesting to sketch the rather adventurous history of the collection.

During his short life of thirty-eight years Mendelssohn wrote, to various persons, well over three thousand letters, most consisting of more than two closely penned pages. The family letters alone number about seven hundred lengthy items; they begin in his twelfth year and end ten days before his death on November 4, 1847. Nearly all are written in the same meticulous hand that characterizes his musical writing and his many fine drawings and paintings. Sir George Grove, in the fourth edition of Grove's *Dictionary of Music*, justly compared Mendelssohn's letters with his paintings: "For these letters are no hurried productions, but are distinguished, like the drawings, for the neatness and finish which pervade them. An autograph letter of Mendelssohn is a work of art."

[5]

Most — not all — of the family letters were collected after the composer's death by his brother Paul, chiefly from his sisters and the estate of his parents. Paul bequeathed the collection to his son Ernst von Mendelssohn Bartholdy, who in turn left it to his children. After the death of his son Paul III, the letters were left in trust of his oldest sister and deposited in a vault of the Dresdener Bank, together with other papers. The incendiary bombardment of Dresden in the spring of 1945 totally destroyed the bank building, but the vaults remained intact. The letters, bound in five volumes, were found, turned over to the attorney of the trustee, and eventually entrusted to a great granddaughter of the composer, living in Switzerland. They have now come to rest in New York.

Most music lovers are acquainted with some Mendelssohn letters, either from anthologies or from collected volumes of his correspondence. Yet in all published editions the printed texts differ from the actual letters to a larger or lesser degree — to use diplomatic language. If we avail ourselves of plain speech, we must confess that the editors of the printed editions (all near relatives of the composer) have not hesitated to alter the language, to suppress names and incidents, to misrepresent, and even to omit entire sentences and insert inauthentic ones. Their reasons are understandable enough. At the time of the first edition of letters, 1861, most of Mendelssohn's contemporaries were still alive, and it seemed mandatory to omit most passages containing their names. Richard Wagner meanwhile had published his notorious pamphlet *Judaism in Music*, attacking the master he had formerly admired as one who had corrupted the style and spirit of German music. According to Wagner, Mendelssohn had, by his shallowness and alienation from the ideals of the German nation, betrayed the immortal patrimony of Beethoven and, in preferring elegance and inanity to Profundity, done irreparable damage to the image of Beethoven and his sole worthy successor — to wit, Wagner himself. Intimidated by this attack, the editors of Mendelssohn's family letters carefully omitted all allusions which might remind the reader of his aristocratic Jewish ancestors.

In the preface of a popular Mendelssohn anthology, Sebastian Hensel's *The Mendelssohn Family*, this principle is plainly and naively stated: "This book ought to be read as the chronicle of a good German citizen's family." Yet there were certain obstacles to be overcome. The celebrated Jewish theologian and philosopher Moses Mendelssohn, grandfather of the composer, hardly represented the image of the "good German citizen." But the editors did what they could to camouflage all indications of the ancestral faith.

Other considerations also influenced the editors. The mid-Victorians saw in Mendelssohn the paragon and embodiment of their moral and social virtues. To protect this "copy-book saint" image, every flaw in the letters had to be removed, especially the frequently naughty remarks of their writer — who was, after all, a lively and lusty young anti-Philistine. Nor can the editors be blamed for omitting references to little domestic disagreements, such as those between Mendelssohn's wife and his sisters — for his wife, a very beautiful and very shy and reserved daughter of a Hugenot pastor of Frankfort, was not always in harmony with her sisters-in-law. But to the latter sort of lacunae no tactful and judicious person is likely to take exception unless he takes a special interest in Mendelssohn's *Familiengeschichte*.

These various suppressions and distortions were first noted by Sir George Grove, and quite explicitly deplored by Miss Selden-Goth, editor of the most recent English edition of the letters.[1] However, in her preface, writing with penetration but not always with full information, Miss Selden-Goth treats certain omissions as if they were Mendelssohn's own and remarks on the absence of love-letters, letters to his wife, and his apparent indifference to Jewish problems as well as to "the spiritual problems of his era."

As for love letters, indeed, none written *by* Mendelssohn have come down to us; for even Cécile, his wife, burned all the letters that had been exchanged between them. She felt quite strongly about their being "too sacred" for publication. Other ladies may have felt likewise. Yet to assume he had no amourous adventures before his marriage would be quite unwarranted. For there are still extant several love letters addressed *to him*. And we know well that, even as a married man, he liked flirtation. In fact we know the names of some of the ladies in question.

That he was anything but indifferent to matters of European Jewry I have demonstrated elsewhere.[2] As for his interest in "the spiritual problems of his era," it may be seen in his correspondence with the celebrated historian and politician Gustav Droysen and in some of his letters to Klingemann and Devrient, especially after 1840.

In a comment on the minister Eichhorn, Miss Selden-Goth misses the point entirely. She believes that " . . . the reactionary activities of his staunchest protector at the Prussian court, Minister von Eichhorn, [did not engross] Mendelssohn's attention." Nothing could be further from the truth. Far from liking Eichhorn, Mendelssohn detested the man and his policy, in unmistakable terms. Nor was Eichhorn his protector at the Prussian court; this

---

[1] *Felix Mendelssohn's Letters*, ed G. Selden-Goth (New York 1945).

[2] The full scope of these interests will be shown in my forthcoming biography of Mendelssohn.

role fell to two men of much greater stature, Baron G. J. von Bunsen and his friend Wilhelm von Humboldt. Whenever Mendelssohn mentions Eichhorn, he adds a derogatory epithet to his name. But Miss Selden-Goth, not having seen the original letters, could not be aware of the extent of the censorship practised by the editors of the first edition — from which all subsequent editions have derived.

Only now, with the manuscript letters available, is it possible to make comparisions and see how many interesting passages — and indeed whole letters — have been omitted from the printed editions. First, here are two examples of letters that have been altered beyond recognition, by the omission of passages here given in angle brackets ⟨ ⟩.

March 30, 1840:

> Die Philister, denen es am meisten um die theuren Preise und darum zu thun ist, dass es einem tuechtigen Kerl nicht gar zu wohl in seiner Haut werden moechte, und deshalb raisonnieren — die koennen mir gar gestohlen werden! — ⟨Und Liszt, der sich einen albernen Geschaeftsfuehrer mit auf Reisen nimmt — aber nun auf der anderen Seite das Zeitungsschreiben!⟩

> The philistines, who are grumbling because of the expensive tickets and who never like to see an able fellow feel well in his own skin — let them go to the dickens! — ⟨And Liszt, too, who takes with him on all journeys a fool of a business manager — and the journalists to boot.⟩

March 31, 1835:

> Anders als in Berlin, wo sie wohl die Lust haben Haendel abzuaendern oder gar zu verbessern, aber nicht einmal das koennen sie ordentlich. . . . ⟨Aber fuer uns . . . ist es gar keine Wonne, solch einem Ruepel zu sehen . . . es sind die Oboen in fis-moll in der Tiefe zum Ausfuellen zugefuegt, vor denen jedes Oboenherz schaudern muss; und eine armselige Bassposaune! die klingt wie ein alter Kamm; dann wollen sie G. F. Haendel instrumentieren und wuerden vor Angst unter den Tisch kriechen, wenn der dicke Herr noch lebte . . .⟩

> As far as Berlin [the Singakademie] is concerned, they'd like to alter and even improve upon Handel, but they aren't able to manage that. ⟨As for me, it is no pleasure for me to see such a boor [as Rungenhagen, director of the Singakademie] or to hear him — he has added low oboes in f sharp minor to pad the score — every oboist's heart will shudder! and *one* feeble bass trombone! It sounds like an old comb; such a gang of nitwits would reorchestrate G. F. Handel! They would creep under the next table in terror, if that stout gentleman were still alive.⟩

Rungenhagen was the man whom the members of the Singakademie in Berlin had preferred to Mendelssohn, when both had aspired to the directorate in succession to Zelter. Rungenhagen was a mediocrity, to be sure, but Mendelssohn felt less bitter about his ineptness than about his presumption in rearranging Handel. The omitted passage is obviously the most interesting part of the whole letter.

We fare even worse when entire letters are suppressed. From several that are strongly critical of leading musicians of the time, here are a few selections. First some passages from an unpublished letter of April 6, 1825, from Paris:

About Rossini:

> Der hat ein verzwicktes Gesicht, eine Mischung von Schelmerey, Fadaise und Ueberdruss . . . da habt ihr den grossen Maestro Windbeutel! Der setzte sich an's Clavier und accompagnirte das Ave Verum von Mozart. . . . Da wollte er, als gelahrter Componist alle Dissonanzen vorhalten, und so praeparirte er denn die Terz, die Quinte, die Octave, zu Nutz und Frommen aller zuhoerenden, oder vielmehr nicht zuhoerenden, Damen.

> He has a pinched up face, a mixture of roguery, boredom, and weariness . . . there is your great maestro humbug! He sat down at the piano and accompanied Mozart's *Ave verum*. . . . But he wanted to show off his profound musical erudition and made suspensions before every dissonance, thus "preparing" the third, the fifth, the octave, to the great admiration of all listening, or rather not listening, ladies.

About Meyerbeer:

> Meyerbeer sprach lehrreich ueber die Natur des F-Horns; die Tage der Welt vergess' ichs nieht . . . Ich fiel vor Lachen beinahe von der Bank.

> Meyerbeer expounded the nature of the French horn in F; I shall never in my life forget it . . . I almost fell from the bench from laughter.

About Liszt:

> Nun spielte Liszt . . . er hat viel Finger, aber wenig Kopf, die Improvisation war erbaermlich und flach, lauter Tonleitern und Triller.

> Liszt played a lot of music . . . he has many fingers, little brains. His improvisation was miserable and shallow, nothing but scales and trills.

Thus wrote the fresh boy of sixteen, from Paris. He is even more interesting when he discusses seriously the notables of his maturer years, or questions concerning the lot of the Jews.

London, July 23, 1833:

> Heut frueh haben sie die Juden emancipiert, das amuesirt mich praechtig, zumal da vor ein paar Tagen Eure lumpigen Posener Ordnungen hier runtergemacht worden sind, nach Recht und Billigkeit; die Times fuehlte sich vornehm, und meinte, in England sey es doch besser, und nachdem gestern eine Menge Judenhasser: Mr. Finn und Mr. Bruce, und der Rohsche [2a] Inglis gesalbadert hatten, schloss Robert Grant, der die Bill einbringt, indem er fragte, ob sie glaubten, dass sie da seien, um die Prophezeiungen zu erfuellen . . . und sagte er hielte sich an das Wort "Glory to God, and good will to men" . . . und darauf waren ayes 187, und noes 52. Das ist ganz nobel und schoen . . . ünd erfuellt mich mit Dankbarkeit gegen den Himmel . . .

> This morning they have emancipated the Jews [in Parliament]. This pleases me mightily, the more so as, a few days ago, your wretched Posen statutes were torn to pieces in the English newspapers, just as they deserve.[3] The *Times*, being noble, observed that our lot here in England is certainly better. Yesterday a number of Jew-baiters, Mr Finn and Mr Bruce and the villain Inglis, twaddled unctuously; then Mr Robert Grant, the sponsor of the bill, concluded with the question, whether they believed they existed in order "to fulfill the prophecies of Scripture" . . . and stated that he himself followed the word "Glory to God and good will to men" . . . and thereupon followed ayes 187 and noes 52. This is quite noble . . . and fills me with gratitude to Heaven. . . .

Düsseldorf, November 28, 1833:

> Was ich zu schaffen suche, das sind Fortschritte . . . und die bestehen da [in Berlin] nicht reichlich . . . und ich habe fuer diese Erdenzeit mit der Berliner Singakademie nichts gemein, und da sie im Himmel nicht besteht, ueberhaupt nichts. . . . In den letzten Tagen hab' ich die Partitur der Hebriden zum Druck fertiggemacht. Die Ouverture ist viel besser geworden durch dreimalige Verbesserungen . . .

> What I try to achieve is advancement in music . . . and Berlin does not offer much potential for such an aim . . . upon earth I have nothing in common with the Berlin Singakademie, and, as it does not exist in the Heavens, nothing at all. . . . During the last few days I have finished the score of the *Hebrides* for the printer. Now the overture is much better than before, after three revisions. . . .

2a Hebrew, *villain*.

3 The edicts of Posen provided, as preliminary to the emancipation of the Jews, the recognition of two different classes. The privileges would be for the upper class only.

Düsseldorf, May 28, 1834:

> Beim Musikfest sah ich Fetis; er kam mit ausgestreckter Hand auf mich zu; jetzt gab ich ihm dafuer cut dead, nickte nur mit dem Kopf und drehte mich um. Er mag nun auf mich herziehen, ich liebe in solchen Dingen Aufrichtigkeit und suche durch mein Betragen moeglichst kund zu geben, was ich empfinde, naemlich in diesem Falle: 'Lassen Sie sich haengen'.

> At the festival [in Cologne] I saw [F. J.] Fétis.[4] He approached me with outstretched arms, but I replied to this gesture with a cold "cut dead," nodded slightly and turned about. Let him curse me and criticize me; in such matters I like blunt sincerity and wish to let my behavior show my sentiments, in this case: Let him go hang himself.

Düsseldorf, January 2, 1835:

> . . . Ein Philosoph bin ich aber ebensowenig wie du, und wenn du mich so nennst und "uns nicht verstehst," so beklege ich dich beim Friedensrichter Jungblut; Potz tausend, ich und ein Philosoph. Oder nur ein Aesthetiker — ich kriege immer mehr grimm auf diese Kerls. . . .

> . . . A philosopher, however, I am just as little as you, and if you call me one and imply you "do not understand us," I shall bring a lawsuit against you to Justice of the Peace Jungblut. What the devil, and me a philosopher? Or even an aesthetician — I am getting more and more indignant over these churls. . . .

Düsseldorf, March 28, 1835:

> Von Bettina habe ich die Vorrede gelesen, und fuer alle Ewigkeit genug an diesem gespreizten, unwahren Wesen. . . .

> I just read the preface of Bettina's book [Brentano's *Goethe's Brief-wechsel mit einem Kinde*] and I have enough of it for all eternity — of this stilted, affected air. . . .

Düsseldorf, January 3, 1835:

> Diejenigen, die schwoeren, es sei ueberhaupt vorbei, die haben wohl Recht, dass es fuer sie keine Kunst mehr gibt, aber dann sollen sie mir auch nicht weis machen, dass ihnen die Vergangenheit viel Plaisir macht

---

[4] The hostility between Fétis and Mendelssohn lasted from 1829 to 1842, when Fétis recognized him as the most celebrated living composer. Both men had lost all sense of proportion in their quarrel.

und sollen es andern nicht trueben mit ihrer Leichenbitteraesthetik; eine hoechst trockne Rasse. Eigentlich aber koennen mir doch alle Aesthetiker, Recensenten, und wie sie heissen moegen, gestohlen werden, sie sind zu faul und leben von anderer Glueck. . . .

Gestern haben sie mir von Leipzig aus eine Professorstelle an der Universitaet angeboten, die meinetwegen creiert werden solle, ich habe sie aber ausgeschlagen. Collegia ueber Musik lesen kann ich nicht, und hinge auch mein ganzes Glueck davon ab.

Those who always lament that it [the era of true art] has passed for good, may be right in believing that there is no art left *for them*. But they shall not make me believe that the art of the past has truly given them pleasure; at any rate, they shall not spoil it for others by their funereal aesthetics. This is a sad and dry race. As a matter of fact, all these aestheticians, critics, and whatever they may call themselves, can go hang themselves. They are too lazy and live upon the fortune of others. . . .

Yesterday Leipzig University offered me a professorship, which is to be created especially for me; but I have declined it. I could not give lectures on music, even if my sole happiness were to depend upon it.

During a short life Mendelssohn came into contact with nearly every important contemporary, from kings and queens to such revolutionaries as Saint-Simon and Herwegh. His correspondence with the musicians of his age is prodigious in extent and in content. To name only the most famous names, there are Hector Berlioz, Robert Schumann, Richard Wagner, Louis Spohr, J. F. Fétis, Ferdinand Hiller, Frederic Chopin, Franz Liszt, Gioacchino Rossini, Giacomo Meyerbeer, Luigi Cherubini, Sterndale Bennett, Heinrich Marschner, the young Joseph Joachim (Mendelssohn was his guardian angel), Jenny Lind, Moritz Hauptmann — and many more.

When we compare his letters to his family with those to his friends we notice that the changing relationship between the composer and his contemporaries — and the world at large — is more clearly reflected in the letters to his friends. The intimate friends who witnessed Mendelssohn's not generally known change from an optimistic reformer and radical to a world-weary, world-famous, and world-frightened conservative were Carl Klingemann, secretary of the Hanover legation in London, Ignace Moscheles, famous pianist and former disciple of Beethoven, Gustav Droysen, whom we noticed above, and Eduard Devrient, a celebrated actor.

The family letters incline — especially in Mendelssohn's younger years — to smart banter, gossip, and occasional outbursts of the volatile temper of a highly sensitive and irascible personality. Their tenor is determinedly and consistently optimistic; they are filled to the brim with events, personalities, opinions; their language appears easygoing and nonchalant: yet surviving drafts of some of these "casual" letters show that their impression of artlessness is deceptive. Conversely, in the letters to his friends, Mendelssohn, always warm-hearted and sincere but considerably more reserved, hardly stoops to gossip or small talk. These letters reveal more of the thinking, worrying, and suffering Mendelssohn.

What are the qualities most characteristic of Mendelssohn's letters? Their artistry, as prose, is equaled among the letters of composers only by those of his friend Berlioz. Yet their lasting appeal is probably most due to Mendelssohn's ability to describe the world he saw with such vividness that the reader 120 years later feels an active participation. A few examples may illustrate the point.

From a letter to his family written in Rome June 6, 1831:

> Um als grosse Stadt eigenthuemlich zu sein, dafuer erscheint mir Neapel zu klein. . . . Die Idee des Mittelpunktes fuer ein grosses Volk, die London so wunderbar schoen macht, giebt mir Neapel nicht, und zwar, weil eben das Volk fehlt; denn die Fischer und Lazzaroni kann ich kein Volk nennen. Sie sind mehr wie Wilde, und ihr Mittelpunkt ist nicht Neapel, sondern das Meer. Die Mittelklassen, die gewerbetreibenden, arbeitenden Buerger, die in den andern grossen Staedten die Grundlage bilden, sind hier ganz untergeodnet; man moechte sagen, es fehlt ganz daran. Das ist es, was mir eigentlich den Aufenthalt in Neapel selbst oft verdriesslich gemacht hat. . . .
>
> Das Klima ist fuer einen grossen Herrn eingerichtet, der spaet aufsteht, nie zu Fuss zu gehen braucht, nichts denkt, (weil das erhitzt), nachmittags seine paar Stunden auf dem Sopha schlaeft, dann sein Eis isst und nachts ins Theater faehrt, wo er wieder nichts zu denken findet, sondern da Besuche machen und empfangen kann. Auf der andern Seite ist das Klima wieder ebenso passend fuer einen Kerl im Hemde mit nackton Beinen und Armen, der sich ebenfalls nicht zu bewegen braucht, — sich ein paar Gran erbettelt, wenn er einmal nichts zu leben hat, — nachmittags sein Schlaefchen macht auf der Erde, am Hafen, oder auf dem Steinpflaster. . . . , der dann sich seine *frutta di mare* etwa selbst aus dem Meere heraufholt, dann da schlaeft, wo er abends zuletzt hinkommt, -kurz, der in jedem Augenblick das thut, was ihm gerade gemuethlich ist, wie ein Thier. Das sind denn nun auch die beiden Hauptklassen in Neapel. Bei weitem der groesste Theil der Bevoelkerung des Toledo [5] besteht

5 Toledo Street, now Via·Roma.

aus zierlich geputzten Herren und Damen oder schoenen Carossen, in denen sich Mann und Frau einander spazieren fahren, oder aus diesen braunen *Sans-culottes*, die 'mal Fische zum Verkauf tragen und graesslich dazu bruellen oder Last tragen, wenn es an Gelde fehlt. . . .

Naples is too small, in my opinion, to give the proper impression of a great city. . . . The idea of the capital of a great people, which London so wonderfully well fulfills, is not conveyed to me by Naples at all, chiefly because it actually lacks a people. For I can't consider the fishermen and *lazzaroni* as constituting a people. They are more like savages, and their true capital is not Naples but the sea. The middle classes, the tradesmen and working citizens, who constitute the basic populace of other great towns, are quite subordinate and one might say virtually nonexistent here. It is this circumstance, I believe, which has often spoiled my stay in Naples. . . .

The climate is suitable for a great lord who rises late, never has to go out on foot, never thinks (for this makes one hot), sleeps a couple of hours on a sofa in the afternoon, then eats his sherbet and drives to the theatre at night, where he again finds nothing to think about, but simply makes and receives visits. On the other hand this climate is also suitable for a fellow in a shirt, with naked legs and arms, who likewise has no reason to move about; who begs for a couple of grans when he has nothing more to live on and who takes his afternoon siesta lying on the ground, or on the quay, or on the street pavement. . . . He fetches his *frutti di mare* himself out of the sea, and sleeps wherever he may happen to be at night; in short, who does every moment what he likes best, just like an animal. These are the two principal classes in Naples. By far the largest part of the population of the Toledo consists of dolled-up ladies and gentlemen, or elegant carriages in which husbands and wives drive together, or of those tawny sans-culottes who sometimes peddle fish, yelling hideously, or carry burdens when they are penniless.

From a letter to K. F. Zelter written in London July 20, 1829 (unpublished):

. . . es ist mir ein Beduerfnis, auszusprechen, dass ich Ihnen das alles groesstenteils verdanke, und Ihnen zu sagen, wie ich das weiss und anerkenne. Am liebsten hielte ich wohl solchen Dank zurueck, denn man sollte lieber verschweigen, was man doch nicht recht vollkommen und erschoepfend ausdruecken kann; aber es draengt sich mir so bei Vielem, an das ich mich erinnere, gerade heut der Gedanke auf, Ihnen und Ihnen allein es schuldig zu sein, dass ich heut nicht verschweigen kann . . . ich dachte an Sie, und danke Ihnen, dass Sie mich nicht in der Steifheit einzwaengender Lehrsaetze, sondern in der wahren Freiheit, das heisst in der Kenntnis der rechten Graenzen erzogen haben.

. . . I feel the urge of expressing to you that all I know and have mastered I owe to you; I want you to know that I am fully aware of it. Perhaps I should not talk about it at all and reserve my gratitude for another occasion, for one should be silent if one is unable to express one's thoughts perfectly and exhaustively. Yet the thought came forcibly to my mind time and again, that I owe all this mastery to you and to you alone. . . . I thank you for not having pressed me into the strait-jacket of rigid rules, and for having educated me in the only true freedom, that is, in the knowledge of the true frontiers of art and taste.

From a letter from Leipzig to his family in Berlin, October 6, 1835 (translation from Miss Selden-Goth's edition):

. . . den Tag, nachdem ich Hensels nach Delitzsch begleitet hatte, war Chopin da; er wollte nur einen Tag bleiben und so waren wir diesen auch ganz zusammen und machten Musik. Ich kann Dir nicht leugnen, liebe Fanny, dass ich neuerdings gefunden habe, dass Du ihm in Deinem Urtheile nicht genug Gerechtigkeit widerfahren laessest; vielleicht war er auch nicht recht bei Spiellaune, als Du ihn hoertest, was ihm wohl oft begegnen mag; aber mich hat sein Spiel wieder von Neuem entzueckt, und ich bin ueberzeugt, wenn Du und auch Vater, einige seiner besseren Sachen so gehoert haettest, wie er sie mir vorspielte, Ihr wuerdet dasselbe sagen. Es ist etwas Grundeigenthuemliches in seinem Clavierspiel, und zugleich so sehr Meisterliches, dass man ihn einen recht vollkommenen Virtuosen nennen kann; und da mir alle Art von Vollkommenheit lieb und erfreulich ist, so war mir dieser Tag ein hoechst angenehmer. . . . Es war mir lieb, wieder einmal mit einem ordentlichen Musiker zusammen zu sein, nicht mit solchen halben Virtuosen und halben Classikern, die gern *les honneurs de la vertu et les plaisirs du vice* in der Musik vereinigen moechten, sondern mit einem, der seine vollkommen ausgepraegte Richtung hat. Und wenn sie auch noch so himmelweit von der meinigen verschieden sein mag, so kann ich mich praechtig damit vertragen;- nur mit jenen halben Leuten nicht.

. . . The day I accompanied the Hensels to Delitzsch, Chopin came; he intended to remain only one day, so we spent this entirely together and made music. I cannot deny, dear Fanny, that I have lately found that you are not doing him sufficient justice in your judgement; perhaps he was not in the right humor for playing when you heard him, which can often be the case with him. But, as for myself, his playing has enchanted me afresh, and I am persuaded that if you, and Father also, had heard him play some of his better pieces as he played them to me, you would say the same. There is something entirely original in his piano playing, and it is at the same time so masterly, that he may be called a perfect virtuoso; and as, in music, I like and rejoice in every kind of perfection, that day was most agreeable to me. It was so pleasant to be once more with a thorough musician, and not with those semi-virtuosi and semi-classicists who would gladly combine in music *les honneurs de la vertu et les plaisirs du vice*, but with one who has his own perfect and well-defined way; however far asunder we may be in our different spheres, I can still get on famously with such a person — but not with those semi-demi people.

By inclination and education Mendelssohn was a classic humanist, espousing a system of values which harmonized beautifully with his deep Christian religiosity and owed much to the decisive influence of Schleiermacher. Four other men of towering stature made strong impressions on the composer and left their traces in his ideas on ethics and the arts: Goethe, Hegel, Moses Mendelssohn, and G. E. Lessing. His epistolary style, however, is indebted mainly to Goethe, Lessing, and Zelter.

Goethe warmly loved the young composer, whom he first met as a twelve-year old boy and exchanged a number of letters with him. In turn Felix, as everyone who came near Goethe's orbit, could not remain unaffected by the poet's style, the less so as he set many of Goethe's poems to music. Here is the young Mendelssohn at twenty-one, reporting a recent visit with the grand old man (Weimar, May 24–25, 1830):

> . . . Vormittags muss ich ihm ein Stuendchen Clavier vorspielen, von allen verschiedenen grossen Componisten, nach der Zeitfolge und muss ihm erzaehlen, wie sie die Sache weiter gebracht haetten; und dazu sitzt er in einer dunklen Ecke wie ein *Jupiter tonans*, und blitzt mit den alten Augen. An den Beethoven wollte er gar nicht heran. — Ich sagte ihm aber, ich koenne ihm nicht helfen, und spielte ihm das erste Stueck der C-moll Symphonie vor. — Das beruehrte ihm nun ganz seltsam. Er sagte erst: "Das bewegt aber gar nichts; das macht nur Staunen; das ist grandios," und dann brummte er so weiter und fing nach langer Zeit wieder an: "Das ist sehr gross, ganz toll, man moechte sich fuerchten, das Haus fiele ein; und wenn das nun alle die Menschen zusammenspielen!"
> . . . Da ich Goethe gebeten hatte, mich 'Du' zu nennen, liess er mir den folgenden Tag durch Ottilie sagen, dann muesse ich aber laenger bleiben als zwei Tage, wie ich gewollt haette, sonst koenne er sich nicht wieder daran gewoehnen. Wie er mir das nun noch selbst sagte und meinte, ich werde wohl nichts versaeumen, wenn ich etwas laenger bliebe, und mich einlud, jeden Tag zum Essen zu kommen, wenn ich nicht anderswo sein wollte; wie ich denn nun bis jetzt auch jeden Tag da war und ihm gestern

von Schottland, Hengstenberg, Spontini und Hegels Aesthetik erzaehlen
musste, wie er mich dann nach Tiefurth mit den Damen schickte, mir aber
verbot nach Berka zu fahren, weil da ein schoenes Maedchen wohne, und
er mich nicht ins Unglueck stuerzen wolle, und wie ich dann so dachte,
das sei nun der Goethe, von dem die Leute einst behaupten wuerden, er
sei gar nicht *eine* Person, sondern bestehe aus mehreren kleinen Goeth-
iden:- da waer' ich wohl recht toll gewesen, wenn mich die Zeit gereut
haette.

. . . Mornings I must play to him on the piano for about an hour, from
the various great composers, in chronological order, and must explain
what each had done to further the art. He all the while sits in a dark
corner like a *Jupiter tonans*, his old eyes flashing fire. At first he would not
venture upon Beethoven at all, but I declared I could not help him, and
played the first movement of the C-minor symphony. It had a stunning
effect on him. First he said: "That arouses no emotion; nothing but aston-
ishment; it's grandiose." He continued to grumble in this way for a while,
and after a pause he began again: "That is very great, quite wild, enough
to bring the house down about one's ears; and what it must be when all
the people are playing at once!" [6]

. . . I had asked Goethe to call me "Du" [as before] and he sent me
word by Ottilie [his daughter-in-law] that in this case I must stay more
than two days, or else he could not get into the way of it again. And then
he repeated the same thing to me himself, and said I should not miss anything if I stayed a little longer, and invited me to come to dinner every
day, unless I wanted to go elsewhere. I have been there every day, and
yesterday I had to tell him all about Scotland, Hengstenberg, Spontini,
and Hegel's Aesthetics — and he sent me to Tiefurth with the ladies, for-
bidding me however to go on to Berka, because there was a beautiful girl
living there and he did not wish to plunge me into misery. And as I felt
that this was the very Goethe of whom people will one day declare that
he is not all *one* person but is made up of several small *Goethides* — I
should have been very foolish indeed if I had begrudged the time. . . .

The robust and often malicious outpourings of Zelter, as we know them
from his voluminous correspondence with Goethe, reflect faithfully the spirit
and temper of that sober and pragmatic man, who loved his Felix like a son.
Zelter's manly and blunt personality left its imprint on Mendelssohn's epistolary style, especially in early letters in which he imitated Zelter, consciously
or unconsciously. A few examples of Mendelssohn's essays in Zelterian lan-

---

[6] A more detailed account of this visit, from Mendelssohn's diary, is quoted in his son Carl
Mendelssohn Bartholdy's *Goethe und Mendelssohn* (Leipzig 1871).

guage may serve as tokens of this influence. The first is from an unpublished letter dated Paris, December 11, 1831:

> . . . Dr. Boerne, der mir mit seinen langsamen Impromptus, seinen abge-quaelten Einfaellen, seiner Wuth auf Deutschland und seinen franzoes-ischen Freiheitsphrasen ebenso zuwider ist wie Dr. Heine mit allen dittos.

> . . . Dr Boerne, who, with his slow impromptus, his cramped and laboured fancies, his rage against Germany, and his French claptrap of "liberty," is just as loathsome to me as that Dr Heine with all the same items.

The second, from an unpublished letter from Rome, December 14, 1830, is a response to news of Goethe's illness:

> Er [Goethe] ist der letzte und schliesst eine heitere, glueckliche Zeit vor uns zu. . . . moege das uebergrosse Glueck, das uns allen in allen Dingen geschenkt war, noch eine lange Zeit dauern . . . bei aller Lustigkeit vergesse ich nie, dass der Kern und das Eigentliche von allen Dingen ernsthaft, ja oft tragisch ist, und dass ich wieder beim Ernst daran denke, dass der rechte Ernst heiter und nicht eben finster und kalt sein muss . . . dessen bin ich gewiss.

> He [Goethe] is the last and closes a serene and happy era before our eyes . . . may the huge good fortune which has accompanied all of us in all respects, last for many years to come . . . in the midst of gaiety I never forget that the kernel and essence of all things is serious and often tragic; on the other hand, speaking of seriousness, I am convinced that the truly serious is serene and not at all grim and cold.

The third is a comment on Berlioz in Rome, March 12, 1831 (letter un-published):

> . . . wir spielten dann seine Symphonie . . . 'episode de la vie d'un artiste' und zu der ein gedrucktes Programm ausgetheilt wird, wie der arme Kuenstler im letzten Satz zum Teufel faehrt, waehrend die Zuhoerer schon laengst desselben werden moechten — nun und da haben alle Instrumente den Katzenjammer und vomiren Musik und man wird sehr unglueklich dabei, und doch ist er ein sehr angenehmer Mensch und spricht gut und hat feine Ideen, und man muss ihn liebgewinnen.

> . . . we then played [on the piano] his symphony . . . *"episode de la vie d'un artiste."* [7] For it a printed program will be given out, wherein the poor artist goes to the devil in the last movement, while the listeners long before have felt that they are possessed by the devil anyway [8] — at this juncture all instruments have a bad hangover and vomit music, and one

[7] This was, of course, Berlioz' *Symphonie Phantastique*. Berlioz recognized the high gifts of Men-delssohn and acclaimed him without envy or rivalry. Mendelssohn thought Berlioz a musician without genuine talent, yet befriended him and, during Berlioz's German tour placed the Gewandhaus orchestra at his disposal.
[8] The German pun is not translatable.

gets most unhappy about it. And yet he [Berlioz] is a most pleasant man
and speaks well and has fine ideas, and one must love him just the same.

Another influence occasionally apparent in the letters is that of the pointed
aphorisms of Lessing, especially when the young Mendelssohn is shooting
his barbed arrows of contempt at the target of contemporary French opera
and musical commercialism. On the whole, however, it is surprising what
scant use he made of his command of six languages (French, English, Italian, Latin, Greek, besides German) and his vast reading in three or four
literatures. Quotations in foreign tongues are rare in his letters, and the composer who studied the original texts of Sophocles' *Antigone* and *Oedipus in
Colonos* and wrote incidental music for them was prone rather to fall into
Berlinese slang than into high-sounding or pompous diction.

Nevertheless the informal, even naive, appearance of the letters is deceptive. Not one to parade his erudition, their author is yet capable of subtle
allusions to matters of philosophy, history, any of the arts; an intellectual
who despises in equal measure the uneducated and the professional intellectuals, the "aesthetes." His facility is not altogether spontaneous. The
graceful casualness of many of his letters is carefully contrived, in the best
sense of the word, as we can see from some surviving drafts. Yet his sincerity
is never impaired, and his composing never does violence to his inner feelings.
A magnificent sense of humor and of self-detachment, inherited from his
father and grandfather Mendelssohn, fairly radiates from most of his letters;
yet his judgment of art and men is sharply critical; if usually just, it is often
satiric, even to the point of malice. Mendelssohn was one who frequently
indulged a choleric temper, and several of his letters reflect an irascible
nature; yet he never, never expressed it toward his parents or other "persons
of respect," so strongly entrenched was the Jewish patriarchal command of
filial respect. Diplomacy marks his expression of differences with his mother.
In all the letters there are to be found no outbursts of anger or even impatience vis-a-vis his parents. His humor transcends all difficulties and, indeed,
affords us the best measure of the man Mendelssohn — able to see himself
objectively, without self-love or pity.

Certainly these family letters cast a bright light on Mendelssohn as a person; yet, chronologically clustered though they are, they never served auto-
biographical intentions. Nor do they convey more than incidental and
peripheral information concerning his musical creativity, his ideas and practice of composition. Perhaps the most captivating aspect of the letters, that
which makes their reading a continually fresh delight, is their subtle and
honest revelation of his inner nature.

The older musical historians listed Mendelssohn among the romanticists. The newer, no longer sure of the watershed between musical classicism and romanticism, have had to attempt hybrid formulas for his quality, such as "romantic classicist" or "classic romanticist." We are inclined to consider him a "classic mannerist," a composer who looked back to classicism though his most original and spontaneous works reveal a sympathy with romantic ideas. Yet his letters bespeak most clearly an inclination to the classic tradition of manifest simplicity. In them his romantic temper is represented by his irony and satire, perhaps also by an occasional but relatively rare lyricism. For the deeper understanding of this highly complex artist the probative value of these letters is invaluable. Not in vain did he all through his life stress the motto: "Life and Art are not divisible."

Mendelssohn's signature on a family letter, April 11, 1825

Mendelssohn's Fame and Tragedy

Reprinted with permission of *Reconstructionist*, 25, 1959-1960, pp. 9-14.

THE destiny of Mendelssohn's work has been much more adventurous since his death than in his lifetime. Music, as any art, knows of many fluctuations of taste or fashion, and the *oeuvre* of any creative artist has its ups and downs in posthumous criticism. In the case of Mendelssohn's work, however, these fluctuations display a violence and amplitude during the past century, incomparable which that of other masters. The destiny of Schumann's, Chopin's, and even Berlioz' music, (to name his most significant contemporaries) was not free from the vicissitudes of changing styles either; but none of these became in the least as controversial as Mendelssohn's music, indeed his stature in the history of music. Adored beyond reason during his lifetime, his music seemed to fall rapidly into oblivion during the Wagnerian era; it rose again in the esteem of the critics at the beginning of the 20th century, when neoclassicists "rediscovered" him. Under the impact of Nazism it fell again into contempt, and not only in Germany and Italy, but even in his beloved England, which had adopted him, like Handel, as one of her favorite composers. After the collapse of Nazism his music regained its earlier popularity, and if the catalogues of recording firms and the statistics of concert-halls are of any scientific value, it is now almost at par with that of his archenemy Wagner. Yet, if popularity increased, the scope of his living music has shrunk to about a dozen works: the overtures to "Midsummernight's Dream," "Hebrides," "Fair Melusina," the great Violin concerto, the Italian and Scottish symphonies, the oratorio "Elijah," two organ-sonatas, one trio, (d-minor), a few piano pieces, (Rondo Cappriccioso, Songs without words), the incidental music to "Midsummernight's Dream," and one or two of his great psalm-motets.

TWO CONTROVERSIES

What were—and are—the reasons behind these fluctuations, controversies, and the gradual diminution of his regularly performed and living music? Let us not forget that we are not discussing a man of second-rate importance, but a master, whose shadow influences even today many facets of music, mostly those of choral and piano-compositions. We venture to say: his status has become controversial just because he declined to take sides in the two essential controversies of his life and art: Judaism vs. Germanism,

and Romanticism vs. Classicism. This evasiveness permeated his entire thinking and feeling and made him an "elliptic personality," a man with two foci, of which neither was ever clearly defined by himself. This was by no means an oversight, for Mendelssohn took the problem of being a German Jew-Christian very seriously, and was also fully aware of his hedging attitude between classic and romantic styles. Being a student of Hegel's, a protegé of Goethe, a most precious and deeply reflective person, he cannot be exculpated by the usual supercilious remarks of "intelligent" critics, that as a musician he did not concern himself with religious, political, or aesthetic problems. No; everybody familiar with his letters, (even in the distorted and forged text, in which they were published) must know that his power of thinking, his profound erudition, and his brilliant intellect encompassed all issues of his time. In this respect he had only two peers in the nineteenth century: Berlioz and Wagner. Nonetheless, he evaded the two crucial controversies of his day, and so he himself has become controversial.

Even we, who remember him at the occasion of his 150th birthday, must ask ourselves: what does he mean to us? which redounds to the more interesting question, what did we—that is, Judaism, —mean to him?

THE PROBLEM OF JEWISHNESS

Once or twice Mendelssohn did face the problems of his Jewish descent of his own volition; three times he was confronted with it under traumatic circumstances. The following letter indicates the difference of opinion between Felix Mendelssohn and his father Abraham, Moses' second son. It was motivated by Felix' habit of appearing in London under the name of Mendelssohn without the added Bartholdy. Here the stern father (Abraham) forces his son, eleven years after he had him baptized, to confront the problem of his Jewishness. He writes:

Berlin July 8, 1829

Dear Felix:

Today's family sheet will run full without my contribution . . . I will therefore write you separately because I have to discuss with you a most serious matter.

The suspicion has come to me that you have suppressed or neglected or allowed others to suppress or neglect the name which I have taken as the name of our family, the name Bartholdy. In the concert programs you have sent me, likewise in newspaper articles, your name is given as Mendelssohn. I can account for this only on the supposition that you have been the cause.

Now, I am greatly dissatisfied about this. If you are to blame, you have committed a huge wrong.

After all, a name is only a name, neither more nor less. Still, so long as you are under your father's jurisdiction, you have the plain and indisputable duty to be called by your father's name. Moreover it is your ineffaceable, as well as reasonable, duty to take for granted that, whatever your father does, he does on valid grounds and with due deliberation.

On our journey to Paris after that neck-breaking night you asked me the reasons why our name was changed. I gave you those reasons at length. If you have forgotten them, you could have asked me about them again. If my reasons seemed unconvincing, you should have countered with better reasons. I prefer to believe the former, because I am unable to think of any reasons countervailing. I will here repeat my arguments and my views.

My grandfather was named Mendel Dessau. When my father, his son, went forth into the world and began to win notice and when he undertook the project which can not be too highly praised, that noble project of lifting his brethren out of the vast degradation into which they had sunk, and to do this by disseminating among them a better education, my father felt that the name, Moses ben Mendel Dessau, would handicap him in gaining the needed access to those who had the better education at their disposal. Without any fear that his own father would take offense, my father assumed the name Mendelssohn. The change, though a small one, was decisive.

As Mendelssohn, he became irrevocably detached from an entire class, the best of whom he raised to his own level. By that name he identified himself with a different group. Through the influence which wisely and worthily he exerted by word and pen and deed,—an influence which, ever growing, persists to this day,—that name Mendelssohn acquired a Messianic import and a significance which defies extinction. This, considering that you were reared a Christian, you can hardly understand. A Christian Mendelssohn is an impossibility. A Christian Mendelssohn the world would never recognize. Nor should there be a Christian Mendelssohn; for my father himself did not want to be a Christian. "Mendelssohn" does and always will stand for a Judaism in transition, when Judaism, just because it is seeking to transmute itself spiritually, clings to its ancient form all the more stubbornly and tenaciously, by way of protest against the novel form that so arrogantly and tyrannically declared itself to be the one and only path to the good.

The viewpoint, to which my father and then my own generation committed me, imposes on me other duties toward you, my children, and puts other means of discharging them into my hands. I have learnt and will not until my dying breath, forget that, while truth is one and eternal, its forms are many and transient. That is why, as long as it was permitted by the government under which we lived, I reared you without religion in any form. I wanted you to profess whatever your convictions might favor or, if you prefer, whatever expediency might dictate. But it was not so to be. I was obligated to do the choosing for you. Naturally, when you consider what scant value I placed on any form in particular, I felt no urge to choose the form known as Judaism, that most antiquated, distorted, and self-defeating form of all. Therefore I reared you as Christians, Christianity being the more purified form and the one most accepted by the majority of civilized people. Eventually, I myself adopted Christianity, because I felt it my duty to do for myself that which I recognized as best for you. Even as my father found it necessary to adjust his name to conditions, filial devotion, as well as discretion, impelled me to adjust similarly.

Here I must reproach myself for a weakness, even if a pardonable one. I should have done decisively and thoroughly that which I deemed right. I should have discarded the name Mendelssohn completely. I should have adhered to the new name exclusively. I owed that to my father. My reason for not doing so was my long established habit of sparing those near to me and of forestalling perverted and venomous judgments. I did wrong. My purpose was merely to prepare for you a path of transition, making it easier for you that have no one to spare and nothing to care about. In Paris, when you, Felix, were about to step into the world and make a name for yourself, I deliberately had your cards engraved: Felix M. Bartholdy. You did not accept my way of thinking. Weakly enough I failed to persist. Now I only wish, though I neither expect nor deserve it, that my present intervention may not have arrived too late.

You can not, you must not carry the name Mendelssohn. Felix Mendelssohn Bartholdy is too long; it is unsuited for daily use. You must go by the name of Felix Bartholdy. A name is like a garment; it has to be appropriate for the time, the use, and the rank, if it is not to become a hindrance and a laughing-stock. Englishmen, otherwise a most formal lot, change their names frequently. Seldom is anyone renowned under the name conferred at baptism. And that is as it should be. I repeat: There can no more be a Christian Mendelssohn than there can be a Jewish Confucious. If Mendelssohn is your name, you are *ipso facto* a Jew. And this, if for no other reason than because it is contrary to fact, can be to you of no benefit.

Dear Felix, take this to heart and act accordingly.

Your Father and Friend

This letter, while meticulously honest, was at the same time unrealistic in the extreme. Its Kantian minimizing of "form," its reasoning in terms of 18th century philosophy was inapplicable to life's actualities.

The rather lame reply of Felix to this letter evades the issue; but his actions speak for themselves. In the four concerts given by Felix in London during 1829, (*after* Abraham's letter was received), his name appears as Mendelssohn, in open contradiction to his father's wishes. Felix' entire outlook differed from that of Abraham; he actually toyed with the idea of dropping the name Bartholdy altogether.

ANTI-SEMITISM

We know nothing about his reaction, when during the "Judensturm" of 1819 a royal prince of Prussia encountered Felix, then ten years of age, spat before him and cried: "Hep, hep, Jewboy." This was the first time that his Jewishness was put to shame from the outside; the second time the shock was even worse: his teacher and paternal friend Zelter, had designated Felix his successor as director of the Berlin *Sing-Akademie*. Yet at the election, Felix was rejected by an overwhelming majority in favor of a hopeless mediocrity; the real reason was, as we know from contemporary sources, Mendelssohn's Jewish descent. This was considered incompatible with the direction of a Christian choral institution. The third time Felix himself was not concerned, but many of his Jewish friends and relatives were affronted by the posthumous publication of the correspondence between Goethe and his friend Zelter. (Here it must be stated in fairness to Goethe, that in these letters he never indulged in vulgarities or anti-Jewish remarks, which cannot be said of Zelter.) The two last mentioned insults hurt Felix, where he was most vulnerable, in his relation with beloved men.

How did he react to these shocks? Did they give him a better insight into the roots of his being, did they remind him of the old people that had born him? The question must remain unanswered. For with Abraham Mendelssohn, who died in 1835, died also the image of the "great father," in which many features of Moses Mendelssohn had been alive. The reaction of the broken-hearted son became apparent on two levels: in a conscious and intentional purification of his religious thought, in this case in a turn towards true, pious, and sincere Christian religiosity of Schleiermacher's tint; yet on the other hand towards a definite identification with the people of his ancestors. There are many instances of this apparent (but not real) antinomy of his sentiments. We shall mention only a few.

Upon the invitation of the Hamburg Tempelverein Mendelssohn composed for their 25th anniversary the hundredth psalm; he supported in every way the orthodox Polish Jew Gusikow, a xylophonist, whom he called "a genius": he had a plaque put on the door of Moses Mendelssohn's house in Dessau; but before doing so, he inquired carefully if the present owner could be considered worthy and appreciative of so signal an honor; when he composed Psalm 114 "When Israel out of Egypt came" he felt "over his head the wings of his ancestors, he saw the Lord's pillar of fire." It is hardly a coincidence that this became his best and most impressive psalm-composition; Grove, in his dictionary, makes this observation: "The Jewish blood of Mendelssohn must surely for once have beat fiercely over this great triumph of his forefathers, and it is only the plain truth to say that in directness and force his music is a perfect match for the splendid words of the unknown Psalmist." Mendelssohn's "Elijah" is the only great oratorio of the 19th century and has, up to this day, remained a landmark in the musical interpretation of the Bible. Many more instances could be quoted to demonstrate that he identified himself with the Jewish people as well as with the Germans, but also with Protestantism of Schleiermacher's color. Indeed, Mendelssohn had no use for trinitarian ideas; he was, what might be called today a devout "liberal Protestant"—the descendant of R. Moses Isserles and Moses Mendelssohn!

WAGNER ON MENDELSSOHN'S DILEMMA

R. Wagner had sensed intuitively somewhat of Mendelssohn's dilemma between Judaism and German Christianity; in the first (anonymous) edition of his otherwise biased and unfair pamphlet "Judaism in Music" he said:

> "Where can we better elucidate . . . this deep conflict than in the works of a musician of Jewish descendence, by nature equipped with a specific talent as very few musicians before him? . . . All the inherent contradictions of this (Jewish) mentality and its antagonism against us, its whole inability to live with us, being alien to our soil, and yet eager to further our soil's output, are climaxed in the altogether tragic conflict in the nature, the life, and work of the early deceased Felix Mendelssohn. He has demonstrated that a Jew of abundant specific talent may possess the most refined . . . culture, the highest and most rarefied sense of honor; and yet all these virtues do not enable him to impress our hearts and souls in their profound recesses even once. . . ."

THE ALTERNATIVES

Yet, where was there an alternative for him? Let us make a mental experiment: supposing Mendelssohn had taken a positive attitude to Judaism; would his "Elijah," his Psalms, his overtures to the "Hebrides" or to "Midsummernight's Dream" be better, be different to any measurable extent? I doubt it very much. For these chief works of the master are peaks in musical history, they are in their way perfect, they cannot be better! Let us remember that Mendelssohn's music was a product of rich hereditary gifts, of strict and intelligent training, but also of his dissident attitude to the style of his contemporaries. His grandfather Moses had occupied himself with problems of music theory, both his parents were keen judges of music and enthusiastic music lovers, and his great aunt Sarah Levy, nee Itzig, had been the favorite disciple of Wilhelm Friedemann Bach and the patroness of Philip Emanuel Bach.

And now let us consider another mental experiment: let us assume that Felix Mendelssohn had been born before the emancipation, before assimilation! What would have become of him? Either an excellent *Klezmer* or, at best, a fine and creative *hazan,* forgotten today and without any significance for the development of music.

For it was the emancipation and, let us face it, the assimilation of European Jewry which placed at his (or his parents') disposal the means of training the young genius. As irrelevant and even harmful, as the legalistic achievements of the emancipation were for European Jewry, as wholesome and fruitful was the assimilation for the elevation of Jewry to the cultural standard of Western Europe—and that was very high, probably higher than it is today. Here we can fully appreciate the great merit of the "Science of Judaism" which had the vision of profiting from European culture without abandoning the principles of Judaism.

The question has been raised, if traces of synagogue-chant are apparent in Mendelssohn's music; it has generally, if cautiously been denied, because most of the musicologists who had raised the question were not sufficiently familiar with traditional Jewish chant to affirm or deny it categorically. To my knowledge there are only two passages in his music, where ancient echoes from the synagogue emerge and come to life: The first, in the chorale-paraphrase: "Wir glauben all' an einen Gott," (We all believe in one God) from his oratorio "Paulus" (!). There we hear quite unmistakably the closing trope of Tora-cantillation with the characteristic *sof-pasug* cadence. Secondly, in the prophetic Theophany of the "Elijah": "Behold, God the Lord passed by," where the traditional mode of the *"Adonoi, Adonoi"* is mysteriously and magnificently paraphrased. Is this merely accidental? If subconscious reminiscences can be termed accidental, this instance is a case in point. On the other hand, it seems plausible that the monumental concept of this piece had aroused his dormant Jewish feelings to a point, where subconscious memories from childhood arose and implanted themselves in his creative and conscious mind. However that may be, this and similar choruses from the "Elijah" and the Psalms would adorn every synagogue; and I for one cannot understand why only the concert-hall or the Protestant chuch should have the privilege of performing Mendelssohn's religious music.

CONTEMPORARY VIEWS

Had it not been for a handful of his compositions, especially his violin concerto, the darling of every violin-virtuoso, Mendelssohn's music might have disappeared during the twenties altogether; he had not identified himself with the romantic school like Schumann or Berlioz, nor could he be considered a "true classic." Thus he was caught "between two stools." But while popular taste is loyal and faithful, that of the connoisseurs and critics is highly changeable, not to say fickle, and thus Mendelssohn is again being received graciously as one of the forerunners of "objective" music, whatever that term may mean. At the same time, popular taste sifts, over many decades, much more rigorously than the connoisseur's, until only a handful of works of a favored composer remain truly alive. The criteria of this sifting process seem mysterious to us; yet I suspect that subliminal associations and perhaps symbolic functions of music play a part in it.

The attitude of the modern professional critic to Mendelssohn is best represented in this passage:

> "Composer's craftsmanship having taken a new turn and having reached an impasse, the ease with which Mendelssohn progressed had become an object of admiration, perhaps of envy. He has joined the select band of composers, Mozart and Ravel among them, who know just how many notes to write and where to put them . . ."

Significantly enough, the few works that remain in general favor, reflect the more volatile side of Mendelssohns music—its neo-classic and anti-romantic facets. This is in tune with our current musical fashion. Neither does his music engender very profound emotions, nor does it exact the audience's painstaking endeavors to penetrate the composer's lofty and esoteric intentions, as Wagner often requires. Mendelssohn's absence of pretentiousness appeals anew to that sociological stratum for which his music was written in the first place, the European bourgeoisie. When it declined, his music faded; when it reasserted itself, as e.g., after the second World War, his music came to life again.

GERMAN AND JEW

On the eve of the 90th anniversary of his death in 1937, the aldermen of Leipzig scrapped the Mendelssohn statue in front of the *Gewandhaus*, which he had made world-famous. Today, the Leipzig Conservatory, the oldest German academy of music, also founded by Mendelssohn, calls itself "Mendelssohn Academy." Between these two facts lies his whole tragedy, and that of German Jewry as well.

What does Mendelssohn and his music mean to us, to Jews who assert Judaism as a civilization? The answer to this question should be simple: wherever his identification with the Bible has avoided christological interpretations (as in his Psalms, The "Hymn of Praise," and "Elijah"), it has produced masterpieces of religious music and warrants our recognition of his native Judaism; his personal concern with matters Jewish can but vindicate our limited acceptance.

His personal conflict foreshadowed the tragedy of the German Jew, assimilated or not; hence Mendelssohn stands out as a representative of that segment of Jewish civilization, without which we would be much poorer in the arts, the sciences, and the knowledge of Judaism.

WITHDRAWN